A READER'S GUIDE TO
THE
POLICE PROCEDURAL

Reader's Guides to Mystery Novels
Susan Oleksiw, Series Editor

A READER'S GUIDE TO THE POLICE PROCEDURAL

Jo Ann Vicarel

G.K. Hall & Co.
An Imprint of Simon & Schuster Macmillan
New York

Prentice Hall International
London   Mexico City   New Delhi   Singapore   Sydney   Toronto

Copyright © 1995 by Jo Ann Vicarel

All rights reserved. No part of this book may be reproduced or transmitted in any form or by any means, electronic or mechanical, including photocopying, recording, or by any information storage and retrieval system, without permission in writing from the Publisher.

G.K. Hall & Co.
An Imprint of Simon & Schuster Macmillan
866 Third Avenue
New York, NY 10022

Library of Congress Catalog Card Number: 94-33650

Printed in the United States of America

Printing number
1 2 3 4 5 6 7 8 9 10

Library of Congress Cataloging-in-Publication Data

Vicarel, Jo Ann.
    A reader's guide to the police procedural / Jo Ann Vicarel.
      p.   cm. — (Reader's guides to mystery novels)
    Includes bibliographical references.
    ISBN 0-8161-1801-9
    1. Detective and mystery stories—Stories, plots, etc.
2. Detective and mystery stories—Bibliography. 3. Bibliography—
Best books—Detective and mystery stories. 4. Fiction—20th
century—Stories, plots, etc.   I. Title. II. Series.
PN3448.D4V49 1995
016.80883'872—dc20   94-33650
                                                                                               CIP

The paper used in this publication meets the minimum requirements of American National Standard for Information Sciences—Permanence of Paper for Printed Library Materials. ANSI Z39.48-1984.∞™

Contents

Preface   vii

1. Pseudonyms   1
2. Creators and Series Characters   3
3. Series Characters and Creators   17
4. Police Procedurals   31
5. Period of Story (1700–1992 and Beyond)   297
6. Locations   337
7. Serial Killers   373
8. A Lighter Touch   379
9. Police Personnel or Ex-Police Personnel   391
10. Police Agencies   393
11. One Hundred Classics of the Genre   397

Preface

A long time ago, while browsing in the public library, I found a book by J. J. Marric. There is no way to be sure which one of the George Gideon novels it was, but the enjoyment I got from the reading sent me back to find all of the Marric titles. Next came Maurice Proctor, John Creasey, and Ed McBain. Thus, an avid reader of the police procedural was born. What makes the genre so appealing to me is that the books are, for the most part, based in reality. There is no super-brain who comes into the case and makes pronouncements about cigar ash, train timetables, or the precise whereabouts of the ten prime suspects. Please do not misunderstand me. I like all of the other types of mystery novels and have read widely in every area. Yet I tend to enjoy reading about the police solving a crime more than I do reading about most amateur sleuths and some private eyes.

The main difference between a police procedural and a traditional mystery is that the procedural is a novel about police life and work first, and a mystery second. Sometimes the crime is secondary to the personal lives of the police, as Joseph Wambaugh illustrates so perfectly in his well-structured novels about cops going about their daily routines yet never losing sight of their individual situations. Frequently in a procedural, the perpetrator is known to the police and to the reader. Often, the investigating officers have very little to direct them to the criminal, although at times there are a few leads or some forensic evidence to follow. Mainly, the police slog through a mass of detail, knocking on doors, telephoning, plugging away at a thin trail of fact until the pieces fall into place. The focus, then, becomes how to bring the criminal to justice.

We need only look from Inspector Cuff, the investigator in Wilkie Collins's *The Moonstone* published in 1868 and definitely not a procedural, to the 1930s and Inspector Christopher McKee (made popular by Helen Reilly) and Inspector Roderick Alleyn, who stars in Ngaio Marsh's classic tales, to understand that the policeman has been in fiction for years.

Therefore, the difference between a traditional mystery and a police procedural becomes moot. When the mystery is no longer the sole purpose of the story, when the actual work of the police officer becomes the focus of the plot, when the investigation is center stage and the police are the main characters, you are reading a police procedural.

To give a precise definition of the police procedural is difficult because these novels take many forms. To say you know one when you see one is right on target. The procedural must feature a police officer or a police department, precinct, or division as the protagonist of the story. There must be a crime or crimes to solve. The story has to be told from the point of view of the police officers. The details are given to us as we follow along to the scene of the crime, go inside the morgue for the autopsy, listen as witnesses are questioned, watch the arrests being made. The reader knows everything the officer does.

Sometimes the most difficult feature of the procedural is how the police will identify the guilty party. There is much painstaking piecing together of very small bits of information, until a picture begins to emerge. In some stories the identity of the criminal is known, and the difficulty may be putting together the evidence that will convict him or her. In any case, all must be carried out logically and realistically. The author cannot pull a perpetrator from left field, even though the criminal may not make an appearance until the end of the novel. The facts must fit the overall nature of the story and the crime; the procedure must be as close to the correct way as possible.

As difficult as it is to write a working definition of the genre, it is even harder to figure out who wrote the first one. It is generally agreed that the police procedural novel made its appearance in the late 1940s. I believe that the prototype was John Creasey's *Inspector West Takes Charge*, which was published in 1942 and introduced Roger West. Although the books provide West with a reporter friend to serve as alter ago and legman, the stories fit securely into the procedural niche rather than into the classic British mystery genre typified by Ngaio Marsh's books. Creasy's stories follow Roger West as he solves crimes and interacts with his compatriots at Scotland Yard. The Roger West tales have held up over time and are just as readable today as they were fifty years ago. One fault, perhaps, of the first stories and perhaps of the series overall is that West usually focuses on only one case. More realistic procedurals show several concurrent investigations—prime examples of which are the books by Marric and McBain.

Lawrence Treat has consistently been credited as the father of the genre. He wrote *V as in Victim* in 1945, yet he has denied that he was attempting a new direction in crime fiction. His books contain the rudiments of the procedural but not the substance.

Along with Treat, Hillary Waugh is recognized as a pioneer in the development of the police novel. To me, Waugh, in his early books, spends too much time on the suspects and usually does not start focusing on the investigation of the crime until halfway through the story. I do admit to a personal preference for his Frank Sessions books, which take place in New York City and are to my mind the real thing. Published in the late Sixties, they are too recent, however, to be considered trend-setting books.

A major contributing force to the demand for books featuring police personnel was the introduction of *Dragnet* on American television in 1949. In 1950 MacKinley Kantor wrote *Signal Thirty-Two*, a documentary novel that follows the steps of the personnel of New York City's 23rd precinct. In 1951, Maurice Procter, himself a policeman, wrote *The Chief Inspector's Statement*, the first true procedural and a breakthrough book for two reasons. First, it follows the investigating officer around in his professional and private life, and second, Procter was a real working policeman with years of on-the-job experience. The fact that a policeman is always suspicious of everyone, relates past experience to the case in hand, and must be single-minded in his duty comes through in all of Procter's work. Yet there is a human quality to his characters that gives them dimension and makes them true protectors of the citizenry.

A mystery novel does not need the authenticity that a police procedural must have. In a traditional mystery a crime has been committed and the detective follows clues until the guilty person is caught and/or unmasked. The procedural is a bit out of step with the detective story, as frequently the perpetrator is known to the police and they must figure out a way to gather evidence to prove in a court of law that he or she is guilty. Also, the police begin under the handicap of rules and the laws that must be followed in the apprehension of a criminal.

The narration of a procedural is usually a third person's voice but the story must focus on the police investigation. There are several books that split the story into the detailing of the crime, the police investigation, and a follow-up section with a separate running stream of consciousness or relating of events from the criminal, often a serial killer. If the writer is able to maintain the integrity of the policeman's job and actions as the primary focus of the tale, then so be it. Lawrence Sanders's *The First Deadly Sin* is one of the first and best examples of this juxtaposing of several narrators. The true police procedural is a walk-through of the daily events as told by the police personnel responsible for apprehending the guilty. That often means the reader is treated to a firsthand account of gruesome murder scenes, minute renderings of autopsies, the routine attention to detail that must be accomplished if evidence is to be gathered. As an added bonus the reader often is given a close look at the personal lives of those individuals who keep us safe. This is why having a police background or exposure to firsthand knowledge of the investigation of crime is very important for the would-be author.

The modern police novelist comes in many varieties. Former and acting police officers head the list with William J. Caunitz, James Barrett, and

Joseph Wambaugh very prominent. Investigative reporters like Roger Busby and Peter Turnbull, a former social worker, have an edge over someone who has never experienced the mean streets. There are writers, such as Patricia Cornwell, who immersed themselves in the daily grind of crime investigation in order to prepare for a career in writing police novels. But wherever they are coming from, the criterion remains the same: they must get the procedure right.

The procedural assumes different shapes and focuses. Some are so graphic in detail that only the hardcore reader can stay with the story. It takes a strong stomach to read Thomas Harris's *Red Dragon* and an even stronger one to stay with Michael Slade's *Headhunter*. To counterbalance the more gory tales, I have included some that take a lighter approach. There are also novelists, like William Marshall, who make a reader laugh out loud while his stories are dealing with events that are very painful to witness. The humor allows the reader a brief respite from stark reality. Read *Sci Fi* or *The Far Away Man* to understand this literary technique.

Included in this book are a few authors who could (and some will most assuredly say should) have been left out. A case could be made against Elizabeth Linington, who romanticized her policemen until they became larger-than-life heroes, members of the family, and sometimes too delightfully fanciful to bear any resemblance to the real thing. Nevertheless, her works are included here to balance the atrocities found in the hardboiled side of the genre. While Simenon's Maigret books are not procedurals at their best, they do follow him as he solves crimes within the confines of his policeman's role. Janwillem van de Wetering and Maj Sjöwall and Per Wahlöö can be read for procedure and reality in the life of a European cop.

The procedural does not have to be filled with gore and torture and mental illness to be effective. Read Tony Hillerman for poignancy, John Harvey for a sense of balance between the ugly and the ordinary, Tom Philbin for the gritty truth, and John Wainwright for an all-encompassing view of the police hierarchy at work. These are some of the authors one points to when asked for something good to read.

I was able to read and annotate over 1,115 books by 271 authors. There are 76 titles listed but not read, mainly because I could not find the books. This was a difficult volume to compile at times. A number of paperback books display a police badge on the cover but turn out to have very little to do with police investigation. I read many books that I ultimately rejected, and I am still finding titles that just might fit the parameters of this work.

I have included hard-to-find authors as well as those displayed on library shelves and in bookstores. The police procedural may have gotten off to a slow start but the number of titles currently being published is impressive. I was forced to stop examining books somewhere in 1993 because the sheer volume of them was interferring with the completion of this book. The growing popularity of the genre is matched by the resurgence of police shows on prime-time television and reruns of oldies on late-night. There is also a plethora of true-crime books and volumes in which the police are interviewed for their views on crime, life, the job, and everything else on their minds.

I have tried to list all the titles in a given series except for the Maigret works, which are catalogued frequently and are easy to find elsewhere, and which, although they are not true procedurals, must at least be touched upon in any work about the genre.

I have attempted to be as all-inclusive as possible, yet, realistically, some titles surely have been omitted unintentionally. Using the book as a browsing tool for help in finding something interesting to read is one of the volume's aims. To my knowledge, only two other works deal with the police procedural: George N. Dove's *The Police Procedural* (Bowling Green, OH: Bowling Green University Press, 1982) and George N. Dove and Earl F. Bargainnier's *Cops and Constables* (Bowling Green, OH: Bowling Green University Press, 1986). Neither book attempts to be a near-complete compendium of the genre.

The most difficult part of writing any reference source is the verification of title, publisher, and publication dates. In most cases I used the publishing information given in the book. As anyone knows who has set out to document titles with pertinent information, there are many discrepencies and omissions in the publishing records of books. When I could find no British publisher or date I used only the American one available. Frequently, there was no American edition, so only the British is listed. When information about publisher and date could not be verified and several sources listed different information, I chose what I thought made the most sense. Using *First Search*, an online database included in the OCLC megacatalog of publications that includes *World Cat*, I verified publishing information for both American and British titles. I also used Allen J. Hubin's *Crime Fiction II: A Comprehensive Bibliography 1749–1990* (New York: Garland, 1994) as a source for both publishing data and title verification. All three editions of *Twentieth Century Crime and Mystery Writers* (Chicago and London: St. James Press, 1980; 1985; 1991) were consulted.

Because this volume is one in the Readers' Guides to Mystery Novels series, you can check for your favorite author in another of the books if you do not find her or him listed here. An example is the Charlotte and Thomas Pitt novels by Anne Perry, included in Susan Oleksiw's *The Reader's Guide to the Classic British Mystery*, which also contains the works of P. D. James and Ruth Rendell, among many others.

The inclusion of an asterisk indicates that the author has written other books that are not police procedurals and so are not listed, or that a title has not been read by me. Books included in supplemental lists are in chronological order. The annotations are strictly story outlines and contain no critical material. I hope I gave away no endings or ruined any plots for would-be readers.

In any undertaking of this sort there are bound to be mistakes, omissions, and perhaps a slight bias toward one's favorite authors. All of these faults, mistakes, and omissions are my own.

As in the writing of any book there are people to thank. I wish to acknowledge my gratitude to all of the men and women writing police novels for the many hours of reading enjoyment they have given me. To say that these are my favorite books is an understatement. The police procedural has been and will always be my reading matter of choice.

My heartfelt thanks to Jeff Meyerson, Brooklyn bookseller extraordinaire, who found British police procedurals that I had never seen before, along with the titles that I desperately needed to read.

A special thank you to my husband, Don, who spent his summer vacation typing hundreds of annotations without a complaint. To my mother, Elvera Genaro, and my children, Daniel and Angela, who never doubted that the book would be written. And to my friends and staunch supporters Rebecca Katzenmeyer, Mary Murphy, Linda Chopra, and Rita Knight-Gray, who listened and empathized throughout the writing process.

A READER'S GUIDE TO THE POLICE PROCEDURAL

1

Pseudonyms

Listed here are the few writers of police procedurals who use or have used a pseudonym.

PSEUDONYM	REAL NAME(S)
K. C. Constantine	Carl Kosak
E. V. Cunningham	Howard Fast
Alison Drake	T(rish) J(aneshutz) MacGregor
John Kevin Dugan	W. E. B. Griffin
Jack Early	Sandra Scoppettone
Joe Gash	Bill Granger
Mark Hebden	John Harris
Bill James	(Allen) James Tucker
Mike Lundy	a former New York City policeman
J. J. Marric	John Creasey
Lee Martin	(Martha) Anne (Guice)Wingate
Jennie Melville	Gwendoline Butler
Gil North	Geoffrey Horne
Robert Pike	Robert L. Fish
Erica Quest	John Sawyer and Nancy Buckingham Sawyer
Derek Raymond	Robin (Robert William Arthur) Cook
John Sandford	John Camp

PSEUDONYM	REAL NAME(S)
Jack S. Scott	Jonathan Escott
Francis Selwyn	Donald Thomas
David Serafin	Ian Michael
Dell Shannon	Elizabeth Linington
Michael Slade	John Banks, Jay Clarke, and Richard Covell
Pamela West	Pamela West Katkin and Samuel Leonard Rubenstein

2

Creators and Series Characters

CREATOR	SERIES CHARACTER(S)
Thomas Adcock	Detective Neil Hockaday
Warren Adler	Detective Fiona FitzGerald
Gary Alexander	Superintendent Bamsan Kiet
Noreen Ayres	Smokey Brandon
John Ball	Detective Virgil Tibbs; Chief of Police Jack Tallon
Dallas Barnes	Sergeant Lee Hollister; Investigator Virgil Fox
James Barnett	Detective Chief Superintendent Owen Smith
William Bayer	Lieutenant Frank Janek; David Bar-Lev
Greg Bear	Inspector Mary Choy
Paul Bishop	Calico Jack Walker; Tina Tamiko
Eleanor Taylor Bland	Detective Marti MacAlister
Peter Blauner	Probation Officer Baum
K. Arne Blom	Chief Inspector Seved Olofsson
John Brady	Sergeant Matthew Minogue
Anthony Bruno	FBI Special Agent Cuthbert "Bert" Gibbons; FBI Special Agent Mike Tozzi
James Lee Burke	Lieutenant/Detective Dave Robicheaux

CREATOR	SERIES CHARACTER(S)
Rex Burns	Detective Gabriel Wager
Roger Busby	Detective Inspector Leric; Detective Inspector Eddie Quick; Detective Sergeant Roger Goodman; Detective Inspector Tony Rowley
Gwendoline Butler	Detective Chief Superintendent/Chief Inspector John Coffin
Robert Cain	Lieutenant Christopher Drake; ROD (a combat robot)
William Camp	Captain Ken Others
William J. Caunitz	Lieutenant Dan Malone; Lieutenant Teddy Lucas; Major Andreas Vassos; Lieutenant Tony Scanlon; Lieutenant John Vinda
Robert Chambers	Detective Hank Moody
Nick Christian	Sergeant Arnold Ross
Marten Claridge	Detective Inspector Frank McMorran
Ernest Clark	Detective William Ruffin
Jon Cleary	Inspector Scobie Malone
Andrew Coburn	Rupert Goetz, Chief of Homicide; Frank Chase; Sergeant Sonny Dawson
Max Allan Collins	Eliot Ness, Director of Public Safety
Michael Connelly	Detective Hieronymus Bosch
K. C. Constantine	Chief of Police Mario Balzic
Thomas H. Cook	Detective Tom Jackson; Lieutenant Frank Clemons; Sergeant Ben Wellman
Susan Rogers Cooper	Chief Deputy Sheriff Milton Kovak
Patricia D. Cornwell	Medical Examiner Kay Scarpetta; Lieutenant Lou Marino
E. W. Count	Lieutenant Andrew Flynn

CREATOR	SERIES CHARACTER(S)
John Creasey	Detective Superintendent/Chief Inspector Roger West
Bill Crider	Sheriff Dan Rhodes; Detective Howland; Police Psychologist Romain
E. V. Cunningham	Sergeant Masao Masuto
Jack Curtis	Inspector Robin Cully; Sergeant Mike Dawson
Claire Curzon	Detective Superintendent Mike Yeadings
Robert Daley	Chief of Detectives Earl Eischied; Commissaire Robert Bellarmine; Inspector Joseph Hearn
John Danica and Lucy Freeman	FBI Special Agent Joseph Lerza
Harold R. Daniels	Lieutenant Daniel Nalon; Sergeant Charlie Wilentz
Frank DeFelitta	Chief Inspector Martin Bauer
Nelson De Mille	Sergeant Joe Ryker
O'Neil de Noux	Detective Dino LaStanza
Joseph P. De Sario	Detective Brenda Collins
Michael Dibdin	Commissioner of Police Aurelio Zen
D. J. Donaldson	Chief Medical Examiner Andy Broussard; Police Psychologist Kit Franklin
Alison Drake	Detective Aline Scott
John Kevin Dugan	Staff Inspector Peter Wohl
Robert L. Duncan	Detective Picone; Detective Rizzutto
Susan Dunlap	Detective Jill Smith
John Dunning	Detective Cliff Janeway
Lew Dykes	Lieutenant Vercingetorix Fort; Detective Babs Bladenbauer
Jack Early	Lieutenant Dina Donato; Sergeant Michael Donato
John Eller	Detective Charlie Rope

CREATOR	SERIES CHARACTER(S)
James Ellroy	Policeman Freddy Underhill; Policeman Wacky Walker; Sergeant Lloyd Hopkins; Detective Bucky Bleichert
Earl W. Emerson	Fire Chief MacKinley Fontana
Robert L. Fish	Captain José da Silva
Richard Fliegel	Sergeant Shelly Lowenkopf
Peter Fox	Detective Inspector Jack D. Lamarre; Detective Sergeant Alison Prendergast
Edward J. Frail	Inspector Matt Senacal
Kristopher Franklin	Deputy Sheriff Murphy Davis
Nicolas Freeling	Inspector Van der Valk; Inspector Henri Castang
Stephen Gallagher	Officer Johnny Mays; Officer Nick Frazier
Joe Gash	Sergeant Terry Flynn
Kenneth Goddard	Sergeant Walter Anderson; DEA Task Force
Paula Gosling	Lieutenant Mike Malchek; Lieutenant Jack Stryker; Lieutenant Jake Chase
Laurence Gough	Detective Jack Willows; Detective Claire Parker
James Grady	Sergeant Devlin Rourke
Bill Granger	Sergeant Terry Flynn
Michael Grant	Lieutenant Brian Shannon; Lieutenant Alex Rose
Richard Grayson	Inspector Jean-Paul Gautier
W. E. B. Griffin	Staff Inspector Peter Wohl; Sergeant Jason Washington; Detective Matthew Payne
Ken Gross	Detective Jack Mann
Batya Gur	Chief Inspector Michael Ohayon
A. B. Guthrie, Jr.	Sheriff Chick Charleston; Deputy Sheriff Jason Beard
Jean Hager	Chief of Police Mitchell Bushyhead
Nan Hamilton	Isamu Ohara

CREATOR	SERIES CHARACTER(S)
Joseph Harrington	Lieutenant Frank Kerrington; Detective Jane Boardman
Alfred Harris	Detective Lou Baroni
Thomas Harris	FBI Forensic Specialist Will Graham
Ray Harrison	Sergeant Joseph Bragg; Constable James Morton
Roy Hart	Superintendent Douglas Roper
James Neal Harvey	Lieutenant Ben Tolliver; Chief of Police Jud MacElroy
John Harvey	Inspector Charlie Resnick
Mark Hebden	Chief Inspector Clovis Pel
Keith Heller	Parish Watchman George Man
Laurence Henderson	Detective Inspector Durant; Sergeant Arthur Milton; Station Sergeant Newcombe
Sue Henry	State Trooper Sergeant Alex Jensen
Nat Hentoff	Detective Noah Green
Olga Hesky	Inspector Tami Shimoni
Joan Hess	Chief of Police Arly Hanks
Peter Hill	Detective Chief Superintendent Bob Staunton; Detective Inspector Leo Wyndson; Commander Allan Dice; Superintendent Ray Corelli
Tony Hillerman	Lieutenant Joe Leaphorn; Detective Jim Chee
Chester Himes	Detective Coffin Ed Johnson; Detective Grave Digger Jones
Timothy Holme	Inspector Achille Peroni
Ruby Horansky	Detective Nikki Trakos; Detective Dave Lawton
John Hough, Jr.	Chief of Police Nye Gifford; Lieutenant Tom O'Rourke
Robert Houston	Special Agent, U.S. Customs Service, Quintus Paz
Gary Hunter	Detective Garrick Travis
Jack D. Hunter	Inspector Fred Stabile

CREATOR	SERIES CHARACTER(S)
Joe Hyams	Captain Phillip "Punch" Roberts
Peter Inchbald	Chief Inspector Frank Short (Franco Corti)
Graham Ison	Detective Chief Superintendent John Gaffney; Detective Chief Inspector Harry Tipper
Jon A. Jackson	Sergeant "Fang" Mulheisen
Michael Jahn	Lieutenant Bill Donovan; Sergeant T. L. Jefferson
Bill James	Detective Chief Superintendent Colin Harpur
J. A. Jance	Detective Jones Piedmont "J. P." Beaumont
Trish Janeshutz	Detective John Conway; Lieutenant Deidre O'Malley
Hamilton Jobson	Detective Superintendent/ Inspector Matt Anders
Matti Joensuu	Detective Timo Harjunpaa
E. Richard Johnson	Detective Tony Lonto; Detective Pat Runnion; Sergeant Ross Hogan; Detective Mose Hamilton; Lieutenant Joseph Kinsmiller
Bruce Jones	Sergeant Eustes Tully; Sergeant William Brumeister
R. W. Jones	Detective Inspector Huw Evans
Cyril Joyce	Detective Superintendent Bragge; Detective Sergeant Luke Spicer; Detective Constable Tim Cox; Detective Sergeant Jerome; Chief Superintendent Patrick Stockton
Stuart M. Kaminsky	Chief Inspector Porfiry Rostnikov; Inspector Emil Karpo; Inspector Sasha Tkach
MacKinlay Kantor	23rd Precinct, New York City
Herbert Kastle	Sergeant Eddy Roersch; Detective Willis Jones
William Katz	Lieutenant Leonard Karlov
John Katzenbach	Detective Mercedes Barren

CREATOR	SERIES CHARACTER(S)
Faye Kellerman	Detective Peter Decker
Jonathan Kellerman	Chief Inspector Daniel Shalom Sharavi
Bill Kelly and Dolph Le Moult	Detective Vince Crowley
Alanna Knight	Detective Inspector Jeremy Faro
Bill Knox	Detective Chief Inspector Colin Thane; Detective Inspector Phil Moss
John Lantigua	Inspector David Cruz
Philip Lauben	Captain Homer Clay; Sergeant Ernest Manion
John Leslie	Lieutenant Patrick Bowman
Bob Leuci	Captain Marjorie Butera
J. R. Levitt	Detective Jason Coulter; Detective Dave Warren
Michael Z. Lewin	Lieutenant Leroy Powder
Roy Lewis	Chief Inspector John Crow
Herbert Lieberman	Chief Medical Examiner Paul Konig; Detective Francis Xavier Haggard; Sergeant Edward Flynn; Lieutenant Francis (Frank) Mooney
David L. Lindsey	Sergeant Stuart Haydon; Detective Leo Hirsch; Lieutenant Bob Dystal; Detective Carmen Palma
Elizabeth Linington	Sergeant Ivor Maddox; Detective Sue Maddox
Jayson Livingston	Detective Stu Redlam
Tom Logan	14th Precinct, Detroit Police
Ed McBain	87th Precinct, Isola Police Department: Detective Arthur Brown; Lieutenant Peter Byrnes; Detective Steve Carella; Detective Richard Genero; Detective Cotton Hawes; Detective Bert Kling; Detective Meyer Meyer; Detective Hal Willis

CREATOR	SERIES CHARACTER(S)
James McClure	Lieutenant Tromp Kramer; Sergeant Mickey Zondi
Vincent McConnor	Chief Inspector Damiot; Vidocq; Lieutenant Victor Lolo
Sharyn McCrumb	Sheriff Spencer Arrowood
Jill McGown	Detective Chief Inspector Lloyd; Detective Sergeant/Inspector Judy Hill
William McIlvanney	Detective Inspector Jack Laidlaw
Joseph D. McNamara	Police Chief Fraleigh
Michael Malone	Lieutenant Justin Savile; Lieutenant Cudberth "Cuddy" Mangum
Anthony Mancini	Lieutenant David Torino
Terry Marlowe	Sergeant Bill Clark
Margaret Maron	Lieutenant Sigrid Harold
Max Marquis	Chief Inspector Ted Greening; Inspector Harry Timberlake; Superintendent Charles Harkness
J. J. Marric	Commander/Chief Superintendent George Gideon
William Marshall	Detective Chief Inspector Henry Feiffer; Lieutenant Felix Elizalde; Detective Vergil Tillman; Detective Ned Muldoon
Ian Kennedy Martin	Inspector Jack Regan
Lee Martin	Detective Deb Ralston; Chief of Police Alberto Salazar
Edward Mathis	Lieutenant Benjamin Cloud
Seicho Matsumoto	Inspector Imanishi Eitaro; Detective Yoshimura Hiroshi; Detective Jutaro Torigai
Archer Mayor	Lieutenant Joseph Gunther
Henry Meigs	Inspector Tetsuo Mori
James Melville	Superintendent Tetsuo Otani; Inspector Jiro Kimura

CREATOR	SERIES CHARACTER(S)
Jennie Melville	Inspector Charmian Daniels
D. R. Meredith	Sheriff Charles Timothy Matthews; Deputy Meanie
Hugh Miller	Inspector Michael Fletcher
Rex Miller	Detective Jack Eichord
John Minahan	Detective John "Little John" Rawlings
Kirk Mitchell	Detective John Kost (Ivan Mikhailovich Kostoff)
Marcel Montecino	Lieutenant Jack Gold
David J. Murphy	Inspector Edward Malone
Stephen Murray	Detective Inspector Alec Stainton
Ed Naha	Lieutenant Kevin Broskey
Janet Neel	Detective Inspector John McLeish; Detective Sergeant Bruce Davidson
David Nemec	Parole Officer Frank Reppa
Christopher Newman	Lieutenant Joe Dante; U.S. Treasury Agent Robert McElliot; U.S. Treasury Agent Stan Torbeck
Fridrikh Neznansky	Investigator Alexander Borisovich "Sasha" Turetsky; Investigator Konstantin Dmitriyevich "Kostya" Merkula; Forensic Pathologist Margarita N. Kolayevna "Rita" Shchastlivaya
Kyotaro Nishimura	Inspector Totsugawa; Detective Sergeant Honda
Gil North	Detective Sergeant Caleb Cluff; Detective Inspector Mole; Superintendent Kofi Katt
Lillian O'Donnell	Police Officer/Detective/Sergeant/Lieutenant Norah Mulcahaney; Sergeant/Lieutenant Joseph Capretto; Lieutenant/Captain Emmanuel; Detective Gary Reissig

CREATOR	SERIES CHARACTER(S)
Freny Olbrich	Chief Inspector Frank Desouza
D. J. Olivy	Superintendent Ken Hollis
Jack Olsen	Watch Commander Lieutenant Packer Lind
Paul Orum	Inspector Jonas Morck; Inspector Knud Einarsen
Jerry Oster	Sergeant Joe Cullen; Sergeant Robert Redfield; Lieutenant Jacob "Jake" Neuman; Lieutenant David Milner; DEA Agent Susan Van Meter
T. Jefferson Parker	Detective Tom Shephard
James Patterson	Lieutenant John Stefanovitch; Detective Isiah Parker
Paul Patti	Lieutenant Andy Amato; Sergeant Gabrielle Amato
Barbara Paul	Sergeant Marian Larch; Detective Foley
Laurence Payne	Detective Chief Inspector Sam Birkett; Detective Sergeant Saunders
Michael Pearce	Mamur Zapt Captain Gareth Cadwallader Owen
Ridley Pearson	Sergeant Lou Boldt; Sergeant James Dewitt; FBI Special Agent Cameron Daggett
Dave Pedneau	D. A.'s Investigator Whit Pynchon
Anne Perry	Detective Inspector William Monk
Gerald Petievich	Treasury Agent Charles Carr; Treasury Agent Jack Kelly; Sergeant Jose Stepanovich
Tom Philbin	Detective Joe Lawless
Robert Pike	Lieutenant Clancy; Lieutenant James Reardon; Sergeant Dondero
Joyce Porter	Detective Chief Inspector Wilfred Dover; Detective Sergeant Charles Edward MacGregor

Creators and Series Characters

CREATOR	SERIES CHARACTER(S)
Maurice Procter	Detective Chief Inspector Philip Hunter; Detective Inspector Robert Fairbrother; Detective Chief Inspector Harry Martineau
Mary Monica Pulver	Sergeant Peter Brichter
Erica Quest	Detective Chief Inspector Kate Maddox
Hugh C. Rae	Detective Chief Superintendent McCaig; Detective Inspector Ryan
Julian Rathbone	Commissioner Jan Argand
Derek Raymond	Nameless Detective
Robert Sims Reid	Detective Leo Banks; Detective Red Hanrahan; Sergeant Sam Blieker
John Lawrence Reynolds	Lieutenant Joe McGuire; Lieutenant Ollie Schantz
Shepard Rifkin	Sergeant Damian McQuaid
Jack Ripley	Constable John George Davis
Peter Robinson	Chief Inspector Alan Banks
Charles G. Rogers	Detective Steve Cates
Robert Rosenberg	Commander Avram Cohen; Chief Inspector Nissim Levy
Dennis St. Pierre	Lieutenant Frank Evans
Lawrence Sanders	Captain Edward X. Delaney
John Sandford	Lieutenant Lucas Davenport
J. G. Sandom	Inspector Nigel Lyman
Soledad Santiago	Police Officer Toni Conroy; Police Officer Errol Stutz
Eric Sauter	Detective Patrick Paige
Alan Scholefield	Detective Superintendent George Macrae; Detective Sergeant Leopold Silver
Monte Schulz	Chief of Police Carroll Howser
Jack S. Scott	Detective Inspector Alfred Rosher; Detective Sergeant Cruise; Detective Chief Inspector Pete Parsons; Detective Sergeant Wammo Winbush

CREATOR	SERIES CHARACTER(S)
Owen Sela	Senior Chief Inspector Richard Chan; Inspector Peter Winston
Francis Selwyn	Sergeant William Clarence Verity; Sergeant Martock
David Serafin	Superintendent Luis Bernal
Steve Shagan	Lieutenant Jack Raines
Dell Shannon	Lieutenant Luis Mendoza
Georges Simenon	Superintendent Maigret
V. L. Sims	Sergeant Dixie Struthers; Lieutenant Tony DiFranco
Maj Sjöwall and Per Wahlöö	Chief Inspector Martin Beck
Michael Slade	Superintendent Robert DeClercq; Chief Superintendent Hilary Rand; Inspector Zinc Chandler
Ben Sloane	Detective Max Horn; Detective Dan Riddle
Alison Smith	Chief of Police Judd Springfield
D. W. Smith	Chief Inspector Harry Fathers
Julie Smith	Detective Skip Langdon
Mark Smith	Detective Magnuson
Martin Cruz Smith	Chief Inspector Arkady Renko
Stephen Solomita	Sergeant Stanley Moodrow; Detective Jim Tilley
Richard Martin Stern	Lieutenant Juan Felipe "Johnny" Ortiz
J. Michael Straczynski	Detective Susan Warwick; Detective Jordan Cayle
L. A. G. Strong	Chief Inspector Ellis McKay
Carsten Stroud	Detective Frank Keogh
Rob Swigart	Lieutenant Cobb Takamura; Microbiologist Chazz Koenig
Jeffrey Tharp	Lieutenant John Branch
Donald Thomas	Detective Inspector Alfred Swain; Detective Sergeant Oliver Lumley
Roderick Thorp	Lieutenant Mike Gallagher
Laurence Treat	Detective Mitch Taylor; Detective Jub Freeman

Creators and Series Characters

CREATOR	SERIES CHARACTER(S)
Joseph Trigoboff	Detective Alvin Yablonsky
Peter Turnbull	P Divison, Glasgow Police
Dorothy Uhnak	Detective Christie Opara; Sergeant Joe Peters
Derek Van Arman	VICAT Director John F. Scott
Janwillem van de Wetering	The Commissaris (unnamed); Adjutant Grijpstra; Sergeant Rinus de Gier
Peter Van Greenaway	Detective Inspector Cherry
John Holbrook Vance	Sergeant Joe Bain
Conrad Voss Bark	Detective Sergeant Lune
Per Wahlöö	Inspector Jensen
John Wainwright	Chief Superintendent Lewis; Superintendent Gilliant; Chief Superintendent Charles Ripley; Detective Superintendent Lyle Lennox; Chief Inspector Bardoph Sawyer; Assistant Chief Constable Robert Harris; Chief Superintendent Robert Blayde; Inspector Lye; Inspector Chris Tallboy; Inspector Edmund Caan; Chief Superintendent Ralph Flensing; Chief Inspector David Hoyle; Chief Superintendent Harry Barstow; Inspector James Riddle; Inspector Faber; Sergeant Jackson
Peter N. Walker	Detective Sergeant James Aloysius Carnaby-King; Constable Jock Patterson
Randall Wallace	Detective Scarlet Mc Cullers; Detective Tom Ridge
Joseph Wambaugh	Officer Serge Duran; Officer Gus Plebesly; Officer Roy Fehler; Officer William A. "Bumper" Morgan; Sergeant Cruz Segovia; Commander Hector Moss; Detective Valnikov; Sergeant Al Mackey; Martin Welborn;

CREATOR	SERIES CHARACTER(S)
Joseph Wambaugh (*cont.*)	Sergeant Mario Villalobos; Sergeant Sidney Blackwell; Sergeant Otto Stringer; Chief of Police Paco Pedroza; Detective Lynn Cutter
Hillary Waugh	Captain Mike Danaher; Detective Dave Malone; Chief of Police Fred C. Fellows; Detective Frank Sessions
Irving Weinman	Inspector Lenny Schwartz
Pamela West	Detective Inspector West
Robert Westbrook	Lieutenant Nicholas Rachmaninoff
John Westermann	Detective "Tree" Nelson; Detective Jimmy Tibaldi; Police Officer Orin Boyd; Detective Jack Mills; Detective Claire Williamson
Collin Wilcox	Lieutenant Frank Hastings; Lieutenant Pete Friedman
Charles Willeford	Sergeant Hoke Mosley
Timothy Williams	Commissario Piero Trotti
David Wiltse	Lieutenant Sandy Block; Detective Lou Florio; Special Agent John Becker
Anne Wingate	Chief of Police Mark Shingata; Sergeant Al Quinn
Pauline Glen Winslow	Detective Chief Superintendent Merle Capricorn; Detective Inspector Al Copper
Ted Wood	Chief of Police Reid Bennett; Sam, a police dog
Daniel Woodrell	Detective Rene Shades
Eric Wright	Inspector Charlie Salter
L. R. Wright	Staff Sergeant Karl Alberg

3

Series Characters and Creators

SERIES CHARACTER	CREATOR
Staff Sergeant Karl Alberg	L. R. Wright
Lieutenant Andy Amato	Paul Patti
Sergeant Gabrielle Amato	Paul Patti
Detective Inspector Matt Anders	Hamilton Jobson
Sergeant Walter Anderson	Kenneth Goddard
Commissioner Jan Argand	Julian Rathbone
Sheriff Spencer Arrowood	Sharyn McCrumb
Sergeant Joe Bain	John Holbrook Vance
Chief of Police Mario Balzic	K. C. Constantine
Chief Inspector Alan Banks	Peter Robinson
Detective Leo Banks	Robert Sims Reid
David Bar-Lev	William Bayer
Detective Lou Baroni	Alfred Harris
Detective Mercedes Barren	John Katzenbach
Chief Superintendent Harry Barstow	John Wainwright
Chief Inspector Martin Bauer	Frank DeFelitta
Probation Officer Baum	Peter Blauner
Deputy Sheriff Jason Beard	A. B. Guthrie Jr.
Detective Jones Piedmont "J. P." Beaumont	J. A. Jance
Chief Inspector Martin Beck	Maj Sjöwall and Per Wahlöö
Special Agent John Becker	David Wiltse
Commissaire Robert Bellarmine	Robert Daley
Chief of Police Reid Bennett	Ted Wood
Superintendent Luis Bernal	David Serafin

SERIES CHARACTER	CREATOR
Chief Inspector Sam Birkett	Laurence Payne
Sergeant Sidney Blackwell	Joseph Wambaugh
Detective Babs Bladenbauer	Lew Dykes
Chief Superintendent Robert Blayde	John Wainwright
Detective Bucky Bleichert	James Ellroy
Sergeant Sam Blieker	Robert Sims Reid
Lieutenant Sandy Block	David Wiltse
Detective Jane Boardman	Joseph Harrington
Sergeant Lou Boldt	Ridley Pearson
Detective Hieronymus Bosch	Michael Connelly
Lieutenant Patrick Bowman	John Leslie
Police Officer Orin Boyd	John Westermann
Sergeant Joseph Bragg	Ray Harrison
Superintendent Bragge	Cyril Joyce
Lieutenant John Branch	Jeffrey Tharp
Smokey Brandon	Noreen Ayres
Sergeant Peter Brichter	Mary Monica Pulver
Lieutenant Kevin Broskey	Ed Naha
Chief Medical Examiner Andy Broussard	D. J. Donaldson
Detective Arthur Brown	Ed McBain
Sergeant William Brumeister	Bruce Jones
Chief of Police Mitchell Bushyhead	Jean Hager
Captain Marjorie Butera (Captain Butterfly)	Bob Leuci
Lieutenant Peter Byrnes	Ed McBain
Inspector Edmund Caan	John Wainwright
Lieutenant Joseph Capretto	Lillian O'Donnell
Detective Chief Superintendent Merle Capricorn	Pauline Glen Winslow
Detective Steve Carella	Ed McBain
Detective Sergeant James Aloysius Carnaby-King	Peter N. Walker
Treasury Agent Charles Carr	Gerald Petievich
Inspector Henri Castang	Nicolas Freeling
Detective Steve Cates	Charles G. Rogers
Detective Jordan Cayle	J. Michael Straczynski

Series Characters and Creators

SERIES CHARACTER	CREATOR
Senior Chief Inspector Richard Chan	Owen Sela
Inspector Zinc Chandler	Michael Slade
Sheriff Chick Charleston	A. B. Guthrie Jr.
Frank Chase	Andrew Coburn
Lieutenant Jake Chase	Paula Gosling
Detective Jim Chee	Tony Hillerman
Detective Inspector Cherry	Peter Van Greenaway
Inspector Mary Choy	Greg Bear
Lieutenant Clancy	Robert Pike
Sergeant Bill Clark	Terry Marlowe
Captain Homer Clay	Philip Lauben
Lieutenant Frank Clemons	Thomas H. Cook
Lieutenant Benjamin Cloud	Edward Mathis
Detective Sergeant Caleb Cluff	Gil North
Detective Chief Superintendent/ Chief Inspector John Coffin	Gwendoline Butler
Commander Avram Cohen	Robert Rosenberg
Detective Brenda Collins	Joseph P. De Sario
The Commissaris (unnamed)	Janwillem van de Wetering
Police Officer Toni Conroy	Soledad Santiago
Detective John Conway	Trish Janeshutz
Detective Inspector Al Copper	Pauline Glen Winslow
Detective Superintendent Ray Corelli	Peter Hill
Detective Chief Inspector Franco Corti (Frank Short)	Peter Inchbald
Detective Jason Coulter	J. R. Levitt
Detective Constable Tim Cox	Cyril Joyce
Detective Chief Inspector John Crow	Roy Lewis
Detective Vince Crowley	Bill Kelly and Dolph Le Moult
Detective Sergeant Cruise	Jack S. Scott
Inspector David Cruz	John Lantigua
Sergeant Joe Cullen	Jerry Oster
Inspector Robin Cully	Jack Curtis
Detective Lynn Cutter	Joseph Wambaugh
Captain José da Silva	Robert L. Fish
FBI Special Agent Cameron Daggett	Ridley Pearson
Chief Inspector Damiot	Vincent McConnor

SERIES CHARACTER	CREATOR
Captain Mike Danaher	Hillary Waugh
Inspector Charmian Daniels	Jennie Melville
Lieutenant Joe Dante	Christopher Newman
Lieutenant Lucas Davenport	John Sandford
Detective Sergeant Bruce Davidson	Janet Neel
Constable John George Davis	Jack Ripley
Deputy Sheriff Murphy Davis	Kristopher Franklin
Sergeant Mike Dawson	Jack Curtis
Sergeant Sonny Dawson	Andrew Coburn
Sergeant Rinus de Gier	Janwillem van de Wetering
Detective Peter Decker	Faye Kellerman
Superintendent Robert DeClercq	Michael Slade
Captain Edward X. Delaney	Lawrence Sanders
Detective Inspector Delaval	Roy Lewis
Chief Inspector Frank Desouza	Freny Olbrich
Sergeant James Dewitt	Ridley Pearson
Commander Allan Dice	Peter Hill
Lieutenant Tony DiFranco	V. L. Sims
Lieutenant Dina Donato	Jack Early
Sergeant Michael Donato	Jack Early
Sergeant Dondero	Robert Pike
Lieutenant Bill Donovan	Michael Jahn
Detective Chief Inspector Wilfred Dover	Joyce Porter
Lieutenant Christopher Drake	Robert Cain
Officer Serge Duran	Joseph Wambaugh
Detective Inspector Durant	Laurence Henderson
Lieutenant Bob Dystal	David L. Lindsey
Detective Jack Eichord	Rex Miller
87th Precinct, Isola Police Department	Ed McBain
Inspector Knud Einarsen	Paul Orum
Chief of Detectives Earl Eischied	Robert Daley
Inspector Imanishi Eitaro	Seicho Matsumoto
Lieutenant Felix Elizalde	William Marshall
Captain Emmanuel	Lillian O'Donnell
Detective Inspector Huw Evans	R. W. Jones

SERIES CHARACTER	CREATOR
Lieutenant Frank Evans	Dennis St. Pierre
Inspector Faber	John Wainwright
Detective Inspector Robert Fairbrother	Maurice Procter
Detective Inspector Jeremy Faro	Alanna Knight
Detective Chief Inspector Harry Fathers	D. W. Smith
Officer Roy Fehler	Joseph Wambaugh
Chief Inspector Henry Feiffer	William Marshall
Chief of Police Fred C. Fellows	Hillary Waugh
Detective Fiona FitzGerald	Warren Adler
Chief Superintendent Ralph Flensing	John Wainwright
Inspector Michael Fletcher	Hugh Miller
Lieutenant Andrew Flynn	E. W. Count
Sergeant Edward Flynn	Herbert Lieberman
Sergeant Terry Flynn	Joe Gash
Detective Lou Florio	David Wiltse
Detective Foley	Barbara Paul
Fire Chief MacKinley Fontana	Earl W. Emerson
Lieutenant Vercingetorix Fort	Lew Dykes
Fourteenth Precinct, Detroit Police	Tom Logan
Investigator Virgil Fox	Dallas Barnes
Police Chief Fraleigh	Joseph D. McNamara
Police Psychologist Kit Franklin	D. J. Donaldson
Officer Nick Frazier	Stephen Gallagher
Detective Jub Freeman	Laurence Treat
Lieutenant Pete Friedman	Collin Wilcox
Detective Chief Superintendent John Gaffney	Graham Ison
Lieutenant Mike Gallagher	Roderick Thorp
Inspector Jean-Paul Gautier	Richard Grayson
Detective Richard Genero	Ed McBain
FBI Special Agent Cuthbert "Bert" Gibbons	Anthony Bruno
Commander George Gideon	J. J. Marric
Chief of Police Nye Gifford	John Hough, Jr.
Rupert Goetz, Chief of Homicide	Andrew Coburn
Lieutenant Jack Gold	Marcel Montecino

SERIES CHARACTER	CREATOR
Detective Sergeant Roger Goodman	Roger Busby
FBI Forensic Specialist Will Graham	Thomas Harris
Detective Noah Green	Nat Hentoff
Detective Chief Inspector Ted Greening	Max Marquis
Adjutant Grijpstra	Janwillem van de Wetering
Lieutenant Joseph Gunther	Archer Mayor
Detective Francis Xavier Haggard	Herbert Lieberman
Detective Mose Hamilton	E. Richard Johnson
Chief of Police Arly Hanks	Joan Hess
Detective Timo Harjunpaa	Matti Joensuu
Detective Superintendent Charles Harkness	Max Marquis
Lieutenant Sigrid Harold	Margaret Maron
Detective Chief Superintendent Colin Harpur	Bill James
Assistant Chief Constable Robert Harris	John Wainwright
Lieutenant Frank Hastings	Collin Wilcox
Detective Cotton Hawes	Ed McBain
Sergeant Stuart Haydon	David L. Lindsey
Inspector Joseph Hearn	Robert Daley
Detective Sergeant Judy Hill	Jill McGown
Detective Yoshimura Hiroshi	Seicho Matsumoto
Detective Leo Hirsch	David L. Lindsey
Detective Neil Hockaday	Thomas Adcock
Sergeant Ross Hogan	E. Richard Johnson
Superintendent Ken Hollis	D. J. Olivy
Sergeant Lee Hollister	Dallas Barnes
Chief of Detectives Martin Holmberg	K. Arne Blom
Detective Sergeant Honda	Kyotaro Nishimura
Sergeant Lloyd Hopkins	James Ellroy
Detective Max Horn	Ben Sloane
Detective Howland	Bill Crider
Chief of Police Carroll Howser	Monte Schulz
Chief Inspector David Hoyle	John Wainwright
Sergeant Jackson	John Wainwright

SERIES CHARACTER	CREATOR
Detective Tom Jackson	Thomas H. Cook
Lieutenant Frank Janek	William Bayer
Detective Cliff Janeway	John Dunning
Sergeant T. L. Jefferson	Michael Jahn
Inspector Jensen	Per Wahlöö
State Trooper Sergeant Alex Jensen	Sue Henry
Sergeant Jerome	Cyril Joyce
Detective V. K. Jessenovik	Eleanor Taylor Bland
Detective Coffin Ed Johnson	Chester Himes
Detective Grave Digger Jones	Chester Himes
Detective Willis Jones	Herbert Kastle
Lieutenant Leonard Karlov	William Katz
Inspector Emil Karpo	Stuart M. Kaminsky
Superintendent Kofi Katt	Gil North
Treasury Agent Jack Kelly	Gerald Petievich
Detective Frank Keogh	Carsten Stroud
Lieutenant Frank Kerrington	Joseph Harrington
Superintendent Bamsan Kiet	Gary Alexander
Inspector Jiro Kimura	James Melville
Lieutenant Joseph Kinsmiller	E. Richard Johnson
Detective Bert Kling	Ed McBain
Microbiologist Chazz Koenig	Rob Swigart
Chief Medical Examiner Paul Konig	Herbert Lieberman
Detective John Kost (Ivan Mikhailovich Kostoff)	Kirk Mitchell
Detective Karen Kovac	Joe Gash
Chief Deputy Sheriff Milton Kovak	Susan Rogers Cooper
Lieutenant Tromp Kramer	James McClure
Inspector Jack Laidlaw	William McIlvanney
Detective Inspector Jack D. Lamarre	Peter Fox
Detective Skip Langdon	Julie Smith
Sergeant Marian Larch	Barbara Paul
Detective Dino LaStanza	O'Neil de Noux
Detective Joe Lawless	Tom Philbin
Detective Dave Lawton	Ruby Horansky
Lieutenant Joe Leaphorn	Tony Hillerman
Detective Superintendent Lyle Lennox	John Wainwright

SERIES CHARACTER	CREATOR
Inspector Leric	Roger Busby
FBI Special Agent Joseph Lerza	John Danica and Lucy Freeman
Chief Inspector Nissim Levy	Robert Rosenberg
Chief Superintendent Lewis	John Wainwright
Watch Commander Lieutenant Packer Lind	Jack Olsen
Detective Chief Inspector Lloyd	Jill McGown
Lieutenant Victor Lolo	Vincent McConnor
Detective Tony Lonto	E. Richard Johnson
Sergeant Shelly Lowenkopf	Richard Fliegel
Lieutenant Teddy Lucas	William J. Caunitz
Detective Sergeant Oliver Lumley	Donald Thomas
Detective Sergeant Lune	Conrad Voss Bark
Chief Inspector Lyle	John Wainwright
Inspector Nigel Lyman	J. G. Sandom
Detective Marti MacAlister	Eleanor Taylor Bland
Detective Chief Superintendent McCaig	Hugh C. Rae
Detective Scarlet McCullers	Randall Wallace
U.S. Treasury Agent Robert McElliot	Christopher Newman
Chief of Police Jud MacElroy	James Neal Harvey
Sergeant Charles Edward MacGregor	Joyce Porter
Lieutenant Joe McGuire	John Lawrence Reynolds
Chief Inspector Ellis McKay	L. A. G. Strong
Detective Inspector John McLeish	Janet Neel
Detective Inspector Frank McMorran	Marten Claridge
Sergeant Damian McQuaid	Shepard Rifkin
Sergeant Al Mackey	Joseph Wambaugh
Detective Superintendent George Macrae	Alan Scholefield
Sergeant Ivor Maddox	Elizabeth Linington
Detective Chief Inspector Kate Maddox	Erica Quest
Detective Sue Maddox	Elizabeth Linington
Detective Magnuson	Mark Smith
Superintendent Maigret	Georges Simenon
Lieutenant Mike Malchek	Paula Gosling

Series Characters and Creators

SERIES CHARACTER	CREATOR
Lieutenant Dan Malone	William J. Caunitz
Detective Dave Malone	Hillary Waugh
Inspector Edward Malone	David J. Murphy
Inspector Scobie Malone	Jon Cleary
Parish Watchman George Man	Keith Heller
Lieutenant Cudberth "Cuddy" Mangum	Michael Malone
Sergeant Ernest Manion	Philip Lauben
Detective Jack Mann	Ken Gross
Lieutenant Lou Marino	Patricia D. Cornwell
Detective Chief Inspector Harry Martineau	Maurice Procter
Sergeant Martock	Francis Selwyn
Sergeant Masao Masuto	E. V. Cunningham
Sheriff Charles Timothy Matthews	D. R. Meredith
Officer Johnny Mays	Stephen Gallagher
Deputy Meanie	D. R. Meredith
Lieutenant Luis Mendoza	Dell Shannon
Investigator Konstantin Dmitriyevich "Kostya" Merkula	Fridrikh Neznansky
Detective Meyer Meyer	Ed McBain
Detective Jack Mills	John Westermann
Lieutenant David Milner	Jerry Oster
Sergeant Arthur Milton	Laurence Henderson
Sergeant Matthew Minogue	John Brady
Detective Inspector Mole	Gil North
Detective Inspector William Monk	Anne Perry
Sergeant Stanley Moodrow	Stephen Solomita
Detective Hank Moody	Robert Chambers
Lieutenant Francis (Frank) Mooney	Herbert Lieberman
Inspector Jonas Morck	Paul Orum
Officer William A. "Bumper" Morgan	Joseph Wambaugh
Inspector Tetsuo Mori	Henry Meigs
Detective Constable James Morton	Ray Harrison
Sergeant Hoke Mosley	Charles Willeford
Commander Hector Moss	Joseph Wambaugh
Detective Inspector Phil Moss	Bill Knox

SERIES CHARACTER	CREATOR
Lieutenant Norah Mulcahaney	Lillian O'Donnell
Detective Ned Muldoon	William Marshall
Sergeant "Fang" Mulheisen	Jon A. Jackson
Lieutenant Daniel Nalon	Harold R. Daniels
Nameless Detective	Derek Raymond
Detective "Tree" Nelson	John Westermann
Eliot Ness, Director of Public Safety	Max Allan Collins
Lieutenant Jacob "Jake" Neuman	Jerry Oster
Station Sergeant Newcombe	Laurence Henderson
Isamu Ohara	Nan Hamilton
Chief Inspector Michael Ohayon	Batya Gur
Chief Inspector Seved Olofsson	K. Arne Blom
Lieutenant Deidre O'Malley	Trish Janeshutz
Detective Christie Opara	Dorothy Uhnak
Lieutenant Juan Felipe "Johnny" Ortiz	Richard Martin Stern
Superintendent Tetsuo Otani	James Melville
Captain Ken Others	William Camp
Mamur Zapt Captain Gareth Cadwallader Owen	Michael Pearce
P Divison, Glasgow Police	Peter Turnbull
Detective Patrick Paige	Eric Sauter
Detective Carmen Palma	David L. Lindsey
Detective Claire Parker	Laurence Gough
Detective Isaiah Parker	James Patterson
Detective Chief Inspector Pete Parsons	Jack S. Scott
Constable Jock Patterson	Peter Walker
Detective Matthew Payne	John Kevin Dugan
Detective Matthew Payne	W. E. B. Griffin
Special Agent, U.S. Customs Service, Quintus Paz	Robert Houston
Chief of Police Paco Pedroza	Joseph Wambaugh
Chief Inspector Clovis Pel	Mark Hebden
Inspector Achille Peroni	Timothy Holme
Sergeant Joe Peters	Dorothy Uhnak
Detective Picone	Robert L. Duncan
Officer Gus Plebesly	Joseph Wambaugh

SERIES CHARACTER	CREATOR
Lieutenant Leroy Powder	Michael Z. Lewin
Detective Sergeant Alison Prendergast	Peter Fox
D. A.'s Investigator Whit Pynchon	Dave Pedneau
Detective Chief Inspector Eddie Quick	Roger Busby
Sergeant Al Quinn	Anne Wingate
Lieutenant Nicholas Rachmaninoff	Robert Westbrook
Lieutenant Jack Raines	Steve Shagan
Detective Deb Ralston	Lee Martin
Chief Superintendent Hilary Rand	Michael Slade
Detective John "Little John" Rawlings	John Minahan
Lieutenant James Reardon	Robert Pike
Sergeant Robert Redfield	Jerry Oster
Detective Stu Redlam	Jayson Livingston
Inspector Jack Regan	Ian Kennedy Martin
Detective Gary Reissig	Lillian O'Donnell
Chief Inspector Arkady Renko	Martin Cruz Smith
Parole Officer Frank Reppa	David Nemec
Inspector Charlie Resnick	John Harvey
Sheriff Dan Rhodes	Bill Crider
Detective Dan Riddle	Ben Sloane
Inspector James Riddle	John Wainwright
Detective Tom Ridge	Randall Wallace
Chief Superintendent Charles Ripley	John Wainwright
Detective Rizzutto	Robert L. Duncan
Captain Phillip "Punch" Roberts	Joe Hyams
Lieutenant Dave Robicheaux	James Lee Burke
ROD (a combat robot)	Robert Cain
Sergeant Eddy Roersch	Herbert Kastle
Police Psychologist Romain	Bill Crider
Detective Charlie Rope	John Eller
Superintendent Douglas Roper	Roy Hart
Lieutenant Alex Rose	Michael Grant
Detective Inspector Alfred Rosher	Jack S. Scott
Sergeant Arnold Ross	Nick Christian
Chief Inspector Porfiry Rostnikov	Stuart M. Kaminsky
Sergeant Devlin Rourke	James Grady

SERIES CHARACTER	CREATOR
Detective Inspector Tony Rowley	Roger Busby
Detective William Ruffin	Ernest Clark
Detective Pat Runnion	E. Richard Johnson
Detective Inspector Ryan	Hugh C. Rae
Sergeant Joe Ryker	Nelson De Mille
Chief of Police Alberto Salazar	Lee Martin
Inspector Charlie Salter	Eric Wright
Sam, a police dog	Ted Wood
Detective Sergeant Saunders	Laurence Payne
Lieutenant Justin Savile	Michael Malone
Chief Inspector Bardoph Sawyer	John Wainwright
Lieutenant Tony Scanlon	William J. Caunitz
Medical Examiner Kay Scarpetta	Patricia D. Cornwell
Lieutenant Ollie Schantz	John Lawrence Reynolds
Inspector Lenny Schwartz	Irving Weinman
Detective Aline Scott	Alison Drake
VICAT Director John F. Scott	Derek Van Arman
Sergeant Cruz Segovia	Joseph Wambaugh
Inspector Matt Senacal	Edward J. Frail
Detective Frank Sessions	Hillary Waugh
Detective Rene Shades	Daniel Woodrell
Chief Inspector Daniel Shalom Sharavi	Jonathan Kellerman
Forensic Pathologist Margarita N. Kolayevna "Rita" Shchastlivaya	Fridrikh Neznansky
Lieutenant Brian Shannon	Michael Grant
Detective Tom Shephard	T. Jefferson Parker
Inspector Tami Shimoni	Olga Hesky
Chief of Police Mark Shingata	Anne Wingate
Chief Inspector Frank Short (Franco Corti)	Peter Inchbald
Detective Sergeant Leopold Silver	Alan Scholefield
Detective Jill Smith	Susan Dunlap
Chief Superintendent Owen Smith	James Barnett
Detective Sergeant Luke Spicer	Cyril Joyce
Chief of Police Judd Springfield	Alison Smith
Inspector Fred Stabile	Jack. D. Hunter
Detective Inspector Alex Stainton	Stephen Murray

Series Characters and Creators

SERIES CHARACTER	CREATOR
Detective Chief Superintendent Bob Staunton	Peter Hill
Lieutenant John Stefanovitch	James Patterson
Sergeant Jose Stepanovich	Gerald Petievich
Detective Chief Superintendent Patrick Stockton	Cyril Joyce
Sergeant Otto Stringer	Joseph Wambaugh
Sergeant Dixie Struthers	V. L. Sims
Lieutenant Jack Stryker	Paula Gosling
Police Officer Errol Stutz	Soledad Santiago
Detective Inspector Alfred Swain	Donald Thomas
Lieutenant Cobb Takamura	Rob Swigart
Inspector Chris Tallboy	John Wainwright
Chief of Police Jack Tallon	John Ball
Tina Tamiko	Paul Bishop
Detective Mitch Taylor	Laurence Treat
Detective Chief Inspector Colin Thane	Bill Knox
Detective Jimmy Tibaldi	John Westermann
Detective Virgil Tibbs	John Ball
Detective Jim Tilley	Stephen Solomita
Detective Vergil Tillman	William Marshall
Inspector Harry Timberlake	Max Marquis
Detective Chief Inspector Harry Tipper	Graham Ison
Inspector Sasha Tkach	Stuart M. Kaminsky
Lieutenant Ben Tolliver	James Neal Harvey
U.S. Treasury Agent Stan Torbeck	Christopher Newman
Detective Jutaro Torigai	Seicho Matsumoto
Lieutenant David Torino	Anthony Mancini
Inspector Totsugawa	Kyotaro Nishimura
FBI Special Agent Mike Tozzi	Anthony Bruno
Detective Nikki Trakos	Ruby Horansky
Garrick Travis	Gary Hunter
Commissario Piero Trotti	Timothy Williams
Sergeant Eustes Tully	Bruce Jones
Investigator Alexander Borisovich "Sasha" Turetsky	Fridrikh Neznansky

SERIES CHARACTER	CREATOR
23rd Precinct, New York City	MacKinlay Kantor
Policeman Freddy Underhill	James Ellroy
Inspector Van der Valk	Nicolas Freeling
Detective Valnikov	Joseph Wambaugh
DEA Agent Susan Van Meter	Jerry Oster
Sergeant William Clarence Verity	Francis Selwyn
Vidocq	Vincent McConnor
Sergeant Mario Villalobos	Joseph Wambaugh
Lieutenant John Vinda	William J. Caunitz
Detective Gabriel Wager	Rex Burns
Calico Jack Walker	Paul Bishop
Policeman Wacky Walker	James Ellroy
Detective Dave Warren	J. R. Levitt
Detective Susan Warwick	J. Michael Straczynski
Sergeant Jason Washington	John Kevin Dugan
Sergeant Jason Washington	W. E. B. Griffin
Detective Martin Welborn	Joseph Wambaugh
Sergeant Ben Wellman	Thomas H. Cook
Detective Inspector West	Pamela West
Detective Chief Inspector Roger West	John Creasey
Sergeant Charlie Wilentz	Harold R. Daniels
Detective Claire Williamson	John Westermann
Detective Hal Willis	Ed McBain
Detective Jack Willows	Laurence Gough
Superintendent Richard Wilson	R. W. Jones
Detective Sergeant Wammo Winbush	Jack S. Scott
Inspector Peter Winston	Owen Sela
Staff Inspector Peter Wohl	John Kevin Dugan
Staff Inspector Peter Wohl	W. E. B. Griffin
Detective Inspector Leo Wyndson	Peter Hill
Detective Alvin Yablonsky	Joseph Trigoboff
Detective Superintendent Mike Yeadings	Claire Curzon
Commissioner of Police Aurelio Zen	Michael Dibdin
Sergeant Mickey Zondi	James McClure

4

Police Procedurals

I included all of the books in a series even if they were not strictly police procedurals, unless the main character has retired or become a private investigator. The James Lee Burke and Stephen Solomita novels are prime examples of this. For the remaining nine-tenths of the volume, listing all of the books gives the reader a chance to find most of the stories about a particular character.

Books by certain authors are billed as procedurals even though they are not. Hamilton Jobson is one such writer. His books can be categorized as mysteries or suspense, yet his publishers describe them as police novels even though Matt Anders, his principal character, does not make an appearance until the middle or final section of the story. I can guess that the publisher wanted to advertise the fact that Jobson was a career policeman and the books as authentic in detail as firsthand experience can be. I have included Jobson because many readers in the United States are not familiar with his works since a number of them have not been published here.

Another author who presents a problem is Georges Simenon, whom I have included only in part. His Maigret novels are not all listed here as he would have required about 100 pages of annotations and his books are not strict police procedurals. Maigret has his own way of solving a case and the reader is never cognizant of the official process by which a crime is investigated in France. Only a sampling of the Maigret stories is included here for that reason and because Simenon is touted as the premier European writer of procedurals. Maigret is what I call a cerebral sleuth. He spends more time thinking about information he has received verbally than about autopsies, crime scene evidence, and the difficult and tedious gathering of facts from witnesses.

There are also series with one foot in the procedural camp and the other planted firmly in another genre. A good example is Gwendoline Butler's early Coffin novels, which are ambivalently British classics and police procedurals at the same time. Other writers give the reader a break from the perceived tedium of following the police around by telling part of the story through the eyes of the criminal. John Sandford and Lawrence Sanders do this juxtaposing of narratives best.

Some writers are included because the police are the main characters in the stories and a case can be made for the books being procedurals as well as not. I have stayed away from all police officers whose spouse helps in the investigation and is not an officer as well. Elizabeth Linington's Maddox series is included because Sue Maddox is a policewoman.

The majority of the writers keep to a strict usage of one or two main police characters in their novels. Others, such as Ed McBain and John Wainwright, use a multitude of police personnel to solve crimes. Ed McBain is very easy to describe when it comes to series characters. I chose to list them as the 87th Precinct, and yes, I know that the precinct is often referred to in the books as the 87.

To categorize John Wainwright's series characters neatly is difficult and it is impossible to list a police department as the character because that situation can also change. All the books take place in Yorkshire in Beechwood Brook division and the Bordfield region or in and around the Lessford area. About the time three-fourths of the series had been written, Great Britain redefined its entire police organization and at the same time Wainwright, in order to reflect what was going on in the country, changed his area to the Lessford Divisional Police, an enormous area encompassing all the previously known divisions and counties, in addition to Lessford. If this sounds confusing, try reading his books. He mixes up his detectives and his uniformed branches of each division, as well. The reader is challenged by Wainwright every time.

Thomas Adcock*

Dark Maze *Detective Neil Hockaday*
New York: Pocket, 1991.

An old man known on the street as Picasso introduces himself to Neil Hockaday, a detective in the Street Crimes Unit, New York Police Department (NYPD), and proceeds to talk about killing. The murders that follow are a means of self-expression, creative in much the same way that any art form is. That they are very strange adds to the picture of a mentally unstable person. To find Picasso, Hockaday must begin to understand him as an individual.

Warren Adler*

American Quartet *Detective Fiona FitzGerald*
New York: Arbor, 1981.

An art teacher is shot to death in the National Gallery in Washington, DC. Ballistics prove that the gun was an old model. The victim is a failed artist whose one claim to fame is that he painted one of his students in the nude. The investigation is going nowhere, when there is another murder. Again the weapon is an old model. After no clues can be pieced together in either of the cases, homicide detective FitzGerald of the Washington, DC, police department stumbles on an idea arising from the painstaking work of the medical examiner.

American Sextet *Detective Fiona FitzGerald*
New York: Arbor, 1983.

The body of a beautiful young woman is found under a bridge. There are too many questions to answer before Fiona can accept a verdict of suicide. The victim would engage in sex with prominent men in Washington, then turn over to reporter Jason Martin the secrets they revealed in bed.

Senator Love *Detective Fiona FitzGerald*
New York: Fine, 1991.

Senator Sam Langford is a well-known womanizer. When one of his ex-lovers is murdered, the Senator is the prime suspect.

Immaculate Deception *Detective Fiona FitzGerald*
New York: Fine, 1991.

Congresswoman Frances McGuire is found dead in her bed, a glass of wine laced with cyanide spilled next to her. Did she commit suicide or was she murdered? The congresswoman was the leading pro-life proponent in the House. When the autopsy reveals that McGuire was six weeks pregnant, Fiona knows she did not take her own life.

The Witch of Watergate *Sergeant Fiona FitzGerald*
New York: Fine, 1992.

Polly Dearborn, the most aggressive investigative reporter for the Washington *Post*, is found hanging from her balcony in the Watergate complex. It is soon established that she did not commit suicide. Fiona's new partner, Sergeant Charleen Evans, finds that Dearborn's database contains the dirt on many influential people in the government, including His Honor the mayor.

Gary Alexander*

Pigeon Blood *Superintendent Bamsan Kiet*
New York: Walker, 1988.

Denny McCloud ran a charter and freight service out of the Luong Airport. An American, McCloud turns into a major headache for Superintendent Kiet when he is found murdered in the cockpit of his aircraft. The plane had been searched, the luggage cut into pieces. The police suspect that the cargo Luong Express was supposed to fly was opium since there are inconsistencies in the flight plan and the passenger list. All the intrigues of the fictitious Southeast Asian country are displayed, from political corruption to communist factions jockeying for a more powerful position.

Unfunny Money   *Superintendent Bamsan Kiet*
New York: Walker, 1989.

Luong will be in a state of chaos if Kiet does not stop the person or persons responsible for spreading counterfeit money throughout Hickorn, the capital city. Then Kiet finds a body. Much is made of Kiet's wanting to go around looking for clues to solve the case as opposed to Captain Bink's plan to roll the forensic team and the detectives.

Kiet and the Golden Peacock   *Superintendent Bamsan Kiet*
New York: St. Martin's, 1989.

The Golden Peacock, revered symbol of ancient Luong, is stolen just before the national festival in which the Prince rides an elephant to the museum doors and accepts the Peacock and then leads a celebration parade. If the Peacock is not recovered the country will be covered in shame, not to mention how bad the people will feel. The country is also playing host to a visiting group of Vietnamese headed by the alluring and dangerous Madame Mai.

Kiet and the Opium War   *Superintendent Bamsan Kiet*
New York: St. Martin's, 1990.

Drugs, mainly opium and heroin, have been pouring into Luong ever since a territorial war erupted among the opium dealers of Southeast Asia. Kiet must discover who the villains are. The list runs from the national air force high command to the owner of a sleazy night club to Luong's tiny community of insurgents.

Deadly Drought   *Superintendent Bamsan Kiet*
New York: St. Martin's, 1991.

The monsoon has not come this year and all the crops are dying or not growing. There is not enough food in Luong. The Royal Prince's illegitimate son comes to visit, and a fortune teller puts a curse on Kiet. Other things go wrong as well. The government expects food riots and Kiet is supposed to execute publicly a rice merchant who was caught hoarding his wares.

Noreen Ayres

A World the Color of Salt   *Smokey Brandon, Forensic Specialist*
New York: Morrow, 1992.

A young man on duty in his father's store is gunned down in a particularly vicious manner. Smokey Brandon, a forensic specialist for the Orange County Sheriff's Office, goes to the scene and realizes that she knows the young man. Smokey makes a mistake in taking her friend Patricia to an interrogation of two brothers suspected of the killing. When Patricia begins dating one of the brothers and then disappears, Smokey goes looking for her, leading her to the murderer.

John Ball*

In the Heat of the Night   *Detective Virgil Tibbs and*
New York: Harper, 1965.   *Chief of Police Bill Gillespie*
London: Joseph, 1966.

Maestro Enrico Mantoli, the conductor for the upcoming music festival, is found dead in the road. His wallet is missing. When the police do a sweep of the town looking for suspicious persons they find a black man at the railroad station with a wallet full of money. He is arrested and brought to the police station where he says he is a police officer in California. Virgil Tibbs, a homicide detective in Pasadena, is gradually eased into conducting the case for the inexperienced Wells police force. Set in the segregated South of the 1960s where blacks, looked upon as inferior, were not able to question whites directly.

The Cool Cottontail   *Detective Virgil Tibbs*
New York: Harper, 1966.
London: Joseph, 1967.

The Sun Valley Lodge is a restful and private place for nudists until the caretakers discover the body of a man floating in the lake. Someone has gone to great pains to try to suggest that the victim is a nudist but no one recognizes him. Virgil Tibbs is called in partially because he is a good investigator and also because the police are not very objective about the colony. Dealing with an unidentified corpse and the fact that no one has been reported missing make this a case worthy of Tibbs's skills.

Johnny Get Your Gun *Detective Virgil Tibbs*
Boston: Little, Brown, 1969.
London: Joseph, 1970
Revised Edition: New York: Bantam, 1972

For his ninth birthday Johnny McGuire received a small radio. The McGuire family, new to Pasadena and quite poor, is doing the best it can under hard circumstances. But when a school bully steals Johnny's radio, Johnny gets mad—and he also gets a gun.

Five Pieces of Jade *Detective Virgil Tibbs*
New York: Little, Brown, 1972.
London: Joseph, 1972.

Mr. Wang Fu-sen, a wealthy dealer in jade art, is found stabbed to death with one of his priceless jade daggers. The killing looks to be ritualistic, as Mr. Wang is arranged on the floor with four pieces of jade by his head and the dagger neatly placed in his chest. In addition to attempting to solve the crime, Virgil Tibbs is asked to be the liaison officer between the Pasadena police and the Bureau of Narcotics and Dangerous Drugs.

The Eyes of Buddha *Detective Virgil Tibbs*
Boston: Little, Brown, 1976.
London: Joseph, 1976.

The decomposing body of a young woman who could be missing heiress Doris Friedkin is found in Pasadena. The body is not Doris's, but that leaves Tibbs with two problems—who is the murdered woman and where is Doris Friedkin?

Then Came Violence *Detective Virgil Tibbs*
New York: Doubleday, 1980.
London: Joseph, 1981.

There are a number of robberies and several deaths in Pasadena. One victim is found hanging in the shed used by the Tournament of Roses parade entrants to make their floats. While investigating these crimes, Virgil Tibbs is also providing protection and a cover for the wife and children of the leader of Bakara, an African country in which the Russians, Cubans, and a group of guerrilla fighters are mounting an insurrection.

Singapore *Detective Virgil Tibbs*
New York: Dodd, Mead, 1986.

Miriam Motamboru, widow of the assassinated president of Bakara, is accused of murder. Virgil Tibbs is sent to help her, and while in

Singapore he is invited to help the local police solve the murders of the children of a naval shipyard engineer. Tibbs uses deduction and mysticism in his investigation.

Police Chief *Police Chief Jack Tallon*
New York: Crime Club, Doubleday, 1977.
London: Hale, 1982.

Jack Tallon leaves the hectic pace of the Pasadena police force for what he believes to be the less stressful Whitewater force in Washington. He finds that the police department needs a complete overhauling and the cops need training. He also faces the hostility of a populace with no love for an incompetent, inexperienced police department. In this atmosphere Tallon finds that he is the chief suspect when a number of vicious rapes occur.

Trouble for Tallon *Police Chief Jack Tallon*
New York: Crime Club, Doubleday, 1981.
London: Hale, 1982.

City Council member Wilson Sullivan is beaten to death. In his clenched hand is an Ankh, the ancient Egyptian symbol of peace. With his dying breath, Sullivan accuses four members of Dharmaville, an eight-hundred-acre village run by Swami Dharmayana, an American who has renounced all the amenities of life to study for years in India to become a spiritual leader. Chief of Police Jack Tallon organizes his small force into teams, each concentrating on one aspect of the investigation.

Chief Tallon and the S.O.R. *Police Chief Jack Tallon*
New York: Dodd, Mead, 1984.

A group known as the Society for Open Relationships decides to hold a convention in Whitewater, much to the distress of the town. The Reverend Moses is going to go to any extreme to drive the group out of his area. Tallon is also investigating a hit and run and then he has a murder on his hands.

Dallas Barnes*

Yesterday Is Dead *Sergeant Lee Hollister and Investigator Virgil Fox*
New York: Signet, 1976.

Ellen Shane and her little daughter live with David Wilson, a cop at the LAPD's Southwest station. One night Ellen is brutally raped and murdered, leaving Wilson as suspect number one. The Southwest homicide team of Hollister and Fox catches the case.

James Barnett

Head of the Force *Chief Superintendent Owen Smith*
London: Secker and Warburg, 1978.
New York: St. Martin's, 1979.

Metropolitan Police Assistant Commissioner for Crime Roger Hicks is late for his meeting with the Commissioner. But the Commissioner does not mind—he's been murdered. The interesting fact about the body is that its head has been cut off but not in the Scotland Yard Office since there is an absence of blood. How the body was transported to the Yard is another problem facing Chief Superintendent Owen Smith, the Metropolitan police's bad boy and number one troublemaker, who is called in to handle the investigation.

Backfire Is Hostile *Chief Superintendent Owen Smith*
London: Secker and Warburg, 1979.
New York: St. Martin's, 1979.

The Royal Air Force base at Cladenham is experiencing a number of unusual incidents. A Russian bomber is seen flying off the coast of England. When intercepted, the bomber signals in Morse code. The British fighter plane involved in the intercept crashes while landing and the crew is killed. Then a young RAF flight lieutenant, Alison Maude Cumberley, is murdered. Her body is left in such a way that it appears she was raped and strangled, but the postmortem reveals that she was dead before being strangled. Chief Superintendent Owen Smith does not believe in coincidence and soon is linking all the mysterious happenings at the base with the murder.

Palmprint *Chief Superintendent Owen Smith*
London: Secker and Warburg, 1980.

An American named Eli Voden is found throttled on the island of Baracana. This is the second murder in the area, which is about to gain its independence from the United Kingdom. Chief Superintendent Owen Smith is sent to the Caribbean island to conduct the investigation, which turns out to be quite complex and leads him to an international assassin and to Canada.

The Firing Squad *Chief Superintendent Owen Smith*
London: Secker and Warburg, 1981.
New York: Morrow, 1981.

A man is found tied to a chair in a pit. He has been executed by a firing squad of five. When his body is examined, a small tattoo is found and recognized as a Nazi SS identification mark. Then a retired policeman arrives with the news that there was an identical killing in Scarborough in 1945.

The case gets even more complicated when a sizable gift to the Police Widows and Orphans Fund is made in Krugerands, one of which has the dead man's thumbprint on it.

Marked for Destruction *Detective Chief Superintendent*
London: Secker and Warburg, 1982. *Owen Smith*

The body of a baby is found in a laundry bag tossed in the trash in an alley. Marks on the bag lead to a home where the baby may have lived for awhile. Detective Chief Superintendent Owen Smith, who has been transferred to the quiet borough of Cobb Common, is bored and pays no attention to the details relating to the dead baby. He therefore does not properly supervise his newest and youngest detective, Inspector Murdock. Murdock goes off on his own and ends up viciously beaten to death. Smith cannot head the investigation into his inspector's death because it took place in another jurisdiction. He investigates anyway.

William Bayer

Switch *Lieutenant Frank Janek*
New York: Linden Press/Simon & Schuster, 1984.

Two women are killed the same night. Amanda Ireland is decapitated, her head carried across town and placed on the body of Brenda Thatcher, a call girl. Thatcher's head is set on Ireland's corpse. The problem is to decipher what the murderer is trying to convey with this bizarre arrangement. Frank Janek is generally the one to handle unusual cases, but Janek has retreated into himself because he is finding it difficult to deal with reality, such as the suicide of his old mentor on the force.

Wallflower *Lieutenant Frank Janek*
New York: Villard, 1991.

While he is on a much needed holiday, Janek's goddaughter is murdered. He comes back to find that she has been the latest victim in a series of ritualistic killings being kept under wraps by the FBI.

Pattern Crimes *David Bar-Lev*
New York: Villard, 1987.

The Pattern Crimes Squad in Jerusalem is handed several ugly mutilation deaths. The first victim is a young Arab woman who has been disowned by her family. The fact that she is Arab leads to racial tensions between that community and the Israeli police.

Greg Bear*

Queen of Angels *Inspector Mary Choy*
New York: Warner, 1990.

The discovery of eight students murdered in the apartment of poet Emanuel Goldsmith and forensic evidence pointing to his guilt make the poet the only suspect in this rare murder case in 2047 A.D. Los Angeles. Mary Choy sets out to find Goldsmith before he is apprehended by the Selectors, a band of fanatics dedicated to irradicating the misfits of society.

Paul Bishop*

Citadel Run *Calico Jack Walker and Tina Tamiko*
New York: TOR, 1988.

Calico Jack Walker has accepted a challenge to race from Los Angeles to Las Vegas, take a picture in front of a casino, then race back. All in a few hours. He is about to retire so he feels he has nothing to lose. When he and Tina get to Vegas they witness a crime and both believe that even though they have no jurisdiction, they must act.

Sand Against the Tide *Calico Jack Walker and Tina Tamiko*
New York: TOR, 1992.

Calico Jack has retired but his dream of peace and quiet fades as the lure of participating in another case catches up with him as he teams up with his old partner Tina to fight against a powerful drug cartel.

Eleanor Taylor Bland

Dead Time *Detective Marti MacAlister*
New York: St. Martin's, 1992.

Lauretta Dorsey dies in her hotel room. Marti MacAlister is a mother of two, a widow, Chicago street-smart, and now a small-town detective in Lincoln Prairie, Illinois, and the officer on the scene. She and her partner, Vik Jessenovik, think that a group of runaway children may have witnessed Dorsey's murder. They must find the kids before the murderer does.

Peter Blauner

Slow Motion Riot *Probation Officer Baum*
New York: Morrow, 1991.

When Darryl King, a crackhead and a vicious killer, violates his parole, Baum, his parole officer, must decide what kind of action to take against him. Baum, who has many personal problems, makes some fundamental errors in his handling of King. King, who is unstable, reacts in a way Baum never suspects and catches him in an impossible and deadly situation.

K. Arne Blom*

The Moment of Truth *Chief Inspector Seved Olofsson*
New York: Harper, 1977.

The wives of uniformed policemen in the Swedish town of Lund are being beaten to death by a man using a heavy club. The murdered women have nothing in common except their policemen husbands. Olofsson and Holmberg work round the clock but the killer is elusive, his motive unknown, until they make an unexpected discovery and find a witness.

John Brady

A Stone of the Heart *Sergeant Matthew Minogue*
London: Constable, 1988.
New York: St. Martin's, 1988.

A student found in the bushes of Trinity College, Dublin, has been murdered. Jarlath Walsh, an idealist, does not fit the pattern of a drug dealer and his murder does not appear to be the random killing it is being made out to be. Sergeant Minogue, almost killed a year ago in an attempt on a diplomat's life, is a bit of a maverick and just what is needed here. This is a sad tale full of the heartbreak and anguish that drives Ireland, both North and South.

Unholy Ground *Sergeant Matthew Minogue*
London: Constable, 1989.
New York: St. Martin's, 1992.

Arthur Combs, the murdered man, was seventy-three and had been strangled to death with a rope. Everything in his home was smashed and broken as if a cyclone had gone through the place. Combs was English and living alone in Dublin. Minogue finds a link between Combs and the British spy organization, MI5. His death may be a deterrent to the talks between England and the Irish government, so the Sergeant must act fast.

Kaddish in Dublin *Inspector Matthew Minogue*
London: Constable, 1990.
New York: St. Martin's, 1992.

The man found on the beach has been shot three times; the murder is execution style. The victim is Paul Fine, a Jew living in Dublin. A PLO terrorist group claims responsibility. Inspector Minogue must piece together all the facts before discovering that all is not as it first appears.

Anthony Bruno*

Bad Guys *Special Agents Cuthbert "Bert" Gibbons*
New York: Putnam, 1988. *and Mike Tozzi, FBI*

With Gibbons in retirement the Bureau has sent Tozzi to Butte, Montana, so that he will learn to take orders. Now they call in Gibbons to inform him that someone is cleaning up the unsolved cases he and Tozzi had worked on together. They believe Tozzi has turned renegade and is killing off such people as Vinnie Clams, a vicious drug dealer. Gibbons finds Mike Tozzi but is faced with deciding whether to join his friend or arrest him.

Bad Blood *Special Agents Cuthbert "Bert" Gibbons*
New York: Putnam, 1989. *and Mike Tozzi, FBI*

A Volkswagen is discovered floating in the river between Manhattan and New Jersey. When it is lifted from the water it is found to contain two very dead bodies. Because the car has New Jersey license plates but is now in New York, the local homicide unit calls in the FBI and Gibbons is assigned. Soon he and Tozzi, his renegade partner, know something very strange is going on as the bodies have been cut almost in half. They also find that the Mafia chief, Mr. Antonelli, and his Yakuza (Japanese "mafia") counterpart, Mr. Nagai, are working together in a very lucrative scam.

Bad Luck *Special Agents Cuthbert "Bert" Gibbons*
New York: Delacorte, 1990. *and Mike Tozzi, FBI*

Mike Tozzi goes deep undercover to infiltrate the organized crime element in Atlantic City. Gibbons is worried about his ex-partner so he determines to find out whether Tozzi is losing it or enjoying his walk among the mob elite. He learns that Tozzi is carrying on an affair with a married woman. The agents need all their ingenuity to extricate themselves from these complications.

Bad Business   *Special Agents Cuthbert "Bert" Gibbons*
New York: Delacorte, 1991.   *and Special Agent Mike Tozzi, FBI*

There are not too many airtight cases, but the one handed U.S. Attorney Tom Augustine is. Special agents Gibbons and Tozzi know they did their homework perfectly. What they do not know is that Augustine has sold himself to the Mafia for a contribution to finance his campaign for New York City mayor. The price is a few cases lost and this is one of them. Soon Gibbons and Tozzi are on a hit list, sought by organized crime and crooked cops alike.

Bad Moon   *Special Agents Cuthbert "Bert" Gibbons*
New York: Delacorte, 1992.   *and Special Agent Mike Tozzi, FBI*

The question facing Gibbons and Tozzi is, who killed Sabatini Mistretta? Mistretta was a powerful crime boss and a number of vicious people could have had him killed in order to benefit or enhance their positions in the organization. But when the prime suspect is murdered, Tozzi and Gibbons must rethink the case.

James Lee Burke[*]

The Neon Rain   *Lieutenant Dave Robicheaux*
New York: Holt, 1987.

Dave Robicheaux learns that he is about to be killed and it looks like a Nicaraguan drug dealer is behind the desire to be rid of the New Orleans homicide detective. As Robicheaux puts pressure on Julio Segura, Segura fights back and is killed. There are three guys after Robicheaux and they are not above torture and murder. But the motives in the case remain clouded until the end.

A Stained White Radiance   *Detective Dave Robicheaux*
New York: Hyperion, 1992.

Weldon Sonnier is a big-money oil man in New Iberia, Louisiana. Someone tries to shoot him while he is standing in his own house. Robicheaux gets nothing from Weldon, but his evangelist preacher brother, Lyle, details a violent event from their past. Called to Weldon's house at the scene of an in-progress breaking and entering, Robicheaux finds three killers who almost get him, and who have already executed Garrett, a new patrolman on the force. It becomes apparent that Weldon Sonnier is in trouble, and his sister Drew is trying to protect him. Their brother, Lyle, is the only one talking sense until he invites the man with the burned face into his home—the man who could very well be their father, and not only hates them, but has reason to kill them.

Rex Burns*

The Alvarez Journal *Detective Gabriel Wager*
New York: Viking, 1975.
London: Hale, 1976.

Working on a tip that a store called The Rare Things Import Shop is really a front for a marijuana operation, Detective Gabriel Wager, a member of the Denver Organized Crime Unit, finds that the shop is owned by a high school acquaintance. The man, Alvarez, is doing something illegal and it is up to Wager to find out what.

The Farnsworth Score *Detective Gabriel Wager*
New York: Harper & Row, 1977.
London: Hale, 1978.

A drug bust in the making for months, which has Denver's Organized Crime Division and the DEA working together, fails because of a cocaine test incorrectly done by an undercover police officer. Or so everyone says. Gabe Wager is picked to bring in Farnsworth, the dealer. Wager goes in deep cover, changing his appearance and becoming a lowlife in order to convince the group around Farnsworth that he can be trusted.

Speak for the Dead *Detective Gabriel Wager*
New York: Harper & Row, 1978.
London: Hale, 1980.

Gabe Wager has been transferred from the Organized Crime/Narcotics Unit to Homicide where he is now considered a rookie. He starts out in the graveyard shift. His first call is to the Botanical Gardens where the head of a once-beautiful young woman has been found. Before he can catch a killer he must find out who the victim is and locate the rest of her body. Wager has his work cut out for him as Homicide reluctantly accepts him as he proves his worth as a detective.

Angle of Attack *Detective Gabriel Wager*
New York: Harper & Row, 1979.
London: Hale, 1980.

The Marco Scorvelli incident—Scorvelli was shotgunned to death in what appeared to be a true gangland killing—has been in the pending file for awhile. Then a man calls Wager with information about Frank Covino, who is subsequently murdered. Wager now has an open case that points to one of the most powerful crime figures in Denver.

The Avenging Angel *Detective Gabriel Wager*
New York: Viking, 1983.

A dead male is found with his arms outstretched, and a drawing of an angel holding a sword in his hand is found on the body. Soon copies of the drawing begin arriving at the police station. The sheriff takes a look at the drawing and confirms Wager's worst fears. It is the avenging angel—a part of Mormon lore. When the next murder is committed, Gabe runs into a group of people who believe in retribution brought about by the arm of the Lord. They have formed a religious cult that just might be producing real avenging angels. Or is this the work of a serial killer?

Strip Search *Detective Gabriel Wager*
New York: Viking, 1984.

The body of Annette Sheldon, dancer at a topless, bottomless bar on East Colfax, is found among the hollyhocks in someone's backyard. Another body is found in Adams County; this woman had been an exotic dancer, too. Wager goes undercover to look into Denver's vicious world of sex and drugs.

Ground Money *Detective Gabriel Wager*
New York: Viking, 1986.

While looking for John and James Sanchez, ranch managers, rodeo riders, and the sons of an old friend, Wager becomes involved in a murder investigation. The brothers are into something not quite legitimate, or so it seems to Wager. He and his girlfriend, Jo Fabrizio, vacation near the ranch from which the Sanchez boys operate.

The Killing Zone *Detective Gabriel Wager*
New York: Viking, 1988.

In a grubby lot in a depressed area in Denver the body of Horace Green is found. Green was a black councilman respected by all who served on the zoning commission with him. Wager soon finds that Green was having an affair with a woman who may have been engaged in a little money-making racket on the side. Meanwhile, racist feelings have been stirring in the city and Wager is being pressured into solving the case before a full-blown riot erupts.

Roger Busby*

Robbery Blue *Detective Sergeant Leric*
London: Collins Crime Club, 1969.

A young policeman dies while taking part in a failed attempt to stop a payroll robbery, in which $250,000 is stolen. There is the distinct possibility that the robbers were tipped off by a member of the police force. The organized group behind the job plans to escape to Ireland but the police get a break in the case and have a good chance to put paid to a very efficient bunch of criminals.

The Frighteners *Detective Inspector Leric*
London: Collins Crime Club, 1970.

A very dangerous and vicious London crime ring is moving into the big, unnamed Midlands city featured in Busby's books. The gang is using an unknown weapon that can cause severe burns. The Assistant Commissioner forms a crime squad to fight the takeover of the organized crime operations in his city.

Deadlock* *Detective Inspector Leric*
London: Collins Crime Club, 1971.

A Reasonable Man *Detective Inspector Leric*
London: Collins Crime Club, 1972.

Leric is in court waiting to testify when a bag containing a human right leg is found under a chair. Then the left leg is found in a florist box on a commuter train. Soon the torso is located in a case for a bass viol. Leric is not only having trouble identifying who belongs to the human parts but his boss is giving him grief because of political pressure, and Leric's personal life is blowing up in his face.

Pattern of Violence *Detective Inspector Leric*
London: Collins Crime Club, 1973.

Checks from a stolen checkbook are being spread all over the city. Leclerc's men are also watching out for a big job that is supposed to go down in a few days. Trouble is they do not know what is going to happen. The man passing the checks is a psycho and the crime about to happen is a big bank job.

New Face in Hell   *Detective Chief Inspector Eddie Quick*
London: Collins Crime Club, 1976.   *and Sergeant Roger Goodman*

The Cloud Nine Club, a gambling casino in Cornwall, is the scene of a shooting spree that leaves three dead, more wounded, and a vicious killer on the loose. Every level of the police investigation is examined, every individual style is shown, and the arming of police officers is an intregal part of the plot.

The Hunter   *Detective Inspector Tony Rowley*
London: Collins, 1985
New York: Doubleday, 1989.

Finally getting the brutal Pollard twins in jail, Tony Rowley of Scotland Yard receives the bad news that the only witness for the prosecution, John Francis Duffy, has murdered two people in Cornwall. Rowley must clear Duffy or the case against the twins and his own career go up in smoke. Politics at the Yard is shown to be tough and dirty.

Snowman   *Detective Sergeant Tony Rowley*
London: Collins, 1987.
New York: Doubleday, 1989.

Helen Linden, six days a detective sergeant newly assigned to the National Drugs Intelligence Unit, dies in a bomb blast while accompanying an American DEA agent around the London area. At the same time in Germany the police arrest a master criminal in a house of prostitution. And in London Tony Rowley (in this book a detective sergeant) is asking for help from the British equivalent of godfather Frank Spinelli.

Gwendoline Butler*
(also Jennie Melville, q.v.)

Dead in a Row*   *Detective Sergeant John Coffin*
London: Bles, 1957.

The Dull Dead*   *Detective Sergeant John Coffin*
London: Bles, 1958.
New York: Walker, 1962.

Five-year-old Minny Duveen has been terribly frightened while on her way to school. She says she saw a man with no face. The Duveens' neighbors are three young professional men—one of whom gets himself murdered.

The police investigate only to find more puzzles. Mrs. Duveen is a flagrant adultress. Minny grows even more withdrawn.

Death Lives Next Door *Detective Sergeant John Coffin*
London: Bles, 1960.

Dine and be Dead
New York: Macmillan, 1960.

Death Lives Next Door.
New York: St. Martin's, 1992.

A man is watching Marion Manning, a popular and admired professor at Oxford. Manning is under extreme pressure and beginning to lose her grip on reality. The watcher moves next door to Marion so that he can observe her better and perhaps be there when she dies. John Coffin arrives in Oxford looking for a missing person. When he begins his search he finds that a man recently stabbed and Marion Manning figure into his case.

Make Me a Murderer* *Detective Sergeant John Coffin*
London: Bles, 1961.

Coffin in Oxford* *Detective Sergeant John Coffin*
London: Bles, 1962.

Coffin for Baby *Detective Inspector John Coffin*
London: Bles, 1963.
New York: Walker, 1963.

Mrs. Cox is viciously murdered in the room she rented to Mrs. Bishop, a poor woman and generally thought to be an unfit mother. Mr. Bishop has disappeared. In searching the rooms of the Cox boardinghouse, the police find the body of the Bishops' baby. But the neighbors as well as the local medical clinic have recently seen the Bishop baby alive and well and this infant has been dead for several months. With his usual understated competence, Coffin sorts out the complications presented by the murder and those in his own life.

Coffin Waiting *Detective Chief Inspector John Coffin*
London: Bles, 1964.
New York: Walker, 1963.

Juliet brings a dead pigeon to Coffin's office. The pigeon was found on the front steps of Roxanne Roland's house. Roland is one of the leaders of the community. Mysterious things are going on in the house as milk is being delivered there to a family who does not exist and things are disappearing. Then three neighborhood women die in one of the rooms as they wait for Roxanne to return home.

Coffin in Malta *Detective Chief Inspector John Coffin*
London: Bles, 1964.
New York: Walker, 1965.

In Valletta, Malta, the severed head of a young man is found by his mother. The murder throws the whole town into a tizzy. When the boy's sister disappears, the police decide they need John Coffin's help.

A Nameless Coffin* *Detective Chief Inspector John Coffin*
London: Bles, 1966.
New York: Walker, 1967.

Coffin Following* *Detective Chief Inspector John Coffin*
London: Bles, 1968.

Coffin's Dark Number* *Detective Chief Inspector John Coffin*
London: Bles, 1969.

A Coffin from the Past *Detective Chief Inspector John Coffin*
London: Bles, 1970.
New York: Dell, 1982.

Member of Parliament Thomas Barr and his secretary, Sheila Daly, are murdered. They had been working, waiting for local people with problems to come to them for help. When found, Barr and Daly are not wearing much in the way of clothing, causing something of a scandal and raising questions about their relationship, since Barr was a married man. The house where they died is quite close to the Museum of London History and to a cemetery where the bodies of the Steinberg family are buried. The Steinbergs were murdered in 1820 and now Coffin suspects that those killings may have something to do with his case.

A Coffin for the Canary *Detective Chief Inspector John Coffin*
London: Macmillan, 1974.
Olivia
New York: Coward, 1974.

Olivia's car is stolen—then it is returned. The police believe it has been used in a robbery. On her way back to London Olivia meets a young man who intrigues her; she visits him at his apartment where he is shot. Olivia seems to be living in a surreal world where nothing is quite what it seems. Inspector John Coffin enters the drama and finds the murderer.

Coffin in Fashion *Detective Sergeant John Coffin*
London: Collins, 1987.
New York: St. Martin's, 1990.

In the 1960s Coffin bought a house in the southeastern part of London and found himself in the midst of the Mouncy Street murders. The body of a small boy who had been dead for a year is found in the floor of Coffin's house. When the body is removed another body, that of an old man, is discovered under it. All evidence points to Steve Hilaire, the son of a wealthy businesswoman in the community. But the case is a little more complicated than that and leaves Coffin with more questions than answers.

Coffin Underground *Detective Superintendent John Coffin*
London: Collins, 1988.
New York: St. Martin's, 1989.

Coffin, newly appointed head of TAS (Tactical Activity Squad), based in South London, has his hands full when a man bent on revenge and recently released from prison is found murdered. The man's son-in-law, an informer and dangerous in his own right, is on the run. But the real story centers around a house where an entire family is found at the dinner table—all poisoned.

Coffin in the Black Museum *Commander John Coffin*
London: Collins, 1989.

Coffin in the Museum of Crime
New York: St. Martin's, 1990.

Heading the new crime unit in Second City, an amalgamation of four old London boroughs, John Coffin moves into an apartment in an old church that has been turned into a theater. His discovery of a disembodied head in an urn in the theater focuses attention on the Black Museum, which is part of the complex. Then the body of a missing woman is found and actress Stella Pinero finds a human hand in her freezer.

Coffin and the Paper Man *Commander John Coffin*
London: Collins, 1990.
New York: St. Martin's, 1991.

At first, Coffin thinks the brutal rape and stabbing death of sixteen-year-old Anna Mary Kinver is just a routine case of violence. Then the people in Coffin's neighborhood begin to die and messages about them, signed "The Paper Man," are arriving for Coffin.

Coffin in Murder Street *Chief Commander John Coffin*
London: HarperCollins, 1991.
New York: St. Martin's, 1992.

A bus from Terror Tour, which visits London crime scenes, disappears with all its tourists on board. Then Nell Casey, an American actress who has come to perform in one of Stella Pinero's productions, finds that she has brought all her problems with her to London.

Robert Cain

Cybernarc *Lieutenant Christopher Drake, Project*
New York: Harper, 1991. *RAMROD, and ROD (Rand Artificially Intelligent Military Robotic Device), a combat robot*

Project RAMROD has produced a lifelike male combat robot who is now ready for action. Lieutenant Drake has been involved with the project for several years and, now a Navy SEAL, gets to take ROD into a war zone—that of the drug cartels. The growing trust between Drake and his partner, ROD, makes them a formidable team.

Cybernarc: Gold Dragon *Lieutenant Christopher Drake, Project*
New York: Harper, 1991. *RAMROD, and ROD (Rand Artificially Intelligent Military Robotic Device), a combat robot*

Sent to Hong Kong to kill the heads of the world's drug empires, ROD and Lieutenant Drake run into trouble when ROD is blasted to bits. Drake puts ROD's face and body back together in a somewhat reasonable fashion. They are soon back on the trail of Feng, one of the most vicious Chinese drug leaders, but Drake falls into his clutches and ROD must mount a rescue.

William Camp

The Jacobs Park Killings *Captain Ken Others*
New York: Vanguard, 1978.

Three men, two white and one black, are executed—shot in the head and their hands cut off. The investigation leads the Sedona County, California, sheriff's department to Crown Point, an industrial town plagued by burglaries.

William J. Caunitz

One Police Plaza *Lieutenant Dan Malone*
New York: Crown, 1984.
London: Century, 1984.

The body of a travel agent found in her bathtub leads Lieutenant Malone to the CIA, the Israeli Mossad, the U.S. Army, Moslem terrorists, and a possible coverup by political officials. The complex plot ends in a massive battle on the Pulaski Bridge joining Queens and Brooklyn.

Black Sand *Lieutenant Theodore "Teddy" Lucas and*
New York: Crown, 1989. *Major Andreas Vassos*
London: Century, 1989.

Two American gunmen fire into a crowd of vacationers in Voula, Greece. Several people are killed, including the wife and young son of Major Andreas Vassos of the Hellenic National Police. The purpose of the attack was to kill two Greek policemen. Vassos is sent to New York City to work with Lieutenant Teddy Lucas, who speaks fluent Greek and is an excellent detective. The object of the investigation is to recover the fabulous treasure of Priam, which amateur archaeologist Schuliemann discovered when he dug up the ruins of Troy. But all is not what is appears to be as the detectives uncover secrets and hidden motives.

Suspects *Detective Lieutenant Tony Scanlon*
New York: Crown, 1986.
London: Century, 1987.

Police lieutenant Joseph P. Gallagher and shopkeeper Yetta Zimmerman are shot down in Yetta's candy store. Scanlon, as investigating officer, finds that the dead policeman had girlfriends, rented a crash pad where he conducted his liaisons, was a heavy gambler, and was in debt to the wrong people. Then Yetta's son and daughter-in-law are murdered in their bedroom. Scanlon is caught between the politicians who want to keep the image of the police pristine and the grieving Zimmerman family, who want justice.

Exceptional Clearance *Lieutenant John Vinda*
New York: Crown, 1991.

Two poor black women are murdered—their throats ripped out. When a wealthy young white woman is killed in the same way, the New York Police Department realizes that a serial killer with an agenda is on the loose. John Vinda is given the unenviable task of finding the killer, who leaves no clues.

Robert Chambers

The Neon Preacher *Detective Second Grade Hank Moody*
New York: Mason/Charter, 1977.

Detective Moody is injured in a building explosion that kills the informer who was going to give him the name of a drug dealer. When Moody gets out of the hospital, his inspector assigns him a special job—try to discover what was behind the explosion as Moody does not remember what he witnessed that night. All the while the mad bomber goes about his work blowing up bits of New York City and Moody, who has seen him, cannot remember.

Nick Christian

Ronin *Detective Sergeant Arnold Ross*
New York: TOR, 1986.

During a robbery at an exclusive aerobics gym in Manhattan, the security guard is murdered. Sergeant Ross, a martial arts expert and commander of the Homicide Squad Zone Four, believes that the man was killed by a karate chop. What he does not know is that Hiroo Matsushima, the last of the samurai, has taught a number of young Hispanic men self-respect, zen, and karate. They are ready to become a maurading gang dedicated to crime.

Marten Claridge

Nobody's Fool *Detective Inspector Frank McMorran*
New York: Walker, 1991.

The body of a fourteen-year-old female is found in a trash bag in a ravine and McMorran is called out of suspension to investigate quietly. Three young people have been murdered with the same modus operandi, but there are no clues to the identity of the person responsible. McMorran is also fighting against his former boss, Chief Inspector Kettle, whose fondest ambition is to become Commander of the Scottish Special Crimes Squad.

Ernest Clark

Fatal Rose *Detective William Ruffin*
New York: Dell, 1986.

An old man is murdered and left on the railroad tracks. Psychiatrist Rose Wood is murdered in her apartment. The names of six prominent men make up a list of possible suspects. The seventh name belongs to Detective William Ruffin, who is investigating the killings but has a hatred for Rose. Then a teenage boy is found in a dumpster covered with freshly poured concrete, and Ruffin must speed up his search for the killer before he murders again.

Jon Cleary*

The High Commissioner *Sergeant Scobie Malone*
London: Collins, 1966.
New York: Morrow, 1966.

The Premier of New South Wales orders Sergeant Scobie Malone to London where he is to arrest the High Commissioner of Australia. Malone goes to London but falls victim to the personal charm of John Quentin, the Commissioner. Quentin is in London trying to negotiate a ceasefire in Vietnam and he is the only respresentative likely to be successful. But there is danger in the form of a group of assassins ready to kill him and anyone who gets in their way.

Helga's Web *Sergeant Scobie Malone*
London: Collins, 1970.
New York: Morrow, 1970.

During the renovation of the Sydney Opera House the body of a young woman is found. The beautiful Helga had been strangled and hidden in the building. Her life is revealed to be a tangled web of deceit and manipulation.

Ransom *Inspector Scobie Malone*
London: Collins, 1973.
New York: Morrow, 1973.

Scobie Malone is finally able to take his wife on a honeymoon to New York City. While they are there the mayor's wife is kidnapped and the ransom is the release of five political prisoners to be sent to Cuba upon their release. An Australian woman, Lisa Malone, in the elevator when the mayor's wife is taken, is held hostage as well.

Dragons at the Party *Inspector Scobie Malone*
London: Collins, 1987.
New York: Morrow, 1988.

The deposed president of Palucca, one of the Spice Islands, is being sheltered by the Australian government. One of his assistants is killed and

Inspector Malone tries to stop the assassination of President Timori himself. The plot turns around who is doing what to whom and why.

Now and Then, Amen *Inspector Scobie Malone*
London: Collins, 1987.
New York: Morrow, 1988.

A nun's body is found on the steps of a brothel. As Scobie Malone investigates, he finds that she comes from a prominent Australian family. Her uncle is an archbishop, her grandfather quite wealthy, and her mother a recognized artist. It seems that the Hourigan family does not want it known that Sister Mary Magdalene had any ties to them. Then Malone receives a telephone threat urging him to stop pursuing his inquiries.

Babylon South *Inspector Scobie Malone*
London: Collins, 1989.
New York: Morrow, 1990.

When Walter Springfellow, head of the Australian Security Intelligence Organization, vanished in 1966, Scobie Malone, then a young constable, worked on the case because he was temporarily assigned to Missing Persons. Twenty-one years later Springfellow's remains are found in the mountains near Sydney. Venetia Springfellow has a reputation for enjoying male company, and her daughter is trying to take over the family business her mother has made so successful. Then there is another death.

Murder Song *Inspector Scobie Malone*
London: Collins, 1990.
New York: Morrow, 1990.

A construction worker is shot while on the job. Next, a policeman getting out of his car in his driveway is gunned down. Then a woman is killed in an apartment and she, too, has been shot with a high-powered rifle. The apartment where she died is kept for the employees of the O'Brien Cossach, a merchant bank, for the purpose of sexual assignations. The Cossach is run by Brian Boru O'Brien, who attended police academy twenty years before with Scobie Malone.

Pride's Harvest *Inspector Scobie Malone*
London: HarperCollins, 1991.
New York: Morrow, 1991.

The local police prove ineffective in handling the death of Kenji Sagawa in Collanmundra. When he arrives Malone finds that although the cotton mill that Sagawa managed has brought jobs and stability to the region, it has also caused racial tensions. Everyone hates the local policeman, an Aborigine. They resent the fact that Sydney had to send someone to clean up their mess, and tension builds just as the town begins filling up with people who have come to see the annual horse race.

Andrew Coburn*

Off Duty *Rupert Goetz and Frank Chase*
New York: Norton, 1980.
London: Secker, 1981.

Frank Chase, retired Boston police detective, has a dead man placed neatly on his front lawn. Chase and Goetz are up to their ears in a nasty situation that involves people who play for keeps.

Love Nest *Sergeant Sonny Dawson*
New York: Macmillan, 1987.
London: Secker, 1987.

A woman is killed in a motel room and Sergeant Sonny Dawson is assigned the task of finding her killer. He must wade through an assortment of townspeople, all of whom have something to hide.

Max Allan Collins*

The Dark City *Eliot Ness*
New York: Bantam, 1987.

In 1935 Eliot Ness was appointed Director of Public Safety in Cleveland. The first order of business was to clean up the police and fire departments and rid them of corrupt personnel. When Ness, ever uncorrupted, discovers that the leader of the crooked officers is a policeman known as the "outside chief," it is a challenge to root him out—a challenge Ness cannot refuse.

Butcher's Dozen *Eliot Ness*
New York: Bantam, 1988.

One of the first recorded serial killers in the United States, the Butcher of Kingsbury Run, murdered people in Cleveland in the 1930s. The corpses were dismembered and beheaded, and pieces left scattered in the ravine known as Kingsbury Run or dumped in the Cuyahoga River, which runs beside it. This was the case that haunted Eliot Ness. Collins offers a solution and a reason why Ness could not reveal that he had solved the mystery.

Bullet Proof *Eliot Ness*
New York: Bantam, 1989.

Cleveland is about to erupt into a seething volcano fueled by union unrest. Eliot Ness is caught between the wealthy industrialists who accuse him of having too much sympathy for the workers, and the union poised to launch a strike even though they believe Ness has too many ties to big business and will not protect them. A group of men calling themselves union leaders turns attention to the produce industry, but must face Ness himself.

Michael Connelly

The Black Echo *Detective Hieronymus Bosch*
Boston: Little, Brown, 1992.

The body of a man is found in a drainage pipe near Mulholland Dam high above Los Angeles. The man, an apparent victim of a heroin overdose, is a Vietnam veteran and known to Detective Bosch, who is in charge of the case. The dead man had been a tunnel rat (a member of a military unit used to clear the enemy from tunnels where they hid and stored equipment) while serving in Vietnam. Bosch was in the same unit and had had to leave the man behind during an unsuccessful mission. The man is somehow tied in with a bank heist that brings in the FBI. Greed, vengeance, betrayal, and the war must be sorted out before the truth of several deaths is revealed.

K. C. Constantine
(Pseudonym of Carl Kosak)

The Rocksburg Railroad Murders *Chief of Police Mario Balzic*
New York: Saturday Review Press, 1972.

Chief of Police Mario Balzic solves a brutal murder. The interpersonal reactions of the people of Rocksburg, Pennsylvania, the personal lives of the police, and some well-placed clues lead Balzic to the murderer.

The Man Who Liked to Look at Himself *Chief of Police Mario Balzic*
New York: Saturday Review Press, 1973.
London: Hodder, 1986.

Chief Balzic goes hunting with Lieutenant Minyon of the state police and his Weimaraner. The dog discovers a bone—a human thighbone. From this meager evidence, Balzic begin a murder investigation.

The Blank Page   *Chief of Police Mario Balzic*
New York: Saturday Review
   Press/Dutton, 1974.

The discovery of a young female student strangled to death in her rented room near the college campus presents Balzic with a fine puzzle. On her body is a blank sheet of paper. Looking into her life he finds that she knew no one at school, had no friends, talked to no one, and did poorly in class; in short, she was a complete blank. So why did someone kill her?

Always a Body to Trade   *Chief of Police Mario Balzic*
Boston: Godine, 1983.
London: Hodder, 1985.

A woman is shot with a heavy-duty-calibre gun. She was standing on the sidewalk outside of a bar. The same day two beautiful apartments are trashed, one while a state narcotics agent was watching the place from his car. Add to this a new mayor who knows nothing about law enforcement, resulting in Balzic explaining every move to him as the cases progress. The only help Balzic is getting is from the Reverend Rutherford, a man deeply entrenched in Rocksburg's vice world.

Upon Some Midnight's Clear   *Chief of Police Mario Balzic*
New York: Godine, 1985.
London: Hodder, 1986.

Christmas should be a quiet time in Rocksburg but Mario Balzic has his hands full when fighting between two groups of Vietnam veterans breaks out. The local bad boy shoots someone and a bitter woman perpetrates a scam that causes endless trouble and ruins the remnants of Balzic's peace of mind.

Joey's Case   *Chief of Police Mario Balzic*
New York: Mysterious, 1988.
London, Hodder, 1988.

The only son of Albert Castelucci, a retired grievance man for the miners' union, was killed five months ago while Balzic was in Pittsburgh. The killing took place outside of Rocksburg's jurisdiction and the case has not been worked on for months because the state police believe it to be closed. Castelucci wants Chief Balzic to look into it, resulting in some painful surprises for all concerned.

Sunshine Enemies   *Chief of Police Mario Balzic*
New York: Mysterious, 1990.
London, Hodder, 1990.

The pornography store that has opened outside of town is the target for the anger of the Reverend P. Shaner Weier. Balzic must also deal with a stabbing death in the store's parking lot. The horrors do not quit there, for his beloved mother has a massive stroke and he must face the inevitability of her mortality.

Thomas H. Cook*

Tabernacle *Detective Tom Jackson*
Boston: Houghton Mifflin, 1983.

Jackson, a former New York City homicide detective, now with the Salt Lake City police department, is present when the body of a hooker is found in a hotel room. She had been strangled. Her body is dressed and groomed to make her appear perfect in death. The story deals with the Mormon community in which a serial killer is murdering because he believes God wants him to.

Sacrificial Ground *Lieutenant Frank Clemons*
New York: Putnam, 1988.
London: Collins, 1988.

A sixteen-year-old girl is found murdered. Clemons had a daughter who committed suicide three years before, so it is difficult for him not to feel a personal connection to the case. Angelica Devereaux was beautiful and attracted to the art world. Clemons must expose her personal life before he discovers a reason for her death.

Streets of Fire *Sergeant Ben Wellman*
New York: Putnam, 1989.
London: Collins, 1990.

The body of a little black girl is found in a baseball field in a shallow grave. Sergeant Wellman walks a tightrope between Birmingham's white community and the black people, who are fighting for their civil rights. The year is 1963 and Martin Luther King Jr. is about to lead his famous Freedom Marches.

Susan Rogers Cooper

The Man in the Green Chevy *Chief Deputy Sheriff Milton Kovak*
New York: St. Martin's, 1989.

Deputy Sheriff Milt Kovak is caught in a dangerous situation between his growing infatuation with a woman who is the victim of an abusive husband and a murder case.

Houston in the Rear View Mirror   *Chief Deputy Sheriff Milton Kovak*
New York: St. Martin's, 1990.

Milton Kovak travels to Houston, Texas, where his sister has allegedly killed her husband and then tried to shoot herself. The brother and sister have been estranged for years but Kovak wants to get to know his nephews and niece better. He ends up taking care of them while their mother is in the hospital. He also tries his hand at investigating what happened to his sister, her marriage, and what her husband was really doing to get himself killed. Although this is not a true procedural, Kovak uses his police training.

Other People's Houses   *Chief Deputy Sheriff Milton Kovak*
New York: St. Martin's, 1990.

Lois Bell is dead in her car in the garage. The gas tank is empty, the ignition key is turned on. Her husband and three children are dead in the house. It looks as if they all died of carbon monoxide poisoning but things do not add up in the Bells' past. There are no family records, no work history, no photographs, and Lois Bell knew things no first-time bank teller should know. Then a U.S. Marshall arrives and takes the bodies away, leaving Milt with an even greater mystery to solve.

Chasing Away the Devil   *Chief Deputy Sheriff Milt Kovak*
New York: St. Martin's, 1991.

It is Pioneer Week in Prophesy County, Oklahoma, and three guys rob a clothing store. Kovak, dressed in a stylized cowboy outfit and very uncomfortable, has a shootout with them. Not in the best of moods, he picks this day to ask his longtime girlfriend, Glenda Sue, to marry him. She gets mad and declines. Next morning the sheriff informs Milt that Glenda Sue has been murdered and he, as her long-term boyfriend, might be the chief suspect. While going through Glenda Sue's possessions, Milt finds an airline ticket to Paris. He now knows that she was keeping something secret because she never had money enough for that kind of trip before.

Patricia D. Cornwell

Postmortem   *Dr. Kay Scarpetta, Chief Medical Examiner,*
New York: Scribner's, 1990.   *and Lieutenant Lou Marino*

Medical Examiner Kay Scarpetta places herself in danger when her job gives her high visibility in a serial murder case. The murderer grows increasingly concerned that she is a threat to him.

Body of Evidence *Dr. Kay Scarpetta, Chief Medical Examiner,*
New York: Scribner's, 1991. *and Lieutenant Lou Marino*

The brutal murder of novelist Beryl Madison leads Kay Scarpetta into a nightmare world, as she flees a man who makes threatening innuendoes on the phone and gradually hunts her down. Madison was working on her memoirs, which would have revealed personal things about Pulitzer Prize winner Cary Harper, and the manuscript is now missing. The medical examiner's office comes under attack from attorney Robert Sparacino, and an old lover comes back into Kay's life.

All That Remains *Dr. Kay Scarpetta, Chief Medical Examiner,*
New York: Scribner's, 1992. *and Lieutenant Lou Marino*

Deborah Harvey and Fred Cheyney are just another couple missing in the Richmond, Virginia, area. Four other couples have vanished, their bodies found months later in remote fields or woods. Harvey is the daughter of the federal government's antidrug administrator. The other couples died mysteriously but Deborah Harvey was shot and cut with a knife before she died. The question facing Scarpetta and Lieutenant Marino is whether the killings were done by a serial killer or if Harvey's and Cheyney's are copycat murders done for a different reason.

Cruel & Unusual *Dr. Kay Scarpetta*
New York: Scribner's, 1993.

While Dr. Scarpetta awaits the body of soon-to-be-executed convicted murderer Ronnie Joe Waddell, someone is busily attacking thirteen-year-old Eddie Heath. Eddie is found the next morning, mortally wounded and propped up against a dumpster. There is a bad feeling about the crime scene from the beginning because it looks so much like those that the now dead serial killer, Waddell, used to leave. Another death, which at first appears to be a suicide and later proves to be murder, also has a few very strange clues left at the site.

E. W. Count

The Hundred Percent Squad *Lieutenant Andrew Flynn*
New York: Warner, 1990.

Flynn has put together a squad that has solved 100 percent of its homicides for the last two years. Trying to make that three years in a row, they run into two cases that have them stumped. The murder of two drug dealers and the brutal slaying of a ballet dancer, which is attracting the attention of the press and the mayor, bring the squad up against deadly Irish Viera, drug lord and possible murderer.

John Creasey*
(also J. J. Marric, q.v.)

Inspector West Takes Charge *Inspector Roger West*
London: Paul, 1942.
Revised Edition: London: Pan, 1943.
New York: Scribner's, 1972.

Three members of the very wealthy Prendergast family are dead, leaving only Claude and his wife, Maisie, to inherit. Then Maisie begins talking in her sleep and to Claude it sounds like she wants to kill him—perhaps she *has* killed his relatives. Then he learns that he has a cousin he never knew existed. Prendergast is very much afraid when he seeks help from Roger West.

Inspector West Leaves Town* *Chief Inspector Roger West*
London: Paul, 1943.

Go Away to Murder
London: Lancer, 1972.

Inspector West at Home *Chief Inspector Roger West*
London: Paul, 1944.
Revised and First American Edition: New York: Scribner's, 1973.

Roger takes his wife, Janet, out for lunch on his afternoon off and sees Tiny Martin, a sergeant who works for Superintendent Abbott, lurking where he has no business being. Then Abbott arrives at West's house and searches it. Next he subjects Roger and Janet to a body search. Even though nothing is found West must clear his name, as someone has accused him of taking a bribe.

Inspector West Regrets—* *Chief Inspector Roger West*
London: Paul, 1945.
Revised Edition: London: Hodder, 1965.
New York: Lancer, 1971.

Holiday for Inspector West *Chief Inspector Roger West*
London: Paul, 1946.

While Roger West is vacationing with his family, a member of Parliament is murdered; someone has hacked off Riddel's head. Riddel knew he was in danger because he asked for protection shortly before his death. Going back to London is West's duty, but the investigation leads him into a great deal of danger.

Battle for Inspector West*   *Chief Inspector Roger West*
London: Paul, 1948.

Triumph for Inspector West   *Chief Inspector Roger West*
London: Paul, 1948.

The Case Against Paul Raeburn
New York: Harper, 1958.

Paul Raeburn is wealthy and very corrupt. When a man with whom he had done business gets out of jail and attempts to blackmail him, Raeburn runs him over with his car. A policeman witnesses the murder but during the trial a surprise witness for the defense testifies that it was all an accident. Then Raeburn, a free man, begins heckling the police and subtly challenging them to a showdown.

Inspector West Kicks Off   *Chief Inspector Roger West*
London: Paul, 1949.

Sport for Inspector West
New York: Lancer, 1971.

Guy Randal, successful salesman for a packaging firm, secures a large order (eight million boxes) to be made up for Perriman's, the U.K.'s largest producer of packaged foods. That evening as Guy returns to his boarding house he is shot and killed. His briefcase, which contained the Perriman order and his sample packages, has vanished. To add to the mystery, Guy Randal looks quite a lot like Roger West.

Inspector West Alone   *Chief Inspector Roger West*
London: Evans, 1950.
Revised and First American Edition: New York: Scribner's, 1973.

Roger West is lured to an abandoned cottage and framed for the brutal murder of a young woman. The police are also looking for a man known as Arthur King, the master criminal behind the plot to destroy West. Roger has his face altered by plastic surgery to assume the identity of Charles Rayner, another criminal. Through complex twists of plot and psychological maneuvering, West is placed in grave danger.

Inspector West Cries Wolf   *Chief Inspector Roger West*
London: Evans, 1950.

The Creepers
New York: Harper, 1952.

A gang of thieves led by the vicious Lobo is creating havoc for the Metropolitan Police. Someone calling herself Miss Lobo has been telephoning

Janet West remarking on Roger's being away so much, how overworked he is, and how his children must miss him. The fight to get Lobo becomes personal when Janet reacts in a very emotional and jealous way. West must save his marriage and children while trying to get results for his bosses at the Yard.

A Case for Inspector West *Chief Inspector Roger West*
London: Evans, 1951.

The Figure in the Dusk
New York: Harper, 1952.

The murder of Wilfred Arlen is not a random killing; his keys are taken and his house entered and robbed. Then Lionel Bennett, another businessman, is murdered. Arlen and Bennett were cousins. The trail leads to Ralph Latimer, who was having an affair with Arlen's wife and every other woman he met. Latimer eludes the police at every turn until they happen upon another girlfriend and her sister.

Puzzle for Inspector West *Chief Inspector Roger West*
London: Evans, 1951.

The Dissemblers
New York: Scribner's, 1967.

James Liddel is arrested by West for the arsenic murder of Lancelot Hay, nephew and blackmailer of Liddel and the rest of the Liddel family. The evening of the arrest Francesca Liddel arrives at West's home and convinces him that her mother is in grave danger of suicide and needs a police nurse, which West supplies. Later he finds Francesca and her brother Tony tied up in Tony's apartment.

Inspector West at Bay *Chief Inspector Roger West*
London: Evans, 1952.

The Blind Spot
New York: Harper, 1954.

The Case of the Acid Throwers
New York: Avon, 1960.

Someone throws acid at Roger West's face (but hits him in the hand) and burns a young woman walking past. As Janet West is getting ready to go to the hospital she is given a message at her front door: "This is only the beginning." West now must try to find the person who hates him so much that they would hurt his wife and children to get at him.

A Gun for Inspector West *Chief Inspector Roger West*
London: Hodder, 1953.

Give a Man a Gun
New York: Harper, 1954.

There is something strange about the murder of old Benny, a known receiver of stolen goods. Also, it was too easy to catch and convict his killer. Benny's niece, Ruth Linder, takes over his shop and makes no bones about the fact that she hates cops. Then vicious attacks occur resulting in death. Add to this a crime wave and the fact that Ruth Linder appears to have taken over her uncle's operation and Roger West has his hands full.

Send Inspector West *Chief Inspector Roger West*
London: Hodder, 1953.

Revised Edition: **Send Superintendent West**
London: Pan, 1965.
New York: Scribner's, 1976.

A young boy is kidnapped from his home in London. The United States Embassy summons West for help. The boy's father is on a special mission of negotiations between East and West. What is needed here is someone known for his expert handling of delicate situations.

A Beauty for Inspector West *Chief Inspector Roger West*
London: Hodder, 1954.

The Beauty Queen Killer
New York: Harper, 1956.

So Young, So Cold, So Fair
New York: Dell, 1958.

A beautiful young woman has been strangled and Inspector Turnbull believes the police have solved the case when her boyfriend commits suicide. However, Roger West finds that another woman has been murdered in the same fashion and then a third is found dead. The Beauty Queen Killer becomes a priority for Scotland Yard.

Inspector West Makes Haste *Chief Inspector Roger West*
London: Hodder, 1955.

The Gelignite Gang
New York: Harper, 1956.

Night of the Watchman
New York: Berkley, n.d.

Murder Makes Haste
New York: Lancer, n.d.

The London department store Jefferson's is robbed by the Gelignite gang. In the course of the robbery they kill one of the night watchmen. Rose Mulcaster, his daughter, is married to one of the gang though she does not know it. West is the officer in charge and soon his suspicions are raised by Billy Mulcaster and Gerald Sarkey, the head of Jefferson's.

Two for Inspector West   *Chief Inspector Roger West*
London: Hodder, 1955.

Murder, One, Two, Three
New York: Scribner's, 1960.

Murder Tips the Scales
New York: Berkley, 1962.

Anthony Reedon, a traveling salesman, has not been seen for a while. West and a colleague find his body in his home. Michael Mallow, a close friend of the deceased, is supposed to be in Scotland, but he cannot be found. And then Mallow's wife disappears.

Parcels for Inspector West   *Chief Inspector Roger West*
London: Hodder, 1956.

Death of a Postman
New York: Harper, 1957.

Tom Bryant, a postal worker, is found murdered in a courtyard next to the River Way post office where he worked. In the few days before Christmas West must deal with telling Bryant's family about his death, the investigation of many bloody parts of a human body placed in parcels and sent to the post office as mail, and the brutal attack on Derek Bryant's fiancée.

A Prince for Inspector West   *Chief Inspector Roger West*
London: Hodder, 1956.

Death of an Assassin
New York: Scribner's, 1960.

West is called from his vacation in Paris to Milan where an attempt on the life of Prince Asir of Jardia has failed. Asir's trusted confidant Colonel Yahuni is dead and an Englishman has been murdered. The chief suspect is a young woman named Anne Pegler. She also happens to be the only witness to both murders. West and his wife, Janet, fly to Milan where West saves the lives of the Prince and Anne. It looks like the assassins from the Brotherhood of Zara are closing in and mean to kill Asir and anyone who gets in their way.

Accident for Inspector West *Chief Inspector Roger West*
London: Hodder, 1957.

Hit and Run
New York: Scribner's, 1959.

Mrs. Bray is run down while walking a child to school. Then Mrs. Kitt, a justice of the peace, is savagely beaten with a chain while in her own home. When it becomes apparent that Charles Jackson, who prepares briefs for an important barrister specializing in criminal cases, is the object of a hate campaign, West slowly begins to recognize the one thing that links these people together.

Find Inspector West *Chief Inspector Roger West*
London: Hodder, 1957.

The Trouble at Saxby's
New York: Harper, 1959.

Doorway to Death
New York: Berkley, 1961.

Michael Quist has discovered that the father of his fiancée is an embezzler. Curiously, Quist is framed for the murder of a woman who is somehow involved with his future father-in-law. West is in trouble at the Yard because the new Assistant Commissioner, Colonel Jay, believes that West was promoted because of his friendship with the former Commissioner. Jay places West in an impossible position and then sits back to watch him fail.

Murder, London–New York *Superintendent Roger West*
London: Hodder, 1958.
New York: Scribner's, 1961.

Margaret Roy, a beautiful young woman, is murdered. West is promoted to Superintendent and the Roy case is handed to him. An attempt is made on Vanity Roy's life and all the paintings of her sister, Margaret, are slashed. When an art dealer is killed in New York City the evidence points to a connection with West's London case.

Strike for Death *Superintendent Roger West*
London: Hodder, 1958.

The Killing Strike
New York: Scribner's, 1961.

In the middle of a laborers' meeting where tensions are running high, Malcolm Munro, son of the CEO and a director of the company, drives through in his new Rolls-Bentley. The car is like a red flag to the people who work hard in the big automotive plant. The stage is set for a fierce labor-management confrontation but what results is a situation where a strike can hardly be avoided. Young Munro has been completely discredited and the ensuing melee ends in a death. Roger West uses all his diplomatic ability to avoid disaster.

Death of a Race Horse *Superintendent Roger West*
London: Hodder, 1959.
New York: Scribner's, 1962.

The Foley family, in its passion for horse racing, has gambled away its entire fortune. The latest horse thought to be their salvation is sent to the Gale stables to be trained but disaster strikes, leaving the promising Silver Monarch dead from a gunshot wound to the head and a trainer murdered. The Reading police send for help and Superintendent West goes to sort it all out.

The Case of the Innocent Victims *Chief Inspector Roger West*
London: Hodder, 1959.
New York: Scribner's, 1966.

Three babies are suffocated in their cribs and West looks for the killer. The search leads him to Edward Maddison, the owner of an import/export rug company. Chief Inspector Gibson disappears while conducting an investigation at the company's warehouse.

Murder on the Line *Commander Roger West*
London: Hodder, 1960.
New York: Scribner's, 1963.

When the railroad-crossing keeper is murdered, Roger West connects the murder to the fact that millions of pounds' worth of materials are stolen from the British rail system each year. He is ready to go with an assigned team to the port area of Southampton and Liverpool when the murder takes place.

Death in Cold Print *Superintendent Roger West*
London: Hodder, 1961.
New York: Scribner's, 1962.

Roger West must go to the town of Corby where a night watchman has been murdered. The problem as the local police see it is that half the population of the town works at the printing plant and Corby is dependent on the industry for its survival. They do not want to pressure the plant employees. Just as West arrives, the body of a woman is found in a silo close to the property of the printing complex. All the evidence points to the woman's husband as the guilty party in both deaths.

The Scene of the Crime *Superintendent Roger West*
London: Hodder, 1961.
New York: Scribner's, 1963.

A young woman is found strangled in her apartment and suspicion soon falls on the son of her employer, a man who desperately loved her but to no avail. He is arrested. Then his father's housekeeper is murdered and the shop safe robbed of thousands of pounds' worth of antique jewelry.

Policeman's Dread *Chief Superintendent Roger West*
London: Hodder, 1962.
New York: Scribner's, 1964.

Anonymous letters to policemen who are scheduled to appear in court causes them to botch their testimony. Someone is determined to undermine the efforts of the police. West sets up a young policeman as a person ready to take bribes and the results are startling.

Hang the Little Man *Chief Superintendent Roger West*
London: Hodder, 1963.
New York: Scribner's, 1963.

In a three-month period in the Clapham area of London there have been eleven shop robberies. The latest ended in the brutal killing of the pregnant wife of the proprietor. West, working closely with Dan Appleby, the Yard's impressive pathologist, begins closing in on the perpetrators, while the husband of the dead woman is bent on revenge.

Look Three Ways at Murder *Chief Superintendent Roger West*
London: Hodder, 1964.
New York: Scribner's, 1965.

Told from three points of view—those of the criminal, the victim, and the police—the story deals with a robbery and an attempted murder. As the robbers grow bolder and more eager for money, West becomes involved with the family of one of their victims.

Murder, London–Australia *Chief Superintendent Roger West*
London: Hodder, 1965.
New York: Scribner's, 1965.

The body of a young woman is found in an apartment. When the police release her picture she is identified as Denise Morrison, who had traveled on the S.S. *Kookaburra* out of Sydney, Australia. When another of its passengers is murdered at the airport and it is learned that Denise had a sister who has vanished, the Yard goes into action trying to prevent more untimely deaths.

Murder, London–South Africa *Chief Superintendent Roger West*
London: Hodder, 1966.
New York: Scribner's, 1966.

A man leaves South Africa bound for London but never arrives. West is sent to the South African embassy to gather facts but is soon on his way to Pretoria. West's marriage is in trouble again and he meets a beautiful woman who tempts him to the brink of infidelity.

The Executioners *Chief Superintendent Roger West*
London: Hodder, 1967.
New York: Scribner's, 1967.

Cecil Rochester Chayter, convicted of murdering a woman he considered his fiancée, is released after spending twenty years in prison. Chayter has maintained that he killed her in a fit of jealous rage. He says he found his fiancée in bed with another man. The book is somewhat of a departure as the action is divided between West and the Chayter family. Is Cecil insane and getting ready to murder again?

So Young to Burn *Chief Superintendent Roger West*
London: Hodder, 1968.
New York: Scribner's, 1968.

In one evening several groups of young men terrorize people by throwing acid on young couples. West knows that gang violence is a growing menace and he moves to stop it. He also knows that to make judgments before all the facts are in can ruin an investigation so he carefully watches Chief Inspector Moriarty, who is assigned to help him. Moriarty is so convinced of his own importance and ability that he begins to make mistakes and to plan trouble for West.

Murder, London–Miami *Chief Superintendent Roger West*
London: Hodder, 1969.
New York: Scribner's, 1969.

Henrietta Lynn is Sir David Marshall's secretary. Sir David is quite possessive of Henrietta and provokes an emotional scene between them and then fights with Gerald Ward, her would-be suitor. Meanwhile, Lady Marshall is in a hospital for the insane, the victim of a writer of poison-pen letters. Then Lady Marshall is murdered.

A Part for a Policeman *Chief Superintendent Roger West*
London: Hodder, 1970.
New York: Scribner's, 1970.

Popular television star Danny O'Hara is beaten to death and his apartment ransacked. Roger West is called in to handle the case. The trail leads to a young woman who has just undergone an abortion. Her father, who was in O'Hara's apartment as he was being murdered, seems to be a strong suspect. Then there is an attack on another popular television star.

Alibi *Chief Superintendent Roger West*
London: Hodder, 1971.
New York: Scribner's, 1971.

When Mario Rapelli attacked Ricardo Verdi there were witnesses and Rapelli is arrested. At his hearing a young woman swears Rapelli was in bed with her and two others at the time of the attack. Then Verdi dies and West finds himself at odds with his Commander and in charge of a case that is more complex and dangerous than he at first thought.

A Splinter of Glass *Chief Superintendent Roger West*
London: Hodder, 1972.
New York: Scribner's, 1972.

The warehouse on the docks has literally been cleaned out. The place is almost spotless—down to the floor having been scrubbed and waxed. No clues are to be found involving the theft of the huge shipment of bullion except for a splinter of glass left on the floor. Chief Superintendent West uses that splinter as the evidence to get the very professional and elusive thieves.

Theft of Magna Carta *Chief Superintendent Roger West*
London: Hodder, 1973.
New York: Scribner's, 1973.

West is alerted that a known art thief is in England currently spending his time in Salisbury and Bath. The police are stumped because they have been told that there is an art theft being planned involving millions of pounds. Where would the thieves find a buyer willing to pay so much and what could the object be except Magna Carta?

The Extortioners   *Chief Superintendent Roger West*
London: Hodder, 1974.
New York: Scribner's, 1975.

In a three-week period three V.I.P.s have committed suicide. West is drawn into the case when a famous anthropologist comes to the Yard to confess that he is being blackmailed. The story accelerates around an organized gang of motorcyclists who try to kill all the witnesses and even make two attempts on West himself.

A Sharp Rise in Crime   *Chief Superintendent Roger West*
London: Hodder, 1978.
New York: Scribner's, 1979.

As the crime rate in London escalates, three members of the Metropolitan police working undercover are murdered. A photograph of Mr. Invisible, one of the leading crime bosses, is taken by an undercover agent and sent to Scotland Yard. The criminal looks just like Roger West. Then someone tries to kill West.

Bill Crider

Too Late to Die   *Sheriff Dan Rhodes*
New York: Walker, 1986.

The violent beating death of a pretty housewife in Blacklin County, Texas, sets off a hunt for the killer that leads Sheriff Rhodes into a complicated investigation that takes him away from his reelection duties and the campaign trail.

Shotgun Saturday Night   *Sheriff Dan Rhodes*
New York: Walker, 1987.

When a sack of human arms and legs is found in a trash pile in Blacklin County, Sheriff Rhodes must find out whether a homicidal maniac is running free in Texas or if there is a more logical reason for dismembered parts to be lying around. To add to his woes a rough motorcycle gang begins causing trouble in Blacklin County.

Cursed to Death   *Sheriff Dan Rhodes*
New York: St. Martin's, 1988.

A dentist, Samuel Martin, complains to Sheriff Rhodes that a woman has put a curse on him. There are also rumors of witchcraft being practiced in the area. Rhodes is skeptical of this, but the worst happens—the dentist's wife is beaten to death and the dentist disappears.

Evil at the Root *Sheriff Dan Rhodes*
New York: St. Martin's, 1990.

Lloyd Bobbit is a resident in a nursing home and someone has stolen his teeth. While the nurse promises to look out for another resident who is having less trouble eating (thus identifying the guilty party), Sheriff Rhodes goes into town, only to find that he, his deputies, and the county are being sued for neglect and for having a jail that is unsafe for prisoners.

Booked for a Hanging *Sheriff Dan Rhodes*
New York: St. Martin's, 1992.

When used-book dealer Hal Brame tells Sheriff Rhodes that he saw ghostly lights and heard strange sounds coming from one of the buildings on the campus of the old, abandoned college in Obert, the Sheriff decides to ride out there to see for himself. They find Simon Graham, the owner of the property, hanging from the rafters of one of the buildings. Graham was a book dealer not because he loved books but because he enjoyed money and manipulation. He was supposed to have a copy of *Tamerlane and Other Poems*, the first book written by Edgar Allan Poe, and published in 1827. Since the book is very rare, a great deal of interest is stirred up over whether the copy really exists and whether Graham's death was suicide or murder.

Blood Marks *Detective Howland and*
New York: St. Martin's, 1991. *Police Psychologist Romain*

Women are being killed in Houston. There are no clues, the crime scenes are immaculate, and the method of murder varies. Howland, working closely with psychologist Romain, tries to find some kind of link between the women to determine why they were picked for murder. The story is told by the killer and Howland.

E. V. Cunningham[*]
(Pseudonym of Howard Fast)

Samantha *Detective Sergeant Masao Masuto*
New York: Morrow, 1967.
London: Deutsch, 1968.

Al Greenberg, a movie producer and friend of Sergeant Masao Masuto of the Beverly Hills police, is dead, murdered by someone who identifies herself as Samantha when she calls to confess. A long list of prominent movie stars and studio executives believes that they will be the next victims, as long ago twelve young men raped an actress and none of them was ever charged or tried for the crime. When the woman did not get the part she had auditioned for and knowing that she would never get justice for the rape, she vanished. Now it appears that she is back for revenge.

The Case of the One-Penny Orange *Detective Sergeant Masao Masuto*
New York: Holt, 1977.
London: Deutsch, 1978.

The house has been totally ransacked but nothing has been taken, at least nothing obvious. When a stamp dealer and his assistant are found dead Masuto must deal with the murders. Thus begins his quiet search for a small stamp—the One-Penny Orange—one of the most sought after stamps in the world.

The Case of the Russian Diplomat *Detective Sergeant Masao Masuto*
New York: Holt, 1978.
London: Deutsch, 1979.

The body of an unidentified man is found in the pool of the exclusive Beverly Glen Hotel and Masuto must get right on the case. Next, a guest in the hotel who may be a possible witness to murder is killed. The overtones of political intrigue and terrorism are not intimidating to the sergeant until his young daughter is kidnapped.

The Case of the Poisoned Eclairs *Detective Sergeant Masao Masuto*
New York: Holt, 1979.
London: Deutsch, 1980.

No one in the bridge club thinks much of it when dessert is delivered to Laura Crombie's house. None of the women eats any because they are all on diets, but the maid does and dies of botulism the following morning. Since Masuto does not know who was the target of the poison, he puts all four women under guard.

The Case of the Sliding Pool *Detective Sergeant Masao Masuto*
New York: Delacorte, 1981.
London: Gollancz, 1982.

Thirty years ago the owner of a house in Beverly Hills had a swimming pool built on a hill in the backyard. Now it is 1980, Southern California is getting more rain than it can handle, and the pool slides down the hill revealing the skeleton of a man long dead. Why he is there concerns Sergeant Masuto until he finds the pieces to his puzzle. The solution relies on Masuto's skill as a practitioner of Zen and karate.

The Case of the Kidnapped Angel   *Detective Sergeant Masao Masuto*
New York: Delacorte, 1982.
London: Gollancz, 1983.

Actress Angel Barton is kidnapped and her husband, Mike, pays the ransom to have her returned unharmed. After she arrives home Mike Barton is murdered. Now Masuto looks at the case in a different light. Both Bartons have hidden their pasts and cannot be traced beyond their stay in California. To get to the bottom of Mike Barton's death the Beverly Hills detectives must uncover what the couple hid and why.

The Case of the Murdered Mackenzie   *Detective Sergeant Masao Masuto*
New York: Delacorte, 1984.
London: Gollancz, 1984.

Mackenzie's corpse is found in his bathtub. Four people identify it as Mackenzie but his actress ex-wife says the corpse is not her husband.

Jack Curtis

Point of Impact   *Inspector Robin Cully*
New York: Simon & Schuster, 1991.   *and Sergeant Mike Dawson*

A sniper is shooting people at random in London. At first the police believe the killings have no meaning but a witness tells Inspector Cully that one of the victims was meant to die and the motive may be stolen art masterpieces. Cully travels to the United States in an attempt to find who may be responsible for hiring the hitman.

Claire Curzon*

I Give You Five Days*   *Thames Valley Serious Crimes Squad*
London: Collins, 1983.

Masks and Faces*   *Thames Valley Serious Crimes Squad*
London: Collins, 1984.

The Trojan Hearse*   *Thames Valley Serious Crimes Squad*
London: Collins, 1985.

The Quest for K*   *Thames Valley Serious Crimes Squad*
London: Collins, 1986.

Three-Core Lead   *Thames Valley Serious Crimes Squad*
London, Collins, 1988.
New York: Doubleday, 1990.

Two cases engage the attention of the Thames Valley Serious Crimes Squad. A girl's body is found in the trunk of a car. The police, trying to determine who she is, find that there is no missing persons report on a girl answering her description. At the same time Detective Superintendent Mike Yeadings is puzzled by the death of a long-time acquaintance who just happened to be a spy. The newspapers say that the friend, Howard Swaffham, died as a tourist in Prague. Somehow Yeadings feels that an Eastern European country and the scene of much of Swaffham's espionage would not be a smart place for a retired agent to vacation. Swaffham's daughter urges him to investigate as she believes her father was in danger.

The Blue-Eyed Boy   *Thames Valley Serious Crimes Squad*
London: Collins, 1990.
New York: Doubleday Crime Club, 1991.

Several muggings have taken place in and around a commercial district in Reading. The case changes when the latest victim, Joel Sefton, is found dead. His family is questioned, and as the investigation progresses it becomes apparent that young Sefton may have been murdered.

First Wife, Twice Removed   *Thames Valley Serious Crimes Squad*
London: Little, Brown, 1992.
New York: St. Martin's, 1993.

Two women are dead. One is a mother found by her four-year-old daughter at the bottom of the stairs in their home. The police do not know whether she is dead due to an accident or foul play. The second woman's death is clearly murder. Found in an abandoned car, she turns out to be someone Detective Inspector Mott of the Thames Valley Police had met on holiday. The two cases appear to be connected.

Robert Daley*

To Kill a Cop   *Chief of Detectives Earl Eischied*
New York: Crown, 1976.

A group of young street criminals is killing cops. Meanwhile an ex-revolutionary living in exile in Africa comes back to New York when he sees how he can bring about chaos and a people's revolution. His recruits begin by robbing banks to get money for what every revolution needs—heavy guns.

The Dangerous Edge　　　　　　　　*Commissaire Robert Bellarmine*
New York: Simon & Schuster, 1983.
London: Hodder, 1983.

The Banque de Nice is robbed by Edward Lambert, an unsuccessful American playwright. The bank robbery is well planned and executed but Lambert makes one or two mistakes. He and his henchmen kill a derelict who is witness to their theft. And Lambert steals some papers and pornography, which leads to his being hunted by someone other than the police. Commissaire Robert Bellarmine must find him before he is killed.

Hands of a Stranger　　　　　　　　　　*Inspector Joseph Hearn*
New York: Simon & Schuster, 1985.
London: Hodder, 1985.

Joe Hearn is a good cop who loves his job and knows how to play politics. When he is made Inspector, he is given command of the narcotics division, which in turn brings him into contact with Judith Adler, assistant district attorney, who has inherited a vicious rape and drug case from the New Jersey State Police. The story revolves around the growing attraction between Hearn and Adler, but when Mary Hearn is raped, her husband must come to some decisions about his life and his job.

John Danica and Lucy Freeman

Lerza's Law　　　　　　　　　　　　　*Special Agent Joseph Lerza*
New York: St. Martin's, 1991.

Joe Lerza is an FBI agent whose specialty is undercover work. When he is sent to Philadelphia to stop a violent clash between a biker group and the Mafia, he begins to crack under the strain of living under so many assumed identities. He starts using cocaine and sinks into a morass of questionable activity. Lerza is saved by the strangest group of rescuers assembled in recent fiction.

Harold R. Daniels[*]

The House on Greenapple Road　　　　　*Lieutenant Daniel Nalon*
New York: Random House, 1966.　　　　　*and Sergeant Charlie Wilentz*
London: Deutsch, 1967.

The kitchen of the house on Greenapple Road in Holburn, Massachusetts, looked like a slaughterhouse. Blood was splattered everywhere. The owner, Marian Ord, was not to be found. Her husband, away on a business trip, does not have a good alibi. Marian herself was fond of younger men and was a negligent mother. The case is an overnight wonder in this small town. Then everyone loses interest except Lieutenant Nalon, who comes up with a brilliant solution.

Frank DeFelitta*

Oktoberfest *Chief Inspector Martin Bauer*
New York: Doubleday, 1973.
London: Collins, 1974.

A butcher is killed with his own cleaver, then stuffed into his freezer. The man looks like Nazi leader Hermann Goering. Chief Inspector Bauer, who served in the German army in Russia during W.W. II, has flashbacks to what he knew about the Holocaust. The fact that there is still a strong Nazi feeling among people in power in Germany and an element that wants to ignore all Jews as if they and W.W. II can be wished away haunts the telling of the mystery and how it is solved with the help of a German Jew from Israel.

Nelson De Mille*

Ryker #1: The Sniper *Sergeant Joe Ryker*
New York: Leisure, 1974.

A sniper fires at the gas tank of a sports car traveling on the West Side Highway in New York City. Ryker is given the case because the resulting explosion kills the driver of the car.

Ryker #2: The Hammer of God *Sergeant Joe Ryker*
New York: Leisure, 1974.

Ryker faces the Monk, a deranged man who believes he is the hammer of God and must strike down the witches of the world. This vicious killer ties up women then drives a stake through their hearts.

Ryker #3: The Terrorists *Sergeant Joe Ryker*
New York: Leisure, 1974.

The American Freedom Army in the guise of liberating the downtrodden and poor is really stealing, looting, and killing them. Ryker's strike force must end the reign of terror that falls on the city.

O'Neil de Noux

The Big Kiss *Detective Dino LaStanza*
New York: Zebra, 1990.

The body of the son-in-law of Alphonso Badalamente, the local Mafia chief, is found floating off New Orleans's St. Maurice Wharf. Two more murders follow, and LaStanza realizes that he has a whodunit on his hands with no clues to follow.

Blue Orleans *Detective Dino LaStanza*
New York: Zebra, 1991.

The single-handed capture of a gunman who has killed five people in a shooting spree leaves LaStanza with an even bigger reputation than he had previously enjoyed. Soon two corpses are dumped in the streets of New Orleans. One of the men, according to his wife and daughter, was snatched from his couch, leaving only his shirt as evidence he had been there. The daughter seems terrified and LaStanza believes that she may be the link between his murder cases and a drug cartel boss. Then she disappears.

Joseph P. De Sario*

Limbo *Detective Brenda Collins*
New York: Doubleday, 1987.

Detective Brenda Collins goes undercover as a hooker on the mean streets of East LA to find a vicious rapist of women. The primary suspect is Father Cedric Anselm of St. John's Church in El Barrio where the rapes are occurring.

Michael Dibdin

Ratking *Commissioner of Police Aurelio Zen*
London: Faber, 1988.
New York: Bantam, 1989.

When Ruggiero Miletti, a wealthy industrialist, is kidnapped, Aurelio Zen is sent from Rome to Perugia to head the investigation to find the missing man. However, the Miletti family is not cooperating with the authorities and Zen soon realizes that one of them is working with the kidnappers.

Vendetta *Commissioner of Police Aurelio Zen*
London: Faber, 1990.
New York: A Perfect Crime
  Book/Doubleday, 1991.

Oscar Burolo videotapes a small dinner party that turns out to be a massacre of most of the guests. Unfortunately, his cameras did not capture the identity of the killer, nor was the killer detected by the house's state-of-the-art security systems. While Zen tracks him, the killer is allowed to interject his thoughts and reminiscences into the narrative.

D. J. Donaldson

Cajun Nights *Chief Medical Examiner Andy Broussard*
New York: St. Martin's, 1988. *and Psychologist Kit Franklin*

For no apparent reason successful men are murdering their families, then committing suicide. The men are not connected in any apparent way. The city of New Orleans and its darker secret history are major participants in the plot.

Blood on the Bayou *Chief Medical Examiner Andy Broussard*
New York: St. Martin's, 1991. *and Psychologist Kit Franklin*

A young girl is murdered—her throat torn out by a gardening claw. A street musician is killed in the same way. A serial killer is on the loose in New Orleans. The newspapers are having a field day printing all the details of the cases. When the evidence appears to suggest that the killer is a werewolf, Broussard and Franklin look into the reality of lycanthropy.

Alison Drake
(Pseudonym of T[rish] J[aneschutz] MacGregor;
also Trish Janeschutz, q.v.)

Black Moon *Detective Aline Scott*
New York: Ballantine, 1989.

Aline Scott and Ryan Kincaid have separated because nothing seems to be happening in their relationship. Meanwhile the body of a young exotic dancer is found in a dumpster, her fingers cut off. There are other indications that this killing has ties to the "santeria," a Cuban mystery cult resembling voodoo. Aline's house is broken into and personal items of hers are taken. Then she begins to have nightmares.

Lagoon* *Detective Aline Scott*
New York: Ballantine, 1990.

High Strangeness *Detective Aline Scott*
New York: Ballantine, 1992.

At the Wellness Center, a psychiatric clinic, a psychiatrist and an orderly are murdered. Margaret Wickerd, the female patient suspected of having committed the murders, is missing. Aline Scott discovers that Margaret believes she was kidnapped by a UFO. The autopsy shows that the murdered doctor had a strange device implanted in his head and no one knows why it was there or what it did.

John Kevin Dugan
(Pseudonym of W. E. B. Griffin, q.v.)

Badge of Honor *Staff Inspector Peter Wohl*
New York: Jove, 1988.

When Captain Dutch Moffitt goes to meet television reporter Louise Dutton at a restraurant he tells himself it is strictly business but knows it is not. While there, an armed robbery takes place and Moffitt is killed trying to stop the crime in progress. The ensuing investigation is given to Philadelphia's newly formed Special Operations Unit headed by Staff Inspector Peter Wohl and involves everyone from the mayor to the newest rookie cop. (For other books in this series, see W. E. B. Griffin.)

Robert L. Duncan*

The Serpent's Mark *Detective Picone and*
New York: St. Martin's, 1989/1990. *Detective Rizzutto*

Peter Stein, ex-NYPD homicide supercop, runs a service for police departments that provides profiles of serial killers and the date, location, and particulars of the murders. In Las Vegas three people are killed and the man responsible believes Stein is a connection between God and the reason he kills. Reluctantly, Stein is drawn into the insane world of the man, who thinks he is harvesting souls for the coming of God.

Susan Dunlap

Karma *Police Officer Jill Smith*
New York: Raven, 1981.

Berkeley police officer Jill Smith attends a Buddhist meeting where Padmasvana, a holy man from Bhutan, is to address a gathering. During the ceremony Padma is stabbed by a knife thrown through the air. Smith and her partner, Howard West, peel away the layers of jealousy and hate that exist among the followers of Padma to find who had reason to kill him.

As a Favor *Police Officer Jill Smith*
New York: St. Martin's, 1984.

Patrol cars have become the target of a street thief. When Jill Smith is contacted by her ex-husband she does not want to talk to him but he tells her that a friend of his is missing. Jill goes to the woman's apartment, which looks like a murder scene with blood everywhere. Then a young boy finds a heap of blood-stained clothes on the beach.

Not Exactly a Brahmin *Detective Jill Smith*
New York: St. Martin's, 1985.

When the brakes fail on the car of wealthy philanthropist Ralph Palmerston and he dies in the resulting crash, newly promoted homicide detective Jill Smith believes that something is not quite right with the situation. With no suspects and no leads Smith perseveres until she finds the one fact that changes the entire case.

Too Close to the Edge *Detective Jill Smith*
New York: St. Martin's, 1987.

Liz Goldenstein, a wheelchair-bound social and political activist, falls out of her chair and drowns in the Bay. The seat belt that held her in place had been cut. Jill Smith sorts through the Berkeley political scene to find Goldenstein's killer.

A Dinner to Die For *Detective Jill Smith*
New York: St. Martin's, 1987.

The owner of the very popular restaurant Paradise is poisoned in his own establishment. Jill Smith, just back on duty after a helicopter accident, discovers that the successful entrepreneur had a few dark secrets, one of which got him killed.

Diamonds in the Buff *Detective Jill Smith*
New York: St. Martin's, 1990.

Two people—Hasbrouck Diamond, a wealthy dentist, and Leila Sandoval, a masseuse—have been feuding for years. They call the police and complain about each other and have verbal battles until the young man staying with Diamond is murdered.

Death and Taxes *Detective Jill Smith*
New York: Delacorte, 1992.

As Jill Smith is driving home one night she stops to help a lone police officer guarding a man lying in the street. The man is Philip Derm, the most hated IRS auditor in all of California. The police discover that he was married to a recluse who is allergic to everything. One of the suspects in the case had had an appointment to meet Derm, but denies having kept it. To complicate things, Derm has been killed by an ingenious method—a hypodermic needle sticking out of his bicycle seat injected poison into his system.

John Dunning

Booked to Die *Detective Cliff Janeway*
New York: Scribner's, 1992.

The body of Bobby Westfall is found in a Denver alley, discarded like so much garbage. But to Cliff Janeway, a detective with the Denver police and an avid, knowledgeable book collector, Westfall was an amazing person. He was usually poor but possessed an uncanny instinct for finding rare books. Janeway believes that a violent criminal named Jackie Newton is the murderer, and his single-minded pursuit of Newton leads him away from the real motive behind Westfall's death.

Lew Dykes

Choke Hold *Lieutenant Vercingetorix Fort and*
New York: Jove, 1990. *Detective Babs Bladenbauer*

Fort sent Turk Mordoni to jail with a broken arm and the promise of a lengthy prison term, but Turk's boss, the Dancer, engineered his release. Now Turk is killing a policeman per night and leaving a note for Fort as a calling card with the promise that he is getting his revenge. Then the homicide squad discovers that Mordoni has had plastic surgery and they cannot recognize him. The homicide squad senses that this is the set-up for a demand for money, and the Dancer, using Mordoni as his hit man, does not disappoint them.

Jack Early
(Pseudonym of Sandra Scoppettone)

Donato and Daughter *Lieutenant Dina Donato and*
New York: Dutton, 1988. *Sergeant Michael Donato*

Catholic nuns are being slaughtered by a serial killer in New York City. Dina Donato, the officer in charge of the investigation, handpicks a team of expert detectives including her estranged father. The case leads the Donatos into the realm of a sociopathic killer who has no feeling about his victims. Dina and her father get a chance for a better understanding of their love for each other.

John Eller

Charlie and the Iceman[*]   *Detective Charlie Rope*
New York: St. Martin's, 1981.

Rage of Heaven   *Detective Charlie Rope*
New York: St. Martin's, 1982.

Long-time cop Charlie Rope is called to the apartment of a young murdered business executive. The trail leads to the corporation where she worked and the business people with whom she was associated. Suspicion soon falls on her fiancé, but that seems too simple a solution for Rope.

James Ellroy[*]

Clandestine   *Policemen Freddy Underhill and Wacky Walker*
New York: Avon, 1982.
London: Allison, 1984.

In 1951 Freddy Underhill is a rookie cop with dreams of being the best. His partner is Wacky Walker, a guy who has been around for awhile. Underhill is a golf whiz who gives lessons to his lieutenant but when a woman he has known is murdered he sees a way to advance his career, and when his partner is killed in the line of duty, Underhill must grow up.

Because the Night   *Detective Sergeant Lloyd Hopkins*
New York: Mysterious, 1984.
London: Century, 1987.

Supercop Jacob Hertzog of the vice squad always works undercover, and alone in the field, has three citations for bravery and a reputation for being able to disguise himself as anyone. Hertzog has not been seen by anyone for three weeks. At the same time three people are killed in a liquor store with a .41 calibre revolver made before the Civil War. Lloyd is able to connect the two cases when he encounters John Havilland, a psychiatrist who manipulates people for his own reasons.

Blood on the Moon   *Detective Sergeant Lloyd Hopkins*
New York: Mysterious, 1984.
London: Allison, 1985.

Hopkins, a detective with a great deal of intelligence, works in the Rampart Division of LA. A serial killer of women is operating in his territory. The murderer has "saved" more than twenty women. But when the object of the killer's true affections turns out to be Kathleen McCarthy, a girl he idolized in high school, Hopkins finds he, too, is attracted to her and in the position of having to put a stop to the killings—Hopkins style.

Suicide Hill *Detective Sergeant Lloyd Hopkins*
New York: Mysterious, 1986.
London: Century, 1988.

Suspended from duty, Sergeant Lloyd Hopkins is in danger of losing his daughter's love. Unfortunately, the respect went long ago. Assigned as liaison officer to the FBI, Hopkins thinks of it as some kind of Mickey Mouse job until he begins working on a string of bank robberies. Then he comes into some information that will destroy his old nemesis, Fred Jaffrey of the dread Internal Affairs Division.

The Black Dahlia *Detective Bucky Bleichert*
New York: Mysterious, 1987.
London: Mysterious, 1988.

Based on the unsolved real-life case known as the Black Dahlia, the subject of this book is the discovery of the horribly mutilated body of a young woman in a vacant lot in Los Angeles. Bucky Bleichert, ex-prizefighter and maverick cop, becomes involved in the case to the point that it becomes an obsession with him.

Earl W. Emerson*

Black Hearts and Slow Dancing *Fire Chief MacKinley Fontana*
New York: Morrow, 1988.

Fontana lives with his young son in Staircase, Washington. Mayor Maureen Costigan appoints Fontana sheriff in order to have someone investigate the case of a missing man and a trashed house. Fontana, with the help of Satan the police dog, finds Zajack's mutilated and tortured body. His search for clues leads him to Seattle and a fire chief who is less than honest, a multimillionaire and his female martial arts bodyguard, three sadistic crooks, and a mysterious woman named April.

Help Wanted: Orphans Preferred *Fire Chief MacKinley Fontana*
New York: Morrow, 1990.

A ham dosed with rat poison and intended for the fire department's dinner kills one fireman and sets Mac Fontana on the trail of a killer. Aided by Warren Bounty, former sheriff of Staircase, Mac finds deception and danger every step of the way.

Robert L. Fish*
(Also Robert Pike, q.v.)

The Fugitive*   *Captain José Da Silva*
New York: Simon & Schuster, 1962.
London: Boardman, 1963.

Isle of the Snakes*   *Captain José Da Silva*
New York: Simon & Schuster, 1963.
London: Boardman, 1964.

The Shrunken Head*   *Captain José Da Silva*
New York: Simon & Schuster, 1963.
London: Boardman, 1965.

Brazilian Sleigh Ride*   *Captain José Da Silva*
New York: Simon & Schuster, 1965.
London: Boardman, 1966.

The Diamond Bubble*   *Captain José Da Silva*
New York: Simon & Schuster, 1965.
London: Boardman, 1965.

Always Kill a Stranger   *Captain José Da Silva*
New York: Putnam, 1967.

The Organization of American States will be meeting in Rio and the Brazilian police have been ordered to carry guns. An anonymous note has been received that threatens the assassination of one of the delegates. Teaming up with his American colleague, Wilson of the U.S. embassy, Da Silva works against the clock to come up with a clue as to who will be killed, how, and by whom.

The Bridge That Went Nowhere   *Captain José Da Silva*
New York: Putnam, 1968.
London: Long, 1970.

A new bridge that basically goes nowhere is blown up. Then Wilson, of the U.S. embassy, arranges for Da Silva to meet a young American woman whose brother is missing. The two incidents may be connected. Also, Da Silva does not know why anyone would want to stop a settlement of Japanese immigrants in the middle of a wilderness.

The Xavier Affair*   *Captain José Da Silva*
New York: Putnam, 1969.
London: Hale, 1974.

The Green Hell Treasure*   *Captain José Da Silva*
New York: Putnam, 1971.

Trouble in Paradise*   *Captain José Da Silva*
New York: Doubleday, 1975.

Richard Fliegel*

The Art of Death   *Detective Sergeant Shelly Lowenkopf*
New York: Pocket, 1988.

Lowenkopf arrests Pietr Albert Nevshi, a street performer, for shooting a member of a street gang on the Cross Bronx Expressway. The artist thought he was acting in a staged competition and in the running to win a prize. But the boy he shoots dies. Lowenkopf then meets and interrogates Simon Foxdale, a newspaper writer, who believes that death is art. Could he have something to do with the failed acting as art attempt of Nevski or are the people he owes money to out to get him any way they can? Lowenkopf and his partner are also trying to find eighty-year-old Mrs. Cohen, who killed her husband by putting metal filings on his steak. She has escaped arrest by running from the police—literally.

The Next to Die   *Detective Sergeant Shelly Lowenkopf*
New York: Pocket, 1989.

In an attempt to catch the boy who stole his car battery, Shelly Lowenkopf chases him up to the roof of a building. But the kid, for reasons of his own, throws himself from the roof and dies. When he returns to his car Shelley discovers that his briefcase is missing. Lowenkopf is not a textbook detective who strictly follows the rules nor is he very efficient as a policeman. He does his job with passion and a need to get the bad guys. But when his briefcase is found at the scene of a murder he is not only outraged but the prime suspect in killing the boy.

The Organ Grinder's Monkey   *Detective Sergeant Shelly Lowenkopf*
New York: Pocket, 1989.

A state inspector working late in the Rehabilitation Building of a psychiatric institute in the Bronx is butchered, dismembered, and his stomach removed from the scene of the crime. A body found in a dumpster also located on the institute grounds sends Shelly Lowenkopf undercover as a custodian in the building. Every scrap of evidence points to the fact that the authorities are looking for an inmate in the psychiatric hospital, a brilliant criminal mind distorted by mental illness.

Time to Kill[*]   *Detective Sergeant Shelly Lowenkopf*
New York: Pocket, 1990

A Semiprivate Doom[*]   *Detective Sergeant Shelly Lowenkopf*
New York: Pocket, 1991.

Peter Fox*

Kensington Gore   *Detective Inspector Jack D. Lamarre*
London: Macmillan, 1983.   *and Detective Sergeant Alison Prendergast*

The Trail of the Reaper
New York: St. Martin's, 1983.

Famous talk show host Nelson Hogan picks up his golf ball and within five minutes is horribly dead. He has been killed by alconitine, a powerful organic alkaloid poison. A picture of Brueghel the Elder's *Grim Reaper* left behind by the murderer is the only clue. Then other murders are committed.

Edward J. Frail

Cult   *Inspector Matt Senacal*
New York: Onyx, 1990.

A boy is sacrificed on an altar in the dining room of his home. His head is cut off and placed in the getaway vehicle and his body is left slowly roasting on the gas grill. The family dog is also ritualistically murdered, as are the boy's parents. A satanic cult is suspected of the crime wave, which involves nine murders.

Kristopher Franklin

Silvercat   *Deputy Sheriff Murphy Davis*
New York: Bantam, 1990.

There is a killer of women loose in Silvercat, Colorado. The tourist season is just beginning so there are lots of women around. The killer picks his prey, plays games with them, then slices off their eyelids. Deputy Sheriff Murphy Davies has a lot on his plate and is running for sheriff, too. Just to complicate matters, Sara Nichols, the new assistant editor of the town newspaper, openly shows her dislike for him and makes it very plain that she is out to get him.

Nicolas Freeling*

Love in Amsterdam   *Inspector Van der Valk*
London: Gollancz, 1962.

Death in Amsterdam
New York: Ballantine, 1964.

A man is accused of murdering Elsa de Charmoy and an eyewitness places him at the scene. The story is told first by the man, Martin, and then by Van der Valk of the Amsterdam police as he goes about his investigation. This is a tale of love, obsession, and jealousy.

Because of the Cats   *Inspector Van der Valk*
London: Gollancz, 1963.
New York: Harper, 1963.

A gang of six young men breaks into an apartment; they steal what they want, then rape the woman living there. Van der Valk is soon onto a group of teens that hangs out at a coffee shop in the wealthy suburb of Bloemendaal aan Zee. The young men have money, good homes, and parents who provide them with material things but spend no time with their sons. As Van der Valk remarks, this is one of those cases where you know immediately who committed the crime, but why it was done and how the perpetrator will be brought to justice are something else.

Gun Before Butter   *Inspector Van der Valk*
London: Gollancz, 1963.

Question of Loyalty
New York: Harper, 1963.

Arnolf Englebert, a famous conductor, dies in an automobile crash. Sometime later his daughter is assaulted by a gang of youths. Then a man who brought a white Mercedes is shot. His body is found in an empty house. There is an attempt to bribe Van der Valk, and the daughter of the conductor returns after being kidnapped. The Inspector goes to Belgium tracking clues and a dead man.

Double Barrel *Inspector Van der Valk*
London: Gollancz, 1964.
New York: Harper, 1965.

Someone in the town of Drente is writing poison-pen letters containing information about secrets the townspeople wish to remain undisclosed. Several people have not been able to handle the stress and have committed suicide. Van der Valk, along with his wife, Arlette, is sent to Drente to work undercover and find out who is responsible. The locals are rather inbred and suspicious of strangers.

Criminal Conversation *Inspector Van der Valk*
London: Gollancz, 1965.
New York: Random House, 1966.

First an unsigned letter arrives at police headquarters requesting a meeting so that the letter writer can assess whether the police are capable of investigating a death that is a possible murder. A man is dead, and Carl Merckel, a wealthy merchant banker and the author of the letter, believes the man was killed by a doctor who is also treating Merckel's wife. Thus begins a cat-and-mouse hunt with Van der Valk doing the stalking.

The King of the Rainy Country *Inspector Van der Valk*
London: Gollancz, 1966.
New York: Harper, 1966.

The extremely wealthy Jean-Claude Marschal, heir to the Sopex fortune, has disappeared, and Mr. Canisius comes to headquarters to make the report. The trail leads to Cologne where Van der Valk has a friend on the police force working on a similar case in which a young woman is missing.

Tsing-Boum *Commissaire Van der Valk*
London: Hamilton, 1969.

Tsing-Boom!
New York: Harper, 1969.

Esther Marx, a housewife and mother, is cut down by a machine gun in her living room. Her unassuming husband is a sergeant in the military and frequently away from home. For this reason Van der Valk takes Esther's ten-year-old daughter home to his wife, Arlette. The woman's past is shrouded in mystery and involves the French occupation of Vietnam and the first battle of Dien Bien Phu. The Commissaire goes to France to unravel the events that led up to Esther's death.

Over the Side *Inspector Van der Valk*
London: Hamilton, 1971.

The Lovely Ladies
New York: Harper, 1971.

The old man lies on the sidewalk. The witnesses to his collapse cannot agree as to whether he had been hit by the bus, walking, standing still, or had a heart attack. To Van der Valk this is a clear case of assault as an antique dagger is sticking out of the man's chest. The only words the man speaks are "the girls." His wife is younger than he and calls him father. He has three daughters who live in Dublin, so to make sense out of the killing Van der Valk goes to interview them there.

Sand Castles *Commissaire Van der Valk*
London: Deutsch, 1989.
New York: Mysterious, 1990.

Van der Valk takes Arlette on vacation. While at a resort he sees a man selling something in manilla envelopes. The something turns out to be pornography involving children. Meanwhile Arlette is engaging in adventures of her own. Soon they find a mysterious man living in a remote area and a variety of strange occurrences.

A Dressing of Diamonds *Principal Officer Henri Castang*
London: Hamilton, 1974.
New York: Harper, 1974.

The eight-year-old daughter of the judge of juvenile court is kidnapped. Judge Colette Delanique calls her friend Vera's husband, Henri Castang. The police mount a huge search for the child, who is being held by a most peculiar family.

What Are the Bugles Blowing For? *Principal Officer Henri Castang*
London: Heinemann, 1975.

The Bugles Blowing
New York: Harper, 1976.

A man calls Castang and announces that he is a murderer. Castang, along with Agent Lucciani, finds three people—a mother, her daughter, and a painter who lived in Paris—all naked and very dead in a bedroom. The confessed murderer turns out to be highly placed in the French government and Castang must use all his cunning to uncover what really precipitated the deaths.

Lake Isle *Principal Officer Henri Castang*
London: Heinemann, 1976.

Sabine
New York: Harper, 1978.

An elderly woman comes to Castang to say that she is afraid of her adopted son. She is Sabine Arthur, a wealthy poet. Castang sees firsthand that her son is manipulative and cruel to his mother. When Sabine is murdered in her kitchen Castang is sent to investigate.

The Night Lords *Principal Officer Henri Castang*
London: Heinemann, 1978.
New York: Pantheon, 1978.

An English judge and his family, vacationing in France, find the body of a man in the trunk of their Rolls Royce. Then Castang finds his landlady's brother hanging in a lavatory in his apartment building. And then the police find a third body. Nothing is what it seems: a naked woman with no identifying features, a suicide that is a murder, and a death that may be one or the other.

Castang's City *Principal Officer Henri Castang*
London: Heinemann, 1980.
New York: Pantheon, 1980.

A prominent man in the city, Etienne Marcel, is gunned down as he walks to his car. The shooting is right on the street in plain view of the townspeople. While Castang is investigating the murder, his wife, Vera, is expecting their child.

Wolfnight *Commissaire Henri Castang*
London: Heinemann, 1982.
New York: Pantheon, 1982.

Marc Vibert, a well-known French politician, is in an automobile accident from which he walks away, although a young woman does not. Seventeen hours later Vibert goes to Castang's office to relate his story of amnesia and great personal fear of the media circus that will ensue when it is learned what he did. The gendarmerie has already pulled the car up from the ravine but no one was in it. The investigation is impeded by politicians who are trying to protect one of their own.

The Back of the North Wind *Commissaire Henri Castang*
London: Heinemann, 1983.
New York: Viking, 1983.

Castang's caseload is horrendous. He comes back from a holiday to find that a young woman's body parts are scattered in plastic bags over a wide area of his territory. Whoever murdered her also ate her flesh. As a new experience, looking for a cannibal is not one Castang wants.

No Part in Your Death *Commissaire Henri Castang*
London: Heinemann, 1984.
New York: Viking, 1984.

Three cases are interwoven here to show Castang's humanity and skill. He is sent to Munich to a police convention. Vera, his wife, goes with him and involves him in a domestic situation with the wife of an influential doctor, who almost succeeds in getting Castang arrested. The woman wants her child but all the power is with her husband. Her father-in-law is even more powerful and has Castang abducted and interrogated. Castang then investigates the death of the wife of one of his friends to determine whether it was suicide, an accident, or murder.

Cold Iron *Commissaire Henri Castang*
London: Deutsch, 1986.
New York: Viking, 1986.

Newly transferred Castang must tread very carefully as he investigates the strangulation death of Madame Lecat, a woman of means and position. It soon becomes apparent that this is no straightforward case. When the second murder occurs Castang finds that justice and right are hard to come by in this tangle of greed and corruption.

Not as Far as Velma *Commissaire Henri Castang*
London: Deutsch, 1989.
New York: Mysterious, 1989.

A woman, Madame Adrienne Sergent, disappears from her hotel. She kept a wild-bird aviary and has made provision for its maintenance. Next a bomb kills two nuns in a convent where Madame Sergent did volunteer work.

Those in Peril *Commissaire Henri Castang*
London: Deutsch, 1990.
New York: Mysterious, 1991.

Castang is transferred to the inconsequential Fraud Squad in Paris and without a promotion. This is a great blow to him as he has served as a distinguished member of the Serious Crimes Squad for twenty-five years. The story follows the Castang family, who are uprooted and in unfamiliar territory.

Stephen Gallagher

Down River *Johnny Mays and Nick Frazier*
New York: TOR, 1990

All the signs are there. Plainclothes cop Johnny Mays keeps a little black book of the names of females who have done things he did not like. He is violent and a little off-kilter. One day Johnny drives his car off the end of a pier into the river. Then people start dying—people who were listed in his book. When his car is dragged up from the water, Johnny is not in it. His partner, Nick Frazier, must go looking for him. Johnny is killing, but seems to use Nick as a sounding board.

Joe Gash
(Pseudonym of Bill Granger, q.v.)

Public Murders *Sergeant Terry Flynn*
New York: Jove, 1980.
London: New English Library, 1981.

Maj Kirsten, an English teacher from Malmö, Sweden, is raped and murdered in a Chicago lakefront park. Another body, stuck with a bayonet, is found floating in the river. And then there are more murders. Policewoman Karen Kovic is sent into the streets to act as a decoy to lure the killer out. And he comes.

The El Murders *Special Squad Sergeant Terry Flynn*
New York: Holt, 1987.

A young businessman is murdered in a train station. Sergeant Flynn must counteract departmental prejudice against gays in order to conduct his investigation. Meanwhile another member of his team is trying to find a rapist. (See Bill Granger for the other books in this series.)

Kenneth Goddard*

Balefire *Detective Sergeant Walter Anderson*
New York: Bantam, 1983

In Los Angeles the Olympic Games are about to start. A group known as the Committee is in place to ignite a warning to the United States and the world. A terrorist named Thanatos is sent to deliver the message. The small coastal city of Huntington Beach suddenly errupts in violence involving the police department. Three suspects in a robbery attempt are shot by a police officer. The police officers are gunned down; one dies. Soon the attacks become more personal as members of Anderson's team begin receiving threatening calls at their homes.

The Alchemist *DEA Task Force*
New York: Bantam, 1985.

Designer drugs are hitting the streets in large amounts. The drugs produce the effect of real narcotics but they are deadly if the dose is not right. The man responsible for the synthetic compounds is known as the Alchemist. A San Diego DEA task force is assembled and goes underground to stop him and his organization.

Paula Gosling*

A Running Duck *Lieutenant Mike Malchek*
London: Macmillan, 1978.

Revised Edition: **Fair Game**
New York: Coward McCann, 1978.

Lieutenant Malchek specializes in crimes committed by contract killers. Clare Randall has been shot in the arm while walking on the street, but Malchek treats it as a random shooting. When Clare is released from the hospital her ex-boyfriend takes her home and is killed when her refrigerator explodes. Someone is serious about wanting her dead. As the killer follows Clare and Malchek across the state, it finally becomes clear that a police informant is keeping him in touch with their movements.

Hoodwink *Lieutenant Jake Chase*
London: Macmillan, 1988.
New York: Crime Club/Doubleday, 1988.

Whatever is contained in a manuscript being submitted for publication by would-be writer Fred Norris got him killed. The case turns into a dangerous situation for Chase involving organized crime, corruption in high places, and people who have much to hide.

Monkey Puzzle *Lieutenant Jack Stryker*
London: Macmillan, 1985.
New York: Crime Club/Doubleday, 1985.

English professor Aiken Adamson was struck on the head, repeatedly stabbed, and had his tongue cut out. Someone obviously wanted him dead and Lieutenant Stryker has more than enough suspects on the Grantham, Ohio, university campus. When the English department's chairman has his ear almost cut off and an attempt to blind instructor Kate Trevorne fails, the newspapers come up with the Monkey Puzzle Case—see no evil, hear no evil, speak no evil. Stryker must find the assailant before more harm is done.

Backlash *Lieutenant Jack Stryker*
London: Macmillan, 1989.
New York: Doubleday, 1989.

Four police officers in different precincts and on different days are shot and killed by a sniper. The officers have no connection to one another. Then the drunken bum found dead in an alley turns out to be a federal agent and beautiful Dana Marchant from the Justice Department arrives to work on the case with Central Homicide. The gun that killed the federal agent is the same one used on two of the dead policemen.

The Body in Blackwater Bay *Lieutenant Jack Stryker*
New York: Mysterious, 1992.

Stryker and his fiancée, Kate, go to Paradise Island for a vacation while Stryker recuperates from a bullet wound. While they are on the island Michael Grey is murdered on the lawn of their next-door neighbor, whose niece is Grey's estranged wife. Having no jurisdiction but encouraged by Kate and the local sheriff, Stryker takes charge of the investigation.

The Wychford Murder *Chief Inspector Luke Abbott*
London: Macmillan, 1986.

The Wychford Murders
New York: Doubleday, 1986.

A woman is found murdered in the town of Wychford and Detective Inspector Luke Abbott is dispatched to handle the case. When he arrives he finds that the woman was a hardworking house cleaner who never bothered anyone. He has barely started working on the case when another woman is found with her throat cut. It looks very much like the same person committed both murders. One of the facts that comes out is that the women shared the same doctor, Jennifer Eames, an old girlfriend of Abbott's. When a third woman, a wealthy matron of Wychford, is killed, everyone begins to panic, believing that a serial killer is on the loose.

Death Penalties *Chief Inspector Luke Abbott*
London: Macmillan, 1991.
New York: Mysterious, 1991.

Retired policeman Ivor Peters lay dead on his apartment floor. The man in charge of the case is Luke Abbott, who has been transferred to London from the Cotswolds to spend time on the big-city force. Sergeant Tim Nightingale, new to the CID, believes that Peters was murdered because he was interested in a strange incident involving a man who was killed in a car crash. Abbott gives Nightingale unofficial permission to look deeper into the Peters puzzle.

Laurence Gough

The Goldfish Bowl *Detectives Jack Willows and Claire Parker*
London: Gollancz, 1987.
New York: St. Martin's, 1987.

Forty-four-year-old secretary Alice Palm is shot by a sniper while riding the bus. Alice had a habit of getting dressed up every Friday night and going out, but no one knows where she went or what she did. Every once in a while she brought a man home. It soon becomes clear that the killer has knowledge of what the police are doing.

Death on a No. 8 Hook *Detectives Jack Willows and Claire Parker*
London: Gollancz, 1988.

Silent Knives
New York: St. Martin's, 1988.

While on vacation Jack Willows catches the dead body of a human female on the end of his fishing line. The woman is naked except for a wedding ring. Back in Vancouver, his partner, Claire Parker, discovers the body of a young boy with a tattoo on his arm. In addition, a hit man has been hired to take out three teenage prostitutes.

Hot Shots *Detectives Jack Willows and Claire Parker*
London: Gollancz, 1989
New York: Viking, 1990.

An eighty-million-dollar heroin shipment is lost in English Bay, and its owner, millionaire Gary Silk, wants it back but first someone must pay in blood for his loss. A Vancouver businessman down on his luck finds the heroin and tries to sell it, but in the meantime detectives Willows and Parker are looking into a possible murderer.

James Grady*

Razor Game *Detective Sergeant Devlin Rourke*
New York: Bantam, 1985.

The Reaper follows a distinct pattern of killing as he moves from city to city. First he publishes a religious advertisement in the city's newspaper, then he slaughters a prostitute, and finally a child is harvested for God. Two victims per city and now he is on his way to Baltimore where Sergeant Devlin Rourke is under great pressure to find him and put an end to the killing.

Just a Shot Away *Lieutenant Devlin Rourke*
New York: Bantam, 1987.

Four people are gunned down in the parking garage of a new office building in downtown Baltimore. The hit man is obviously a professional. Captain Goldstein, head of the homicide unit, calls in Rourke, the best detective he has, to head the homicide team. Figuring out why these people were killed is a difficult task because only one was the intended victim. Then there is the problem of keeping the only eyewitness safe.

Bill Granger*
(also Joe Gash, q.v.)

Priestly Murders* *Special Squad Sergeant Terry Flynn*
New York: Holt, Rinehart, 1984

A serial killer is murdering members of the Chicago clergy and Terry Flynn's squad is called in to find the killer.

Newspaper Murders *Special Squad Sergeant Terry Flynn*
New York: Holt, Rinehart, 1985.

Francis X. Sweeney, an alcoholic and washed-up reporter, tries to drown his problems in booze and ends up in an alley with his head bashed in. The case brings together a number of individuals and groups with political axes to grind and they all want to influence Sergeant Terry Flynn in one way or another. (Other books in the series are under Joe Gash.)

Michael Grant

Line of Duty *Lieutenants Brian Shannon and Alex Rose*
New York: Doubleday, 1991.

Three men are executed in New York City in exactly the same way. There is not a single clue linking them together nor is there any indication that they may be on a list of people marked for death. Lieutenant Brian Shannon, assigned to the NYPD Chief of Detectives office, and Lieutenant Alex Rose of the Internal Affairs Department are given the case. What they find leads right to the police department and a crack narcotics unit headed by Captain Partick Stone, a man on his way up with his sights set on being the next Police Commissioner.

Richard Grayson

The Murders at Impasse Louvain *Inspector Jean-Paul Gautier*
London: Gollancz, 1978.
New York: St. Martin's, 1979.

Two deaths about four blocks away from where Gautier lives are very unusual, especially when they turn out to be murders. Madame Hassler finds her husband and her mother dead. She is the notorious mistress of the late president of France, who died in a compromising situation while in Madame's company. Right from the start there is something wrong with Madame's attitude.

The Monterant Affair *Inspector Jean-Paul Gautier*
London: Gollancz, 1980.
New York: St. Martin's, 1980.

Gautier, ever on the fringe of the Parisian art world, goes to see Sophie Monterant act in *La Dame aux Camelias*. She is quite good in the part that Sarah Bernhardt made famous. After the performance Monterant is poisoned and her death involves Gautier in a backstage flap of passions and entanglements involving highly placed political figures including the director of the Sureté.

The Death of Abbé Dodier *Inspector Jean-Paul Gautier*
London: Gollancz, 1981.
New York: St. Martin's, 1981.

Gautier attends the gala eighteenth birthday party of the daughter of the rich and powerful Armand de Saules. The next morning the vicar of Sainte-Clothilde is found stabbed to death just outside of the church confessional. The abbé had dined with the de Saules family the evening before but so did a hundred or so other intimate friends. Every bit of information, every clue points back to the de Saules family. With pressure coming from all sides Gautier must solve the case but in doing so sees no way to avoid causing a social scandal.

The Montmartre Murders *Inspector Jean-Paul Gautier*
London: Gollancz, 1982.
New York: St. Martin's, 1982.

Several events take place within a few days. An artist in Montmartre commits suicide, another artist disappears, and an art dealer is stabbed to death. There are three paintings by a minor artist that everyone wants to buy and may be the reason for the three deaths. Gautier must travel to St. Tropez for answers to his questions.

Crime Without Passion *Inspector Jean-Paul Gautier*
London: Gollancz, 1983.
New York: St. Martin's, 1983.

Gautier, coming back to work at the Sureté after solving the Denise de Richemont murder case, inherits another murder case, that of a woman of the streets. But the Denise de Richemont case continues to hold the public interest as well as Gautier's, and leads him to the real reason why Jacques Le Tellier, the famous journalist, was shot.

Death en Voyage *Inspector Jean-Paul Gautier*
London: Gollancz, 1984.
New York: St. Martin's, 1986.

Lady Dorothy Strathy is dead in her hotel room, stabbed. It is believed that Lady Dorothy had withdrawn a substantial sum of money from the bank the day before she died but no money is found in her room. Her traveling companion tells Gautier that she had recently given Lady Dorothy notice that she was leaving her employ. But an unfinished letter reveals that the companion had been fired and also provides the essential clues that solve the case. However, that same day Gautier's estranged wife dies and he is challenged to a duel in which he participates. He is relieved of duty but still the Dorothy Strathy case haunts him.

Death on the Cards *Inspector Jean-Paul Gautier*
London: Macmillan, 1988.
New York: St. Martin's, 1988.

Gautier witnesses a bomb exploding on board a yacht owned by a wealthy Greek entrepreneur. That very morning a list of fifteen names arrived at Sureté headquarters. It is a list of people marked for death. The accompanying note says that the police will receive a playing card because one of the people listed is killed. Two of the people mentioned have already died.

Death Off Stage *Inspector Jean-Paul Gautier*
London: Macmillan, 1991.
New York: St. Martin's, 1992.

A baby is thrown from the window of the apartment where it lives and is crushed on the bricks below. Both mother and father confess to the murder of their child, then retract their confessions. At the same time some strange things are going on around the Russian ballet troupe the Princess

Sophia has imported from Moscow. A French judge is caught with half his clothes off in the room of a male dancer. Then the judge is murdered.

W. E. B. Griffin*
(also John Kevin Dugan, q.v.)

Badge of Honor: Special Operations *Staff Inspector Peter Wohl, Sergeant*
New York: Jove, 1989/1991. *Jason Washington, Patrolman*
Matthew Payne, et al.

A man is going around Philadelphia humiliating and terrorizing women; he is incapable of raping them, so he punishes them. Soon he goes too far, and losing control, he murders one of his victims. Mayor Carlucci assigns the case to the newly formed and empowered Special Operations Division under the command of Staff Inspector Peter Wohl.

Badge of Honor: The Victim *Staff Inspector Peter Wohl*
New York: Jove, 1991. *and the Special Operations Division Staff*

When Matt Payne drives his date to the wedding rehearsal dinner of his best friend, he does not know that he will find the murdered body of Tony De Zega, a small-time drug dealer for organized crime, and the wounded Penny Detweiler, heiress, bridesmaid, and drug addict, who witnessed the murder. The narcotics people think Payne is a drug dealer. MacFadden and Martinez of the Special Operations Division Staff mistakenly become involved in the hit on a pimp turned snitch.

Badge of Honor: The Witness *Staff Inspector Peter Wohl*
New York: Jove, 1992. *and the Special Operations Division Staff*

During a robbery at a furniture store a maintenance man is killed. The I.L.A.—the Islamic Liberation Army—claims it did the crime for the oppressed peoples of the world. When the Special Operations team tries to arrest the seven perpetrators, one of the suspects makes a bid for freedom and is killed by rookie officer Matt Payne, executive assistant to Peter Wohl, head of the division. (See John Kevin Dugan for the first book in the series.)

Ken Gross

Rough Justice *Detective Jack Mann*
New York: TOR, 1991.

Jack Mann has just received the news that his wife is dying of cancer. Not a drinker, he gets drunk (and very ill) but still sees the killer driving away from a Korean deli where three people have been gunned down, one an informer against the Mafia. The killer is Tommy Day, a detective on the Organized Crime Task Force, dedicated to wiping out organized crime. Day kills cats for recreation and people for cash.

Batya Gur*

The Saturday Morning Murder   *Chief Inspector Michael Ohayon*
New York: HarperCollins, 1992.
Jerusalem: Keter, 1988.

One of the consulting doctors is shot and killed in the Jerusalem Psychoanalytic Institute. Ohayon finds that the doctor's home, where she kept a list of her patients, has been searched and the list has disappeared. The staff at the Institute naturally become the chief suspects, especially since one of them reports a missing handgun. Each person is so riddled with guilt maybe they are all guilty.

A. B. Guthrie, Jr.*

Playing Catch-Up   *Sheriff Chick Charleston and*
Boston: Houghton Mifflin, 1985.   *Deputy Jason Beard*

Two young women are brutally raped and murdered and both cases leave Sheriff Charleston without clues to follow. The fact that one of the women is a call girl and the other a sixteen-year-old does not make his job easier.

Jean Hager

The Grandfather Medicine   *Chief of Police Mitchell Bushyhead*
New York: St. Martin's, 1989.

Joe Pigeon, a painter beginning to sell his work, is found in his cabin with his throat cut and two fingers removed from his left hand. Mitch Bushyhead, town chief of police and recent widower, juggles the murder inquiry and his new duties as mother and father to his teenage daughter.

Night Walker   *Chief of Police Mitchell Bushyhead*
New York, St. Martin's, 1991.

A new lodge in Buckskin has been built right on top of what a lot of townspeople believe was an Indian burial ground. When the lodge's owner is found dead there are those who believe he was murdered by a nightwalker, a Cherokee witch. Thornton, the dead man, had a nasty way of alienating people but Mitch Bushyhead goes about finding the killer, who has now eliminated another person from Buckskin's small population.

Nan Hamilton*

The Shape of Fear   *Isamu Ohara*
New York: Dodd, Mead, 1986.

The economic tension in Southern California between Japanese-Americans and the people who work in American-owned industry comes to the fore with the murder of an insurance agent. Ohara must investigate the case, which involves extortion, the Yakuza, drugs, and racial prejudice.

Joseph Harrington*

The Last Known Address   *Detective Frank Kerrington*
Philadelphia/New York: Lippincott, 1965.
London: Hale, 1966.

Kerrington stops a man who is drunk and driving—a man who happens to be from a prominent family. Through political connections Kerrington is busted from detective to beat sergeant in uniform. Kerrington is lent out to all the specialty departments until the D.A. needs a good investigator. Frank and his rookie partner, Jane Boardman, become involved in a court case involving a gambling and drugs crime syndicate. Through routine plodding they illustrate the policeman's lot.

Blind Spot   *Lieutenant Frank Kerrington and*
Philadelphia/New York: Lippincott, 1966.   *Detective Jane Boardman*
London: Hale, 1967.

Laurie Callender was convicted of the second degree murder of her boyfriend and sent to prison. Eight months later a second boyfriend with political connections surfaces and wants the facts reviewed as he believes her innocent. Kerrington reads the interrogation transcripts, and begins a second painstaking look at the death of Neil Jefferson.

The Last Doorbell   *Lieutenant Frank Kerrington and*
Philadelphia/New York: Lippincott, 1969.   *Detective Jane Boardman*
London: Hale, 1966.

Kerrington and Boardman look into an eleven-year-old kidnapping case that had been an obsession with the now dead detective Ernest Detweiler. There is a connection between the Cherie Fondant Company and the kidnapping. Then they find a letter the kidnapper sent to the little girl's mother.

Alfred Harris*

Baroni   *Detective Lou Baroni*
New York: Putnam, 1975.

A woman falls out of her apartment window and plunges to her death five floors below. Baroni, a veteran cop, knows this was murder, but his sergeant and lieutenant, Tate and Perry, want the case cleared up right away and declare it death by misadventure. The team is also working on the highly visible killing of Zakos, a crime figure, and everyone wants that solved yesterday. Baroni must fight Tate and Perry every step of the way.

Thomas Harris*

Red Dragon   *Will Graham*
New York: Putnam, 1981.
London: Bodley, 1982.

An Atlanta family of four and their dog are butchered in their home. Then a family in Birmingham is slaughtered. Will Graham, forensic scientist for the Federal Bureau of Investigation, has a special gift. He can track serial killers by understanding why and how they think and feel. He begins following in the footsteps of the Red Dragon, a murderer who leaves no personal trace of himself and no leads as to how he has singled out the families he kills.

Ray Harrison*

French Ordinary Murder   *Detective Sergeant Joseph Bragg and*
London: Quartet, 1983.   *Detective Constable James Morton*

Why Kill Arthur Potter?
New York: Scribner's, 1984.

Arthur Potter is beaten to death by a group of thugs looking for a bank check. Potter was a hard-working man, a good husband and father. He had just begun making enough money to keep his family from the poorhouse. Bragg and Morton must do their best to find out why someone thought Potter had the check and why he died for it.

Death of an Honourable Member *Detective Sergeant Joseph Bragg and*
London: Quartet, 1984. *Detective Constable James Morton*
New York: Scribner's, 1985.

The Coroner of the City of London, Dr. John Primrose, has been accused of gross dereliction of duty in the death of Sir Walter Greville, one of the city's representatives to Parliament. Sergeant Bragg is asked to conduct an intense look into whether Greville's death was really an accident. He and Morton are to work alone and report directly to the Commissioner, thus incurring the wrath of Inspector Cotton, Bragg's direct supervisor.

Death of a Dancing Lady *Detective Sergeant Joseph Bragg and*
London: Quartet, 1985. *Detective Constable James Morton*
New York: Scribner's, 1986.

The *Dancing Lady* sailed from England to Galveston, Texas, where the cargo was off-loaded and the ship sunk. The owners then made a big insurance claim and the London police became involved because Lloyd's of London knew it had been defrauded. Since Morton is vacationing in Boston he is sent to New Orleans where the *Dancing Lady* should have docked. Morton gets little cooperation from the local police. With Bragg checking the freighting company records in London and Morton in the southern United States, the team thinks everything will be resolved neatly, but then a murder is committed.

Deathwatch *Detective Sergeant Joseph Bragg and*
London: Quartet, 1985. *Detective Constable James Morton*
New York: Scribner's, 1986.

Tortured and then impaled on an iron fence surrounding a church, the body of an unidentified man becomes the focal point of this investigation. Bragg soon learns that the man was a policeman who was working undercover. The City of London police are concerned that union rallies are becoming more and more violent. The Metropolitan Police Special Branch has the temerity to try to stop Bragg from working on the murder case and they succeed in calling him off the union violence investigation. Then Bragg is accused of raping a reverend's daughter and is arrested.

Harvest of Death *Detective Sergeant Joseph Bragg and*
London: Quartet, 1988. *Detective Constable James Morton*
New York: St. Martin's, 1988.

When Sergeant Bragg is knifed while apprehending a burglar he decides to convalesce at the home of his cousin. While he is there, a man is killed and his death leads to a great upheaval in the small village where many secrets have been kept for years.

Tincture of Death *Detective Sergeant Joseph Bragg and*
London: Quartet, 1989. *Detective Constable James Morton*
New York: St. Martin's, 1989.

Two separate events leading to death happen at the same time. Constable Morton investigates a newspaper report about a poisoned tea shipment and Catherine Marsden, the only female reporter for the City Press, is asked to meet a young painter who has more emotion than common sense. At a ceremony admitting him into the Worshipful Company of Saddlers, Sir Fergus Jardine is poisoned. Jardine is the head of the largest opium operation in the East. The next man to die is the Secretary of the Royal Commission for the opium trade.

Sphere of Death *Detective Sergeant Joseph Bragg and*
London: Constable, 1990. *Detective Constable James Morton*
New York: St. Martin's, 1990.

An American disappears and Bragg and Morton begin looking for him. There is something strange going on as he vanished right after exchanging a rather large sum of money into British sovereigns. Constable Morton is beaten up and recruited by Scotland Yard's Special Branch to go underground to infiltrate a group of European revolutionaries.

Patently Murder *Detective Sergeant Joseph Bragg and*
London: Constable, 1990. *Detective Constable James Morton*
New York: St. Martin's, 1991.

Catherine Marsden, reporter for the City Press and friend of James Morton, finds a young girl dead in a yard in Bartholomew Close. The child was stabbed to death in an unusual fashion. The wounds match those found on the corpse of a rich man. No one comes forward to claim the girl. No one knows her name. After the autopsy they know she had syphilis.

Cynthia Harrod-Eagles

Orchestrated Death *Detective Inspector Slider*
London: Macmillan, 1991.
New York: Scribner's, 1992.

The dead young woman lay in a fetal position, her legs drawn up, her body resting on its left side. She had no clothing on and there was nothing in the old apartment to indicate who she was. She has very short fingernails and a callus on her neck. The only clues are a large container of olive oil and a Stradivarius violin.

Roy Hart

Seascape with Dead Figures *Superintendent Douglas Roper*
London: Macmillan, 1987.
New York: St. Martin's, 1987.

Elderly and wealthy George Winterton is found on the rocks at Monk's Cove on New Year's Day. It is soon apparent that he was thrown or pushed off the cliff. Winterton had just changed his will to include his only son, who for some years had been disinherited. Why Winterton had gone out after midnight is a question Roper must answer, and all along he is hampered by young Inspector Miller, who resents the fact that Roper has been sent from County headquarters to be in charge of the case.

A Pretty Place for a Murder *Detective Superintendent Douglas Roper*
London: Macmillan, 1987.
New York: St. Martin's, 1988.

Eighteen-year-old Vera Jackman worked hard to save almost 2,000 pounds. She put together a portfolio of pictures and planned to go to London to seek her fortune. The day she is murdered the village doctor told her she was pregnant. Roper is sent from county headquarters to question those who knew her and to find the reason she died.

A Fox in the Night *Detective Superintendent Douglas Roper*
London: Macmillan, 1988.
New York: St. Martin's, 1988.

Superintendent Roper and Inspector Price must solve the drowning death of the area's wealthiest, most talked-about widow. They are impeded along the way by a local police officer who has something to hide.

Remains to be Seen *Detective Chief Inspector Douglas Roper*
London: Macmillan, 1989.
New York: Scribner's, 1989.

Cassandra Murcheson buys Box Cottage to get away from her old life. She discovers that the place may not have a ghost but it certainly has a violent past. She calls the police about a dead chicken that has been left on her doorstep with its throat cut. Next thing she knows Chief Inspector Roper from the county police is there asking questions. Suspected witchcraft and an old unsolved mystery figure in the case.

Robbed Blind *Superintendent Douglas Roper*
London: Macmillan, 1990.
New York: St. Martin's 1990.

Stella Pumprey is dead at the foot of the stairs, the back of her head severely damaged. The doctor and constable view the scene and declare her dead by accident. Roper looks at the report and decides the case needs more of an investigation. The head injuries were caused by something sharp, not round like the newel post at the foot of the stairs.

Breach of Promise *Superintendent Douglas Roper*
London: Macmillan, 1991.
New York: St. Martin's, 1991.

Zygmunt Komarowski is found dead by his longtime friend Enid Kingsley in his caravan (house trailer), killed with a shotgun. Roper is plagued by a rash of crime. Sheep rustling and arson appear to be on the rise. But he promises Miss Kingsley that he will find the murderer.

Final Appointment *Detective Superintendent Douglas Roper*
London: Little, Brown, 1993
New York: St. Martin's, 1993

First someone finds the body of a man lying at the side of the road. He had been riding a motorcycle and it appears that he had an accident. The terrible thing is that his head is missing. Then a man walking his dog finds the head, but it is several hundred yards from the body. The bike is also quite far from the site. What at first appeared to be a bad accident is now being looked at as a homicide for there is evidence that someone stretched wire across the road. Superintendent Roper is none too happy when he finds that the dead man is Sergeant Pope, a policeman who is a proven criminal. The officer in charge of proving his guilt is Roper.

James Neal Harvey*

By Reason of Insanity   *Lieutenant Ben Tolliver*
New York: St. Martin's, 1990.

The murderer thinks he is an artist. He poses the dead women in stylistic shots, which he sends to a TV reporter possessed by too much ambition. What the photos of the dead women do not reveal is that the killer is vicious. He bites the buttocks of his victims the way an animal might. Ben Tolliver must stop him because his lust for praise is only surpassed by his growing need to kill.

The Headsman   *Chief of Police Jud MacElroy*
New York: Fine, 1991

In Braddock, New York, there is a legend about a headsman who appears at intervals and chops off people's heads, thus Braddock's "headless horseman." A high school cheerleader is at home when the legend comes calling. He leaves her severed head on her dresser. Lacking a detective bureau, Chief of Police Jud MacElroy must suffer the intrusion of the New York State Police and allow them free rein over the investigation. But circumstance draws him in and he soon is working with Karen Wilson, a secretary who is clairvoyant and has witnessed the killing as a vision.

John Harvey

Lonely Hearts   *Detective Inspector Charlie Resnick*
London: Viking 1989.
New York: Henry Holt, 1989.

Two women are murdered in the same way and Resnick must find the killer before he kills again. Resnick's personal life plus his other duties, that is, court appearances and ongoing investigations, are detailed. Through serendipity and plenty of hard work the police come upon the criminal.

Rough Treatment   *Detective Inspector Charlie Resnick*
London: Viking, 1990.
New York: Henry Holt, 1990.

A series of successful burglaries points to their being the result of inside information. The burglars are a mismatched pair, one nasty and one responsible. They lead the police on a merry chase until they steal a kilo of cocaine from the home of a TV director.

Cutting Edge *Detective Inspector Charlie Resnick*
London: Viking, 1991.
New York: Henry Holt, 1991.

Dr. Tim Fletcher is attacked on his way home, his tendons cut, destroying his arms, hands, and legs, thus ending his career as a surgeon before it began. Then the body of a male nurse from the same hospital is found mutilated in a public rest room. Resnick and his crew (Kellogg, Patel, Devine, and Naylor) are looking for a motive and find more than they bargained for.

Off Minor *Detective Inspector Charlie Resnick*
London: Viking, 1992.
New York: Henry Holt, 1992.

The body of a missing child is found in an abandoned yard. Then a second young girl is missing from her yard. Resnick and company must sort out all kinds of information to determine whether this is the work of one person and determine where the second child is. Resnick sorts out testimony from both cases to arrive at a shocking conclusion.

Mark Hebden*
(Pseudonym of John Harris)

Death Set to Music *Detective Chief Inspector Clovis Pel*
London: Hamilton, 1979.
New York: Walker, 1983.

The police are summoned to the house of Madame Chenandier, who lies dead in her bedroom, beaten to a pulp. All the chief suspects appear to be innocent as none of them has missing clothing or clothing covered in blood.

Pel and the Faceless Corpse *Detective Chief Inspector Clovis Pel*
London: Hamilton, 1979.
New York: Walker, 1982.

Pel, struggling with all of his personal problems plus trying to quit smoking (he manages three packs per day), gets a case involving a corpse with its throat cut and its face shot off. The beautiful widow Faivre-Perret makes her first appearance in the series. The facts of the investigation lead Pel to the realization that the murder may have ties to WWII and the French Resistance.

Pel Under Pressure *Detective Chief Inspector Clovis Pel*
London: Hamilton, 1980.
New York: Walker, 1983.

Two bodies are found. One is that of a student and drug addict. He is found naked and tied up on the floor of his room. The other body is that of an insignificant thief. The two cases are tied together by minor clues and it is soon apparent that they may be truly connected.

Pel Is Puzzled *Detective Chief Inspector Clovis Pel*
London: Hamilton, 1981.

Priceless art objects are being stolen from cathedrals and chateaux in the area. Then a man found dead in an auto accident is shown by the coroner to have been killed by a knife plunged into his brain. To solve these cases Pel goes to Paris and to London's Scotland Yard.

Pel and the Staghound *Detective Chief Inspector Clovis Pel*
London: Hamilton, 1982.
New York: Walker, 1984.

Two criminals have long been itching to fight and take over the other's territory. Now Duke, one of the combatants, is dead, but his arch rival was in police custody when the killing occurred. Pel is then given the added responsibility of putting together a flying squad that will cover an expanded region of northern France. Then a very important businessman is kidnapped, whose family does not want him back. Rensselaer, the businessman, keeps a pack of hunting dogs in the country. Pel makes the journey to see them and their keeper and finds that one of the dogs has been badly burned with acid.

Pel and the Bombers *Detective Chief Inspector Clovis Pel*
London: Hamilton, 1982.
New York: Walker, 1985.

On an outing with Madame Faivre-Perret in his home village of Vieilly, Pel is unaware that Sergeant Nosjean is there also, looking for a sniper who had shot at a night watchman and at a woman riding her bike. Nosjean takes exception to the popular idea that it was kids doing the shooting. But then a boy is found murdered in the woods. Some missing detonators from a quarry are used for a bomb that kills three policemen and a civilian. The president of France may be the real target.

Pel and the Predators *Detective Chief Inspector Clovis Pel*
London: Hamilton, 1984.
New York: Walker, 1985.

Now that Pel has been promoted it seems that a crime wave has erupted in Burgundy. Murdered women are being found all over Pel's area of command. What they have in common must be the reason for their deaths and so the team begins looking into their backgrounds and lifestyles.

Pel and the Pirates *Detective Chief Inspector Clovis Pel*
London: Hamilton, 1984.
New York: Walker, 1987.

Pel has married Madame Genevieve Faivre-Perret and they journey to the small island of St. Yves. A taxi driver, murdered the night they arrive, appears to have been trying to contact Pel. The local police ask Pel to help in the investigation. Also, the island is experiencing a crime wave including arson and smuggling, adding a bit of spice to the honeymoon.

Pel and the Prowler *Detective Chief Inspector Clovis Pel*
London: Hamilton, 1985.
New York: Walker, 1986.

Two women are murdered within a two-week period and the police believe there may be a serial killer on the loose. Then a third young woman is killed. All three women have an initial scratched on their face and odd messages left at the crime scenes.

Pel and the Paris Mob[*] *Detective Chief Inspector Clovis Pel*
London: Hamilton, 1986.

Pel Among the Pueblos *Detective Chief Inspector Clovis Pel*
London: Constable, 1987.
New York: Walker 1988.

Working on a double murder in which Mexico keeps cropping up, Pel must turn his attention to a rash of stolen cars that has not been reported to the police. Nosjean is given the case and suspects insurance fraud. Pel and Sergeant DeTrog are sent to Mexico to bring back the only suspect in the double killing but he escapes from jail and the two must race around trying to find him.

Pel and the Touch of Pitch *Detective Chief Inspector Clovis Pel*
London: Constable, 1987.
New York: Walker, 1988.

A man is murdered and left in the woods, covered with dirt and leaves. A famous painting is stolen from architect and financier Claud Barclay but experts believe the artwork to be a fake. Pel goes to a party given by his wife's family and from there is invited to cocktails at the Barclay mansion, thus placing him in a compromising position when Barclay is kidnapped.

Pel and the Picture of Innocence   *Detective Chief Inspector Clovis Pel*
London: Constable, 1988.
New York: St. Martin's, 1989.

Maurice Tagliatti, Dijon's leader of organized crime, is killed gangland style right in front of Pel's ten-year-old friend Yves Pasquier. Yves is going to be a policeman when he grows up. Pel travels to Scotland Yard to get some answers and the team protects Yves.

Pel and the Party Spirit   *Detective Chief Inspector Clovis Pel*
London: Constable, 1989.
New York: St. Martin's, 1991.

Pel's already wealthy and successful wife has gone off to tend another dying relative eager to leave her money. Pel goes to Pulaldome to take charge after a body is found in the thirteenth-century tower in the town. The body is thirty years old. Next there is a murder, and the possibility of illegal drugs shows itself.

Keith Heller[*]

Man's Illegal Life   *George Man*
London: Collins, 1984.
New York: Scribner's, 1985.

Geoffrey Standard was terrified of death. Unfortunately, someone boarded him up in his house and left him to die. Early eighteenth-century London parish watchman George Man does not know whether this means Standard had the plague, (victims were frequently abandoned in this manner during the Great Plague in London) or whether he was murdered. No one appears to have had a need to see him dead.

Man's Storm   *George Man*
London: Collins, 1985.
New York: Scribner's, 1986.

A great storm blew up on November 27, 1703, damaging Westminister, then headed for London. George Man, London watchman and forerunner of the police, is very busy helping to put out fires, finding the injured and carrying them to shelter, and then investigating the murder of a woman who refused to close her husband's shop during the storm.

Laurence Henderson*

With Intent *Detective Sergeant Arthur Milton*
London: Harrap, 1968. *and Station Sergeant Newcombe*
New York: St. Martin's, 1971.

Constable Toms, soon to retire, is on his rounds at two A.M. when he sees a car whose driver is hunched over the wheel. When he gets to the car he hears a snicker, then the world explodes in his face. Toms is blinded by the shot. Through diligent police work Milton and Newcombe find the perpetrator, only to be told that they do not have a good enough case for court.

Sitting Target* *Detective Sergeant Arthur Milton*
London: Harrap, 1970.
New York: St. Martin's, 1972.

Cage Until Tame *Divison Detective Inspector Durant*
London: Harrap, 1972. *and Detective Sergeant Arthur Milton*
New York: St. Martin's, 1972.

Raymond Edward "Tolly" Tollington is one of the best safecrackers in the business but has spent the last eight years in prison for bank robbery and causing grievous injury to a Lloyd's of London guard. Tolly, upon release, finds that everything he once had is gone, including his wife and daughter. Tolly is a hard man and soon sets about getting his own back. But first he must steal a bit of cash to live on and lose Detective Sergeant Milton, who has been given the special assignment of shadowing Tollington.

Major Enquiry *Detective Sergeant Arthur Milton*
London: Harrap, 1976.
New York: St. Martin's, 1976.

When sixteen-year-old Monica Henekey is the sixth victim of a rapist/murderer, the case becomes personal for Sergeant Milton; he has known the girl since she was a baby. Soon the police suspect that Monica knew her killer, which places all males in the district under suspicion.

Sue Henry

Murder on the Iditarod Trail *Sergeant Alex Jensen*
New York: Atlantic Monthly Press, 1991.

The Iditarod dogsled race is going fairly well but on the second day one of the mushers falls asleep, crashes against a tree, and dies. Alaska state trooper Sergeant Alex Jensen arrives in time to get a crash course on the methods and logistics of the race and to meet the lead racers. More deaths follow and soon the police have narrowed their suspects to a handful.

Nat Hentoff*

The Man from Internal Affairs *Detective Noah Green*
New York: Mysterious, 1985.

Two bodies are found cut in half and homicide detective Noah Green catches the case. To compound his problems the Internal Affairs Department is looking at him closely, as they suspect him of corruption in the line of duty.

Olga Hesky*

Time for Treason *Detective Inspector Tami Shimoni*
London: Long, 1967.
New York: Dodd, 1968.

A little dog, about to get a vaccination he does not want, runs away and much to his owner's horror comes back with a human hand in his mouth. The rest of the body is found by the police among the butchered meat in a slaughterhouse. The dead man was the night watchman at the Weitzmann Institute of Science in Tel Aviv where researchers are working with permutations of polymers.

Joan Hess*

Malice in Maggody *Chief of Police Arly Hanks*
New York: St. Martin's, 1987.

Arly Hanks has come home to Maggody, Arkansas, leaving New York City and a failed marriage behind. Now she is the chief of police in this quiet

Southern town. But strange things are happening. Jaylee, one of the servers at Ruby Bee's (Arly's mother's bar and grill), confesses that her husband has escaped from prison and is probably on his way to Maggody. The man from the Environmental Protection Agency vanishes, and when murder is committed, Arly gets a chance to prove her professional abilities.

Mischief in Maggody *Chief of Police Arly Hanks*
New York: St. Martin's, 1988.

Upon Arly's arrival in town her mother, Ruby Bee, fills her in on all that has happened in the town of Maggody. A psychic, Madame Celeste, and her brother, who is described as something akin to Adonis, have rented the old Wockerman place. A group of hippies has moved into the local motel. And Robin Buchanon, the town moonshine maker and lady of ill repute, is dead. Nothing is ever what it appears to be in Maggody.

Much Ado in Maggody *Chief of Police Arly Hanks*
New York: St. Martin's, 1989.

Police Chief Arly Hanks is investigating a charge of sex discrimination at the First National Bank of Farberville. Tempers boil over when some of the women in town side with the ex-head teller of the bank, who is demoted and then fired when she returns from maternity leave. Preacher Verber begins lecturing about the evils of women in the workplace, a feminist lawyer arrives in town, and families begin to come apart at the seams, all because the son of the bank's owner is bent on causing trouble.

Madness in Maggody *Chief of Police Arly Hanks*
New York: St. Martin's, 1991.

Jim Bob's Super Saver Buy 4 Less deluxe supermarket is about to open in Maggody. The store will give many of the town's merchants a big financial problem. Jim Bob goes on to antagonize everyone even more by sponsoring a baseball tournament. Arly's mother, one of the town merchants threatened by Jim Bob, starts another baseball team with Arly coaching. Soon Maggody is in a state of chaos.

Mortal Remains in Maggody *Chief of Police Arly Hanks*
New York: Dutton, 1991.

In the last twenty years there have been only four fires in Stump County, Arkansas. Now, in one month, there have been three. The fires involve abandoned buildings, but Arly Hanks is worried. At the same time, a small California movie company arrives in town to make a film. The arsonist sets a fire in Arly's apartment and the movie turns out to be X-rated. What more can go wrong?

Maggody in Manhattan *Chief of Police Arly Hanks*
New York: Dutton, 1992.

The entire crew from Maggody ends up in Manhattan where Ruby Bee is a finalist in a cooking contest. She also winds up as the prime suspect in a murder investigation and her daughter must bail her out and investigate (not technically a procedural as Hanks is out of her jurisdiction).

Peter Hill

The Hunters *Detective Chief Superintendent Robert Staunton*
London: Peter Davies, 1976. *and Detective Inspector Leo Wyndsor*
New York: Scribner's, 1976.

Twenty-year-old Joy Prentiss is found raped and strangled to death. Staunton and his new partner, Leo Wyndsor, travel to Bacton Ford, the small town in Suffolk where the murder occurred, to find that few are sympathetic to the murdered woman and the authorities sadly lacking in the expertise needed for a murder investigation. All the while the killer waits. He has had a taste of power and wants it again. There is also a group of Satan worshipers thriving in Bacton Ford that begins to cause Staunton trouble.

The Liars *Detective Chief Superintendent Robert Staunton*
London: Peter Davies, 1977. *and Detective Inspector Leo Wyndsor*
Boston: Houghton Mifflin, 1978.

The dead man is found hanging upside down by one leg on an old gibbet. Detective Chief Superintendent Bob Staunton is dispatched to Cornwall to discover what happened. The man's body bears considerable damage—both legs and one arm are broken and he is covered with bruises. The people in the town are all hiding relationships and keeping secrets.

The Enthusiasts *Detective Chief Superintendent Robert Staunton*
London: Peter Davies, 1978 *and Detective Inspector Leo Wyndsor*
Boston: Houghton Mifflin, 1979.

John Williams, a skilled climber, is attempting to scale the upper slopes of Moel Celyn in Wales when he is shot and killed. Then Nurse James is killed after being lured into the night on a false emergency. The killer continues to stalk. A farmer is dead next and Staunton and Wyndsor must act fast.

The Savages *Detective Chief Superintendent Robert Staunton*
London: Heinemann, 1980. *and Detective Inspector Leo Wyndsor*

The scarecrow was immaculately dressed in a three-piece suit, a bowler hat, dress shirt, and tie. The clothing and an abandoned car are owned by Colonel Bannister-Coates but the Colonel is missing. A note left by the scarecrow is signed "Valkyrie." Then two locals are shot, the list of suspects begins to grow, and the Scotland Yard detectives must find Valkyrie before more people die.

The Fanatics* *Commander Allan Dice*
London: Peter Davies, 1977.
New York: Scribner's, 1978.

The Washermen *Commander Allan Dice and*
London: Peter Davies, 1979. *Detective Superintendent Ray Corelli*

Firth of the British S.I.S. and Coleman set up a covert operation to eliminate the security boss of the heroin-dealing Triad and get their own man in place. They hire three thugs from Hong Kong to cause a war among the powerful Triads in London. Commander Dice of the Serious Crimes Squad is called in when the three thugs, known as the Washermen, kill three policemen.

Tony Hillerman*

The Blessing Way *Lieutenant Joe Leaphorn*
New York: Harper, 1970.
London: Macmillan, 1970.

Luis Horseman shoots a man and in a panic hides in the desert. Meanwhile Bergen McKee, an anthropologist, and his colleague Jeremy Canfield set out for the Navaho Reservation to do research. Their paths cross that of Leaphorn, of the Navaho Tribal Police, who is hunting Horseman. Things start going wrong for McKee when he hears several tales of a witch, a man who wears a wolfskin and kills animals.

Dance Hall of the Dead *Lieutenant Joe Leaphorn*
New York: Harper, 1973.

George Bowlegs, a fourteen-year-old Navajo boy, is missing on the Zuni reservation and with him is Ernesto Cato, a Zuni boy. George used to go to an archaelogical dig and watch the crew work. Somehow he stumbled on knowledge that has become dangerous.

Listening Woman *Lieutenant Joe Leaphorn*
New York: Harper, 1978.
London: Macmillan, 1979.

When Captain Largo gives him three old cases to work on, Leaphorn is faced with no clues and the possibility of riding herd on a troop of Boy Scouts if he does not come up with something new very quickly. The double murder of a sick old man and a young girl leads him to the listening woman, Mrs. Cigaret, who is blind but has the gift of listening, a kind of second sight, enabling her to prescribe which healing way is appropriate for an individual's problems. Leaphorn is also looking for a missing helicopter and a great deal of money stolen from a Wells Fargo armored vehicle in Sante Fe. He gets stuck in the desert and must use every survival technique he knows to save himself and the Boy Scouts from violent Indian fanatics.

People of Darkness *Detective Jim Chee*
New York: Harper, 1980.
London: Gollancz, 1982.

Rosemary Vines, wife of wealthy B. J. Vines, calls in Jim Chee and offers him money to find a box of keepsakes belonging to her husband that has been stolen from their house. She believes members of the mysterious cult religion, People of Darkness, have taken it. Then B. J. Vines also offers Chee money to find the box. Conducting a very informal investigation, Chee runs into a hostile sheriff and a hired killer, who must now kill Chee and a teacher at the reservation because they know too much and have seen him.

The Dark Wind *Detective Jim Chee*
New York, Harper, 1982.
London: Gollancz, 1983.

Detective Jim Chee of the Navaho Tribal Police has been transferred to the Tuba City substation where he works under Captain Largo. He has been assigned the task of finding who has been vandalizing the new windmill the federal government has built for the Hopi who will live on the land near it—shared land the Navaho have used for years. While on a stakeout at the windmill Chee hears a plane crash and a gunshot and soon finds himself the prime suspect in a drug sting that is being handled by the D.E.A.

The Ghostway *Detective Jim Chee*
New York: Harper, 1984.
London: Gollancz, 1985.

In the parking lot outside of a Shiprock laundromat, two men are gunned down and the shooter, now wounded, gets away. Captain Largo tells Jim

Chee to find the men and he does. But one is dead in a hogan, which goes against all the Navaho tribal teachings.

Skinwalkers *Lieutenant Joe Leaphorn and Detective Jim Chee*
New York: Harper, 1987.
London: Joseph, 1988.

Leaphorn is working on three murders that look like the work of a Navaho skinwalker. Leaphorn is not superstitious and does not believe in many of the Navaho ways, yet while he works this case, he is drawn into the culture he finds unacceptable. This is the first case in which Leaphorn and Chee are brought together.

A Thief of Time *Lieutenant Joe Leaphorn and Detective Jim Chee*
New York: Harper, 1988.
London: Joseph, 1989.

Joe Leaphorn is looking for a missing archaeologist and Jim Chee is scouting the reservation for a flatbed truck missing from the motor pool of the tribal police. Then a backhoe is taken, but when Chee finds it he also discovers stolen Anasazi artifacts and a dead man. The two policemen, working separately, track clues and bits of information until their paths come together on the site of an ancient ruin.

Talking God *Lieutenant Joe Leaphorn and Detective Jim Chee*
New York: Harper, 1989.
London: Joseph, 1990.

The man is lying next to the railroad tracks. He has no identification on him and his false teeth are missing. Joe Leaphorn is called in to determine how his body got there. At the same time Henry Highhawk sends Indian bones that he has taken from the Smithsonian to a woman on the Navaho Reservation. Jim Chee is waiting for his arrival so that Highhawk can be arrested. Leaphorn and Chee eventually end up in Washington, DC.

Coyote Waits *Lieutenant Joe Leaphorn and Detective Jim Chee*
New York: Harper, 1990.
London: Joseph, 1991.

Tribal policeman Delbert Nez is shot and burned by an old Navaho, Askie Pinto. People do not believe Pinto capable of harming anything and Leaphorn is brought in on the case. Chee, injured while trying to rescue Nez, is on sick leave, attempting to satisfy himself that he did not cause his friend's death. Taking separate tacks, they work toward a solution, which involves a former Vietnamese leader, Navaho folk tales, archaeology, and hidden mystery.

Chester Himes

For Love of Imabella *Detectives Coffin Ed Johnson*
New York: Fawcett, 1957. *and Grave Digger Jones*

A Rage in Harlem
New York: Avon, 1965.
London: Panther, 1969.

Religion and racism play a major part in this tale of counterfeiting. Jackson is caught with the fake money—actually he throws it out the car window but the Marshall is going to arrest him anyway unless Jackson pays him off. So Jackson goes to Clay's Funeral Parlor and steals money from the safe. Later he steals the hearse.

The Crazy Kill* *Detectives Coffin Ed Johnson*
New York: Avon, 1959. *and Grave Digger Jones*
London: Panther, 1968.

The Real Cool Killers* *Detectives Coffin Ed Johnson*
New York: Avon, 1959. *and Grave Digger Jones*
London: Panther, 1969.

All Shot Up *Detectives Coffin Ed Johnson*
New York: Avon, 1960. *and Grave Digger Jones*
London: Panther, 1969.

Coffin Ed and Grave Digger must sort out a series of events involving three men dressed as policemen who have robbed a man, which started a major gun battle in which two people are killed in front of the Paris Bar in Harlem. Then there is the matter of the old woman who was run down while crossing the street and a gold Cadillac that has been stolen by the killers.

The Big Gold Dream *Detectives Coffin Ed Johnson*
New York: Avon, 1960. *and Grave Digger Jones*
London: Panther, 1968

Alberta Wright finds Jesus at a revival, is baptized, then drinks holy water blessed by the Sweet Prophet and dies on the sidewalk at his feet. When her husband, Rufus, sells all her furniture, the used-furniture dealer who buys it is killed by someone looking for the money hidden inside it. Then Rufus is killed. Everyone knows the hidden money has been taken. The detectives from Harlem, Coffin Ed and Grave Digger, must find out where it came from and why Alberta had it.

Cotton Comes to Harlem *Detectives Coffin Ed Johnson*
New York: Putnam, 1965. *and Grave Digger Jones*
London: Muller, 1965.

Deke O'Hara sees the pot of gold at the end of the rainbow when he fronts the Back-to-Africa program and starts raking in large sums of money. Thousands are collected but some white men steal the money. O'Hara hides out while Coffin Ed and Grave Digger hunt for him, but he makes an irreversible mistake.

The Heat's On *Detectives Coffin Ed Johnson*
New York: Putnam, 1966. *and Grave Digger Jones*
London: Muller, 1966.

Come Back, Charleston Blue
New York: Berkley, 1970.

An albino black man who wants to save his father from being robbed and murdered sets off the fire alarm at a nearby church to attract attention. The ensuing brouhaha is typical Himes. When Johnson and Jones get things sorted out, the giant albino has been shot and his father may still be in trouble. The clues lead to a faith healer called Sister Heavenly, who sells drugs on the side and engages in murder. A man gets his throat cut, $3,000,000 goes missing, and Coffin Ed and Grave Digger are suspended from duty for brutality.

Blind Man with a Pistol *Detectives Coffin Ed Johnson*
New York: Morrow, 1969. *and Grave Digger Jones*
London: Hodder, 1969.

Hot Day, Hot Night
New York: Dell, 1970.

Coffin Ed and Grave Digger are present when a white man dies on the streets of Harlem. His throat has been cut and, before dying, he was unable to identify his killer. At the same time the police discover a Mormon preacher advertising for a twelfth wife. In his cellar the police find the buried bodies of three women. Add to this a Black Power movement that is threatening to erupt in a fullscale racial riot.

Timothy Holme

The Neopolitan Streak *Inspector Achille Peroni*
London: Macmillan, 1980.
New York: Coward, McCann, 1980.

The Montagues and the Capulets are at it again. Seventy-four-year-old

Montague descendent General Piantaleone left his house and never returned. The leading suspect is the Red Brigade leader, Policarpo Pellipopoli. Another murder, a maze of crime, and unanswered questions lead Peroni of the Verona police into a most difficult case.

A Funeral of Gondolas *Inspector Achille Peroni*
London: Macmillan, 1981.
New York: Coward, McCann, 1982.

Having solved a case of illegal betting on gondola races run by the gondoliers and a priest at the local church, Peroni moves on to the murder of an attorney. But it looks like a gondolier has something to do with the murder. Then there is a matter of blackmail and a lost manuscript. Peroni goes from boredom to being hip deep in intrigue and mayhem.

The Devil and the Dolce Vita *Inspector Achille Peroni*
London: Macmillan, 1982.
New York: Walker, 1988.

Former Neopolitan police inspector Achille Peroni, now transferred to Venice, is visited by a young woman who explains that her American friend, another young woman, has disappeared. As he looks for Kehzia Michaelis, Peroni becomes obsessed with her. Has she been murdered? What did she talk about in her visit to the priest of Sacro Cuore di Gesú? Who is Luca, a young man with whom she is supposedly in love? What of the wealthy man who invited her to a dinner party?

The Assisi Murders *Inspector Achille Peroni*
London: Macmillan, 1985.
New York: Walker, 1988.

Making a pilgrimage to Assisi with his sister, Assunta, was supposed to be boring. But then Peroni saw the woman in the lime green coat. Next there is a murder. A gun is found near the scene of the crime and it is soon established that the husband of the woman in the green coat bought it. The murdered young man was writing a treatise on St. Francis and the present-day case is related to a thirteenth-century mystery.

At the Lake of Sudden Death *Inspector Achille Peroni*
London: Macmillan, 1987.
New York: Walker, 1988.

A beautiful young Englishwoman is found drowned in Lake Garda. Everyone thinks her death was an accident but Inspector Peroni believes she was too good a sailor to lose control of her boat and she certainly was not suicidal.

The belief that Mussolini's missing gold is hidden in Lake Garda may be the reason she is dead. Peroni has no authority in the case but sets out to find what happened and why.

Ruby Horansky

Dead Ahead *Detectives Nikki Trakos and Dave Lawton*
New York: Scribner's, 1990.

Frankie Sunmann thinks he is going to be rich, but instead, he is murdered. Newly appointed detective Nikki Trakos catches the case. Working with veteran homicide detective Dave Lawton she finds that facts involved in another death caused by an explosion on board a yacht keep cropping up in her case.

John Hough, Jr.

The Guardian *Chief of Police Nye Gifford*
Boston: Little, Brown, 1975. *and Lieutenant Tom O'Rourke*

The body of an unidentified woman is found on Bayberry Hill Road in Lymington, Massachusetts. She has been shot in the face four times. The woman is identified as Kimberly Ann Regan from Boston and her suitcase turns up in a small town forty miles from Lymington. Gifford and O'Rouke go to Boston where they trace Regan's last days. Gifford is horrified at life in the big city.

Robert Houston

The Fourth Codex *Special Agent, U. S. Customs Service,*
Boston: Houghton Mifflin, 1988. *Quintus Pax*

The Mexican government asks for Paz's help in locating a missing Mayan codex discovered by old family friend Baron Von Hummel.

Gary Hunter

Death Warrant *Detective Garrick Travis*
New York: Warner, 1990.

While trying to shut down the drug operation of Solomon Davis, Travis is forced to kill him thus opening up old emotional wounds.

Jack D. Hunter

Judgment in Blood *Inspector Fred Stabile*
New York: Avon, 1986.

Women in Zieglersville are dying horrible deaths. One woman is hanged while another is stoned to death while in bed with someone else's husband. The third victim is tied to a cross and burned. The deaths are part of some bizarre religious cult.

Joe Hyams

Murder at the Academy Awards *Captain Phillip "Punch" Roberts*
New York: St. Martin's, 1983.

The ballots for the Academy Awards have been tampered with. Eva Johnson, about to receive her first award, walks toward the podium, but collapses in pain in full view of 300 million TV viewers and dies. Captain Phillip Roberts heads the Los Angeles Police Department's homicide division. Roberts, ex-marine, ex-Pittsburgh Steeler, is a tough cop. The Johnson case is a puzzle, both because how she died from a perforated aorta is a medical mystery, and why she died is even more inexplicable. The deed keeps homicide busy.

Peter Inchbald*

Tando for Short *Detective Chief Inspector Frank Short*
London: Collins, 1981. *(Franco Corti)*
New York: Doubleday Crime Club, 1982.

Corti of Scotland Yard's Art and Antique Squad is assigned to the case when a masterpiece of Michelangelo is taken from a museum. He travels to Florence and into a world of trouble, including murder.

The Sweet Short Grass   *Detective Chief Inspector Frank Short*
London: Collins, 1982.   *(Franco Corti)*
New York: Doubleday Crime Club, 1982.

Franco Corti has changed his name to Frank Short in an effort to minimize his Italian origins. His father has presented him with a small painting that turns out to be a real Fra Angelico, but it is stolen. Corti is suspended from the police force pending an investigation into why a mere policeman owns such a valuable painting.

Graham Ison*

Confirm or Deny   *Detective Chief Superintendent John Gaffney*
London: Macmillan, 1989.   *and Detective Chief Inspector Harry Tipper*
New York: St. Martin's, 1990.

Special Branch, an elite part of Scotland Yard, is assigned to find and arrest suspected and known spies. Gaffney is told to find the mole (an undercover enemy agent) on an MI5 team that has lost three suspected spies in a row. Someone on the team is warning their prey shortly before the arrest. Gaffney and his selected personnel work all the angles in good police fashion.

Jon A. Jackson

The Diehard   *Detective Sergeant "Fang" Mulheisen*
New York: Random House, 1977.
London: Hale, 1978.

While Jane Clippert is relaxing in her morning bath, a man is busily stealing her VCR, money, and jewelry. He makes the mistake of being seen by her, so he kills her by hitting, shooting, and stabbing her. The homicide investigation is headed by Sergeant Mulheisen of the Detroit PD, who must investigate her husband, Arthur, separating his personal life from his professional life in order to make sense out of the robbery. It is not hard to find a motive, as Jane Clippert was wealthy and had a million-dollar life insurance policy. Arthur is in serious legal and financial trouble. Mulheisen must figure out whether this was a random crime or planned.

The Blind Pig   *Detective Sergeant "Fang" Mulheisen*
New York: Random, 1978.
London: Hale, 1980.

In this action-packed tale, Mulheisen thinks he is getting an easy case when two policemen kill a man seen going into a garage holding a gun. But the corpse has all the earmarks of having been a hit man. The garage belongs to Jerry Vanni, owner of a landscape company and some vending machines, which ties him in with the Detroit family of organized crime—or is he an independent operator?

Grootka *Detective Sergeant "Fang" Mulheisen*
Woodstock, VT: Foul Play, 1990.

The body of Books Meldrim is dumped in a plastic bag and put in the trunk of an old car. Books is found by retired Detroit cop Grootka, who calls Sergeant Mulheisen of homicide to the scene. Books was involved in a famous and still unsolved murder and rape case that took place thirty years previously. Then a widow is viciously murdered and Mulheisen and Grootka keep crossing each other's paths, making Mulheisen very suspicious.

Hit on the House *Detective Sergeant "Fang" Mulheisen*
New York: Atlantic Monthly, 1993.

Big Sid, a crime boss, is gunned down in the front of his home. Soon after, Frosty Tubman and some of his boys are shot and killed. Next Billy Conover, a prominent drug dealer, is blasted as he leaves his favorite restaurant. It appears that someone is killing off the organized crime bosses of Detroit and the murders probably have something to do with missing drug money.

Michael Jahn[*]

Death Games *Lieutenant Bill Donovan and*
New York: Norton, 1987. *Sergeant T. L. Jefferson*

Organized crime leaders in New York are being gunned down by a beautiful hit woman using a Civil War Colt 44. Donovan and Jefferson must discover the motivation for the murders but whether they can stop the brainy hit woman is another question.

City of God *Lieutenant Bill Donovan and*
New York: St. Martin's, 1992. *Sergeant T. L. Jefferson*

People are being killed in the Cathedral of St. John the Divine. The killer strikes with deadly accuracy using a heavy mallet. Only one person has escaped with his life, investigative reporter Avignon, who is also an old friend of Donovan. At the same time a friend of Marcie has been killed while running in a marathon.

Bill James*
(Pseudonym of [Allen] James Tucker)

You'd Better Believe It *Detective Chief Superintendent Colin Harpur*
London: Constable, 1985.
New York: St. Martin's, 1986.

A big-time London thief is going to rob a bank in the town presided over by Harpur, who puts together a team empowered to carry guns when going into dangerous situations. Unfortunately Harpur bungles almost everything about his job. He pays more attention to the wife of the new man he picks for the team than he does to the man on the team who gets himself brutally murdered.

The Lolita Man *Detective Chief Superintendent Colin Harpur*
London: Constable, 1986.
Woodstock, VT: Foul Play, 1991.

A killer known as the Lolita Man is raping and murdering young girls. Chief Superintendent Harpur is on his trail but he must contend with the politics of the upper echelons of the police organization and the petty jealousies of his fellow officers. His ongoing affair with the widow of a police detective killed in the line of duty complicates his life as well. He realizes that something is wrong with one of the young girls he sees going about town. Then Cheryl-Ann disappears.

Halo Parade *Detective Chief Superintendent Colin Harpur*
London: Constable, 1987.
Woodstock, VT: Foul Play, 1992.

Harpur sends a young detective in deep cover to get close to a very dangerous drug gang. The man, Ray Street, is playing way over his head. The man they are after is a killer and Street is very convincing in his role of young thug. He is also dipping into coke and homosexuality. Street's body is found with another corpse, and Harpur needs to establish what connection, if any, there is between them.

Protection   *Detective Chief Superintendent Colin Harpur*
London: Constable, 1988.
Woodstock, VT: Foul Play, 1992.

Harpur has his hands full when the grandson of Bernard Mellick is kidnapped after Mellick attacked Ivor Wright with a blowtorch. Mellick is the snitch of Hubert Scott, who is being retired from the police force because he is believed to have taken bribes. Harpur must move quickly, for lives depend on his ability to get to the bottom of things.

Come Clean   *Detective Chief Superintendent Colin Harpur*
London: Constable, 1989.
Woodstock, VT: Foul Play, 1993.

Assistant Chief Constable Desmond Iles is caught up in a very unprofessional situation when his wife, who has cheated on him for years, is witness to a murder. Sarah Iles and her lover, Ian Aston, have learned too much about the local underworld. Not only are the criminals after them but Colin Harpur is sure that they know more than they are telling.

J. A. Jance*

Until Proven Guilty   *Detective Jones Piedmont "J. P." Beaumont*
New York: Avon, 1985.
London: Curley, 1991.

When a five-year-old girl is found at the bottom of a ravine. J. P. Beaumont of the Seattle police must investigate. Her pink nightgown has been used to strangle her. The child's mother, a member of Faith Tabernacle, blames herself for Angel's death. The pastor of the group has told its members that people outside of the Tabernacle are instruments of the devil and that God abandons those who listen to nonbelievers. The children are beaten in church to make them obey. Most are covered with bruises, all are afraid of Pastor Michael. The only one who was not was Angel. Then Beaumont meets and falls in love with Anne Corley, a woman deeply involved in the case.

Injustice for All   *Detective Jones Piedmont "J. P." Beaumont*
New York: Avon, 1986.
London: Severn, 1993.

The body of Sig Larsen is found on the beach by Ginger Watkins, a friend and co-member of the Washington parole board. As a team, the two of them paroled a rapist who, when free, murdered a woman and her young daughter. The day after Larsen's death Ginger dies in an accident and Beaumont is caught in the complexity of an ugly case that is not even his.

Taking the Fifth   *Detective Jones Piedmont "J. P." Beaumont*
New York: Avon, 1987.

The body of a man is found next to the railroad tracks. He has been stabbed by an object that was definitely not a knife. Also found is a high-heeled shoe with blood splotches on it. It looks as if the man had been stabbed to death by the heel of a shoe. Beaumont falls in love in this one.

Improbable Cause   *Detective Jones Piedmont "J. P." Beaumont*
New York: Avon, 1988.
London: Severn, 1992.

A dentist is found dead in his office in the chair reserved for patients. Blood is everywhere. There are plenty of suspects and an array of zany characters to offset the horror of why Dr. Frederick Nielsen was murdered.

A More Perfect Union   *Detective Jones Piedmont "J. P." Beaumont*
New York: Avon, 1988.
London: Severn, 1992.

Beaumont has been assigned by the mayor's office to watch a movie being made in Seattle and to act as public relations liaison for the company. He is the on-scene detective when the body of a man is found floating in Lake Union where the daily filming is taking place. On the dead man's belt is the word "ironworker." When there is another murder marked with the same message, the ironworkers' union becomes a key figure in the case.

Trish Janeshutz[*]
(also Alison Drake, q.v.)

In Shadow   *Detective John Conway*
New York: Ballantine, 1985.

Conway is called in to investigate the murder of Denise Markham, a research chemist at the University of Miami. Her life is a closed book as she had only two friends and was divorcing her husband. It soon becomes apparent that she was involved with the manufacture of a new drug and that the person responsible for her murder has killed before. Will he kill again?

Hidden Lake *Detective Lieutenant Deirdre O'Malley*
New York: Ballantine, 1987.

Hidden Lake houses a surprising number of psychics. During an experiment at the University of Miami, psychic Gary Lukas gets inside a killer's mind while he murders Hidden Lake's foremost citizen, Anna Lemont. Police lieutenant Deirdre O'Malley finds herself in an ethical bind. Anna was her friend and Deirdre is in charge of the investigation. Lieutenant Moody, Deirdre's ex-lover, is also assigned to the case and she begins to feel a romantic interest in a journalist doing a story on the Florida psychic community.

Hamilton Jobson*

Therefore I Killed Him *Detective Chief Inspector Matt Anders*
London: Long, 1968.

Included because Anders of Scotland Yard appears midway through to begin an investigation. The book is told mainly from a civilian point of view, but is included here because it is the first book in the series.

Smile and Be a Villain *Detective Chief Inspector Matt Anders*
London: Long, 1969.
New York: Abelard-Schumann, 1971.

Computer engineer Alex Blake is successful and happily married until he comes home from a business trip and his wife is not there. He becomes jealous and goes out on the town with an old friend. His drinking spree ends in the death of a policeman and Matt Anders is left to sort out what happened and why.

Naked to My Enemy* *Inspector Matt Anders*
London: Long, 1970.

The Silent Cry* *Inspector Matt Anders*
London: Long, 1970.

The House with Blind Eyes* *Inspector Matt Anders*
London: Long, 1971.

The Sand Pit*   *Inspector Matt Anders*
London: Long, 1972.

Contract with a Killer*   *Inspector Matt Anders*
London: Long, 1974.

The Evidence You Will Hear   *Superintendent Matt Anders*
London: Collins, 1975.
New York: Scribner's, 1975.

Young girls are being murdered in a suburb of London. In a thorough police investigation and canvass of the entire town certain facts point to a man named Pete Mellish. The story follows the police all the way through to the trial.

Judge Me Tomorrow   *Detective Superintendent Matt Anders*
London: Collins, 1978.

Anders gets his murderer but the majority of the story is told by the chief suspect.

Exit to Violence   *Detective Chief Superintendent Matt Anders*
London: Collins, 1979.

The Chief Constable is ill and his deputy, Baxter, has taken over, much to the discomfort of the police. Anders, head of the Criminal Investigations Department, must fend off Baxter's interference while trying to solve the death of a man found lying at the side of the road. The man remains unidentified but evidence mounts that he was a member of a German terrorist group.

Matti Joensuu

Harjunpaa and the Stone Murders   *Detective Timo Harjunpaa*
London: Gollancz, 1986.

The Stone Murders
New York: St. Martin's, 1987.

When a man is stoned to death the Helsinki police look for the perpetrators. The path leads into the realm of child abuse and the ineffectual reality of the criminal justice system.

E. Richard Johnson*

Silver Street *Detective Tony Lonto*
New York: Harper, 1968.

The Silver Street Killer
London: Hale, 1969.

Willie Mack, a Silver Street pimp, is murdered by a prospective customer with a reason to kill. Tony Lonto is called out because his lieutenant knows he grew up in the area. There is another murder and Lonto realizes that he is faced with a killer working with an agenda.

The Inside Man *Detective Tony Lonto*
New York: Harper, 1969.
London: Macmillan, 1970.

Benjamin Solomon, street name, the Nut, is shot in an alley while Nick, another homeless person, witnesses the crime. Tony Lonto, who has been a good detective for years, has now been loaned to the Internal Security Division where he feels like a traitor. Captain Gallagher believes that someone in the police department is protecting the narcotics dealers because drug arrests have fallen off at an alarming rate. Along with this, Lonto is the detective in charge of the Solomon murder investigation.

Blind Man's Bluff *Detectives Tony Lonto and Pat Runnion*
New York: St. Martin's, 1987.

A blind Vietnam veteran is murdered in his apartment, strips of his chest peeled off as he was tortured and left to die. In the routine search of the apartment, the lab people find a bag of uncut heroin and the trail leads to the city's red-light district and super bad guy Julian Shapiro.

Dead Flowers *Detective Tony Lonto*
New York: International Polygonics, 1990.

Raymond DeMeyere, owner of a florist shop, is shot twice in the head with a .45 and dies in his van outside his shop. While trying to find out why he was killed and who took his wallet, credit cards, money, and shoes, an undercover narcotics agent working out of the homicide office is found executed. The narcotics squad is working on a big bust involving Cuban drug kingpin Isidro Torres, but the squad withholds vital information from Lonto.

The God Keepers *Detective Sergeant Ross Hogan*
New York: Harper, 1970.
London: Macmillan, 1971.

A very dead Jackie Sands, wife of Max Sands, ex-cop and alcoholic, is found on the beach of the Playa del Rey section of Los Angeles. Sands was the partner of Sergeant Ross Hogan, who is in charge of the case. Hogan finds it difficult to be as objective as he should when the autopsy reveals that Jackie was a drug addict and had been killed by a massive dose of cyanide injected into her bloodstream. With this knowledge the case takes a different direction.

Case Load—Maximum *Detective First Grade Mose Hamilton*
New York: Harper, 1971. *and Lieutenant Joseph Kinsmiller*

In a three-way narrative the story of Mary Blair's murder unfolds. Detective Moses Hamilton, hardheaded and crabby, follows police procedures until he finds a man who served time for rape. The ex-convict tells his story and his parole officer swims in a mire of guilt.

Bruce Jones

In Deep *Detective Sergeants Eustes Tully*
New York: Crown, 1991. *and William Brumeister*

When a woman is found murdered on a beach in Santa Barbara Tully gets the case. He knows the killing has been done by someone who is mentally ill, but when a paint chip found in the woman's body tests out to be from a police car, he is pulled off the case and sent back to Narcotics where he must infiltrate the gang of Colombian drug dealer Santiago Dias. The suspects all have mothers who play parts in the story and the author allows the reader to hear the murderer's thoughts concerning his own mom, who appears to be the cause of his need to kill.

R. W. Jones*

Saving Grace *Detective Inspector Huw Evans*
London: Joseph, 1986.
New York: St. Martin's, 1986.

Ten-year-old Caroline Yardley, an obedient and lovely child, is kidnapped on her way home from school. Soon she is found dead, and Evans must cope with the investigation as well as to help ease the mother's anguish. The story deals not only with the police attempting to find a killer, but the grief of the victim's family.

Cop Out   *Detective Inspector Huw Evans*
London: Joseph, 1987.   *and Sergeant Roy Beddoes*
New York: St. Martin's, 1987.

Sergeant Beddoes is sent to a convent school to discourage a man who watches the female students at play. He chases him off but is left with a bad feeling about the guy. Next, a streetwalker comes to tell Evans about a man who made her take off her clothes, then held a knife to her throat. When Sarah Holroyd is raped the man wore a mask and held a knife to her throat. The rapist is becoming more violent.

The Green Reapers   *Detective Inspector Huw Evans*
London: Joseph, 1988.   *and Sergeant Roy Beddoes*
New York: St. Martin's, 1989.

British Special Services send Evans and Beddoes to Dublin to find and capture the Green Reapers, a terrorist organization operating from Ireland. Beddoes is sent home in disgrace after committing an indiscretion and getting kneecapped as a punishment. Evans is recalled as well when he does not arrest the head terrorist, who toys with him. All agencies involved are using others as scapegoats. Against the overwhelmingly dangerous world of the Irish underground and the deviousness of the British Secret Service, Evans, with Beddoes guarding his back, triumphs in a negative way.

Cyril Joyce*

The Information Man   *Detective Sergeant Luke Spicer and*
London: Hale, 1976.   *Detective Constable Tim Cox*

The city of Swington has been hit with a rash of burglaries that require several men and an insider's knowledge of the premises to carry out. All the facts in the investigation point to a policeman selling inside knowledge to the criminals. Spicer knows he must walk carefully as this is a major crimes case and he is in the hot seat.

Seize the Passing Stranger
London: Hale, 1978.

*Superintendent Bragge and
Detective Sergeant Jerome*

Industrialist Gerrard Tancred and his secretary, Rosalind Broome, are kidnapped on Christmas Eve. His car—the latest model Mercedes—is found burned, and a young Norwegian sailor gets himself into serious trouble when he is held captive in a hut. Then there is the question of embezzlement concerning Tancred's company.

Murder Is a Pendulum
London: Hale, 1983.

Chief Superintentent Patrick Stockton

The Saltsby Sniper has been going around the town shooting out clocks. When a young policeman is gunned down in the main street, the sniper is the chief suspect. But was PC Alvison shot for other reasons? Shortly thereafter a crime wave hits the area involving armed robbery at a betting shop in Cleeton, a market robbed by four men carrying shotguns in Parkham, and several robberies in three small towns close by; over a million pounds in goods have been taken.

Stuart M. Kaminsky*

Death of a Dissident
New York: Ace, 1981.

*Chief Inspector Porfiry Rostnikov and
Inspectors Emil Karpo and Sasha Tkach*

Rostnikov's Corpse
London: Macmillan, 1981.

Aleksander Granovsky is a Russian dissident about to go on trial for crimes against the state. While writing the speech he will deliver on that occasion he is murdered in his apartment. Since the KGB has the building staked out and the watchers see and hear nothing, the case is a clear embarrassment for the government. Pressure is brought to bear on Rostnikov and his men to solve the crime immediately.

Black Knight in Red Square
New York: Berkley, 1983.
London: Macdonald, 1988.

*Chief Inspector Porfiry Rostnikov and
Inspectors Emil Karpo and Sasha Tkach*

Moscow's Metropole Hotel is the site of a foreign film festival. In a single night four people, two Russian, one Japanese, and an American, are poisoned. The four men had shared two bottles of vodka just before they died. Rostnikov is unaware that the poisonings are a result of an experienced terrorist who enjoys embarrassing the police.

Red Chameleon   *Inspector Porfiry Rostnikov and*
New York: Scribner's, 1985.   *Detectives Sasha Tkach and Emil Karpo*

Rostnikov is looking into the murder of an old man. Along with Tkach and Karpo, he is also working to find an auto theft ring and trying to locate the sniper who shot and killed a policeman. At the book's end, Rostnikov is transferred to the investigative staff of Colonel Snitkovoy (nicknamed the Gray Wolfhound).

A Fine Red Rain   *Inspector Porfiry Rostnikov and*
New York: Scribner's, 1987.   *Detectives Sasha Tkach and Emil Karpo*

In the pouring rain a man jumps from the shoulders of the statue of Gogol in Arbat Square and lands on the concrete at Rostnikov's feet. Rostnikov, demoted from his previous position in the Procurator's Department, now works out of the central MVD headquarters under Colonel Snitkovoy, otherwise known as the Gray Wolfhound. The MVD (the national police) are responsible for taking care of less important, routine policing, and nonpolitical criminal actions. Karpo and Tkach are still with the office of the Procurator General. Whan an aerial trapeze artist does a double flip and falls to the net below (which is not tied down) and is killed, the three old friends go to the circus to investigate. How this man's death and the one in Arabat Square tie together leads them into the shadowy world of Moscow organized crime.

A Cold Red Sunrise   *Inspector Porfiry Rostnikov and*
New York: Scribner's, 1988.   *Inspectors Emil Karpo and Sasha Tkach*
London: Severn House, 1990.

Inspector Rostnikov is sent to Tumsk, Siberia, to discover what happened to two people who have died there. First, the daughter of a notorious dissenter dies. She had been living a lonely, reclusive life in Siberia. Because of this, the government sends Commissar Illya Rutkin to investigate when the dissident dies—and then Rutkin is murdered. Rostnikov, always a careful detective, knows he must work quickly as the eyes of the KGB are everywhere. There are only a few people living in Tumsk so the field of suspects is narrow. However, that does not necessarily mean that this will be an easy case.

The Man Who Walked Like a Bear   *Inspector Porfiry Rostnikov and*
New York: Scribner's, 1990.   *Detectives Sasha Tkach and Emil Karpo*
London: Heinemann, 1991.

A municipal bus and its driver disappear on the same day that a man who walks like a bear invades Sarah Rostnikov's hospital room. Also a woman comes to police headquarters to say that she believes her son is about to kidnap a high-ranking member of the Politburo.

Rostnikov's Vacation   *Inspector Porfiry Rostnikov and*
New York: Scribner's, 1991.   *Detectives Sacha Tkach and Emil Karpo*

Karpo is working on a murder case alone because Rostnikov has been ordered to take a vacation. Tkach and Zelach are posing as computer experts hoping to catch the people who are stealing computer hardware. Rostnikov realizes that something is wrong when an old acquaintance from the GRU (military intelligence) is murdered and more people from all of the police and intelligence factions are assigned vacations. In his own quiet way he sorts out Karpo and Tkach along the way.

Death of a Russian Priest   *Inspector Porfiry Rostnikov and Detectives*
New York: Fawcett Columbine, 1992.   *Sacha Tkach and Emil Karpo*

In the town of Arkush a famous Russian priest is murdered. Rostnikov and Karpo go to Arkush to find the "Oleg" mentioned by Father Merkum as he died. Meanwhile Tkach and his new partner, Elena Petrooka, are looking for an Arab girl who remains elusive but dangerous to people who know her. Each case requires patient questioning and careful piecing together of facts.

MacKinlay Kantor

Signal Thirty-two   *23rd Precinct*
New York: Random House, 1950.

This is a a documentary novel detailing the everyday routine of a New York City police precinct.

Herbert Kastle

Death Squad   *Detective Sergeant Eddy Roersch and Willis Jones*
New York: Dell, 1977.

Three young men steal a car and drive into one of the wealthy areas of Manhattan. As they cruise around they find a man and woman getting into a car. In the process of robbing the couple the young men lose control of the situation and kill their victims, another passerby, and a policeman who happens to be on the scene. The dead police captain is the focus of the investigation because he was carrying a bag containing twenty thousand dollars. Why he had the money and what his business was in that area are big headaches for Sergeant Roersch.

William Katz*

Open House *Lieutenant Leonard Karlov*
New York: McGraw-Hill, 1985.

A killer stalks young women living alone on the West Side of Manhattan. At the scene of each murder the police find a tiny papier-mache gondola left as a calling card.

John Katzenbach*

The Traveler *Detective Mercedes Barren*
New York: Putnam, 1987.
London: Macmillan, 1987.

Told in alternating chapters by the killer and Miami detective Mercedes Barren as they travel across the country. Barren is looking for the murderer of her niece; the killer is torturing his captive.

Faye Kellerman

The Ritual Bath *Lieutenant Peter Decker*
New York: Arbor, 1986.
London: Collins, 1987.

Inside the grounds of a yeshiva a young mother is brutally raped. LAPD lieutenant Decker, the officer in charge, tries to help out but the residents of the school are reluctant to believe that one of their own is a rapist and they do not want an outsider interfering with the orderly running of the place.

Sacred and Profane *Lieutenant Peter Decker*
New York: Arbor, 1987.
London: Coronet, 1989

Using painstaking police procedure and forensic dentistry Decker identifies the burned bodies of two women found on a hill outside of Los Angeles. Young people used in pornography and the ugly realities of the life of a runaway child are the subject matter here.

Milk and Honey *Lieutenant Peter Decker*
New York: Morrow, 1990.

Decker finds a two-year-old girl wandering in the street. He takes her to his station where child welfare authorities pick her up but not before he discovers that her pajamas are caked in blood. Then her family is found. All of them have been killed and it becomes imperative to discover whether the child saw them murdered. Decker is also trying to help a friend who served with him in Vietnam who has been accused of raping a prostitute.

Day of Atonement *Lieutenant Peter Decker*
New York: Morrow, 1991.

Decker and Rina go to New York City for their honeymoon, which includes meeting Rina's former in-laws and celebrating Rosh Hashanah. Even though this tale is not strictly a procedural, Decker, a consummate detective, finds that when a fourteen-year-old boy disappears from his grandmother's house he must act. As he organizes the search, he discovers that the missing Noam Levine is a troubled youth. To add to this, unbeknown to the Levine siblings, Decker is their half brother.

False Prophet *Lieutenant Peter Decker*
New York: Morrow, 1992.

Lilah Brecht had it all. Her mother is actress Davida Eversong, her father a famous director. Lilah runs the Vulcan, a luxurious spa. But when she is viciously raped in her bedroom, Decker begins to see that all is not paradise in her world. Everyone seems to gather round to help, but then her brother is murdered and Decker must find the killer. Lilah thinks the attack and the subsequent robbery of her jewelry were really an attempt to get at her father's memoirs, which contain information that would best be kept undisclosed.

Jonathan Kellerman*

The Butcher's Theater *Chief Inspector Daniel Shalom Sharavi*
New York: Bantam, 1988.
London: Macdonald, 1988.

The fifteen-year-old girl lay in a ravine on the Mount of Olives. She was brutalized, all of her blood drained from her body, then thoroughly washed, dressed, and left. On the off chance that this is the work of the Gray Man, a serial killer who has eluded capture, Sharavi picks an unusual crime task force. Choosing an experienced older detective, an Arab, a Chinese Jew, and a young rookie, Sharavi, himself a Yeminite, covers several ethnic and religious bases. A second body is discovered one week later and the team knows that they are up against a killer of superior intelligence.

Bill Kelly and Dolph Le Moult

Street Dance *Detective Vince Crowley*
New York: Charter, 1987.

A transsexual named Miguel (Marguerita) Ramos is dead in the Bronx River. Ramos was tortured, then emasculated and eviscerated while alive. Crowley, whose personal life is coming apart, works on this case as it becomes almost a lifeline to reality as he plays cat and mouse with the killer.

Dream Street *Detective Vince Crowley*
New York: Charter, 1989.

An ex-pimp is stabbed while riding on the New York subway. The second murder is that of an old woman who was reluctant to sell her home to a construction company. The point of reference seems to be a few blocks of real estate that has been earmarked to become an exclusive land development. The movers and shakers will stop at nothing to accomplish what they want.

Death Spiral *Detective Vince Crowley*
New York: Onyx, 1989.

A woman from a wealthy family is murdered in a sleazy hotel in the Bronx. Her father, a powerful man in the New York media world, wants action and attempts to orchestrate the hunt and capture of her killer. Detective Vince Crowley sees the case not as a crusade but as the taking of a human life. He looks for motive and finds that the dead woman was not the angel her father made her out to be.

Alanna Knight*

Enter Second Murderer *Detective Inspector Jeremy Faro*
London: Macmillan, 1988.
New York: St. Martin's, 1989.

Shortly before Patrick Hymes is executed, he tells Inspector Faro he did not kill Lily Goldie, the second woman he was convicted of murdering. Gradually Faro is enticed into reopening the case, aided by his stepson, Dr. Vincent Laurie. Their growing relationship adds depth to the tale.

Blood Line *Detective Inspector Jeremy Faro*
London: Macmillan, 1989.
New York: St. Martins, 1989.

A man is found on the rocks outside of Edinburgh Castle, his clothes shabby but of good quality. There is nothing to identify him except a tailor's mark and an antique brooch found by Faro near where the man fell. Among the effects of Faro's policeman father is an identical pin. While reading his father's papers he realizes that the pin has been in the collection of the Royal family, that it has something to do with an Egyptian-style curse, and the dead baby found in the walls of Mary Queen of Scots' apartment in the Castle may have a great deal to do with his present case.

Deadly Beloved *Detective Inspector Jeremy Faro*
London: Macmillan, 1990.
New York: St. Martin's, 1991.

Mabel Kellar, wife of the famous police surgeon Melville Kellar, has been missing for two weeks. Mrs. Kellar never arrived at her sister's home in North Berwick. Soon her sable cape and the bloody carving knife missing from the Kellar home are found beside the railroad tracks at Longniddy Station.

Killing Cousins *Detective Inspector Jeremy Faro*
London: Macmillan, 1990.
New York: St. Martin's, 1992.

Inspector Faro is off to apprehend his archenemy, Noblesse Oblige, but once again the master criminal gets away. Faro is therefore free to visit his mother and daughters on the island of Orkney where his stepson, Vincent, is also visiting. When he arrives, Vince tells him that Thora Balfray, wife of their host, is dead and he suspects the cause of death was arsenic.

Bill Knox

Deadline for a Dream *Chief Inspector Colin Thane*
London: Long, 1957. *and Inspector Phil Moss*

In at the Kill
New York: Doubleday, 1961.

A young news reporter, David Renfield, is besotted by a woman from a wealthy background who will only marry a rich man. To get big money

Renfield robs the Swivney factory payroll but panics and kills the young police guard. The take is £7,000. But Renfield, realizing he will never get away with the crime because the police are not fools, decides to help them in their investigation.

Death Department *Chief Inspector Colin Thane*
London: Long, 1959. *and Inspector Phil Moss*

Glasgow's Hillman Department store is hit with an enormous amount of theft. Over a period of three months £4,000 of merchandise has vanished. The store manager believes that this loss is due to organized stealing by employees, not shoplifting. Then the head of women's fashions disappears after a salesperson accuses her of theft. Thane and Moss try to find who would buy odd lots of goods and where they might sell it.

Leave It to the Hangman *Chief Inspector Colin Thane*
London: Long, 1960. *and Inspector Phil Moss*
New York: Doubleday, 1960.

Patrick Kilburn, in jail for murder, is in danger and then someone tries to shoot him—in jail. While the police are attempting to protect him, he escapes from prison. Meanwhile, another man is murdered, and while Thane and Moss look for the killer, Kilburn's young daughter sets out to find her father. So the inspectors must now also find the little girl as well as her father, and discover why someone wants him dead.

Little Drops of Blood *Chief Inspector Colin Thane*
London: Long, 1962. *and Inspector Phil Moss*
New York: Doubleday, 1962.

The man lying dead in the road was an auto mechanic and a member of a gang specializing in stolen cars. Sammy Bell had been run over; the car then reversed and ran over him again. Sammy, in and out of prison, had not had a decent job in years, but he knew all about the stolen car operation that meant big money to someone.

Sanctuary Isle *Chief Inspector Colin Thane*
London: Long, 1962. *and Inspector Phil Moss*

The Grey Sentinels
New York: Doubleday, 1963.

The Scottish Sea Bird Society has hired Lewis Tinemann to live on Sanctuary Isle as warden. But Tinemann is murdered, the case particularly intriguing because there is no access to the isle except by boat and only the man who delivers supplies has been out there. The other interesting fact is that Tinemann was poisoned with aconite. The mystery here requires all of Thane's skill to unearth why someone thought the bird warden had to die.

The Man in the Bottle *Chief Inspector Colin Thane and*
London: Long, 1963 *Inspector Phil Moss*

The Killing Game
New York: Doubleday, 1963.

Thane has been busy organizing a guided tour of Glasgow for General Igor Shashkov, Soviet Minister for Industrial Development. In the Perthshire Highlands is a NATO listening post that records nuclear explosions using a worldwide search method. The Perthshire police find the body of a man who had gone fishing but ended up in the middle of a dynamite explosion. The dead man's companion is missing, his office and his apartment broken into and searched. But then Russian sailors are arrested for stealing explosives and an attempt is made on the Russian general's life.

The Taste of Proof *Chief Inspector Colin Thane*
London: Long, 1965. *and Inspector Phil Moss*
New York: Doubleday, 1965.

The Glen Ault Whiskey Company is robbed of £3,000. At the scene is a bottle of Glen Ault bearing the fingerprints of Frank Humbie, convicted felon several times over. Mrs. Humbie states emphatically that her husband was at home when the robbery occurred. Then she is murdered and the young man Humbie spent the evening with vanishes as does all trace of the money.

The Deep Fall *Chief Inspector Colin Thane*
London: Long, 1966. *and Inspector Phil Moss*

The Ghost Car
New York: Doubleday, 1966.

One of the directors of Hydrostat Drives, Inc., is trapped inside an enameling oven and baked to death. Hydrostat, a company specializing in ways to move liquid under pressure to drive machines, does a considerable business in government contracts, one of which is building sea-to-air warships. The company is just finishing work on what they call the Ghost Car, a vehicle that would revolutionize the automotive industry.

Justice on the Rocks *Chief Inspector Colin Thane*
London: Long, 1967. *and Inspector Phil Moss*
New York: Doubleday, 1967.

During a gang fight broken up by the police, Constable MacGrigor sees a young man behind some wood, dead of a puncture wound to the chest.

Doc Williams is puzzled but soon learns that the murder weapon was a nail gun. The gangs are getting more aggressive toward each other and the dead boy's father is out for revenge. Thane and Moss must go into action to solve this one fast before more people are hurt or killed.

The Tallyman *Chief Inspector Colin Thane*
London: Long, 1969. *and Detective Inspector Phil Moss*
New York, Doubleday, 1969.

Andrew Fergan, admitted killer of a moneylender, is sentenced to life in prison. The judge wants to bring the man behind the moneylenders, the tallyman, to justice. This is a no-win assignment as Colin Thane and Phil Moss must work against the clock to fulfill the magistrate's mandate.

Children of the Mist *Chief Inspector Colin Thane*
London: Long, 1970. *and Inspector Phil Moss*
Who Shot the Bull?
New York: Doubleday, 1970.

A bull, the Marquis of Braedale, has been shot to death. The Perthshire force asks for help from Glasgow's Millside Division and they send Thane and Moss. The problem is that the prime suspect is Inspector Fenn of the local police. There are witnesses against him—his own sergeant and a constable claim they saw Fenn shoot the bull, plus there is a feud between Fenn and Jennings, the bull's owner.

To Kill a Witch *Chief Inspector Colin Thane*
London: Long, 1971. *and Inspector Phil Moss*
New York: Doubleday, 1972.

Margaret Sinclair's body is hauled out of the Clyde River. It is clear that she had been strangled. A white witch, she lived in a town, Monkswalk, where a sizeable coven flourishes. The witches are duped into thinking they are doing good while a hidden evil is guiding them to destruction.

Draw Batons! *Chief Inspector Colin Thane*
London: Long, 1973. *and Inspector Phil Moss*
New York: Doubleday, 1973.

After hours Sergeant Francey Lang sneaks in to take a look at the huge model train and airplane exposition. But to his chagrin he finds the body of a man. The dead man was a used-car dealer and his business practices provide a good starting place for the investigation.

Rally to Kill*
London: Long, 1975.
New York: Doubleday, 1975.

Chief Inspector Colin Thane and Inspector Phil Moss

Pilot Error
London: Long, 1977.
New York: Doubleday, 1977.

Chief Inspector Colin Thane and Inspector Phil Moss

A small plane crashes in the countryside, killing the pilot and his passenger. Both worked for a travel agency and the pilot had been drinking. The plane wreck is searched. Nothing is adding up until another employee of the travel agency dies and Thane and Moss move operations north.

Live Bait
London: Long, 1978.
New York: Doubleday, 1979.

Detective Superintendent Colin Thane

Colin Thane is promoted to Detective Superintendent and reassigned to the Scottish Crime Squad, an elite, hand-picked group covering the entire expanse of Scotland and concentrating on major crimes. He acquires rookie Francey Dunbar as a partner and they do not work well together. A group of whiskey distilleries keeps figuring in the backgrounds of the dead men who continue to crop up.

A Killing in Antiques
London: Hutchinson, 1981.
New York: Doubleday, 1981.

Detective Superintendent Colin Thane

Drum Lodge, a medium-sized Scottish country house owned by Fergie Mackenzie, is robbed by three men, one dressed as a policeman. The silver, some furniture, and the antique firearms collection are stolen. Mackenzie, otherwise known as "Bloody Mac," is a senior judge of the Scottish High Court and a real terror. This is just the tip of an epidemic of robberies involving antiques.

The Hanging Tree
London: Hutchinson, 1983.
New York: Doubleday, 1984.

Detective Superintendent Colin Thane

A Glasgow post office is robbed of bags of pension money. Thane is called in to head the investigation because a passerby was killed during the getaway. Hidden in the dead man's apartment was lots of money, a false passport, and a videotape of an American movie so new that it has not been released in Europe. This leads to the discovery of a videocassette racket with big money potential. The people involved are heavy hitters—running protection rackets, large-scale theft operations, and a ready and willing market for all goods.

The Crossfire Killings *Detective Superintendent Colin Thane*
London: Century Hutchinson, 1986.
New York: Doubleday, 1986.

Detective Sergeant Mary Dutton of the Strathclyde police falls to her death while hiking near Loch Lomond, Scotland. When a postcard arrives saying that she had seen two known criminals there and would try to move on without them seeing her, the Scottish Crime Squad Commander sends Thane to find out what really happened to Mary Dutton.

The Interface Man *Detective Superintendent Colin Thane*
London: Century Hutchinson, 1989.
New York: Doubleday, 1990.

John William Gort, a.k.a. the Interface Man, has returned to Scotland. Gort has the ability to crack electronic security systems and break into protected computer programs. Thane and Sergeant Francey Dunbar are waiting for him at Glasgow Airport. The death of a man who has fallen off a train seems to be tied in to the Gort case. Something big is going on and Thane is in the dark until a woman calling herself Pony begins to phone him. She knows too much for her own good.

John Lantigua[*]

Heat Lightning *Inspector David Cruz*
New York: Putnam, 1987.

The body of a beautiful Latin American woman from El Salvador is found on a street in San Francisco. She has been executed, shot with her thumbs tied behind her back. This leaves a message for her compatriots, as this is the style of killing used by the goon squads of her country to terrorize people into obeying them. The horrors of the streets of El Salvador have followed her to San Franciso, and illegal refugees will begin full-scale riots if Cruz is unable to find a motive for Gloria Sato's death.

Lynda La Plante

Prime Suspect *Detective Chief Inspector Jane Tennison*
New York: Dell, 1993.

The body of a young woman is found in a small apartment. She had been tortured, beaten, stabbed, and raped. Scotland Yard DCI Shefford, in charge of the case, gets a lucky break in that the body secretions from the murderer are of a rare type and those of a known felon. Shefford rushes to get his man and in doing so makes mistakes in his interrogation of the prisoner. Then Shefford dies of a massive hemorrage. DCI Jane Tennison, the only ranking officer with murder investigation experience, takes over to the disgust and suspicion of Shefford's squad.

Prime Suspect 2 *Detective Chief Inspector Jane Tennison*
New York: Dell, 1993.

When the remains of a young female are found in the basement of a house, the Southhampton Row police think they may have discovered the body of Simone Cameron, a young woman missing from the neighborhood for some months. The problems unleashed by the investigation are many. There is racism to contend with and the hope that creating a face for the dead girl will aid in identifying her.

Philip Lauben*

A Nice Sound Alibi *Captain Homer Clay*
New York: St. Martin's, 1981. *and Sergeant Ernest Manion*

The much disliked Clyde Bumpus is found dead on his boat. The people with reason to kill him all have alibis. The only clue is a baby-blue Volkswagen. Then a second murder is committed.

A Surfeit of Alibis *Captain Homer Clay*
New York: St. Martin's, 1982. *and Sergeant Ernest Manion*

Miss Ella Brundage calls the police station and demands that someone come out and remove the dead body in her garage.

John Leslie*

Killer in Paradise *Lieutenant Patrick Bowman*
New York: Pocket, 1990.

Patrick Bowman of the Chicago police is considered to be one of the best homicide detectives in the country. He is on a two-month leave of absence in Key West, Florida, recovering from a gunshot wound he got while trying to break up an argument between two men. On arriving in Florida, he is asked for his opinion on a case involving the murder of a runaway girl. As the body count soars Bowman finds that his beautiful wife of fifteen years is entangled in an affair with a man who has dragged her deeply into a cesspool of deviant behavior.

Bob Leuci

Captain Butterfly *Captain Marjorie Butera (Captain Butterfly)*
New York: NAL, 1989.

Captain Butterfly, Internal Affairs Division, NYPD, must investigate a Brooklyn precinct where corruption and brutality are the order of the day. The main bad guy, Inspector Janesky, intends to go right to the top and become chief of police. Butara, a member of the unpopular Internal Affairs team, does not receive much help from rank and file police personnel.

J. R. Levitt

Carnivores *Detectives Jason Coulter and Dave Warren*
New York: St. Martin's, 1989.

Tracking a serial killer leads Coulter and Warren of the Salt Lake City PD to the Pharaohs, a vicious biker gang. When Coulter's girlfriend, Jennifer Lasser, disappears he goes crazy, killing Fat Eddie, one of the bikers.

Michael Z. Lewin*

Night Cover *Lieutenant Leroy Powder*
New York: Knopf, 1976.
London: Hamilton, 1976.

Lieutenant Powder is forty-eight, has spent most of his adult life as a cop, and now runs the night shift for the Indianapolis Police Department.

Everything is running along smoothly until he becomes involved in a number of random killings, some of which have no way of being solved. He is removed from the graveyard shift and given more cases to take his mind off his personal problems.

Hard Line *Lieutenant Leroy Powder*
New York: Morrow, 1982.
London: Macmillan, 1983.

Powder has been assigned to the Missing Persons Bureau and he begins by acquiring Sergeant Carollee Fleetwood, who was injured in the line of duty and is confined to a wheelchair. So many cases come in at once that Powder and Fleetwood must learn to work together immediately. They make an understaffed, forgotten part of the police force an efficient and unforgettable unit.

Late Payments *Lieutenant Leroy Powder*
New York: Morrow, 1986.
London: Macmillan, 1986.

A twelve-year-old boy asks Powder to find his missing father. Powder, whose own son is on parole and in trouble, feels sorry for the boy so he tries to help him. Then it comes to his attention that handicapped people are dying at an alarming rate and that there may be a serial killer preying on them.

Roy Lewis*

A Lover Too Many *Inspector John Crow*
London: Collins, 1969.
New York: World, 1971.

Peter Marlin, a Solicitor of the Supreme Court, discovers the body of his murdered wife in their home. The coroner finds her death misadventure by person or persons unknown. Marlin is a suspect because he had an affair during the seven-month interval when his wife had left him. Someone has it in for Marlin as his law partners dissolve their business and his ex-lover turns a cold shoulder to his trouble. Inspector Crow arrives from Scotland Yard to find Jeannette Marlin's murderer.

Error of Judgment *Detective Chief Inspector John Crow*
London: Collins, 1971.

Rosemary Harland, secretary to the head of Burton Polytechnic, is found dead on the same morning as a student demonstration is in progress and one of the professors has suffered a heart attack. As Chief Inspector Crow interviews the personnel and the students he finds the college a hotbed of Marxist theory and political unrest, and encounters the arrogant leader of the rebellious students, Sadruddin Khan.

A Secret Singing[*] *Detective Chief Inspector John Crow*
London: Collins, 1972.

Blood Money[*] *Detective Chief Inspector John Crow*
London: Collins, 1973.

A Question of Degree *Detective Chief Inspector John Crow*
London: Collins, 1974.

The dog Gyp falls down a mine shaft in Wales and his owner is winched down in a bucket to save him. But he finds the body of a woman on the ledge along with the dog. Crow is sent to the Rhondda to act in the strictly limited capacity of advisor in the case so when the woman's husband confesses, Crow cannot pursue the investigation, which the local police want solved quickly. During the trial, the Welsh police's case is torn to shreds and Crow must go to Canada for a few answers.

A Part of Virtue *Detective Inspector John Crow*
London: Collins, 1975.

While Andrew Keene's wife is having a baby in their van, Chuck Lindop, a suspected burglar, is being murdered. Andrew is Crow's prime suspect along with Chuck's ex-girlfriend and her current boyfriend. There is also a local man who has hated Lindop for a long time and would do anything to get even.

Nothing But Foxes *Detective Chief Inspector John Crow*
London: Collins, 1977.
New York: St. Martin's, 1977.

James Sweet, a man opposed to hunting and not afraid to speak out about it, is found dead by the dogs leading a fox hunt. Sweet's head has been blown off by a shotgun blast. The Yard, represented by Crow, is called in to find out why Sweet was murdered, as well as to handle all the important people who participated in the hunt, many of whom had reason to dislike the victim.

A Relative Distance *Superintendent John Crow*
London: Collins, 1981.

Mining has been a fact of life in Devonshire for a long time. Now deposits of tungsten-bearing ore have been found but a person unknown wants to stop an American company from setting up a tungsten mining operation. Fred Norman, the company environmental coordinator, is murdered, and John Crow is sent in to found out why. There are any number of people who may have killed Norman, including antipollution groups, local residents, and his colleagues.

Herbert Lieberman*

City of the Dead   *Dr. Paul Konig,*
New York: Simon & Schuster, 1976.   *Lieutenant Francis Xavier Haggard,*
London: Hutchinson, 1976.   *and Detective Sergeant Edward Flynn*

Two bodies are found totally dismembered and the heads missing. A young man is found in his bathtub with an ice pick in his chest, a young woman is raped and murdered—all in a day's work for Konig, NYC chief medical examiner. His artist daughter, Lolly, has left home and is now a captive of a radical group with no regard for life or the well-being of others. The detectives and Konig are in a race to save Lolly Konig. To add to the mystery, bodies are being stolen from the morgue and sold.

Nightbloom   *Captain Francis (Frank) Mooney*
New York: Putnam, 1984.   *and Dr. Paul Konig*
London: Hutchinson, 1984.

A serial killer murders only once a year, by dropping a cement block from the roof of a building into the throngs of people leaving theaters. The story moves back and forth between narratives told by Lieutenant Mooney and Charles Watford, a loner, a Demerol addict, and the one person who knows the identity of the illusive Bombadier.

Shadow Dancers   *Lieutenant Francis (Frank) Mooney*
Boston: Little Brown, 1989.
London: Hutchinson, 1989.

Suki Klink lives in a 150-year-old house full of junk and dirt. She is an amateur herbalist growing her herbs in the backyard, which extends down to the river. The city of New York paid millions for her home, which is on a prime piece of property, but she continues to live there in extreme poverty, stealing to keep alive. Then she acquires a child whom she turns into a killer. The murders are particularly gruesome, leading the police to believe that there is not one but two killers.

David L. Lindsey

A Cold Mind *Sergeant Stuart Haydon, Detective Leo Hirsch,*
New York: Harper, 1983. *and Lieutenant Bob Dystal*
London: Arlington, 1984.

When Sally Steen is pulled from Buffalo Bayou in Houston, there is no apparent cause of her death, even after the autopsy. Steen had been a high-priced call girl with lots of money. Soon Haydon, his partner, Leo Hirsch, and vice cop Ed Mooney are following the elusive trail of someone who is murdering expensive prostitutes. The facts give every indication that the murders will continue.

Heat from Another Sun *Sergeant Stuart Haydon*
New York: Harper, 1984.
London: Arlington, 1985.

A highly placed executive in a large advertising company is murdered. The man had been brought in especially because of his experience with movies. Haydon is recovering from a very bad experience after his last case. He has had five months off and Lieutenant Dystal calls him in to work solely on this murder case, the brutality of which does nothing to help Haydon's state of mind.

Spiral *Sergeant Stuart Haydon*
New York: Atheneum, 1986.
London: Arlington, 1987.

The man had been neatly arranged in death, his clothes adjusted so that he presented as good a picture as could be expected with a spike protruding from his skull. A few hours later a wealthy Mexican and his entourage, consisting of armed guards and business associates, are ambushed and slaughtered by men riding motorcycles, the work of Los Tecos, a Mexican terrorist group. Hayden goes undercover to solve a difficult case involving more murders and violence.

In the Lake of the Moon *Sergeant Stuart Haydon*
New York: Atheneum, 1988.
London: Corgi, 1989.

After receiving several envelopes of photographs of his father and a mysterious and beautiful woman, Haydon gets a death threat and a dead man. The case is linked in some way to the envelopes he has been receiving. Traveling to Mexico City, Haydon discovers his father's deepest secrets and danger in a madman's fantasies.

Body of Truth*   *Sergeant Stuart Haydon*
New York: Warner, 1992
London: Warner, 1992

Mercy   *Detective Carmen Palma*
New York: Doubleday, 1990.
London: Macdonald, 1990.

Two women are murdered within a relatively short time, both bodies laid out in a funereal pose. After the third murder, Detective Palma calls in the FBI's top serial killer profiler and together they track down the murderer. Sadomasochism, sex, and torture are the games of this vicious killer.

Elizabeth Linington*
(also Dell Shannon, q.v.)

Greenmask   *Sergeant Ivor Maddox*
New York: Harper, 1964.

An old shop owner in Los Angeles is found with his head bashed in. The business was taking in about $32 a day. Money was found in the victim's wallet and he still had his watch and a ruby ring so robbery was not the motive. The crime is a copy of an old mystery story and Maddox has to dig through his collection of mystery novels and his knowledge of them to solve the case.

No Evil Angel   *Sergeant Ivor Maddox*
New York: Harper, 1964.
London: Gollancz, 1965.

Maddox asks policewoman Susan Carstairs to help him interview a woman who reports her thirteen-year-old daughter missing. The girl has been gone a week without the mother becoming concerned. A man is found in his car, dead from an overdose of barbiturates. Someone is going around killing people for no apparent reason and an elderly woman has disappeared.

Date with Death   *Sergeant Ivor Maddox*
New York: Harper, 1966.
London: Gollancz, 1966.

A painted pig is found eating the flowers in a garden on Higman Avenue and Wilcox Street police are investigating the shooting deaths of Ruth Evans and a friend.

Something Wrong *Sergeant Ivor Maddox*
New York: Harper, 1967.
London: Gollancz, 1968.

Wilcox Street precinct detectives are looking for a missing baby, a teenage girl who is getting into deep trouble, and a cop killer.

Policeman's Lot *Sergeant Ivor Maddox*
New York: Harper, 1968.
London: Gollancz, 1969.

The worried mother of a twenty-one-year-old man comes in to report her son missing. He is usually dependable and predictable but he never came home from his second job. Then a fortune teller is murdered in her apartment. In the middle of his shift the night supervisor of a hospital emergency room vanishes

Practice to Deceive *Sergeant Ivor Maddox*
New York: Harper, 1971.
London: Gollancz, 1971.

The rapist first steals underwear from his victims. Then he goes back, rapes, and beats them. The police are called to the home of an attorney who has been shot to death in his kitchen. His mother was making the beds when he died and did not hear a thing. He was shot with his own gun. A drunken man breaks his wife's arm for being drunk, and a dismembered body is dug up in Griffith Park, thus rounding out the work facing the Wilcox police.

Crime by Chance *Sergeant Ivor Maddox*
Philadelphia: Lippincott, 1973.
London: Gollancz, 1974.

Dorrie Mayo quit her job and left her apartment with her fifteen-month-old daughter without saying goodbye to any of her friends. Both notes she left were typewritten but Dorrie does not have a typewriter. When Maddox goes back to look at the abandoned apartment he finds the baby's favorite toy left behind. The Wilcox Street station detectives are also looking for two men posing as policemen, trying to find a murderer, and sorting out the brutal attack on an old man.

Perchance of Death *Sergeant Ivor Maddox*
New York: Doubleday, 1977.
London: Gollancz, 1978.

Sue Maddox, wife of Ivor and a detective in the same station, is looking for a young woman who vanished from the porch of her home. The detectives are also working on a series of robberies at gunpoint. A woman named Juanita propositions middle-class men, then robs them of their valuables. There is also a child abuse case and several other murders, including the killing of an elderly woman known in her neighborhood as having a million dollars.

No Villain Need Be *Sergeant Ivor Maddox and Detective Sue Maddox*
New York: Doubleday, 1979.
London: Gollancz, 1979.

The husband and wife team of Ivor and Sue Maddox must persuade Sue's mother to come live with them, which necessitates buying a larger house. Plus, they have a number of burglaries, all of which have taken place during the daytime. A grandmother and her two-year-old granddaughter have been brutally murdered and a number of fatal accidents look suspicious.

Consequences of Crime *Sergeant Ivor Maddox*
New York: Doubleday, 1980.
London: Gollancz, 1981.

The "Gorilla Man," a huge, incredibly strong person, is raping women in laundromats. The police find the body of a prostitute who has been killed and left in the street; they are also looking for two teenage girls from Stockton who ran away from home as a lesson to their parents. A television celebrity is murdered and a series of robberies is causing the team headaches.

Skeletons in the Closet *Sergeant Ivor Maddox*
New York: Doubleday, 1982.
London: Gollancz, 1983.

A thirteen-year-old boy reported missing by his father is found dead in an alley. A number of churches have been vandalized and messages about Satan have been written on the walls of some buildings. The police are also investigating a number of random murders in which the bodies have been left under abandoned houses.

Jayson Livingston

Point Blank *Detective Stu Redlam*
New York: St. Martin's, 1990.

The Sacramento P.D. robbery division on a stakeout goes in to make a bust and one of the cops is killed. His partner thinks he deliberately let himself be killed. That same night a woman is raped and murdered. The police find a rare coin on her back. After searching the murdered woman's apartment, Stu Redlam knows she was into something that produced big money. Then a second woman is murdered, she, too, with a coin on her back, plus she has a little book written in code just like the first victim did.

Tom Logan

Detroit P.D.: Sword of Samos *14th Precinct*
New York: Lynx, 1989.

The situation in Detroit is terrible. Old people are preyed upon, hurt, robbed. When the courts get the perpetrators, they release them. A group of vigilantes known as the Sword of Samos (SOS) has a better response time than the Detroit Police Department. The police are concerned that the SOS's taking the law into their own hands.

Mike Lundy

Raven *Detective Fred Raven*
Secaucus, NJ: Stuart, 1985.

When Bill Lamps and Pat Knees are kidnapped and taken to a building where Pat is raped and murdered, Lamps is charged with her death. Raven and his partner, Higgins, of the NYPD, are assigned to the case as it matches up with at least twelve attacks and rapes committed by a gang of men. The detectives are looking for a man who could be an ex-priest, a cop, or a guy who wears overalls.

Ed McBain*

Cop Hater *87th Precinct, including*
New York: Permabooks, 1956. *Detectives Steve Carella, Meyer Meyer,*
London: Boardman, 1958. *Bert Kling, Cotton Hawes, Richard Genero,*
Hal Willis, Lieutenant Byrne, and Eileen Burke

Mike Reardon, one of the sixteen detectives assigned to the 87th Precinct, located in Isola, a city very much like New York, is shot in the head while on his way to work. His partner is killed the following night. When a third cop is killed, the detectives of the 87th know they must do something to stop the murders.

The Mugger 87th Precinct
New York: Permabooks, 1956.
London: Boardman, 1959.

The mugger preys on women who are out alone at night. He grabs them fast and takes their purses, then thanks them politely, but does not care what he has to do in order to get their cash. He hurts one so badly that she dies. Because this was a seventeen-year-old girl who had met Patrolman Bert Kling at a family dinner, Kling takes this one personally. He also meets Eileen Burke, proposes to Clair, and makes detective.

The Pusher 87th Precinct
New York: Permabooks, 1956.
London: Boardman, 1959.

A young boy is found in a basement with a rope around his neck, an apparent suicide. The boy was a drug addict whose sister gave him his first hit. Then while making an unrelated arrest Carella discovers that the dead boy was also a pusher.

The Con Man 87th Precinct
New York: Permabooks, 1957.
London: Boardman, 1960.

The body of a young woman is found in the Harb River. She had not drowned, but died of arsenic poisoning. Soon another woman is found in the river. She, too, has been poisoned. The only clue to the murders is a tattoo on the hands of each woman. The 87th is also looking for a con man working the mean streets of Isola preying on poor people; he blesses their five and ten dollar bills, then fails to give the money back.

Killer's Choice 87th Precinct
New York: Permabooks, 1958.
London: Boardman, 1960.

Annie Boone is working in a liquor store when she is shot to death and the store wrecked. At the same time Detective Roger Haviland is killed when he is thrown through the plate glass window of a grocery shop where a robbery is taking place. Cotton Hawes, newly transferred from the 30th Precinct, almost gets Steve Carella killed.

Killer's Payoff *87th Precinct*
New York: Permabooks, 1958.
London: Boardman, 1960.

Sy Kramer was handsome, well dressed, and wealthy. He had everything going for him except that he was a blackmailer and now he is dead. The detectives of the 87th work their way through a list of people with many reasons to kill Kramer.

Lady Killer *87th Precinct*
New York: Permabooks, 1958.
London: Boardman, 1960.

In the course of any week big city precinct police will receive crank calls. One hot summer day a boy delivers a letter saying that the writer will kill the lady. But which lady? Is it the prostitute who acts out rape? Is it Lady Jay Astor, singer of pornographic songs? Or is it the wealthy Mrs. Bannister? The detectives have twelve hours to find out which one is the intended victim.

Killer's Wedge *87th Precinct*
New York: Simon & Schuster, 1959.
London: Boardman, 1961.

It is a beautiful October day in Isola and many of the detectives assigned to the 87th are in the office when a woman enters. She pulls out a .38, levels it at them, and demands their guns. She announces that she is waiting for Steve Carella. When he comes in, she is going to kill him.

'Til Death *87th Precinct*
New York: Simon & Schuster, 1959.
London: Boardman, 1961.

Steve Carella's sister is getting married but the bridegroom is in danger. Someone sends him a small box wrapped as a wedding present that contains a black widow spider. The limousine taking the groom and his party to the church goes out of control and crashes. Then a guest is killed.

King's Ransom *87th Precinct*
New York: Simon & Schuster, 1959.
London: Boardman, 1961.

A radio supply store has had several break-ins, the amount of theft not very much. Add to this a few other robberies at radio parts stores and a picture begins to emerge that someone is building something with what he is stealing. Then Bobby King, the son of a businessman, is kidnapped. The 87th goes to work.

Give the Boys a Great Big Hand　　　　　　　　　　　*87th Precinct*
New York: Simon & Schuster, 1960.
London: Boardman, 1962.

First a patrolman, Richard Genero, finds a severed hand in an airline bag dropped by a person getting on a bus. Then the second hand is found in a trash can. A torso is found next.

The Heckler　　　　　　　　　　　　　　　　　　　　*87th Precinct*
New York: Simon & Schuster, 1960.
London: Boardman, 1962.

It is a warm and sunny April Fool's Day and the man lying on his back in the park is naked except for his shoes and socks. He is also dead. A shotgun blast at close range has done considerable damage to him. A partially deaf heckler is calling a businessman and telling him he must move out of his loft even though it houses a part of his business operation. This is the first case featuring the Deaf Man, the 87th's nemesis.

See Them Die　　　　　　　　　　　　　　　　　　　*87th Precinct*
New York: Simon & Schuster, 1960.
London: Boardman, 1963.

Pepe Miranda is wanted by the police. When they trap him in his apartment he gets the drop on them and escapes, enhancing his reputation with the neighborhood gang members. A street gang is getting set to kill a sixteen-year-old boy as an example to the rest of the youth that resistance to them is futile. So the detectives from the 87 must save the boy and stop the violence while searching for Pepe Miranda.

Lady, Lady, I Did It　　　　　　　　　　　　　　　　*87th Precinct*

New York: Simon & Schuster, 1961.
London: Boardman, 1963.

Detectives from the 87th are called to a bookstore where robbery and murder have been committed. Bert Kling discovers that the dead woman is his fiancée, Clair. Three other people have also been killed there and the investigation must determine whether Clair and the others were targets for a reason or innocent victims.

Like Love　　　　　　　　　　　　　　　　　　　　　*87th Precinct*
New York: Simon & Schuster, 1962.
London: Boardman, 1964.

Steve Carella and Cotton Hawes are swamped with puzzling cases. First a young woman jumps from a ledge to her death while Carella is trying to talk her to safety. Next an apartment explodes, killing a woman and a man who may or may not have been having an affair. There are no prints in the ruined apartment.

Ten Plus One *87th Precinct*
New York: Simon & Schuster, 1963.
London: Hamilton, 1964.

Anthony Forrest is shot as he walks down the street, the first victim of a sniper. The next day Randolph Horden is shot between the eyes by an unidentified marksman. When the third murder is committed, the trail leads to Ramsey University where all the victims went to school.

Ax *87th Precinct*
New York: Simon & Schuster, 1964.
London: Hamilton, 1964.

The man on the basement floor has an ax buried in his head. He has numerous wounds where the murderer struck him before delivering the final blow. The victim, a man in his eighties, was superintendent of the apartment building. When Carella and Hawes go to inform the family, they discover a reclusive son who illustrates books, a strange mother who quotes Shakespeare, and a man who chops wood for the murdered man.

He Who Hesitates *87th Precinct*
New York: Delacorte, 1965.
London: Hamilton, 1965.

Roger Broome is a country boy come to the big city to sell the handcrafted wares he and his family make. He has made the acquaintance of a few young women, and now must go to the police about one of them.

Doll *87th Precinct*
New York: Delacorte, 1965.
London: Hamilton, 1966.

Fashion model Tenka Sachs is brutally murdered, stabbed repeatedly, while her five-year-old daughter is in the next room listening to her mother being killed. In piecing the case together Kling is still suffering from the death of his fiancée, so he leaves Carella to work alone. Carella is captured and tortured before his car is found at the bottom of a ravine complete with a charred corpse.

Eighty Million Eyes *87th Precinct*
New York: Delacorte, 1966.
London: Hamilton, 1966.

Stan Gifford, late night comic, dies on screen before millions of viewers. The same day, a young man visits Vollner Audio-Visual Components, a New York-based company, and sits in the office waiting to see Cindy, assistant to the company psychologist. When asked to leave he resists and attacks the patrolman called to expel him. The man becomes obsessed with Cindy and beats her up when she goes out with Bert Kling, one of the detectives from the 87th. Unless the police find a way to stop him, this man is going to kill her.

Fuzz *87th Precinct*
New York: Doubleday, 1968.
London: Hamilton, 1968.

An extortionist is active in Isola. He threatens to kill the parks commissioner if the city does not pay him $5,000. Next on the hit list is the deputy mayor. A list of suspects contains the name Mort Orecchio, Italian for "dead ear." The Deaf Man is back in a big way; he blows up the deputy mayor in his car. Meanwhile, Carella is lurking in alleys, working undercover as a bum, waiting for a gang of hoodlums to set him on fire.

Shotgun *87th Precinct*
New York: Doubleday, 1968.
London: Hamilton, 1969.

A couple is found dead in their upper-middle-class apartment. The murder weapon is a shotgun and both victims have been shot in the face. Soon the detectives know a madman is on the loose in the city, and he is in hiding. They also know that he likes to romance married women and then kill both the woman and her husband.

Jigsaw *87th Precinct*
New York: Doubleday, 1970.
London: Hamilton, 1970.

Two men are found dead in a seedy apartment in Isola. In the hand of one of them is a piece of a photograph. It has the shape of a piece from a jigsaw puzzle. The mystery increases when a man walks into the squad room and announces that he has two more pieces of the photo, which will provide the whereabouts of $750,000, the loot taken during a bank robbery six years ago.

Hail, Hail, the Gang's All Here!   *87th Precinct*
New York: Doubleday, 1971.
London: Hamilton, 1971.

While Meyer Meyer is sitting in a dark house with Adele Gorman waiting for two Dutch ghosts who she believes have stolen her jewelry, Carella is working on the murder of an actress whose claim to fame is that she once played a stripper in a bad play. Kling is after a car thief and three people are killed in the bombing of a church. Willis and Genero handle the case of a young, naked boy who has jumped or was pushed to his death from a fourth floor window into the alley below.

Sadie, When She Died   *87th Precinct*
New York: Doubleday, 1972.
London: Hamilton, 1972.

A murder investigation acts as a backdrop for the unhappiness in the lives of the police of the 87th.

Let's Hear It for the Deaf Man   *87th Precinct*
New York: Random House, 1973.
London: Hamilton, 1973.

The 87th Precinct's nemesis, the Deaf Man, is at it again, setting up a big-time operation that Steve Carella must figure out before the crime is committed. The detectives are also working on a series of burglaries and a murder.

Hail to the Chief   *87th Precinct*
New York: Random House, 1973.
London: Hamilton, 1973.

Six bodies are found in a ditch and Steve Carella and Bert Kling soon know that the deaths are a result of a territorial war between the Death's Heads, a Spanish street gang, the Scarlet Avengers, a black group, and the white Clique gang. The story is told in part by the leader of the Cliques in an attempt to explain why the gangs are fighting.

Bread   *87th Precinct*
New York: Random House, 1974.
London: Hamilton, 1974.

When a warehouse burns down, the owner, Roger Grimm, visits the precinct and asks for help from Carella and Hawes. The case begins to get complicated when Grimm's house also burns down and the day watchman at the warehouse is killed. Another murder and a vicious beating later, the web begins to untangle as the police arrest four members of the Ancient Skulls, a street gang, three employees of a development firm, and Mr. Grimm.

Blood Relatives *87th Precinct*
New York: Random House, 1975.
London: Hamilton, 1976.

After leaving a party, two cousins running home in the rain seek shelter in the doorway of an abandoned building. There they are accosted by a man with a knife who cuts up the fifteen-year-old, then tries to do the same thing to the seventeen-year-old. She escapes and seeks help at the 87th Precinct.

So Long As You Both Shall Live *87th Precinct*
New York: Random House, 1976.
London: Hamilton, 1976.

Detective Bert Kling's wedding night turns into a nightmare when his wife of a few hours disappears from their hotel room. Who would want to harm Kling or his wife becomes the focus of the investigation.

Long Time No See *87th Precinct*
New York: Random House, 1977.
London: Hamilton, 1977.

Steve Carella and Meyer Meyer are working on the murder of a blind man. The next morning his blind wife is killed. A day later another blind woman is murdered. All three have had their throats cut. The evidence is slim, clues are nonexistent. There is nothing to go on except the blind man's army record.

Calypso *87th Precinct*
New York: Viking, 1979.
London: Hamilton, 1979.

A calypso singer and a prostitute have been killed with the same .38 Smith and Wesson. Carella and Meyer interview pimps, streetwalkers, and bartenders in sleazy bars where women sell sex, and drugs are readily available.

Ghosts *87th Precinct*
New York: Viking, 1980.
London: Hamilton, 1980.

First a woman is killed on the sidewalk at 781 Jackson. While Carella and

Hawes and the two detectives from homicide are looking over the scene, they get another call. Gregory Craig, the writer of the bestselling *Deadly Shades*, has been murdered in his apartment in the same building. The police find that $83,000 worth of jewelry was stolen from the Craig apartment.

Heat   87th Precinct
New York: Viking, 1981.
London: Hamilton, 1981.

A woman arrives home from a trip to find that her husband has been dead in their apartment for several days. Although it is sweltering, the air conditioner in the apartment has been turned off. Bert Kling's marriage is in trouble and a psychopath is out to get Kling for sending him to prison.

Ice   87th Precinct
New York: Arbor, 1983.
London: Hamilton, 1983.

The 87th catches the murder of a dancer shot twice in the face. Then they inherit a downtown precinct's case because the cocaine pusher murdered there was killed by the same gun used on the dancer.

Lightning   87th Precinct
New York: Arbor, 1984.
London: Hamilton, 1984.

Women are being raped in the 87th Precinct, not once but three or four different times by the same man. Then a young female athlete is found hanging from a lamppost. A second woman is killed in the same way and the detectives find that both are runners for different colleges. They then decide to use Eileen Burke as a decoy.

Poison   87th Precinct
New York: Arbor, 1987.

Carella and Willis investigate a man's death by nicotine poisoning. Willis becomes romantically involved with the chief suspect and many scenes of sexual depravity are described.

Tricks   87th Precinct
New York: Arbor, 1987.

On Halloween night a magician disappears, a mother is driving a station wagon full of kids dressed for trick or treat who are robbing stores, and an amazing number of body parts are being found in the city.

Lullaby *87th Precinct*
New York: Morrow, 1989.

On New Year's Eve a six-month-old baby and her babysitter are murdered. Is the killer a burglar or is there another reason for their deaths? Kling is trapped into working with a drug pusher hunted by a Jamaican "posse," and Willis is still fighting the fact that his love life is a mess.

Vespers *87th Precinct*
New York: Morrow, 1990.

Father Michael, thinking of Vespers and blackmail as he walks in his garden, is attacked and stabbed to death. When the detectives from the 87th arrive they notice the sign of Baphomet on the garden gate. It is a satanic symbol and there is a cult very close to Father Michael's church. Also, Detective Willis's girlfriend is having trouble with people from her past.

Widows *87th Precinct*
New York: Morrow, 1991.

A beautiful woman is killed and soon her lover, a older man, is dead as well. The suspects include his wife, his ex-wife, and his two daughters. There are more murders the 87th is investigating and a tragedy for Steve Carella.

James McClure*

The Song Dog *Lieutenant Tromp Kramer and*
London: Faber, 1991. *Bantu Sergeant Mickey Zondi*
New York: Mysterious, 1991.

In this prequel to the series, set in South Africa, the characters Kramer, Zondi, and the Widow Flouri meet for the first time. Aman, a detective sergeant with the Jofini police, and the wife of the park ranger are killed in an explosion that reduces her home to rubble. Then Kramer discovers that the victim's clothing has been incinerated at the police station and is not available for evidence. Also there is a suspicious kaffir lurking in the area.

The Steam Pig *Lieutenant Tromp Kramer and*
London: Gollancz, 1971. *Bantu Sergeant Mickey Zondi*
New York: Harper, 1971.

Two women die at about the same time: one was old and had been murdered, the other was young and apparently died from cardiac arrest. The bodies are mistakenly switched by the undertaker and the old woman is cremated and the young one, Theresa le Roux, undergoes an autopsy. Ms. le Roux had a small puncture wound in her armpit where her killer had poked a bicycle spoke up into her aorta. Ms. le Roux led a quiet life, renting a small house on the grounds of a large estate where she gave music lessons. Her life gives no immediate clues as to why someone would want to kill her. But the method used is a favorite of the South African natives so Kramer and Zondi must dig into her background for some reason that anyone would want her dead. This tale typifies the rigid racial and social rules that long governed South Africa.

The Caterpillar Cop *Lieutenant Tromp Kramer and*
London: Gollancz, 1972. *Bantu Sergeant Mickey Zondi*
New York: Harper, 1972.

A twelve-year-old white boy is found on the grounds of a country club, murdered and then emasculated. All signs point to a standard sexual killing until Zondi and Kramer uncover the boy's secret life as a junior detective.

The Gooseberry Fool *Lieutenant Tromp Kramer and*
London: Gollancz, 1974. *Bantu Sergeant Mickey Zondi*
New York: Harper, 1974.

Working simultaneously on a suicide and a road accident, the infamous Colonel Du Plessis (who has never liked Kramer and positively hates Zondi) splits up the two detectives in order to ruin their careers. There are more questions than answers concerning both cases, which are not what they appear to be. The answers Kramer and Zondi manage to unearth involve the two policemen in a race to a solution.

Snake *Lieutenant Tromp Kramer and*
London: Gollancz, 1975. *Bantu Sergeant Mickey Zondi*
New York: Pantheon, 1975.

Kramer and Zondi investigate the death of a stripper who has been strangled by her pet snake. The second case is the death of a black shopkeeper killed in a robbery attempt. As they search for clues and motivation, many of the evils of South African apartheid become apparent.

The Sunday Hangman *Lieutenant Tromp Kramer and*
London: Macmillan, 1977. *Bantu Sergeant Mickey Zondi*
New York: Harper, 1977.

Tollie Erasmus wakes up to find himself in a cell waiting to be hanged. But the execution is not done by the state. Kramer and Zondi have a stake in his fate as Tollie is the one who put a bullet in Zondi's leg causing him endless pain and possible loss of his job. Soon their attention turns to facts dug up by Dr. Strydom, the medical examiner, who contends that evidence reveals that several more men may have been executed by this killer.

The Blood of an Englishman   *Lieutenant Tromp Kramer and*
London: Macmillan, 1980.   *Bantu Sergeant Mickey Zondi*
New York: Harper, 1980.

In the trunk of a car the body of a man is found covered in his own excrement and tied so tightly that his bones are broken. And he has been shot. The possibility that this murder ties in with an assault case keeps Kramer and Zondi busy. Kramer loses interest as his wandering eyes turn to the beautiful Tish, but Zondi, as usual, keeps them on target.

The Artful Egg   *Lieutenant Tromp Kramer and*
London: Macmillan, 1984.   *Bantu Sergeant Mickey Zondi*
New York: Pantheon, 1984.

Naomi Stride, famous novelist, is dead in her home in Morningside, an affluent section of Trekkersburg. Stride won acclaim with her first novel, *The Last Magnolia*, which dealt with apartheid. Each of her novels illustrated South African social and political rigidity and were all banned in the country.

Vincent McConnor*

The Provence Puzzle   *Chief Inspector Damiot*
New York: Macmillan, 1980

When Chief Inspector Damiot is wounded in the line of duty in Paris, his doctor recommends that he convalesce in Provence. That city is under siege by a killer who preys on young women, killing them by slitting their throats. Damiot sits this one out as long as he can, then joins the fray.

The Riviera Puzzle   *Chief Inspector Damiot*
New York: Macmillan, 1981.

The local police have word that a stolen Cézanne has appeared in the Cote d'Azur. Paris sends Damiot to help. The art world is in upheaval as a young artist is missing and an important art dealer is murdered.

The Paris Puzzle *Chief Inspector Damiot*
New York: Macmillan, 1981.

American celebrity and movie star Alex Scott is found murdered in a Paris street. Scott had made enemies. Now Damiot must sort through a list of suspects that includes Scott's wife and his film double.

I Am Vidocq *Vidocq, Chief of Sureté Nationale*
New York: Dodd, 1985.

Vidocq, head of the Brigade de Sureté Nationale, which he has staffed with ex-criminals, keeps a tight rein on crime in Paris and a close eye on criminal activities throughout France. He is aware of the plundering of old chateaux in the countryside and awaits the day when "Le Diable Noir" (the Black Devil), who leads the gang of mauraders, will turn his attention to the treasures in Paris. Vidocq is working on the murder of Clochette, a woman who has been good to his wife, and that of Tessier, the famous jeweler, when Maya, one of three great courtesans, is killed. Vidocq must discover whether these events tie in with the theft of a jeweled bracelet.

Limbo *Lieutenant Victor Lolo*
New York: Mysterious, 1987.

Troubleshooting detective lieutenant Victor Lolo, special investigator, LAPD, is working on the Midnight Jogger Case. The Jogger rapes females who are out alone at night. He stalks his prey until he is ready to enact the fantasies his sick mind has concocted.

Sharyn McCrumb[*]

If Ever I Return Pretty Peggy-O *Sheriff Spencer Arrowood*
New York: Scribner's, 1990.

When Peggy Muryan moves to Hamelin, Tennessee, Sheriff Arrowood is pleased because he always enjoyed her music. Muryan was a popular folksinger in the Sixties. She has come to peaceful Wake County to write music and relax but someone does not want her to live. She receives a postcard that frightens her enough to send for the sheriff. Then a local woman who resembles Muryan vanishes. The passions of the Sixties come home to roost in the Eighties.

Jill McGown*

A Perfect Match *Inspector Lloyd and Sergeant Judy Hill*
London: Macmillan, 1983.
New York: St. Martin's, 1983.

The body of Julia Mitchell is found in the deserted cafe she has inherited from her husband. Chris Wade, a man she has known for all of five minutes, flees because he is the last known person to have seen her alive. This complex case leads Lloyd and Hill into the lives of Mitchell's friends and family.

Redemption *Inspector Lloyd and Sergeant Judy Hill*
London: Macmillan, 1988.

Murder at the Old Vicarage
New York: St. Martin's, 1989.

The vicar's daughter and her husband come to spend Christmas with her parents. The young man is murdered in the vicarage and suspicion falls on his wife, who is very obviously abused. Then someone else emerges with a motive for the killing and Lloyd and Hill put the pieces together.

Death of a Dancer *Chief Inspector Lloyd and Sergeant Judy Hill*
London: Macmillan, 1989.

Gone to Her Death
New York: St. Martins's, 1990.

Diana Hamlyn is killed, her head bashed in by the proverbial blunt instrument. Diana, whose husband is the new headmaster of the small boys' school where they both teach, was a promiscuous woman who chased every male within shouting distance. The secrets kept by the people at the school are enough to keep the police digging until the right pieces fall into place.

The Murders of Mrs. Austin and Mrs. Beale *Chief Inspector Lloyd and Inspector Judy Hill*
London: Macmillan, 1991.
New York: St. Martin's, 1991.

First Leonora Austin is murdered in her home, then Rosemary Beale is found dead—all within an hour or so during the same night. Both are connected with the Austin Pearce Company. Jonathan Austin is the prime suspect for his wife's death as he had phoned Detective Inspector Judy Hill shortly before the murder. She suspects the call was a means to establish an alibi. But what of Mrs. Beale's death?

William McIlvanney

Laidlaw *Detective Inspector Jack Laidlaw*
London: Hodder, 1977.
New York: Pantheon, 1977.

Bud Lawson, a hard man known to the police for assaulting and almost killing someone, reports his eighteen-year-old daughter missing. She is found, raped and brutally murdered. Jack Laidlaw is given the task of interviewing the people involved while Detective Inspector Milligan is in charge of the routine part of the case. Detective Constable Harkness acts as a bridge between them, keeping the lines of communication open.

The Papers of Tony Veitch *Detective Inspector Jack Laidlaw*
London: Hodder, 1983.
New York: Pantheon, 1983.

Laidlaw is called to the hospital to hear the dying words of an old man. Eck Adamson is incoherent but in his jacket pocket is a paper with three names written on it. Laidlaw believes that Adamson was murdered. The only clue is the list, and one of the people on that list has ties to organized crime in Glasgow. Another is a rich woman, and the third name is that of a club.

Strange Loyalties *Detective Inspector Jack Laidlaw*
London: Hodder, 1991.
New York: Morrow, 1992.

Jack Laidlaw's brother Scott dies in what looks like an accident. While on a visit to his home Laidlaw discovers that Scott's wife is gone and that they had been separated before his death. Scott's life had been erratic before the accident and Jack wants to know more about what happened.

Joseph D. McNamara

The First Directive *Sergeant Fraleigh*
New York: Crown, 1984.
London: Collins, 1985.

Homicide sergeant Fraleigh and his team, Paul English and the Block, are assigned to the Lisa Stone case. Lisa, a member of a cult, has been kept from her father, or so he says. Now he is receiving threatening calls concerning her. There are parallels here with a ten-year-old missing-person case that resulted in the death of the victim. The new case leads Fraleigh directly into conflict with city officials, their politics, and the wealthy citizens of Silicon Valley.

Fatal Command *Chief of Police Fraleigh*
New York: Arbor, 1987.

Fraleigh is having an affair with the mayor's wife when he gets caught up in a messy situation concerning drugs, crooked cops, and murder. He calls in his working partners, the Block, Louis Robinson, and Paul English.

The Blue Mirage *Chief of Police Fraleigh*
New York: Ballantine, 1990.

The board of supervisors for Silicon Valley is to decide whether Fraleigh should remain chief of police. A few weeks before the big vote a major bust goes wrong and the S.W.A.T. team allows the drug dealer to escape. The man then shoots a cop, almost killing him, and the press goes wild. Meanwhile Fraleigh and his team are poised to arrest a defense attorney whose brother is on the board of supervisors. To complicate matters Fraleigh is having a raging affair with another member of the board. An active case brings Fraleigh to New York City where he must confront his past in order to meet his future.

Michael Malone*

Uncivil Seasons *Lieutenants Justin Savile*
New York: Delacorte, 1983. *and Cudberth "Cuddy" Mangum*

Cloris Dollard, wife of California state senator Rowell Dollard and aunt of Savile, is murdered and robbed in her home. All trails lead to a reopening of an old case in which Cloris's first husband died in a drowning accident. Joanna Cadmean, a clairvoyant, tells Justin that she fears for her life and soon she is dead. All the evidence points to Rowell Dollard.

Time's Witness *Chief of Police Cudberth "Cuddy" Mangum*
Boston: Little, Brown, 1989.

A sequel to *Uncivil Seasons*. At the very last second, George Hall, convicted murderer, is granted a stay of execution. The next day his brother is murdered. Cuddy is faced with opposition from the town's wealthy and powerful residents along with the Ku Klux Klan.

Anthony Mancini*

Talons *Lieutenant David Torino*
New York: Fine, 1991.

A golden eagle stalks human prey in the streets of Manhattan. Torino heads the investigation and uses the skills of falconer Raven Lokka to track the bird down.

Terry Marlowe

Target Blue *Sergeant Bill Clark*
New York: Putnam, 1991.

The entire Dallas police force is portrayed here as a working unit. Sergeant Bill Clark, in charge of the auto pound, finds the dead body of a young woman in one of the city's impounded cars. The woman had been tortured before her death. Meanwhile there is a drug war in the making and a new substance about to hit the market that will interfere with the Colombian cocaine trade. While this is going on there is a gang of young men who like to torture women and kill people for money, as well as a cop who becomes a druggie and sells out her fellow police officers.

Margaret Maron

One Coffee With *Lieutenant Sigrid Harold*
New York: Raven, 1981.

The art department of Vanderlyn College appears to be a hotbed of seething emotions. Art historian Riley Quinn has plenty of enemies so when he is poisoned Lieutenant Harold has lots of suspects to interview. Quinn had been working on a new book of art criticism and his reputation as a vicious critic led his colleagues to suspect that the new book would be devastating.

Death of a Butterfly *Lieutenant Sigrid Harold*
New York: Doubleday Crime Club, 1984.

Julie Redmond is found on her kitchen floor, the back of her head bashed in. Mother of a small boy, Redmond was also a blackmailer. The murder has taken place while unbeknownst to anyone on the third floor, someone sits and watches Redmond's apartment.

Death in Blue Folders *Lieutenant Sigrid Harold*
New York: Doubleday Crime Club, 1985.

Clayton Gladwell, a successful attorney, is murdered in his office. His personal files, which are kept locked in his desk, are dumped into a wastebasket and set on fire. The blue folders held cases involving important or prominent people. Harold discovers that Gladwell might have been engaged in some blackmail involving a mysterious actress of the Forties and Fifties, a millionaire looking for his missing grandson, a reclusive survivor of the Algonquin Round Table, and a wealthy, frail old man.

Baby Doll Games *Lieutenant Sigrid Harold*
New York: Bantam, 1988.

Five people in black tights and sweatshirts are dancing a Halloween fantasy on the stage of an improvisational theatre. The jack-o-lantern stationed high in a tree catches Emmy, who is dancing the role of a little ghost, soaring through the air to him. Then her tiny form is flung downward onto the spikes of an iron fence. In dying, the diminutive dancer Emmy Mion, the driving force of the troupe, becomes the focus of the investigation. This murder reopens the death of little Amanda Gillespie, killed earlier in the year on her way home from dance class.

Past Imperfect *Lieutenant Sigrid Harold*
New York: Crime Club, 1991.

Detective Mick Cluett, just sixty-one days short of being on the force forty years, is shot to death. Cluett had served under Sigrid Harold and just before his transfer he told her that he and her father had been partners. Thirty years before, Lief Harold was killed in the line of duty. Now it seems there was something funny about his death and Sigrid wants to know what. The trail leads to a bizarre character named Jerry the Canary, who lives on the street and knows more than he should.

Max Marquis*

Vengeance *Chief Inspector Ted Greening, Inspector*
London: Macmillan, 1990. *Harry Timberlake, and Detective*
Superintendent Charles Harkness

The Twelfth Man
New York: St. Martin's, 1992.

Titus Lloyd is run down and killed by an automobile. A burglar breaks into homes, stealing only the inexpensive goods and leaving the valuables. Chief Inspector Ted Greening is raked over the coals about his low rate of crime solving so he must find the thief. Then a local barrister is found with an ax buried in his head. Inspector Harry Timberlake discovers that the murder is a part of a series of killings, which leads him to work with Harkness of Scotland Yard in order to solve them.

J. J. Marric
(Pseudonym of John Creasey, q.v.)

Gideon's Day *Superintendent George Gideon*
London: Hodder, 1955.
New York: Harper, 1955.

Gideon of Scotland Yard
New York: Berkley, 1958.

Gideon's day begins with him in a towering rage—Detective Sergeant Eric Foster has been taking bribes and looking the other way when crimes are committed . Rape, murder, and a variety of robberies round out the twenty-four hours.

Gideon's Week *Commander George Gideon*
London: Hodder, 1956.
New York: Harper, 1956.

Seven Days to Death
New York: Pyramid, 1958.

Gideon's week involves a prison break in which nine men escape. He is asked to look into a murder case that appears to be open and shut, and London thieves are on a stealing spree.

Gideon's Night *Commander George Gideon*
London: Hodder, 1957.
New York: Harper, 1957.

Commander George Gideon likes to be an active, hands-on supervisor of the Criminal Investigation Department of New Scotland Yard so he works all hours of the day and night. During one of his night shifts a series of baby snatchings results in murder. A bad fog is rolling in and the "prowler" is out and about terrorizing young women. A gang rumble is about to occur, as is a series of warehouse break-ins. Gideon has his hands full.

Gideon's Month *Commander George Gideon*
London: Hodder, 1958.
New York: Harper, 1958.

Gideon's month begins with a missing child, a so-called accidental death that turns out to be murder, and a young wife who is kept prisoner and threatened with a knife by her mentally unstable husband.

Gideon's Staff *Commander George Gideon*
London: Hodder, 1959.
New York: Harper, 1959.

Gideon, long aware of a rise in the crime rate in metropolitan London, alerts the Home Office of the necessity to add more staff, not make cuts in order to stay within budget. A man named Ryman is planning the kidnapping of an infant, plus there is a robbery and the murder of two policemen committed simultaneously in order to demonstrate the inability of the police to be everywhere. Meanwhile someone is killing blonde, blue-eyed female children in Bournsea, and Gideon is filling in for the ailing Assistant Commissioner.

Gideon's Risk *Commander George Gideon*
London: Hodder, 1960.
New York: Harper, 1960.

John Borgman, who was nothing without his wife's wealth and influence, murdered her when she was three months pregnant. Now the police are sure he is set to kill his second wife and Gideon means to stop him. The Yard team also is faced with a number of car thefts committed by what looks like an organized gang.

Gideon's Fire *Commander George Gideon*
London: Hodder, 1961.
New York: Harper, 1961.

Eight people, five of them children and one a policeman, die in a fire in a tenement, set by a man who has burned down other slum properties. Scotland Yard CID is also looking into the brutal murder of a fourteen-year-old girl and trying to figure out an embezzlement case. While coping with crime in London, Gideon is faced with a crisis at home.

Gideon's March *Commander George Gideon*
London: Hodder, 1962.
New York: Harper, 1962.

London is to be the site of a high-level meeting between France, Germany, and the United States. Because the head of the uniform branch is ill, CID's Gideon is placed in charged of both branches, causing some hard feelings on the part of the second in command of the uniform branch. Not only do the police have to keep the dignitaries safe but they must worry about opportunists who will prey on the people who gather for the scheduled parade.

Gideon's Ride   *Commander George Gideon*
London: Hodder, 1963.
New York: Harper, 1963.

The female bus conductor is an eyewitness to an attack and robbery on a London bus, and can recognize the miscreant. But there is more trouble for the transportation system. People fall to their deaths from the subway platform; more assaults and robberies occur. Nevertheless, Gideon's plan to thwart the crime wave is met with skepticism on the part of the transit management.

Gideon's Vote   *Commander George Gideon*
London: Hodder, 1964.
New York: Harper, 1964.

The big news is a threat to blow up Parliament by the extremist group known as Fight for Peace, dedicated to stopping nuclear armament any way they can. The Quack, a man who impersonates a doctor in order to take liberties with female patients, is back in business. At this least convenient time Gideon has been ordered to take a vacation.

Gideon's Lot   *Commander George Gideon*
New York: Harper, 1964.
London: Hodder, 1965.

Juggling the kidnapping of a wealthy American's stepdaughter, a killing spree by a rapist-murderer, a fencing operation of stolen goods, and a big counterfeit money operation leaves Gideon little time to consider the offer to become Assistant Commissioner of Police.

Gideon's Badge   *Commander George Gideon*
New York: Harper, 1965.
London: Hodder, 1966.

The Gideons travel to New York on a luxury liner, sent there by Scotland Yard to coordinate an American/British attempt to stop crime. In London an accused killer is protesting his innocence. He is charged with nine poisoning deaths of housewives. Gideon is hesitant about leaving the case in Lemaitre's impetuous hands. Can he take over for Gideon and do the job right?

Gideon's Wrath *Commander George Gideon*
London: Hodder, 1967.
New York: Harper, 1967.

Vandalism in London's churches is increasing at an alarming rate and George Gideon must stop it. It looks as if someone is deliberately trying to embarrass the police, as well as damage the churches. There is also the matter of the photographer who takes pictures of young women in the nude.

Gideon's River *Commander George Gideon*
London: Hodder, 1968.
New York: Harper, 1968.

Scotland Yard is trying to find a young girl who has vanished. Crime is on the rise and the police are pushed to maximum effort. They are looking for a person or persons who beat up a man and left him for dead. Sir Jeremy Pilkington has decided to produce an extravaganza on the Thames. There will be a flotilla of boats carrying models wearing expensive clothing, furs, and jewelry. The event will be a police department's nightmare.

Gideon's Power *Commander George Gideon*
London: Hodder, 1969.
New York: Harper, 1969.

When an old furniture factory burns down, arson is suspected by Superintendent Lemaitre, who asks Gideon for assistance. Sixteen separate incidents of sabotage at London's power plants are causing Gideon to plant plainclothes policemen among the workers in order to catch whoever is responsible.

Gideon's Sport *Commander George Gideon*
London: Hodder, 1970.
New York: Harper, 1970.

It is a hot summer in London and Commander Gideon sees a trend in the rise of crime. The South African cricket team is about to tour England and there have been threats against them. Lemaitre, who is now the head of one of the toughest districts in London, believes there will be trouble and massive cheating at the English Derby. The English sports world appears to be under seige.

Gideon's Art *Commander George Gideon*
London: Hodder, 1971.
New York: Harper, 1971.

Five men are known to be capable of stealing art work from heavily guarded museums and all five are out of prison and in London at the time of a theft from a small Chelsea museum. Gideon is moving in on them when they start dying. He is convinced that each one has been murdered because each knew something about the theft of Velazquez's painting *The Prince*, stolen from the National Gallery. Then the daughter of a famous art collector is kidnapped.

Gideon's Men *Commander George Gideon*
London: Hodder, 1972.
New York: Harper, 1972.

The cases before Gideon are, as usual, the most difficult. The residents of the Notting Hill Gate district, where immigrants are being packed into dilapidated and dangerous housing, are in a mood that could errupt into rioting. There is a big post office robbery, a fraud case that has been going on for years, and the murder of a young woman. Rosamund Lee's death looks like a random killing until certain similarities begin to point to the Entwhistle case in which the husband of the murdered woman is now serving a life sentence.

Gideon's Press *Commander George Gideon*
London: Hodder, 1973.
New York: Harper, 1973.

Amid a dock strike about to turn ugly by a right-wing disturbance, the London press goes on strike as well, thus hampering the relaying of information to the public. The thing the police must do is convince the press that the country is in danger of being underminded as well as threatened by an organization called the "Strike Breakers." Continuation of problems with immigrants begun in *Gideon's Men*.

Gideon's Fog *Commander George Gideon*
New York: Harper, 1974.
London: Hodder, 1975.

During one of the worst fogs in recent memory Gideon sees a young man helping people across the street. While he is feeling good about the helpful youth, he comes back. The observant Gideon knows that he could not have guided the older person through the park and to safety in that short a time. Upon investigating he finds that a gang of young men is waiting not far off to attack people their comrade has led to them. During the fog an off-duty constable comes upon a wounded man in the same area where the gang had been operating. Close by, the body of a woman is found in the shrubbery. Now along with the robbery cases, his men must investigate a homicide.

Gideon's Drive   *Commander George Gideon*
London: Hodder, 1976.
New York: Harper, 1976.

Cases of food poisoning caused by contaminated eel, a vicious prison break, an escaped rapist, a series of hijacked produce trucks, a young woman dead in childbirth possibly caused by malpractice of the physician, and Gideon is in the middle of it all.

William Marshall

Yellowthread Street   *Detective Chief Inspector Harry Feiffer*
London: Hamilton, 1975.   *and the Yellowthread Street Police*
New York: Holt, 1976.

A missing husband from New Jersey believes his wife is lost wandering around the Yellowthread Street area in Hong Kong. No sooner did the police find the husband, then the wife managed to disappear. Feiffer is hunting a man who murdered his wife and her lover. Also a Mongolian who is extorting money from businesspersons in exchange for protection. This book introduces the wacky police at Yellowthread Street Station.

Gelignite   *Chief Inspector Harry Feiffer*
London: Hamilton, 1976.   *and the Yellowthread Street Police*
New York: Holt, 1977.

Letter bombs are being delivered without warning to a number of people, including a man who can neither read nor write. The post office is no help at all. It is up to the Yellowthread Street police to make sense out of the case.

The Hatchet Man   *Chief Inspector Harry Feiffer*
London: Hamilton, 1976.   *and the Yellowthread Street Police*
New York: Holt, 1977.

The Hatchet Man is shooting men who go to movies alone in the afternoon. The description of the murderer is that of an all-around average man. He could, in short, be anyone in Southeast Asia. The one clue Feiffer's team dredges up is that the Hatchet Man pays for everything in coins.

Thin Air   *Chief Inspector Harry Feiffer*
London: Hamilton, 1977.   *and the Yellowthread Street Police*
New York: Holt, 1978.

Harry Feiffer receives a call from an anonymous person who tells him that something bad will happen on board an airplane. The plane is recalled, and on landing it is discovered that all aboard, the crew and fifty-seven Japanese businessmen in the passenger section, are dead. Feiffer must wait until the terrorist (if that is what he is) calls again.

Skullduggery *Chief Inspector Harry Feiffer*
London: Hamilton, 1979. *and the Yellowthread Street Police*
New York: Holt, 1980.

The Yellowthread Street gang must delve into the past to discover why a raft arrives in Hong Kong containing the skeleton of a man who has been dead for twenty years. The dead man's teeth are traced to Putnam—a man who is still alive.

Sci Fi *Chief Inspector Harry Feiffer*
London: Hamilton, 1981. *and the Yellowthread Street Police*
New York: Holt, 1981

The All-Asia Science Fiction and Horror Movie Congress is going strong in Hong Kong and the Yellowthread Street holding cells are full of revelers. Into the midst of the convention comes a Spaceman who cremates things and people with a ray gun that acts like a flamethrower.

Perfect End *Chief Inspector Harry Feiffer*
London: Hamilton, 1981. *and the Yellowthread Street Police*
New York: Holt, 1983.

Six police officers have been executed at a precinct near Yellowthread Street. A typhoon is raging, and Feiffer is the only one close enough to get to the station. He and his team find unbelievable carnage, large claw marks on the walls, and a witness who swears that he saw a great cat leave the building.

War Machine *Chief Inspector Harry Feiffer*
London: Hamilton, 1982. *and the Yellowthread Street Police*
New York: Mysterious, 1988.

In the night the sound is like thunder but the Fireworks Man identifies it as gunfire. Then someone attacks the police station and a construction site next door. A Japanese warrior has returned to seek vengeance for acts committed during World War II.

The Far Away Man *Chief Inspector Harry Feiffer*
London: Secker and Warburg, 1984. *and the Yellowthread Street Police*
New York: Holt, 1984.

During a heat wave the Far Away Man strikes as a one-man killing machine. He never speaks, just fires one shot with precise aim. Each victim is found with an old cholera vaccination certificate on the body. Chief Inspector Harry Feiffer and Inspector Christoper O'Yee must track the illusive Far Away Man with no clues to his identity.

Frogmouth *Chief Inspector Harry Feiffer*
London: Secker and Warburg, 1987. *and the Yellowthread Street Police*
New York: Mysterious, 1987.

Someone kills animals at Yat's Animal and Bird Life Park and Children's Zoo. A sound like high-pitched screaming (dubbed the "Terror That Had No Name") is coming from a wall at the station and driving everyone crazy. And a Tibetan robs the same bank six times in two days.

Out of Nowhere *Chief Inspector Harry Feiffer*
New York: Mysterious, 1988. *and the Yellowthread Street Police*

All five passengers in a van are destroyed in a spectacular blaze following a car crash on a freeway. The medical examiner confirms that one of the passengers had shot another just before the impact. A Dalmation is bent on destroying an apothecary shop, and the police are also trying to find a ten-year-old who has a gun and is carrying it around Hong Kong.

Manila Bay *Lieutenant Felix Elizalde*
London: Secker and Warburg, 1986.
New York: Viking, 1986.

Violence and corruption surround the cockfighting business, and Mendez, Manila's prize fighting cock, is in the center of a murder investigation. Elizalde's squad is also looking into illegal bone hunting, and is on the trail of a bomb thrower and a thief who preys on people in air-conditioned taxis.

Whisper *Lieutenant Felix Elizalde*
London: Mysterious, 1988.
New York: Viking, 1988.

Investigating several bizarre murders, Elizalde must outwit the Whispering Man. The trail leads from the Gnome Home Acrobatic and One-Ring Sawdust Circus Café to a possible illegal trade in skeletons and then back to the diabolical Whispering Man, who turns his attention to Elizalde himself.

Faces in the Crowd *Detectives Vergil Tillman and Ned Muldoon*
New York: Mysterious, 1991.

Miss Lily, a young orphan, worked hard in a house of ill repute. Now she is dead and Tillman and Muldoon are outraged because her money and possessions were taken by the madame. From a crooked and affluent cop to the wealthy owners of New York's brothels, Muldoon and Tillman follow a trail that leads them into grave danger in early twentieth-century New York.

Ian Kennedy Martin*

Regan *Inspector Jack Regan*
London: Barker, 1975.
New York: Holt, 1975.

The Sweeney
London: Futura, 1975.

Patrolman Dennis O'Hagen is found leaning against a tree in California, shot between the eyes at close range. The San Francisco police trace a suspect to the airport where he flew to London. In England Eddie Mavor, driving his new Van Den Plas, races a high-powered Daimler through narrow country roads and wins. When he stops his car the passenger in the Daimler blows Eddie's head off with a shotgun. The San Francisco police department sends Lieutenant John Ewing to London to look for O'Hagen's murderer while Jack Regan is discovering he has one of his own and they may be the same person.

Regan and the Manhattan File *Inspector Jack Regan*
London: Barker, 1975.

The Manhattan File
New York: Holt, 1976.

Eti Awolwe, from Tibouti in North Africa, is murdered in his efficiency apartment in New York City. The gun jammed when fired so the murderer dropped it, ran to the kitchen for a knife, and finished the job. Fingerprints found at the scene belong to Salvatore Cimini, a lawyer for organized crime. London is asked to place two men under surveillance and Jack Regan gets the job. This case, which takes him to Manhattan, involves the FBI, organized crime, and $200 million in stolen military weapons.

Regan and the Deal of the Century *Inspector Jack Regan*
London: Barker, 1977.

The Deal of the Century
New York: Holt, 1976.

Sheikh Hamed bin Haffasa is blown away in his hospital bed. The assailant uses a submachine gun and calmly rides down in the elevator with the unsuspecting Regan. Regan has been assigned to what is clearly a special branch case. He believes the hit man to be foreign. When Regan finally stops being mad that he has been given the case, he begins to realize that the Assistant Commissioner wants an independent to handle the investigation—someone good, incorruptible—this is a big case with dangerous implications for all.

Lee Martin
(Pseudonym of [Martha] Anne [Guice] Wingate, q.v.)

Too Sane a Murder *Detective Deb Ralston*
New York: St. Martin's, 1984.
London: Quartet, 1986.

Deb Ralston, member of the Fort Worth Major Crime Squad, is called out on New Year's Day to investiage a multiple murder. Four adults and a four-year-old child have been shot, gunned down in their home. The owner's son, a longtime schizophrenic, is the most likely suspect.

A Conspiracy of Strangers *Detective Deb Ralston*
New York: St. Martin's, 1986.
London: Quartet, 1988.

Young women are disappearing from the Fort Worth area and only one thing links them—they are all pregnant. Deb Ralston finds one murdered. An abortion clinic is bombed and Deb's life may be in danger.

Murder at the Blue Owl *Detective Deb Ralston*
New York: St. Martin's, 1988.
London: Quartet, 1989.

As part of the series, this novel is not a real police procedural but more of a vintage mystery. Deb Ralston goes to a house party given by movie queen Margali Bowman. Ralston is looking forward to having a relaxing time but Bowman confides in Deb that someone is trying to kill her. She has been poisoned, her brakes have failed, and she has been shot at. When she is killed in the Blue Owl, a small private movie theater, Deb must assume her role of policewoman.

Hal's Own Murder Case *Detective Deb Ralston*
New York: St. Martin's, 1989. *and Chief of Police Alberto Salazar*

Sixteen-year-old Hal Ralston and his fifteen-year-old girlfriend, Lorie, hitchhike to Los Alamos to see the atomic energy museums. A girl is found brutally stabbed in Lorie's sleeping bag. Hal is arrested for the murder and Lorie is missing. Deb Ralston is made a special detective for the Las Vegas PD while she and Police Chief Alberto Salazar investigate.

The Mensa Murders *Detective Deb Ralston*
New York: St. Martin's, 1990.

A city employee dies in her bed of natural causes. When Ralston is routinely called in to look at the scene she knows something is wrong. The room is immaculate, everything spotless, unwrinkled. Soon there are three more victims, all belonging to a church run by Sister Eagle Feather and all members of Mensa.

Deficit Ending *Detective Deb Ralston*
New York: St. Martin's, 1990.

After a bank robbery that not only takes place with Deb Ralston and her three-month-old son present in the bank but results in the murder of a kidnapped teller, Ralston and Captain Millner begin piecing together clues. After another robbery they must look for the missing teller and the Fort Worth PD gets a big break.

Hacker *Detective Deb Ralston*
New York: St. Martin's, 1992.

Eric Huffman is murdered. He and his computer have been hacked to death. Deb Ralston, who should have been away enjoying a three-day rest, is the investigating officer. Deb discovers that her husband knew Huffman for years; they were in the same computer club and trying to find out who was spreading a virus over the local modems. Deb has a young man living in her home who could be a killer, and her son Hal's girlfriend lies in a coma in the hospital, a victim of a hit and run.

Edward Mathis[*]

Only When She Cries *Lieutenant Benjamin Cloud*
New York: Berkley, 1989.

Trinity Square, a small city between Dallas and Fort Worth, is harboring a dangerous sociopath who murders women. Spenser Price has a history of killing, beginning when he was very young and hurt animals. In time, he graduated to rape and assault, and then rape and murder. Lieutenant Cloud's homicide team races against time to find him—or is it a killer named Julian Arrowstone they are after?

Seicho Matsumoto*

Inspector Imanishi Investigates   *Inspector Imanishi Eitaro and*
New York: Kodansha, 1970.   *Detective Yoshimura Hiroshi*

The body of a man is found under a train where he had been placed after being strangled, then his face bashed in. Imanishi follows a complex trail of hints and facts that lead him to an incredible tale of several murders. This novel contains wonderful descriptions of Japanese manners, travel throughout the country, and the life of a policeman, as well as the juxtaposition of the old ways and the new, the city life versus the poor country existence, and the prosperous industrial town and the small resort.

Points and Lines   *Detective Jutaro Torigai*
New York: Kodansha, 1970.

A young waitress in a restaurant asks for a week's leave and then is seen boarding a train with a young man. Soon their bodies are found on a beach, dead of potassium cyanide poisoning.

Archer Mayor

Open Season   *Lieutenant Joe Gunther*
New York: Putnam, 1988.

A woman shoots a man who she believes has been making threatening phone calls to her. The man she shoots has been under the impression that he is going to the home of a person who has kidnapped his beloved dog. They were both on the jury for the Kimberly Harris murder trial three years before. It appears that they are the victims of an elaborate scheme for vengeance.

Borderlines   *Lieutenant Joseph Gunther*
New York: Putnam, 1990.

Joe Gunther goes to Gannett, Vermont, on special assignment with the Essex County State's Attorney. He finds a town divided by philosophical differences and intolerance between the oldtimers and the members of a religious cult, the Natural Order. After a fire in which two adults and three children die, Gunther, working with the state and local police, must also deal with several murders, one involving a longtime friend.

Henry Meigs

Gate of the Tigers *Inspector Tetsuo Mori and Robert Ludlow*
New York: Viking, 1992.

An American woman working in high tech computers dealing with artificial intelligence is killed in the middle of rush hour in the busy Tokyo train station. The woman was being followed by Inspector Mori and is killed right in front of him. The Russians and the Yakuza may be dealing in stolen computer technology. Mori and CIA agent Ludlow use every means at their disposal to find out why the woman was murdered.

James Melville

The Wages of Zen *Superintendent Tetsuo Otani*
London: Secker and Warburg, 1979. *and Inspector Jiro Kimura*
New York: St. Martin's, 1981.

The Foundation for East-West Understanding is a hodgepodge of Japanese and Americans under the guidance of a Zen Buddhist group. Money has poured into the foundation bank accounts but no cash has been spent. When one of the members is murdered Otani begins to check into all aspects of the foundation and learns that there may be a criminal element lurking in its background.

The Chrysanthemum Chain *Superintendent Tetsuo Otani*
London: Secker and Warburg, 1980. *and Inspector Jiro Kimura*
New York: St. Martin's, 1982.

David Murrow, a professor of English at Kobe University, is murdered in his garden. Otani, investigating the case, knows that he must tread lightly, as the dead man was British and a guest in Japan. It becomes increasingly clear, however, that Murrow may have had ties to local criminal elements.

A Sort of Samurai *Superintendent Tetsuo Otani*
London: Secker and Warburg, 1981. *and Inspector Jiro Kimura*
New York: St. Martin's, 1982.

After a bad earthquake during which Migisima, a newly commissioned office aide, saves Otani's life, they drive around the city to make sure the situation is under control. While driving, Otani hears a dog howling and they come upon the body of Richard Liebermann, a German businessman. There are one or two things that add up to very suspicious circumstances.

The Ninth Netsuke *Superintendent Tetsuo Otani*
London: Secker and Warburg, 1982. *and Inspector Jiro Kimura*
New York: St. Martin's, 1982.

Undercover, Otani goes to the Sweet Harmony Room in the Fantasia Hotel where a woman has been murdered. This is Kimura's case but Otani is troubled by it. In the murder room he and his wife, Hanae, find a beautifully carved Netsuke. It is very old and valuable and one of a set. Seven of the small figures are in the National Museum. One is in Otani's possession. But where is the ninth Netsuke?

Sayonara, Sweet Amaryllis *Superintendent Tetsuo Otani*
London: Secker and Warburg, 1983.
New York: St. Martin's, 1983.

Inspector Noguchi, in charge of drug control in the Hyogo Prefecture, uncovers the possibility of a new supplier of narcotics to the area. The unknown person is believed to be a foreigner, possibly British or American. The police send Patrolman Migishima undercover as a member of the Kabe Maid Service in order to have him in attendance at parties and social functions attended by prominent foreigners. When the Carradines give a farewell party for the Baldwins, both Migishima and Inspector Kimura are on the job. But Mrs. Baldwin is murdered and Otani's team must solve the crime without causing an international incident.

Death of a Daimyo *Superintendent Tetsuo Otani*
London: Secker and Warburg, 1984.
New York: St. Martin's, 1984.

The godfather of Japan's organized crime dies and the remaining leaders begin manuvering for a takeover. Otani is in Cambridge, England, when a murder is committed, and it is believed that Otani himself was the intended victim. In Japan the police are desperately trying to avert a full-scale war between the crime factions.

The Death Ceremony *Superintendent Tetsuo Otani*
London: Secker and Warburg, 1985. *and Inspector Jiro Kimura*
New York: St. Martin's, 1985.

During an elaborate tea ceremony presided over by the grand master and head of the House of Iemoto, someone shoots and kills the host. Otani and his wife, Hanae, are in attendance but see nothing to help the investigation. The shot could have been aimed at the British ambassador, who also was attending the tea ceremony. However, Otani's men begin to uncover people who had reasons to hate the Iemoto.

Go Gently, Gaijin *Superintendent Tetsuo Otani*
London: Secker and Warburg, 1986. *and Inspector Jiro Kimura*
New York: St. Martin's, 1986.

In a hot-spring resort an Arab male is shot to death in his bathtub. Another Arab is dead in a hit-and-run, and yet another has been accused of rape. An international group of students figures in the case as does the exclusive Arima Grand View Hotel.

Kimono for a Corpse *Superintendent Tetsuo Otani*
London: Secker and Warburg, 1987. *and Inspector Jiro Kimura*
New York: St. Martin's, 1988.

A large fashion show is arranged for Kobe and Otani and his men are there to provide security. But a chandelier falls in the middle of the visiting dignitaries and then a murder leads to the investigation that peels away the veneer of wealth and sophistication to demonstrate that greed and jealousy are the motivating forces in the realm of haute coutre.

The Reluctant Ronin *Superintendent Tetsuo Otani*
London: Headline, 1988. *and Inspector Jiro Kimura*
New York: Scribner's, 1988.

A building housing a company belonging to the Yakuza (Japanese organized crime) burns and in it is found the body of Marianna Van Wijk, a Dutch marketing assistant studying on a fellowship in Japan. Van Wijk's purse contains a photograph of Otani's grandchild and his son-in-law, Akira. When Akira disappears Otani is forced to remove himself from the investigation because suspicion has fallen on Akira as the chief suspect in the murder.

A Haiku for Hanae *Superintendent Tetsuo Otani*
London: Headline, 1989.
New York: Scribner's, 1989.

In a flashback, Otani remembers a case that took place in 1968 on the island of Awaji. An American missionary is killed in a Shinto shrine. The local police want nothing to do with the murder and Otani takes over only to find the charming town of Sumoto is not what it appears to be.

The Bogus Buddha *Superintendent Tetsuo Otani*
London: Headline, 1990. *and Inspector Jiro Kimura*
New York: Scribner's, 1991.

Keizo Hosoda, an aging crime boss, has made some bad mistakes, one of which has placed him in prison. Now he is out of prison at an inconvenient time and he must be taken care of. He disappears just as Otani becomes interested in his actions. At the same time Otani's sister-in-law is worried that something is wrong at an international summer workshop for academicians.

Jennie Melville*
(Pseudonym of Gwendoline Butler, q.v.)

Come Home and Be Killed *Detective Sergeant Charmian Daniels*
London: Joseph, 1962.
New York: London House and Maxwell, 1964.

The first Charmian Daniels mystery is not a true police procedural. A woman arrives home to find that her stepmother and sister are missing. Some very strange phone calls about them and the fear that something bad has happened causes her to call the police.

Burning Is a Substitute for Loving* *Sergeant Charmian Daniels*
London: Joseph, 1963.

Murderer's House* *Sergeant Charmian Daniels*
London: Joseph, 1964.

There Lies Your Love* *Sergeant Charmian Daniels*
London: Joseph, 1965.

Nell Alone* *Sergeant Charmian Daniels*
London: Joseph, 1966.

A Different Kind of Summer *Sergeant Charmian Daniels*
London: Joseph, 1967.

A coffin arrives in Deerham Hills by train. Inside is the body of a woman without head or hands. This victim is just one in a rash of missing women.

A New Kind of Killer, An Old Kind of Death *Sergeant Charmian Daniels*
London: Hodder, 1970.

A New Kind of Killer
New York: David McKay, 1971.

Charmian's old friend Alda Fearon has left the police force to become Lodging Officer at a university. Alda says that she is worried about a Peeping Tom and the next day she is dead of a brain hemorrhage. Charmian is at the University teaching and studying for a chance at promotion. Soon she is involved with a group of student activists, some angered by the Vietnam War, some with another agenda.

Murder Has a Pretty Face *Police Inspector Charmian Daniels*
London: Macmillan, 1981.
New York: St. Martin's, 1989.

While the Deerham Hills CID is dealing with a probable murder, the robbery of a furrier, and a stolen pedigree dog, a woman comes to town who makes everyone nervous. It is one year since the death of Rupert Ascham, Charmian's husband, and she is packing up his clothes when she finds a picture of her stepson, who vanished one day some years before.

Making Good Blood *Chief Superintendent Charmian Daniels*
London: Macmillan, 1989

Charmian Daniels is attacked on her way home from giving a talk at the Windsor Library. The same night a horse has its throat cut, and then the body of a woman is found, her throat slashed. Now Charmian is receiving threats.

Witching Murder *Chief Superintendent Charmian Daniels*
London: Macmillan, 1990.
New York: St. Martin's, 1991.

It is rumored that a group of women in Windsor make up a coven of witches. Most of the women are visitors of Miss Eagle, who lives next door to Charmian Daniels. When one of the women is murdered in what appears to be a ritualistic killing, Daniels, on sick leave, takes an unofficial but professional interest.

D. R. Meredith

The Sheriff and the Panhandle Murders *Sheriff Charles Timothy*
New York: Walker, 1984. *Matthews and Deputy Meanie*

Billy Joe Williams has seen and partially remembers something he should not have. Now he is dead on the highway after a crop duster sprays him with poison. After the second murder the wealthy citizens of Crawford County, a fictional spot in the Texas Panhandle, demand action.

The Sheriff and the Branding Iron Murders   *Sheriff Charles Timothy*
New York: Walker, 1985.   *Matthews*

The tornado struck hard and fast and Sheriff Matthews gets out to Angie Lassiter's place as fast as he can to make sure she is all right. While he is there, the cowhands find a dead man, Willie Russell, an artist who painted Western scenes and worked on the ranch. Matthews goes through torment when it becomes clear that Angie's younger brother, Johnny, may be the killer.

The Sheriff and the Folsom Man Murders   *Sheriff Charles Timothy*
New York: Ballantine, 1987.   *Matthews*

Deputy Raul Trujillo is accused of murdering his cousin. Enrique Armijo was an anthropologist and had been studying the cultural habits of the prehistoric Folsom Man, personified by a cult of people close to Clayton, New Mexico, who live without modern technology and have adopted the ways of the ancient culture. Armijo had sold his family's land without their permission. The murder weapon is found in Raul's motel room and he is arrested. The group of professionals working with Armijo and staying at the same motel is sure Raul is guilty but all have motives for wanting their colleague dead.

Hugh Miller

An Echo of Justice   *Detective Inspector Michael Fletcher*
London: Gollancz, 1990.
New York: St. Martin's, 1991.

Eyewitnesses say Sergeant Lowther was beaten and kicked to death by an enraged young man with a history of bad judgment. He is a patient of Kate Barbour, Fletcher's girlfriend. The police mount an all-out hunt for McMillan, the man believed to have been responsible for Lowther's death, and none is keener to find him than Sergeant Cullen, Fletcher's archenemy. Meanwhile, a criminal, Derek McKashill, has been brutally attacked while in prison. McKashill's father, needing to blame someone, decides it is all Fletcher's fault, for if he had not arrested Derek he would not be paralyzed today. Therefore, Fletcher must die.

Rex Miller*

Stone Shadow *Detective Jack Eichord*
New York: Onyx, 1989.

A killer kidnaps women, tortures them, repeatedly rapes them, and keeps them in chains.

Iceman *Detective Jack Eichord*
New York: Onyx, 1990.

Eichord is called in to work on a series of mutilation/sex murders in Blytheville, Arkansas. The victims have been tortured and raped, then murdered, dismembered, and beheaded.

John Minahan*

The Great Hotel Robbery *Detective John "Little John" Rawlings*
New York: Norton, 1982.

The Champs-Elysées, an exclusive hotel in Manhattan, is robbed of approximately $3.2 million in jewelry, negotiable bonds, and cash. "Little John" Rawlings follows the almost nonexistent clues from the Village to the Bronx until a double murder breaks the case wide open.

The Great Diamond Robbery *Detective John "Little John" Rawlings*
New York: Norton, 1984.

Tara Alvarad, photographer for the Heritage Gallery in New York, reports a possible robbery attempt. Rawlings learns that a friend has asked for all the specs on the gallery's security system. The diamond collection that is to be auctioned off at the gallery is worth between five and eleven million dollars. There are three suspects and Rawlings must check them out even if it means traveling to England.

The Face Behind the Mask *Detective John "Little John" Rawlings*
New York: Norton, 1986.

In one month there have been a number of robberies and rapes of women at home alone. "Little John" Rawlings is on the case but it becomes more than the ordinary when he gets an anonymous phone call telling him that the rapist is his brother.

The Great Pyramid Robbery *Detective John "Little John" Rawlings*
New York: Norton, 1987

Eight million dollars is stolen from a New York armored car company and Chief of Police Vadney wants the robbers at any cost. One of the thieves kills the other and leaves for Egypt with "Little John" Rawlings in pursuit. The chase that follows is a comedy of errors and culminates in the Great Pyramid of Cheops.

The Great Harvard Robbery *Detective John "Little John" Rawlings*
New York: Norton, 1988.

The Gutenberg Bible is stolen from its case in Widener Library, Harvard University. Commissioner Reilly of the New York Police Department is a Harvard graduate and he wants to help get the Bible back. John Rawlings is guarding Reilly because Chief Vadney believes he is in danger from a satanic cult. Then a threat comes from the robbers that a page of the Bible will be soaked in blood each day that the Harvard Corporation conducts business in South Africa.

The Great Grave Robbery *Detective John "Little John" Rawlings*
New York: Norton, 1989.

In 1966 the International Cryogenics Corporation was robbed of documents and vials of microorganisms valued at twenty-four million dollars. Rawlings traces clues from the twenty-two-year-old crime to Trinidad, Detroit, and Phoenix.

Kirk Mitchell

With Siberia Comes a Chill *Inspector John Kost*
New York: St. Martin's, 1990. *(Ivan Mikhailovich Kostoff)*

A patrolman answers a call concerning a man allegedly abusing his wife. When he arrives at the couple's residence, he is shot, along with the man and woman of the house. Something does not ring true to Inspector John Kost. The time is 1945, and a large delegation of foreign leaders is about to arrive in San Francisco for high-level end-of-the-war talks. A Russian agent arrives in town at the same time as a diplomat's wife with a secret.

Marcel Montecino*

The Crosskiller *Lieutenant Jack Gold*
New York: Arbor, 1988.
London: Bodley, 1988.

Los Angeles synagogues are being defaced by an anti-Semite. When

Lieutenant Gold shoots a robbery suspect he is removed from the prestigious homicide squad and given the innocuous task of finding the graffiti artist. The Crosskiller, as he is known once all of his antisocial tendencies come to the fore, is a violent sociopath whose crimes lead Gold into a world of corruption and prejudice.

David J. Murphy

Inspector Malone Sails In *Inspector Edward Malone*
London: Selwyn and Blount, 1947.

The body of Sergeant John Stroud is pulled from the Thames. Stroud had been beaten to a pulp and the case goes to Inspector Malone of the political branch at Scotland Yard. One of the problems facing the police is that there are too many people out of work, causing unrest to build. It looks like an organized group with political connections reaching to the Balkans is behind the agitation. The challenge for Malone is to figure out why Stroud was killed and what possible connection he had to Eastern European politics.

Stephen Murray*

A Cool Killing *Detective Inspector Alec Stainton*
London: Collins, 1987.
New York: St. Martin's, 1988.

Dr. Swainson, a consultant at Overden Hospital, is missing, but no one seems overly concerned. However, the day after his absence is reported to the police, his body is found in the refrigerator in the hospital mortuary. The doctor had been alive when he was put into the mortuary drawer, and he had taken some time to die.

Salty Waters *Detective Inspector Alec Stainton*
London: Collins, 1988.
New York: St. Martin's, 1989.

Tracy Ashford, a young woman who lived in partial disgrace because of posing seminude for a newspaper, is murdered. Stainton is vacationing at a small seaside resort when Tracy's body is pulled from the sea. Because the force is small and the town is in the regional district in which Stainton works, he is assigned the case.

The Noose of Time   *Detective Inspector Alec Stainton*
London: Collins, 1989.
New York: St. Martin's, 1989.

Justin Hamilton, a schoolmaster, is found hanging from a meat hook in his apartment. His arms and legs were bound and a hood placed over his head, making him look as if he had been executed. Once Stainton begins to investigate he turns up any number of people who wanted to kill Hamilton. The school where he taught caters to the upper classes, which gives the police a few stumbling blocks to overcome.

Fetch Out No Shroud   *Detective Chief Inspector Alec Stainton*
London: Collins, 1990.
New York: St. Martin's, 1990.

Andrew Hunter is researching a book on a group of South African pilots who were stationed in England during World War II. He goes to the now-abandoned Hartfield Park airfield where he hopes to find information but he is gunned down. Stainton must solve the murder and find the secrets the old airfield is hiding.

Fatal Opinions   *Detective Chief Inspector Alec Stainton*
London: HarperCollins, 1991.
New York: St. Martin's, 1992

After Kate Randall is murdered, Stainton realizes that she was right about someone trying to harm CAMEX (Campaign Against Medical Experimentation). She had brought her concerns to the Chief Inspector, who discounted them. It looks like the killer wants to draw attention away from where Kate worked, so her death is staged to look like an attempted rape/murder.

Ed Naha*

On the Edge   *Lieutenant Kevin Broskey*
New York: Pocket, 1989.

A young college woman is found tortured, raped, and murdered. The two detectives who are supposed to be investigating her background miss the fact that she was in a pornographic movie. The mayor of Bay City, California, launches an all-out attack on vice and the police department. Meanwhile, another college student is murdered who had also been in a porno film, and Lieutenant Kevin Broskey must solve the cases.

Razzle-Dazzle *Lieutenant Kevin Broskey*
New York: Pocket, 1990.

A teenager putting up political posters is attacked and thrown against the curb, splitting open his head. The posters were for the mayoral challenger, who is waging a vicious fight against the incumbent. Sergeant Amos Goldstein, forensics, who has answered the call, tries to stop the three men responsible for the attack and is mortally wounded when one of them blasts him with a shotgun. The case has political implications reaching right up to the mayor.

Cracking Up *Lieutenant Kevin Broskey*
New York: Pocket, 1991.

While driving around with a visiting actor who intends to play a cop in a new television show, Bay City police lieutenant Broskey responds to a call. A homeless man has been bashed to death and left under the pier. The mayor wants immediate action; the Chief pushes the case onto Broskey, who is still not recovered from the death of his partner.

Janet Neel*

Death's Bright Angel *Detective Inspector John McLeish*
London: Constable, 1988. *and Detective Sergeant Bruce Davidson*
New York: St. Martin's, 1989.

The body of a Yorkshire businessman is found in the London Edgeware district. McLeish finds himself attracted to Francesca Wilson, a member of the team sent from the Department of Trade and Industry to monitor the dead man's company. Something is not quite right and McLeish must find out what because Francesca appears to be involved in it.

Death on Site *Detective Chief Inspector John McLeish*
London: Constable, 1989.
New York: St. Martin's, 1990.

While on vacation, McLeish and his girlfriend, Francesca Wilson, see a rock climber fall. Alan Fraser had been hit on the head with loose rocks and Francesca believes she saw someone moving around above him just before the rocks came down. When they are back in London Fraser falls again, only this time he dies. McLeish suspects murder. This novel is not a strict police procedural as too much action takes place away from and outside of the usual workplace.

David Nemec

Mad Blood *Frank Reppa*
New York: Dial, 1983.

When convicted killer de Spirit comes up for parole, parole officer Frank Reppa finds himself reviewing the facts of the twelve-year-old Behrman-Moffett murder case. Reppa inadvertently stirs things up and a witness in the murder case is killed. Now the possibility of de Spirit being innocent is even stronger.

Christopher Newman[*]

Midtown South *Detective Joe Dante*
New York: Fawcett, 1986.

Coming out of deep cover is never easy for a cop. Joe Dante is greeted by hostile media and the need to explain a few bodies. All undercover personnel must be deprogrammed slowly, so the Police Commissoner decides to send Dante to New York's Tenth Precinct in Midtown South. He is to handle the case of a prostitute whose death was witnessed by a man with very good connections. Five years of undercover work have not prepared Dante for by-the-book cop Rosa Lasada, his new partner. More prostitutes are murdered and the case becomes highly visible.

Knock-Off *Sergeant Joe Dante*
New York: Fawcett, 1989.

Newly promoted Sergeant Joe Dante of Manhattan South Borough Command's Special Task Force is called in when a murdered man is found to be a well-known designer of women's clothes and the brother of Janet Lake, high-priced haute couture model. While Dante scrutinizes the fashion industry he discovers that more is going on here than he first suspects. Then an attempt is made on the life of Janet Lake and he must work fast.

Midtown North *Lieutenant Joe Dante*
New York: Fawcett, 1991.

Internal Affairs watchdog Warren Mott is found shot to death in an alley in Hell's Kitchen. Dante, as the new whip of the major crimes squad, is assigned the case even though he had been investigated by Mott five years before. When a drug pusher is found in possession of Mott's gun, the New York brass are jubilant at the easy solution to a sticky case. But Dante is a tenacious detective and he pursues the meager trail to a violent and stirring conclusion.

19th Precinct *Lieutenant Joe Dante*
New York: Fawcett, 1992.

A double murder, that of a millionaire Ralph Kane and his employee/lover, computer whiz Veronica Tierney, is caught by Dante and the major case squad. On his way to interview Kane's widow, Dante runs into Irish terrorist Billy Mannion, who, while fleeing, causes the death of the only child of a wealthy New Yorker. Dante voluntarily goes undercover to escape the inevitable suspension from the force that comes when the dead girl's father puts pressure on the mayor. Dante is being blamed for the girl's death and no one believes that an IRA killer is doing business in New York City.

Backfire *U. S. Treasury/Secret Service Agents*
New York: Fawcett, 1990. *Robert McElliott and Stan Torbeck*

McElliot and Torbeck are undercover keeping a protective eye on Assistant U. S. Attorney Marilyn Hunt, whose life has been threatened in connection with a case she is trying. When McElliot's grandfather, multimillionaire Michael Harrington, passes away, his death becomes the catalyst for an investigation into the botched abortion of a young woman in 1963 and the murders of several people close to the Harrington family.

Fridrikh Neznansky*

The Body in Sokoliniki Park *Alexander Borisovich "Sasha" Turetsky,*
New York: Bantam, 1987. *Junior Investigator, Konstantin Dmitriyevich "Kostya" Merkula, Serious Crimes Investigator, and Margarita N. Kolayevna "Rita" Shchastlivaya*

A man is found hanging in Moscow's Sokoliniki Park. It is quickly determined that he was dead before he was hanged. In another part of the city the man's lover, a ballerina, is shot by the same two men seen in the park prior to discovery of the first body. The KGB wants the case because they say the dead man was meeting an American journalist who is also a known spy. Young Sasha Turetsky and the prosecutor's office must work fast.

Kyotaro Nishimura

The Mystery Train Disappears *Inspector Totsugawa and*
New York: Debner, 1990. *Detective Sergeant Honda*
Tokyo: Shinchosha, 1982.

The mystery train leaves Tokyo and no one on or off the train knows its destination. On its way to Osaka the train with its 400 passengers disappears and soon the Japanese National Railroad (JNR) is asked for a ransom of one billion yen. Finding the train leads to murder and then the problem of locating the hostages.

Gil North*
(Pseudonym of Geoffrey Horne)

Sergeant Cluff Stands Firm* *Sergeant Caleb Cluff*
London: Chapman, 1960

The Methods of Sergeant Cluff *Sergeant Caleb Cluff*
London: Chapman, 1961. *and Detective Inspector Mole*

Jane Trundle is dead, her body found lying in the rain. Sergeant Cluff, although on leave, is called in because he is the only detective in the little village. Jane was the town's bad girl and no one except Cluff cares if her killer is found.

Sergeant Cluff Goes Fishing* *Sergeant Caleb Cluff*
London: Chapman, 1962.

More Deaths for Sergeant Cluff *Detective Sergeant Caleb Cluff*
London: Chapman, 1963.

The shop had been broken into, the safe opened, and £50 taken. Sergeant Cluff is looking for the burglar when the money turns up in the drawer of a table belonging to the shop owner. Then the arm of a woman is found and the police must find the rest of her.

Sergeant Cluff and the Price of Pity[*] *Sergeant Caleb Cluff*
London: Chapman, 1965.

The Confounding of Sergeant Cluff *Detective Sergeant Caleb Cluff*
London: Hodder, 1966.

Women are being stalked and attacked in the town of Gunnarshaw. The attacks get more violent until finally Mrs. Derrycraft is murdered.

A Corpse for Kofi Katt *Superintendent Kofi Katt*
London: Hale, 1978.

The seaport capital city of an African country where Superintendent Katt plies his trade is plagued with a series of muggings. A beggar, a man without family or friends, is found dead and Katt begins an investigation that leads him to a possible heroin smuggling operation and more death.

Jack O'Donnell

Box Nine *Detective Lenore Thomas*
New York: Mysterious, 1992.

Lenore Thomas is working undercover to snare a top drug lord but she is in way over her head. She is becoming a drug addict, is engaged in a dangerous relationship, and is ignoring the signs that her brother, Ike, is in serious trouble. The DEA comes to Quinsigamond carrying a small jar of a new designer drug (a major side effect of which is homicidal rage) about to hit the streets. Ike's problems at work could be related to the drug traffic in town but Lenore pays no attention until it is too late.

Lillian O'Donnell[*]

The Phone Calls *Police Officer Norah Mulcahaney*
New York: Putnam, 1971. *and Sergeant Joseph Capretto*
London: Hodder, 1972.

Women are receiving threatening phone calls and the only common thread is that they are all recent widows. Two of the women have been driven to suicide by the caller and their resulting feelings of guilt. Officer Mulcahaney works with the homicide team, finally acting as a decoy in an attempt to trap the killer.

Don't Wear Your Wedding Ring *Detective Norah Mulcahaney*
New York: Putnam, 1973. *and Sergeant Joseph Capretto*
London: Barker, 1974.

The decapitated body of a woman is found in a Manhattan hotel room. When she is identified as a wealthy housewife and mother from Long Island and discovered to be working as a high-priced call girl, the homicide squad must cut through the evasive answers given by her clients, all wealthy businessmen.

Dial 577 R-A-P-E *Detective Norah Mulcahaney*
New York: Putnam, 1974. *and Sergeant Joseph Capretto*
London: Barker, 1974.

Norah Mulcahaney is asked to help the daughter of a neighbor after the girl is raped on the back stairs of their building. Norah, as usual, gets personally involved in the case and continues to investigate even after she is reassigned. Following a few scant clues Norah learns that the suspect is a murderer as well as a rapist.

The Baby Merchants *Detective Norah Mulcahaney*
New York: Putnam, 1975. *and Lieutenant Joseph Capretto*
London: Bantam, 1976.

Desperate for a baby, Norah and Joe, now married, discover that they are unable to have children. When they begin the adoption process Norah cannot make sense of all the bureaucratic rules that go along with acquiring a child. Joe is handling a big case involving organized crime and heroin smuggling and the murder of a soldier in the Nerone crime family. Meanwhile Norah gets involved in a private adoption scheme.

Leisure Dying *Sergeant Norah Mulcahaney*
New York: Putnam, 1976.

The attack on an old man walking in Central Park focuses attention on the plight of the elderly as preyed-upon victims. Norah is given the go-ahead by Captain Felix to organize a task force concentrating only on crimes committed against old people. When the police get a confession from a seventeen-year-old who has killed several old ladies in their apartments, Norah feels quite proud of her work. The case collapses, however, and there are strong implications that Lieutenant Joseph Capretto, Norah's husband, has been negligent in his duties as the head of the homicide unit.

No Business Being a Cop *Sergeant Norah Mulcahaney*
New York: Putnam, 1978.
London: Hale, 1980.

First Katie Chave is killed by a bomb planted in Macy's department store.

Then Pilar Nieves is gunned down by a man she thought was a mugger. Next Audrey Ochs is garroted in an elevator. All three women have one thing in common—they were all cops. The homicide squad under the command of Captain James Felix is investigating, but the killings seem random, as if the one responsible has only one mission—to kill female police officers. The fourth killing gives Norah a clue to follow, but no motive.

The Children's Zoo *Sergeant Norah Mulcahaney*
New York: Putnam, 1981.
London: Hale, 1982.

The animals at the petting zoo in Central Park are slaughtered and the night watchman killed. Joe's niece, who has been staying with the Caprettos, is raped by a group of girls in school. Then a famous musician, who is paralyzed, is killed by someone using a baseball bat. Norah has more than she can handle so the special task force Joe oversees is called in to help. In the meantime Norah is trying to decide whether to accept an offer to join Lieutenant Felix and the special task force.

Cop Without a Shield *Sergeant Norah Mulcahaney*
New York: Putnam, 1983.

Joe Capretto is killed in the line of duty and Norah leaves the city to grieve. She finds that she is a policewoman wherever she is.

Ladykiller *Sergeant Norah Mulcahaney*
New York: Putnam, 1984.

A young woman is murdered in Central Park. Her throat has been cut and she has taken a long time to die. Sergeant Mulcahaney realizes they are looking for a repeater when she goes out to Far Rockaway where another young woman has had her throat cut. More women die and Norah must come to terms with the violence on the streets as well as with a man who wants to rule her every thought.

Casual Affairs *Lieutenant Norah Mulcahaney*
New York: Putnam, 1985.

Christina Isserman, a very wealthy woman, has a drinking problem. She is also very jealous of her husband. At a gala affair she drinks too much, argues with her husband, and goes home and continues drinking. In the morning she is comatose. It is determined that she took Valium. As this is the third time that she has consumed both drink and Valium, no one is suspicious except her sister, who goes to the police. Christina, lying in a coma in an exclusive private hospital, has the plug on her respirator pulled and now Norah comes into the picture.

A Private Crime *Lieutenant Norah Mulcahaney*
New York: Putnam, 1991. *and Captain Emmanuel*

In the middle of a schoolyard where a crafts bazaar is in progress a man with an AK-47 shoots and kills a young woman and her infant. The baby's carriage, which was to be examined by the laboratory, is signed out by someone using the name of one of Norah's trusted detectives. The carriage had been filled with cocaine. Randall Tye, talk-show host, prominent newsman, and the current man in Norah's life, begins an investigation on his own. Then he disappears.

Pushover *Lieutenant Norah Mulcahaney*
New York: Putnam, 1992.

A big-time movie star, now retired, is battered in her apartment and left for dead. Her ten-year-old grandson, who was visiting, is kidnapped. While searching for the boy Norah must also try to find the person responsible for the unrelated deaths of several women pushed under subway trains.

The Other Side of the Door *Detective Gary Reissig*
New York: Putnam, 1987.

Alyssa Hanriot, a teacher of music appreciation, is stabbed with a knife and left for dead in the basement of the school in which she teaches evening classes. It was her testimony that convicted Roy Easlick of child molesting. Now he is back, released from prison. Alyssa believes that Easlick is her attacker and the man responsible for the terrifying phone calls she has been receiving. Gary Reissig calls for assistance from Norah Mulcahaney, now a lieutenant and head of fourth zone homicide.

Freny Olbrich*

Desouza Pays the Price *Chief Inspector Frank Desouza*
London: Heinemann, 1979.

When a formal complaint is lodged to stop a cremation, Desouza must act. The body is that of the wife of the wealthy Mr. Shah, known as the Maharajah of Bombay. Religious prejudice is the backdrop for this tale of corruption and murder. Mrs. Shah had died of a knife wound to the spleen. She had been struck on the legs and back, but the coroner could not tell if the bruises were received at the same time as her death. To make matters worse her family was not informed of her death. All the information points to Mr. Shah as a murderer.

Desouza in Stardust *Chief Inspector Frank Desouza*
London: Heinemann, 1980.

The famous Indian film star Sanjiv Saboonder was thrown over his balcony and he died at the bottom of a cliff. It is up to Desouza and his crew to prove whether Saboonder committed suicide or was murdered. The people who found the body moved it to the house, thus destroying the crime scene.

D. J. Olivy

Never Ask a Policeman *Acting Detective Superintendent Ken Hollis*
London: Gollancz, 1970.
New York: Coward, McCann, 1970.

Miss Dracott is murdered and Sheila Yates, a young woman Hollis knows, is accused of harassing and terrorizing her. Yates is fired from her job as a result and shortly thereafter commits suicide. But something does not ring true for Hollis so he begins an investigation even if it means going against the direct orders of his superior officer at Scotland Yard.

Jack Olsen[*]

Night Watch *Watch Commander Lieutenant Packer Lind*
New York: Times Books, 1979.

Lieutenant Packer Lind, night watch commander, goes out on a call. A woman is down, a possible murder and rape. The woman has been strangled, and forced to drink acid. The story involves a number of police personnel working the night shift. As they look for the acid murderer, more killings occur.

Paul Orum

The Whipping Boy *Detective Inspectors Jonas Morck*
London: Gollancz, 1975. *and Knud Einarsen*

Scapegoat
New York: Pantheon, 1975.

A young nurse is murdered while answering a midnight call for help not far from her home in Vesterso, West Jutland. Since her face has been battered and the local police have little experience with homicide, the Copenhagen Flying Squad is called and Morck and Einarsen do the investigating. The village is small but people there are more complicated than they appear to be at first.

Nothing But the Truth *Detective Inspectors Jonas Morck*
London: Gollancz, 1976. *and Knud Einarsen*
New York: Pantheon, 1976.

Alcoholic newspaper reporter Peter Magnussen is found floating in the ocean off the coast of Denmark. Morck is called to a small coastal town to handle the investigation. This is another tale of complex people with secrets to hide.

Jerry Oster[*]

Internal Affairs *Sergeant Joe Cullen*
New York: Bantam, 1990.

Newly appointed NYPD police commissioner Charles Storey supposedly dies in an apartment building fire. He was already dead, however, shot in the chest, his middle finger cut off and placed in his mouth. On the wall of Storey's apartment the word "Raleigh" is written. The Raleigh was the scene of another fire where a social worker died. Joe Cullen of Internal Affairs is assigned the task of solving the murder and determining whether political corruption is connected with the case. He must also baby-sit Storey's movie star sister, who just happens to be an old girlfriend of Cullen.

Sweet Justice *Lieutenant Jacob "Jake" Neuman*
New York: Harper, 1985. *and Sergeant Robert Redfield*

A young man, a television star, a drug dealer, and a feminist author are all killed. It becomes apparent that the killer has inside information on what the police are doing, and during one of the attacks identifies himself as a cop. This book came out at the same time as the Bernard Goetz killing on the New York subway and was quickly described as fiction anticipating reality.

Nowhere Man *Lieutenant Jacob "Jake" Neuman*
New York: Harper, 1987.

While running in Greenwich Village a man is gunned down. He has no identification on him, just a lottery ticket, which is stolen by a garage attendant. Next, the star in a new play is murdered in her dressing room. Her name appears on a list of women who may have been marked for death by a now-dead serial killer. Lieutenant Jake Neuman comes out of retirement to head the investigation and soon has another murder on his hands.

Club Dead *Lieutenant Jacob "Jake" Neuman*
New York: Harper, 1988. *and Lieutenant David Milner*

Frances McAlistair is the shining star on the federal prosecutor's staff. However, she is in a world of trouble when reporter Charles Ives falls from her penthouse terrace. Ives was there to interview McAlistair for his newspaper. The case, a potential time bomb and certainly one of high visibility, is given to two lieutenants who dislike each other—Neuman and Milner.

Saint Mike *Susan Van Meter*
New York: Harper, 1987.

Narcotics agent Paul Van Meter is shot while in a cab. His bosses believe he went rogue while in deep cover. His wife, Susan, who works in the research department of the office, is offered the job of finding the woman who killed him. Susan must solve the murder of her husband while trying to maintain a good relationship with her daughter, who fears that Mom will die as well.

T. Jefferson Parker*

Laguna Heat *Detective Tom Shephard*
New York: St. Martin's, 1985.
London: Bodley, 1986.

His career as a policeman in Los Angeles in ruins, Tom Shephard returns home to makes some sense of his life. The only homicide detective on the tiny Laguna Beach police force, he must investigate when several of the more prominent townspeople are burned to death.

James Patterson*

The Midnight Club *Lieutenant John Stefanovitch*
New York: Little, Brown, 1989. *and Detective Isaiah Parker*

Crime lord Alexandre St.-Germain, the Grave Dancer, has ruled the criminals of the world's major cities by a strict code of street law. Stefanovitch, in an attempt to break St.-Germain, plans a major drug bust, but instead walks into a trap, which places him in a wheelchair and kills his wife. A year later someone begins killing the leaders of the criminal world one by one; the mysterious Midnight Club just might be the key to what is going on.

Paul Patti

Silhouettes *Lieutenant Andy Amato*
New York: St. Martin's, 1990. *and Sergeant Gabrielle Amato*

A double homicide—an old man found executed in his bed and the killer murdered in his car—leads the Amatos on a hunt that involves protected witnesses of the FBI. It becomes increasingly obvious that someone with inside knowledge is systematically killing these witnesses.

Barbara Paul*

You Have the Right to Remain Silent *Sergeant Marian Larch*
New York: Scribner's, 1992. *and Detective Foley*

Four men are found in NYC's East River Park. They were all executed, shot once in the right eye. Sergeant Larch must juggle the investigation, interference by her boss, Captain De Falco, and a possible takeover of the case by either the major crimes unit or the FBI.

Laurence Payne*

The Nose on My Face *Chief Inspector Sam Birkett*
London: Hodder, 1961. *and Sergeant Saunders*
New York: Macmillan, 1961.

Twenty-one-year-old Ursula Twist is found lying on her bed shot to death. Her mother, who was at home at the time, found the body. Chief Inspector Birkett and Sergeant Saunders of Scotland Yard follow a trail of drug addiction and nymphomania to a private club where Birkett meets a former opera diva, who later disappears, and a TV personality once friendly with Ursula and later murdered.

Michael Pearce

The Mamur Zapt and the Return of the Carpet *Captain Gareth*
London: Collins, 1988. *Cadwallader Owen*
New York: Doubleday Crime Club, 1990

It is 1908 and Cairo, Egypt, is the scene of an important Islamic festival, the Return of the Holy Carpet from Mecca. It is feared that a major terrorist attack is planned to ruin the festival. An assassination attempt is made and the head of Mamur Zapt (the Political Criminal Investigation Department) is given the unenviable task of finding, then stopping the group.

The Mamur Zapt and the Night of the Dog *Captain Gareth*
London: Collins, 1989. *Cadwallader Owen*
New York: Doubleday Crime Club, 1991.

Tensions are rising in Cairo between the Copts, the direct descendants of the ancient Egyptians, and the Islamic majority. When a dead dog is placed in the doorway of the tomb of an important Copt, Owen believes that someone is out to start trouble. At the same time an English member of Parliament and his attractive niece, Jane Postlethwaite, are complicating the personal life of the Mamur Zapt. Then a Muslim dervish is murdered with Jane the only witness.

The Mamur Zapt and the Donkey-vous* *Captain Gareth Cadwallader Owen*
London: Collins, 1990.
New York: Mysterious, 1992.

Ridley Pearson

Undercurrents *Sergeant Lou Boldt*
New York: St. Martin's, 1988.
London: Joseph, 1989.

Sergeant Lou Boldt of the Seattle homicide squad is pursuing the serial killer known as the Cross Killer, who has been terrorizing the city for six months. The body pulled from Puget Sound bears the destinctive trademarks of the Cross Killer but something is wrong: the method is very sloppy. Boldt, using the expertise of a police psychologist, pieces together a scenario that leads him to a solution and a murderer.

Probable Cause *Detective Sergeant James Dewitt*
New York: St. Martin's, 1990.
London: Macdonald, 1991.

Sergeant James Dewitt was once a forensic scientist. Now, as a detective sergeant on the Carmel police force, he looks at the body of a man dead from carbon monoxide poisoning. It looks like suicide but Dewitt has a funny feeling about it. There are several other deaths that appear to be suicide but Dewitt's previous hunch and his forensic training lead him into a full homicide investigation.

Hard Fall *Special Agent Cameron Daggett*
New York: Delacorte, 1992.

A terrorist is called in to destroy the 959, an airplane used in flight simulations and training sessions. The same group is responsible for the death of Daggett's wife and the crippling of his young son. The plot follows Daggett as he makes contact with police department forensic investigators and other FBI agents.

Dave Pedneau

A.P.B.[*] *Whit Pynchon, Special Investigator*
New York: Ballantine, 1987. *for the District Attorney*

D.O.A. *Whit Pynchon, Special Investigator*
New York: Ballantine, 1988. *for the District Attorney*

When a mother is found bathing the body of her dead daughter, the police of Milbrook assume she is the murderer. D.A. Danton and his special investigator, Whit Pynchon, recognizing that something is clearly wrong, take the woman to the hospital. Emergency room physicians find a bullet lodged at the base of her skull. She had been shot at the time of her daughter's death. The wound has developed a massive infection but if she survives, she will be able to talk in a week. Meanwhile, Pynchon must find the person who intended to murder her and why.

B.O.L.O *Whit Pynchon, Special Investigator*
New York: Ballantine, 1989. *for the District Attorney*

Two state patrolmen, two drug dealers, a woman, and a small infant are massacred on a lonely mountain road in Raven County, West Virginia. Whit Pynchon's investigation for the D.A. is hampered by the hatred the other police officers have for Whit, the interference of the brother of the two dead drug dealers, and by Anna Tyree, editor of the town newspaper, whose investigative techniques lead her directly into danger.

A.K.A.: Also Known As *Whit Pynchon, Special Investigator*
New York: Ballantine, 1990. *for the District Attorney*

Whit Pynchon's ex-wife, Julia, is the college librarian. Julia switches her schedule with another staff member and the woman is killed by an avalanche of heavy books falling from the second floor of the library. The real target is Whit himself and in order to get to him the murderer kidnaps Whit's live-in girlfriend, Anna Tyree, and his daughter.

B & E: Breaking and Entering *Whit Pynchon, Special Investigator*
New York: Ballantine, 1991. *for the District Attorney*

In the course of a residential breaking and entering the man of the house is stabbed, and the policeman responding to the call is gunned down. Pynchon finds a chaotic crime scene and the new chief of police in charge. And it looks as if firearm theft in and around Millbrook has become big business.

N.F.D. *Whit Pynchon, Special Investigator*
New York: Ballantine, 1992. *for the District Attorney*

District Attorney Tony Danton sends Pynchon to Myrtle Beach to intercept a man he believes kidnapped his young daughter. Pynchon finds that there has been a murder involving the father, Willie Winters. One of Marcia Winters's classmates says she saw a clown steal her. Then another child is threatened.

Anne Perry*

The Face of a Stranger *Inspector William Monk*
New York: Fawcett, 1990.

After a nasty accident in a hansom, William Monk of Scotland Yard comes to in the hospital with no memory of his previous life or what he was doing in the cab. When he returns to work he does not tell his boss, Runcorn, that he has amnesia. Runcorn gives him a six-week-old murder case, which causes Monk personal terror and a change in personality. The principal investigator, he also finds that he is the prime suspect for the murder.

Dangerous Mourning *Inspector William Monk*
New York: Fawcett, 1991.

The murder of the widowed daughter of the influential Sir Basil Moidore rapidly becomes a complicated affair when Monk shows that no one could have entered the house the evening of her death. Someone living in the Moidore residence is guilty but the Victorian social structure and conventions stop the police from using forceful and effective means to find the murderer. The family is not above pointing fingers at the dead woman, and the footman becomes the likely suspect. Monk thinks otherwise but is unable to stop another death.

Defend and Betray *Inspector William Monk*
New York: Fawcett, 1992

General Thaddeus Carlyon has returned to England after a brilliant military career spent mainly in India. While attending a dinner party, Carlyon falls over a bannister onto a suit of armor, a part of which pierces his body, killing him. The police believe his death is an accident until Carlyon's young wife confesses that she killed him, while offering no other details. This series, which began by focusing on Monk, now widely includes sleuthing by nurse Hester Latterly and the legal machinations of barrister Oliver Rathbone.

Gerald Petievich[*]

One-Shot Deal *Charles Carr, Treasury Agent*
New York: Harcourt Brace, 1981.

Someone has stolen sheets of security paper in preparation for printing ten million dollars in treasury notes. Treasury agent Charles Carr is sent to Los Angeles to find out what the forgers' next move will be.

To Die in Beverly Hills *Charles Carr, Treasury Agent*
New York: Arbor, 1983.

Treasury agent Charles Carr, in an ongoing organized crime investigation, begins to suspect that a cop or cops are responsible for a number of burglaries. As he sifts through the sleaze of the oh-so-glamorous and wealthy he must walk a tightrope between his boss, who does not want him to antagonize anyone, and the rogue policemen who are just waiting for him to make a mistake.

The Quality of the Informant *Charles Carr and*
New York: Arbor, 1985. *Jack Kelly, Treasury Agents*

Paul LaMonica is a high-priced forger and he is setting himself up to make $50,000 in traveler's checks. Treasury agent Charles Carr is working with a female informant who turns LaMonica in. As soon as LaMonica posts bail he murders the woman. Carr and Kelly find that the forger is a far more cunning criminal than they first thought.

Earth Angels *Detective Sergeant Jose Stepanovich*
New York: NAL, 1989.

A new police unit (C.R.A.S.H.) is formed to combat gang-related violence. Three detectives and one sergeant form the group. The nature of their work takes them to the backstreets of the barrio. The gangs of East LA are tough and soon the C.R.A.S.H. unit officers are responding in kind.

Tom Philbin*

A Precinct Siberia Novel: Cop Killer *Felony Squad Commander*
New York: Fawcett, 1986. *Joe Lawless*
London: Sphere, 1990.

Crime never ceases at Fort Siberia, the Bronx, and Joe Lawless's felony squad is working hard to keep abreast of it. A cop—ruthless, aggressive, womanizing, and on the pad (taking money from civilians)—is shot in the hallway of a tenement and left to die in a pile of dog feces. George Benton, a detective with a number of personal problems, is given three assault cases involving the robbery of old people in the precinct. Piccolo and Edmunton are working on a missing baby case as well as looking for a team of robbers. Lawless keeps his eye on all of the cases.

A Precinct Siberia Novel: Street Killer *Felony Squad Commander*
New York: Fawcett, 1989. *Joe Lawless*

Jimmy Toolan is the leader of a vicious gang engaged in crimes ranging from drugs to murder. Jerry Collins is in jail but wants to cut a deal with the authorities. He has been convicted of murder, but protests his innocence. He wants to get even with Toolan, whom he blames for his plight; now all the police have to do is keep Collins alive long enough to testify against Toolan. The felony squad is also faced with an obscene phone caller and a very strange case in which superstition has caused death. And Joe Lawless is in charge of it all.

A Precinct Siberia Novel: Death Sentence *Felony Squad Commander*
New York: Fawcett, 1990. *Joe Lawless*

As Joe Lawless looks for a bomber who wants to destroy all abortion clinics, detectives Piccolo and Stein are out to bust an interstate car-and-truck-stealing operation. Detective Barbara Babalino hunts for a vicious rapist, and the precinct is its usual violent self.

Robert Pike
(Pseudonym of Robert L. Fish, q.v.)

Mute Witness *Lieutenant Clancy*
New York: Doubleday, 1963.
London: Deutsch, 1965.

Bullitt
New York: Avon, 1968.

Johnny Rossi, the head of organized crime on the West Coast, is in New York City waiting to testify before the State Crime Commission. It is not known why Rossi chose to come east to give evidence. Lieutenant Clancy is ordered to guard him around the clock, but there is a slip-up in procedure: Rossi fakes being sick and the detective guarding him inadvertently admits a hit man, who shotguns Rossi and the police. The assistant district attorney blames Clancy, but Clancy knows something has not been right from the beginning.

Quarry* *Lieutenant Clancy*
New York: Doubleday, 1964.
London: Deutsch, 1965.

Police Blotter *Lieutenant Clancy*
New York: Berkley, 1965.
London: Deutsch, 1966.

A man falls or jumps in front of a subway train. Another man is beat to death in his apartment, and a policeman is attacked in Central Park. When Lieutenant Clancy investigates the subway case, he realizes that the dead man is not someone likely to commit suicide.

Reardon *Lieutenant James Reardon*
New York: Doubleday, 1970. *and Sergeant Dondero*

It seems like an open-and-shut case. Ralph Crocker killed a man with his car. The man had walked out in front of the moving vehicle and Crocker could not stop in time. Yet Reardon senses something is wrong and begins finding little things that do not add up. Meanwhile weapons are being smuggled into San Francisco.

The Gremlin's Grandpa* *Lieutenant James Reardon*
New York: Doubleday, 1972.

Bank Job *Lieutenant James Reardon*
New York: Doubleday, 1974.
London: Hale, 1975.

In the course of a bank robbery a policeman comes upon the thieves and they kill him. Lieutenant Reardon knows that one of the robbers has been wounded but there is little else with which to work. The case becomes very complicated as the police realize that the perpetrators are either professional thieves or very skilled first-timers.

Deadline 2 A.M. *Lieutenant James Reardon*
New York: Doubleday, 1976.
London: Hale, 1977.

On the last day of Sergeant Mike Holland's career as a policeman he is kidnapped from his own driveway. Jim Reardon can find no reason why Holland was chosen. He is being held hostage, to be exchanged for a prisoner named Guillermo Lazaretti. When Lazaretti was arrested he was carrying a knife and gun, and because it is illegal for aliens to bear arms, he is now awaiting extradition to Italy. Reardon must find why Lazaretti is important enough for someone to go to all this trouble.

Joyce Porter

Dover One *Detective Chief Inspector Wilfred Dover and*
London: Cape, 1964. *Detective Sergeant Charles Edward MacGregor*
New York: Scribner's, 1964.

Juliet Rugg, maid and mistress to Sir John Counter, is missing. Dover and MacGregor are sent to Creekshire Creedon where they meet an extraordinary group of suspects. Rugg was happy to entertain men and may not have been above a little blackmail. Then comes the ransom note.

Dover Two *Detective Chief Inspector Wilfred Dover and*
London: Cape, 1965. *Detective Sergeant Charles Edward MacGregor*
New York: Scribner's, 1965.

Isabel Slatcher is shot in the head and left for dead. She lingers for eight months in the hospital before she dies. Dover begins the investigation only to find that Isabel may have been smothered in her hospital bed. Are there two murderers or one? And does the fact that Protestants and Catholics are warring in the town of Curdley have anything to do with Isabel's death?

Dover Three *Detective Chief Inspector Wilfred Dover and*
London: Cape, 1965. *Detective Sergeant Charles Edward MacGregor*
New York: Scribner's, 1966.

The village of Thornwick is in the grip of a poison-pen writer. The letters are full of dirty language and every woman in the town except one has been a recipient. Then Dover and MacGregor are sent to Thornwick as a result of a bit of string pulling by the local grande dame. But things are bleaker than at first glance as a young schoolteacher commits suicide. Then another woman takes a whole bottle of sedatives and dies.

Dover and the Unkindest Cut of All *Detective Chief Inspector Wilfred*
London: Cape, 1967. *Dover and Detective Sergeant Charles*
New York: Scribner's, 1967. *Edward MacGregor*

The Dovers are on holiday. As they are driving along in a pouring rainstorm Mrs. Dover sees a man go over a cliff. He is a policeman and the nephew of the local chief constable. On the chief constable's insistence, Dover has to stay to conduct an investigation and naturally MacGregor is dragged into the fray. There is a matter of an unsolved murder that may be the motivating force behind the young policeman's death.

Dover Goes to Pott *Detective Chief Inspector Wilfred*
London: Cape, 1968. *Dover and Detective Sergeant Charles*
New York: Scribner's, 1968. *Edward MacGregor*

Dover and MacGregor go to Pott to investigate the brutal murder of Daniel Wibbley, the town's chief citizen. Dover settles on the wrong suspect as usual and MacGregor painstakingly follows clues.

Dover Strikes Again *Detective Chief Inspector Wilfred*
London: Weidenfeld, 1970. *Dover and Detective Sergeant Charles*
New York: McKay, 1970. *Edward MacGregor*

The little town of Sully Martin has had a run of bad luck—first an earthquake, then a murder, which Scotland Yard has sent Dover to investigate. When Dover discovers that there is no whiskey to be had in the village, he turns particulary nasty. His accommodations turn out to be a disaster, and none of the villagers will talk to him about the murder victim, who was the town busybody. Dover lets MacGregor do most of the work, while he mostly lies in bed resting and complaining; yet he himself solves the crime.

It's Murder with Dover *Detective Chief Inspector Wilfred*
London: Weidenfeld, 1973. *Dover and Detective Sergeant Charles*
New York: McKay, 1973. *Edward MacGregor*

The murder at Beltour, the stately home of Lord Crouch, finds Dover and MacGregor investigating. Dover, who is staying at the mansion, does nothing but complain. MacGregor, much better placed in town, has an opportunity to observe firsthand the numerous suspects, virtually conducting the investigation alone.

Dover and the Claret Tappers   *Detective Chief Inspector Wilfred*
London: Weidenfeld, 1977.   *Dover and Detective Sergeant Charles*
Woodstock, VT: Foul Play, 1989.   *Edward MacGregor*

A gang calling themselves the Claret Tappers kidnaps Dover. They want the release of two prisoners and a large sum of money. Much to their surprise, Scotland Yard is not going to give anything to get Dover back, which comes as a shock to Dover as well.

Dead Easy for Dover   *Detective Chief Inspector Wilfred*
London: Weidenfeld, 1978.   *Dover and Detective Sergeant Charles*
New York: St. Martin's, 1979.   *Edward MacGregor*

The discovery of an unidentified body of a young, pregnant woman dismays the people of Frenchy Botham. The chief constable calls in Scotland Yard, and Dover and MacGregor are dispatched. The girl's skull was crushed, and it is difficult finding someone who knows her as she is not a local. Dover works hard on this one as the very lucrative job of security chief for Pomeroy Chemicals Limited is open and he wants it badly. He and MacGregor find the small village of Fenchy Botham to be a hotbed of secrets, problems, and strange people but Dover just steamrolls over them all to his solution.

Dover Beats the Band   *Detective Chief Inspector Wilfred*
London: Weidenfeld, 1980.   *Dover and Detective Sergeant Charles*
Woodstock, VT: Foul Play, 1991.   *Edward MacGregor*

The naked body of a murdered man is discovered in the Muncaster municipal dump. The search into who he is leads Dover and MacGregor straight into a special branch operation investigating a violent cult.

Maurice Procter[*]

The Chief Inspector's Statement   *Detective Chief Inspector Philip Hunter*
London: Hutchinson, 1951.

The Pennycross Murders
New York: Harper, 1953.

Eight months ago the mutilated body of a little girl was found in a wooded area just outside the small village of Pennycross. Now another child is missing and Chief Inspector Hunter has been sent to the village to head the investigation. Focus soon narrows on several of the townsmen.

I Will Speak Daggers *Detective Superintendent Philip Hunter*
London: Hutchinson, 1956.

The Ripper
New York: Harper, 1956.

The Ripper Murders
New York: Avon, 1957.

Janey Elliott stopped her car in narrow Frog Lane. Someone approached her, slit her throat, stabbed her several times, cleaned the knife on her skirt, and left. The Yarborough police call in Scotland Yard. Hunter finds that Mrs. Elliott's dog is missing and the friends she had visited on the night of her murder are acting strangely.

The Pub Crawler *Detective Inspector Robert Fairbrother*
London: Hutchinson, 1956.
New York: Harper, 1957.

Rookie policeman Bill Knight is sent to Champion Road, a squalid area of Airechester to live undercover. He works as a laborer in the Champion Foundry, but is keeping an eye out for illegal betting operations. Then Sam Gilmour, owner of the Starving Rascal, the area lounge, is murdered and robbed of his fine gold coin collection.

Hell Is a City *Detective Chief Inspector Harry Martineau*
London: Hutchinson, 1954.

Somewhere in this City
New York: Harper, 1954.

Murder, Somewhere in this City
New York: Avon, 1956.

The Granchester police are looking for a murderer. He is vicious and now well hidden in Granchester. His one aim in life is to kill Martineau.

The Midnight Plumber *Detective Chief Inspector Harry Martineau*
London: Hutchinson, 1957.
New York: Harper, 1958.

The Granchester police are faced with finding a gang of well-organized burglars. They have stolen a fortune in money and jewelry and have so terrorized their victims that no one will give the detectives any information.

Man in Ambush *Detective Chief Inspector Harry Martineau*
London: Hutchinson, 1958.
New York: Harper, 1959.

Detective Inspector McQuade is killed while investigating a man named Bassey, who is suspected of embezzling other people's money. Martineau's men must backtrack looking for whatever McQuade knew that resulted in his death. Someone sets up Martineau, and when that fails, pours petrol on his house and sets it on fire.

Killer at Large *Detective Chief Inspector Harry Martineau*
London: Hutchinson, 1959.
New York: Harper, 1959.

Guy Ranier was sent to prison for murdering his fiancée's lover. When he escapes, Martineau must deal with the people who believe Rainer will hurt them now that he is out. When a nine-year-old child disappears, the police wonder whether this is connected with the jailbreak or a separate crime.

Devil's Due* *Detective Chief Inspector Harry Martineau*
London: Hutchinson, 1960.
New York: Harper, 1960.

The Devil Was Handsome *Detective Chief Inspector Harry Martineau*
London: Hutchinson, 1961.
New York: Harper, 1961.

Martineau believes that there is a connecting link between the rape of a woman, the murder of another woman, and the theft of a large amount of heroin.

A Body to Spare *Detective Chief Inspector Harry Martineau*
London: Hutchinson, 1962.
New York: Harper, 1962.

The general hospital has discovered an extra body in the morgue. A man had died in an accident, was examined, and supposedly cremated. Now his body has been found in one of the hospital's body boxes. Who was the cremated corpse? Missing is one Verney Barton and the sizable amount of £29,000 belonging to Northern Steel. Then another unaccounted for body is left at the morgue.

Moonlight Flitting* *Detective Chief Inspector Harry Martineau*
London: Hutchinson, 1963.

The Graveyard Rolls
New York: Harper, 1964.

Two Men in Twenty *Detective Chief Inspector Harry Martineau*
London: Hutchinson, 1964.
New York: Harper, 1964.

Scotland Yard has its hands full with crimes committed by the XXC gang, so named because no one knows who its members are. However, things are getting a bit too close for comfort for them in London so they move to Granchester. When Martineau is faced with a series of safecrackings and skillfully executed crimes, he realizes that the XXC gang is on his home turf.

Death Has a Shadow *Detective Chief Inspector Harry Martineau*
London: Hutchinson, 1965.

Homicide Blonde
New York: Harper, 1965.

Lily Ellis, a blonde twelve-year-old, is strangled and the Granchester CID fears she will not be the only one. Two days later another girl is murdered—this one blonde and thirteen. The murderer is not only killing blonde girls, but takes a piece of jewelry from their bodies as a souvenir. The police narrow the list of suspects to two.

Rogue Running *Detective Chief Inspector Harry Martineau*
New York: Harper, 1965.
London: Hutchinson, 1966.

Detective Constable Brabant, on a job at the football game, has his wallet stolen. His police warrant card was in the wallet. Next a businessman goes missing, and his mistress, who is also his secretary, is married to a football player. Brabant, following clues and innuendo, shows police work at its best as he ties all of this together.

His Weight in Gold[*] *Detective Chief Inspector Harry Martineau*
London: Hutchinson, 1966.
New York: Harper, 1966.

Exercise Hoodwink *Detective Chief Inspector Harry Martineau*
London: Hutchinson, 1967.
New York: Harper, 1967.

Two policemen discover an abandoned automobile. It is completely empty except for the blood. The body of a man is found farther down the road and a murdered woman is found in a garage. She almost fits the pattern of a number of serial deaths of young women. Then a diamond merchant is robbed of forty parcels of industrial diamonds. Dixie Costello, head of the local organized crime, is in the thick of the action and it is up to Martineau's men to discover why.

Hideaway   *Detective Chief Inspector Harry Martineau*
London: Hutchinson, 1968.
New York: Harper, 1968.

Chief Superintendent Clay meets a Granchester businessman who is being blackmailed with pictures of him and a woman in compromising positions. The man identifies the blackmailer as Martineau. A man named Merrill is orchestrating the plot to ruin the chief inspector but right behind Merrill is crime boss Costello. When Vanessa, the woman used to reel in the men, is found dead in Yorkshire, Martineau and his team are hot on Costello's trail.

Mary Monica Pulver*

Ashes to Ashes   *Sergeant Peter Brichter*
New York: St. Martin's, 1988.

Brichter investigates a case of arson at Crazy Dave's TV and Appliance, while life is not too pleasant on the home scene as Brichter and his wife, Kori, battle about starting a family. The case is complicated by evidence that points to a possible police connection to criminal activity. (Note: this is the only title in this series that uses procedure to solve crime.)

Erica Quest

Death Walk   *Detective Chief Inspector Kate Maddox*
London: Piatkus, 1987.
New York: Doubleday, 1988.

It is Maddox's first day on the job and Belle Latimer is murdered. There are many people in town who disliked the woman. Maddox must prove to her new staff that she is a top-notch policewoman and detective. There is another death and Kate must locate the killer despite her personal involvment with the locals.

Cold Coffin *Detective Chief Inspector Kate Maddox*
London: Piatkus, 1990.
New York: Doubleday Crime Club, 1990.

First, Sir Noah Kimberley, owner of Croptech, a manufacturer of agricultural chemicals, is missing. Then the body of Gavin Trent, chief biochemist at Croptech, is found in a small pond in the woods. When Sir Noah's body is discovered in his deep freeze Kate must sift through a number of suspects and their conflicting stories to get to the truth.

Model Murder *Detective Chief Inspector Kate Maddox*
London: Piatkus, 1991.
New York: Doubleday, 1991.

The body of Corinne Saxon is found in the woods. Her clothing ripped off, she appears to have been raped then strangled. However, no rape occurred and Kate is left with a number of suspects including Richard Gower, Kate's current boyfriend. The secrets of Corinne's past and her less than stellar present existence add up to many reasons for someone wanting her dead.

Hugh C. Rae*

A Few Small Bones *Detective Chief Superintendent McCaig*
London: Blond, 1968. *and Detective Inspector Ryan*

The House at Balnesmoor
New York: Coward, McCann, 1968.

A sixteen-year-old girl is found buried on the Langs' property. When their yard is dug up, a second body is found. Both girls had disappeared from Glasgow. Why were the girls transported forty miles from the city and buried in the tiny village of Balnesmoor? The answers are not simple to find and a lot of slogging police work goes into tracking down the murderer.

The Shooting Gallery *Detective Chief Superintendent McCaig*
London: Constable, 1972. *and Detective Inspector Ryan*
New York: Coward, McCann, 1972.

Nineteen-year-old Tom McDowell dies after an automobile crash. When the autopsy is performed it is discovered that he was under the influence of a massive heroin dose. But Tom's mother insists that he was no addict.

Julian Rathbone*

The Euro-Killers *Commissioner of Police Jan Argand*
London: Joseph, 1979.
New York: Pantheon, 1979.

Wealthy Wolfgang Heim, founder of EUREAC, is kidnapped. Disappearances are not Commissioner Argand's business but his superior asks him to find Heim. EUREAC, a chemical and plastics manufacturer, has fostered an image that it is a caring, ecologically sound company. But the fact remains that the new project, Sportshaven, may be very detrimental to the environment. Argand interviews business associates of Heim and his family, then two requests for ransom are made, which are followed by death threats.

Derek Raymond*
(Pseudonym of Robin [Robert William Arthur] Cook)

The Devil's Home on Leave *An Unnamed Detective Sergeant in the*
London: Secker and Warburg, 1984. *Department of Unexplained Deaths*
New York: Ballantine, 1987.

The body of a man is found in five plastic trash bags. The body had been sectioned, then boiled so that no identifying marks exist. The nameless policeman from the Department of Unexplained Deaths in London makes a case from nothing. Following innuendo, suggestions, and hunches, he unearths a cold-blooded murderer with ties to another case having far-reaching consequences.

He Died with His Eyes Open *An Unnamed Detective Sergeant in the*
London: Secker and Warburg, 1984. *Department of Unexplained Deaths*
New York: Ballantine, 1987.

The unnamed sergeant becomes caught up in discovering why a man is beaten to death. Among his possessions are audiocassettes containing his recorded musings of agony and personal suffering. The cassettes contain a few leads to places where the detective meets a woman who had known the dead man, and dark obessions come to light.

How the Dead Live *An Unnamed Detective Sergeant in the*
London: Secker and Warburg, 1986. *Department of Unexplained Deaths*
New York: Ballantine, 1989.

Mrs. Marianne Mardy has been gone for six months. No one knows where she is. No one has seen her. Now the nameless detective from the Department of Unexplained Deaths is looking for her, as her friends are concerned for her well-being. Mardy's husband, a doctor who has not practiced for some time, seems oblivious to her plight and the town appears to be either hiding something or operating under extreme guilt.

I Was Dora Suarez *An Unnamed Detective Sergeant in the*
London: Macdonald, 1990. *Department of Unexplained Deaths*
New York: Ballantine, 1990.

The unnamed detective sergeant has been relieved from duty for insubordination. When two women are brutally murdered the Yard calls him in, as he is the only investigator capable of solving the case. One of the butchered women, Dora Suarez, has left a diary, and through reading it, the sergeant learns about her life, her fears, and her knowledge of her approaching death.

Robert Sims Reid

Cupid *Detectives Leo Banks, Red Hanrahan,*
New York: Bantam, 1991. *and Sergeant Sam Blieker*

Leo Banks, detective, had his throat cut, was stabbed in the kidneys, and left for dead by drug dealer Sky King Hudson. Banks's life was saved by Marian Towney, Hudson's woman and the person who identified Banks as an undercover cop. Now Hudson has been murdered and a young woman is found dead in a shallow grave with a crossbow bolt in her heart. Then the FBI asks the Rosette, Montana, police to back off.

Benediction *Detective Leo Banks*
New York: Bantam, 1992.

As a young cop, Leo Banks wanted to help the mother of an eighteen-year-old girl involved with a rich man who was into cocaine, violence, and pornographic movie making. But he was ordered to back off by his boss and the town mayor, who felt that the man had brought money and an economic upsurge to Rosette. Now Banks, older and wiser, is called to a woman's home and is told of a brutal beating and rape that has been videotaped by one of the assailants. The same rich man is involved and Banks wants to bring him to justice this time.

John Lawrence Reynolds

And Leave Her Lay Dying   *Lieutenant Joe McGuire and Ollie Schantz*
New York: Viking, 1990.

During a rape trial the lawyer for the defense, in a vituperous display of taunting, pushes McGuire so far that he assaults attorney Rosen in court. Because of this incident McGuire is assigned the grey files—those cases that are open but inactive. McGuire brings the cases to the home of Ollie Schantz, his former partner, who is now paralyzed from the neck down. As they go over the evidence and facts, their lives change. Ollie begins to function again and McGuire faces up to Schantz's disability.

Whisper Death   *Lieutenant Joe McGuire*
New York: Viking, 1991.

When McGuire returns to Boston after his self-imposed retirement/exile in the Bahamas, he finds that he can have his job back with a new partner, who just happens to be the current lover of his old flame. The two detectives are sent to Palm Springs to retrieve a prisoner. They find a terrorized man who is more than a mild-mannered postal inspector, a super-secret government security agency sniffing around, and the very wealthy and beautiful widow of a South American millionaire. The prisoner is soon dead and Joe's partner seriously injured.

Shepard Rifkin[*]

McQuaid   *Sergeant Damian McQuaid*
New York: Putnam, 1974.
London: Hale, 1975.

Damian McQuaid is leaving for a vacation in Antigua when he discovers the murdered body of his friend Shimmy in a telephone booth at Kennedy Airport. Shimmy, part owner of a jewelry shop, was on his way to Los Angeles to sell a $150,000 diamond necklace. Shimmy's death was caused by a pin inserted into his ear and then shoved into his brain. McQuaid begins looking for a person with great strength in his or her arms and for the woman seen trying to get into the phone booth with Shimmy just before his death.

The Snow Rattlers *Sergeant Damian McQuaid*
New York: Putnam, 1977.
London: Hale, 1978.

Oliver Sorensen is wealthy and spends money wisely—he collects art and Americana. When the police are called to his home, they find him dead in his private museum, run through with a tribal spear. Missing are some very valuable Indian carvings and a first printing of the Declaration of Independence. McQuaid believes the killer has gone home to the Navaho Reservation in New Mexico and follows him there, where a big-city cop is way out of his depth.

Jack Ripley
(Pseudonym of John Wainwright, q.v.)

Davis Doesn't Live Here Any More *Constable John George Davis*
London: Hamilton, 1971.
New York: Doubleday, 1972.

Constable Davis finds a dead man outside his home. Because he is the first policeman on the scene, it becomes his case. More people are murdered and Davis is up to his ears in problems—he has never handled a murder case before and because the town is small, he knows everyone involved.

The Pig That Got Up and Slowly Walked Away* *Constable John George Davis*
London: Hamilton, 1971.

My God How the Money Rolls In* *Constable John George Davis*
London: Hamilton, 1972.

My Word You Should Have Seen Us* *Constable John George Davis*
London: Hamilton, 1972.

Peter Robinson*

Gallows View *Chief Inspector Alan Banks*
London: Macmillan, 1990.
New York: Scribner's, 1990.

Banks has moved his family from London to Eastvale in Yorkshire. There they find that a Peeping Tom is terrifying women and a gang of young thugs is preying on the elderly of the town.

A Dedicated Man *Chief Inspector Alan Banks*
London: Macmillan, 1988.
New York: Scribner's, 1991.

Harry Steadman is found in a field, his head bashed in with a blunt instrument. Steadman was writing a book on local history involving visits to Roman ruins and old mines. The only person who knows anything is a sixteen-year-old village girl, who decides to play detective, putting herself in grave danger.

A Necessary End *Chief Inspector Alan Banks*
London: Macmillan, 1992.
New York: Scribner's, 1992.

At a demonstration against nuclear power many are wounded in a battle between the police and the demonstrators. But a policeman is killed—stabbed to death—and a murder investigation is much different than mopping up after a fight. There are too many suspects, so headquarters sends Superintendent "Dirty Dick" Burgess to head the investigation.

Charles G. Rogers

1199 *Detective Steve Cates*
Ontario, Canada: Worldwide, 1988.

When San Diego homicide detective Steve Cates goes to look at the apartment of a woman who has vanished he does not know that this case will lead him into grave danger. There is a man who kills using "noi cun," meaning the death touch—he touches someone and the person dies. An FBI agent assigned to work with Cates seems too good to be true.

Robert Rosenberg

Crimes of the City *Commander Avram Cohen and*
New York: Simon & Schuster, 1991. *Chief Inspector Nissim Levy*

The investigation into who is responsible for throwing hand grenades into a crowd of innocent people is bogged down and then two Russian Orthodox nuns are murdered. Commander Cohen of the Jerusalem police is harassed by the politicians who believe that Jews are not capable of crime and thus that there is no need for a police force, the press wanting fresh news and easy answers, and the KGB representative at the convent, who knows something but will not talk.

Dennis St. Pierre

The Marshal *Lieutenant Frank Evans*
New York: Warner, 1981.

Lieutenant Frank Evans, a special assignment troubleshooter, is at loose ends now that his long-time partner is retired and moving to Florida. Evans is sent to East LA to meet with Captain Mason, a Western history buff and ex-Texas Ranger. One of Mason's men has been shot by three robbers. Two of the thieves have been killed by a self-styled vigilante known as the Marshal because of his resemblance to Wyatt Earp. But Earp has been dead since 1929. So who is this guy?

Lawrence Sanders*

The First Deadly Sin *Captain Edward X. Delaney*
New York: Putnam, 1973.
London: Allen, 1974.

Daniel Blank meets a mysterious woman at a dinner party who begins to feed his fantasies. When she asks him to murder someone he picks a person at random and kills him with an ice ax. Captain Delaney of the NYPD is stumped. Even the medical examiner cannot tell what kind of weapon was used. Meticulous police work leads to Blank but there is no evidence or legal proof to convict him. Blank kills again and again, all the while growing more corrupt.

The Second Deadly Sin *Edward X. Delaney*
New York: Putnam, 1977.
London: Hart Davis, 1978.

The dead body of Victor Maitland, famous American artist, is found in his studio. Maitland alive was a sick individual; Maitland dead presents the police with a giant headache. Delaney, called out of retirement, believes this to be a premeditated murder and looks closely at the people who hated the artist most.

The Third Deadly Sin   *Edward X. Delaney*
New York: Putnam, 1981.
London: Granada, 1981.

A Swiss Army knife is used by a serial killer to eliminate men. They are killed in hotel rooms after being picked up by a beautiful woman wearing a different disguise each time. The killer leaves no trace, no clues. The murders are on a schedule—Delaney can almost predict when the next one will occur.

The Fourth Deadly Sin   *Edward X. Delaney*
New York: Putnam, 1985.
London: New English Library, 1985.

The bashed-in head of psychiatrist Simon Ellerbee presents the New York police with a high-profile murder case and no clues. They call in Edward X. Delaney to head the investigation. Ellerbee's wife is forced to divulge the names of her husband's most violent patients, leading to a horrifying view of the realm of the mentally unstable.

John Sandford*
(Pseudonym of John Camp)

Rules of Prey   *Lieutenant Lucas Davenport*
New York: Putnam, 1989.
London: Grafton, 1990.

When the Mad Dog Killer strikes out at a woman he has been stalking, she surprises him by macing him in the face, then beating him with a lead pipe. Now he must get his own back. He rapes and stabs a real estate woman who was showing him a house. The interval between killings gets shorter as Mad Dog gets more gruesomely violent. Vuillion, the Mad Dog, plays these life and death situations much like a game and considers Davenport a worthy opponent.

Shadow Prey   *Lieutenant Lucas Davenport*
New York: Putnam, 1990.
London: Grafton, 1990.

In Minneapolis two men, a slum landlord and a probation officer, both known for their hatred and exploitation of Indians, are killed by men using sharp obsidian knives. Then a prominent New Yorker is butchered in the same way. Lucas Davenport and the Minneapolis police department must deal with the interference of the FBI, the investigation of more murders, and the realization that they have no working network of informants in the Indian community as they race against time to make sense of the killings.

Eyes of Prey *Lieutenant Lucas Davenport*
New York: Putnam, 1991.

Stephanie Bekker is beaten to death in her kitchen. Her lover, who had been taking a shower, sees the murderer and hides until he can escape. Lucas Davenport must find the killer but he suspects that this is no random breaking and entering. The case becomes a contest between Davenport and the guilty person.

Silent Prey *Lieutenant Lucas Davenport*
New York: Putnam, 1992.

Just as the jury is ready to begin deliberation, the mentally disturbed murderer from *Eyes of Prey* escapes from the courthouse. He makes his way to New York City where he begins a series of vicious killings. At the same time Lily Rothenberg, Davenport's ex-lover and New York City policewoman, is quietly investigating thirteen murders of prominent people—murders bearing all the earmarks of professional hits. Lily suspects that police personnel are committing the murders.

J. G. Sandom

Gospel Truth *Detective Inspector Nigel Lyman*
New York: Doubleday (A Perfect
 Crime Book), 1992.

Inspector Lyman is given an impossible case to solve. An Italian banker named Pontevecchio has been hanged under the Blackfriars Bridge. His death was ruled a suicide. Now there are indications that he was murdered. Lyman goes to Amiens, France, to learn that his old mentor was somehow connected to the Pontevecchio killing. The cathedrals at Amiens and Chartres are somehow tied to more murders, a clandestine group of freemasons, and the possibility of an existing original gospel of Saint Thomas.

Soledad Santiago*

Undercover *Rookie Police Officer Toni Conroy*
New York: Bantam, 1988. *and Officer Errol Stutz*

Toni Conroy's nineteen-year-old brother robs a lot of money from her drug-dealer husband and gets murdered for it. Conroy's six-year-old daughter also dies. Two years later Conroy is a NYPD rookie police officer attempting to clean up Sixth Street so a Hollywood movie can be made. She goes undercover to avenge her family but her ex-husband is the powerful Cobra and he hooks her on drugs.

Eric Sauter*

Skeletons *Detective Patrick Paige*
New York: Onyx, 1991.

Patrick Paige's wife was murdered by a serial killer and now Paige is called in to solve the crimes of a man who kills in the same way. Paige gets too close for comfort and the hunter becomes the hunted.

Alan Scholefield*

Dirty Weekend *Detective Superintendent George Macrae*
London: Macmillan, 1990. *and Sergeant Leopold Silver*
New York: St. Martin's, 1991.

A talk-show host is found in a bad neighborhood under a bridge, stabbed to death. At the same time a businessman is leaving Hong Kong with a bag full of money and a Japanese hit man in hot pursuit. Macrae and Silver must sift throught hostile witnesses and come to grips with racial prejudice.

Thief Taker *Detective Superintendent George Macrae*
London: Macmillan, 1991. *and Detective Sergeant Leopold Silver*
New York: St. Martin's, 1992.

A wealthy businessman is murdered. His neighbor relates that the man entertained young women in his home. As the investigation leads them into the victim's world, the team becomes entangled in a dangerous stalking situation with Leopold Silver as the intended victim.

Monte Schulz

Down by the River *Chief of Police Carroll Howser*
New York: Viking, 1991.

A seventeen-year-old girl is raped and beaten. When questioned she blames tramps camping in an old railroad yard. Some of the more upstanding men in town shoot up the place and kill one of the old tramps. The horror continues in this sleepy California town as one by one the girl and the group of boys she was with that night begin turning up dead.

Jack S. Scott*
(Pseudonym of Jonathan Escott)

The Poor Old Lady's Dead *Detective Inspector Alfred Stanley Rosher*
London: Hale, 1976. *and Sergeant Cruise*
New York: Harper, 1976.

In less than one year three old ladies in a small English village have died, apparently all victims of accidents. Inspector Rosher, however, suspects that someone is behind the deaths, but his motive for solving the crimes is self-advancement. He wants respect from his fellow policemen at any cost.

The Shallow Grave *Detective Inspector Alfred Stanley Rosher*
London: Hale, 1977. *and Sergeant Cruise*
New York: Harper, 1977.

In a quiet village Miss Ellie Beavis is murdered. She was a good person, who kept to herself. The autopsy proves that she was at least three months pregnant.

A Clutch of Vipers *Detective Sergeant Alfred Stanley Rosher*
London: Collins, 1979. *and Inspector Cruise*
New York: Harper, 1979.

Demoted, depressed, and separated from his wife, Sergeant Rosher needs a housekeeper. When he places an ad in the town newspaper it is seen by Mad Frankie, a criminal with a grudge against Rosher. Mad Frankie manuevers the wife of a now-dead prison inmate into the Rosher home. Meanwhile Rosher has more agony at work because Cruise has become his boss. Cruise is keeping a surveillance on Mad Frankie and the development of his latest criminal caper.

The Gospel Lamb *Detective Sergeant Alfred Stanley Rosher*
London: Collins, 1980.
New York: Harper, 1980.

In the midst of preparaton for a musical festival, the Avenger goes to work. He preys on young women because he thinks they are all whores. Rosher is assigned to the police units on guard at the festival. Rosher finds himself in a tight spot when a young woman is murdered.

A Distant View of Death *Detective Sergeant Alfred Stanley Rosher*
London: Collins, 1981.

The View from Deacon Hill
New Haven, CT: Ticknor and Fields, 1981.

While enjoying the view from the Three Bears, a hill outside of town, Detective Sergeant Rosher is astonished to see a man with a gun sneaking into a van. The man falls out of the van, which was apparently occupied; a car roars out from the bushes alongside the van and races down the road with the van in cold pursuit. When the car is found in a maze of country lanes, there are two dead men inside. A visiting American policeman, his alcoholic wife, a couple whose son hides in the attic, and Rosher's troubles with his nemesis, Superintendent Percy, add spice to solving the murders.

An Uprush of Mayhem *Detective Inspector Alfred Stanley Rosher*
London: Collins, 1982.
New Haven, CT: Tichnor and Fields, 1982.

A young woman goes out on a date with an older, very attractive man who wines and dines her—then she is found dead. The police are soon after Freddie Lugge because his fingerprints are found all over the crime scene. But he was up to something else when Eve was killed. So Rasher must solve two mysteries.

The Local Lads *Detective Inspector Alfred Stanley Rosher*
London: Collins, 1982.
New York: Dutton, 1983.

Rosher is returning to London with Mr. Dunfreet, a solicitor. Dunfreet, also a pilot of some reknown, crashes his plane just short of the runway. Dunfreet dies; Rosher ends up in the hospital. At the same time, two men kill another man who just happens to be the brother of Rosher's nurse. Rosher begins an impromptu investigation from his hospital room.

All the Pretty People *Detective Inspector Alfred Stanley Rosher*
London: Collins, 1985.
New York: St. Martin's, 1984.

Detective Inspector Rosher stops a young man from committing suicide. Soon afterward, the man is murdered.

A Death in Irish Town *Detective Inspector Alfred Stanley Rosher*
London: Collins, 1984.
New York: St. Martin's, 1985.

Rosher's first beat was in Irish Town and he has fond memories of the place. Thirty years later there is a warehouse fire and Rosher just happens to be on hand when a badly charred body is found in the rubble. The man is burned beyond recognition and his skull is caved in, pointing to murder. The questions pile up about the identity of the man, why he was killed, and what was going on in the warehouse.

A Little Darling Dead   *Detective Chief Inspector Pete Parsons*
London: Collins, 1985.   *and Sergeant Wammo Winbush*
New York: St. Martin's, 1986.

A girl of twelve is found dead at the bottom of Lovers' Leap, strangled. Her mother, while cleaning the dead child's room, discovers gold jewelry under the bed. The girl comes from an ordinary family and none of her friends has money. So where did the jewelry come from? The girl's school friends are hiding knowledge that would help the police.

A Knife Between the Ribs   *Detective Inspector Alfred Stanley Rosher*
London: Collins, 1986.
New York: St. Martin's, 1987.

A man is killed in a crowded bar during Festival week but no one saw anything. The man, Harvey Grebshaw, had quite a past. He spent time in prison, he consorted with criminals, and he was a police informer. Then he became Born Again. Rosher must sort all the information to come to a conclusion.

Owen Sela[*]

The Bengali Inheritance   *Senior Chief Inspector Richard Chan*
London: Hodder, 1974.   *and Inspector Peter Winston*
New York: Pantheon, 1975.

An Indian man, Delonath Raghavan, tortured, is shot in the back of the head, and left in a taxi on Yee Wo Road. As a reporter for the Asian *Clarion*, he had written a series of articles on a secret, right-wing Japanese group called the Blue Storm headed by Hiroshi Watanabe. Watanabe is secretly working a deal with Peter Winston to trade atomic secrets and information about student uprisings, and illegal arms for money and safe passage to Hong Kong.

Francis Selwyn
(Pseudonym of Donal Thomas, q.v.)

Cracksman on Velvet   *Sergeant William Clarence Verity*
London: Deutsch, 1974.
New York: Stein and Day, 1974.

Sergeant Verity and the Cracksman
London: Futura, 1975.

It was difficult being a policeman in Victorian England, and William Verity, a sergeant in the Private Clothes Detail, finds it hard going indeed. Verity is set up for a beating and discrediting when he seeks information in a brothel and it looks as if he used violence on a whore. Tied to this is the execution of Private Thomas McCaffery in Bombay. It appears as if McCaffery was killed to stop him from talking about something. Now, in London, Verity faces the combined force of whoremaster Ned Roper and the violent Verney Dacre, who intend to steal a shipment of gold bullion.

Sergeant Verity and the Imperial Diamond　　*Sergeant William Clarence*
London: Deutsch, 1975.　　　　　　　　　　　　*Verity and Sergeant Martock*
New York: Stein and Day, 1976.

Verity searches the dark places of Calcutta for a sixteen-year-old girl who has been kidnapped by the leader of an Indian uprising in Bengal. A magnificent diamond, the Kaiser-i-Hind, is missing. Along the way Verity and Martock face an ugly death at the hands of Nava Sahib, the rebel leader, and horrid consequences when they search a harem.

Sergeant Verity and the Blood Royal　　*Sergeant William Clarence*
London: Deutsch, 1979.　　　　　　　　　　　*Verity and Sergeant Martock*
New York: Stein and Day, 1979.

Verney Dacre, a bank robber, is planning to rob the U.S. Mint in Philadelphia. To this end he has kidnapped a beautiful slave who knows the floor plan of the Mint. The American authorities get William Clarence Verity to help run Dacre to earth, aided by Captain Thomas Crowe of the United States Marines and an incredible lady named Miss Jolly. The story takes place around the time of John Brown's Raid and most of the action is in American brothels.

Sergeant Verity and the Swell Mob　　*Sergeant William Clarence*
London: Deutsch, 1980.　　　　　　　　　　　*Verity and Sergeant Martock*
New York: Stein and Day, 1981.

The Shah Jehan Clasp, a priceless jewel meant to be worn on a turban, is stolen from Baron Lansing's safe in his Sussex mansion. Joe O'Meara is immediately arrested as he is the thief on the scene at the time of the robbery. Verity is in for a bad time as he runs into a nasty group of lowlifes.

David Serafin*
(Pseudonym of Ian Michael)

Madrid Underground *Superintendent Luis Bernal*
London: Collins, 1982.
New York: St. Martin's, 1984.

Spain is anticipating its first general election in more than forty years when two dummies are found on subway trains with blood pouring from their mouths. The body of a young woman is also found in a subway train, but the police know she was murdered elsewhere and placed on the train. The blood from the dummies does not match the dead girl's. Then another woman is found in the subway, murdered. Bernal moves his team into the subway tunnels as the case must be solved before the election is held.

The Body in Cadiz Bay *Superintendent Luis Bernal*
London: Collins, 1985.
New York: St. Martin's, 1985.

Bernal has asked his wife, Eugenia, for a divorce. She has always placed the Church and religion above the marriage, their son, and him. They are spending Holy Week in Cadiz so she can meditate on his request when a frogman is caught in the nets of local fishermen. The man did not drown so the police must discover who he is, how he died, who killed him, and why.

Port of Light *Superintendent Luis Bernal*
London: Collins, 1987.
New York: St. Martin's, 1987.

Ordered to guard the President of the Council of Ministers who are visiting the Canary Islands, Bernal and company go there to make arrangements. Consuelo, Bernal's mistress, is to meet him at the airport, but she is kidnapped.

The Angel of Torremolinos *Superintendent Luis Bernal*
London: Macmillan, 1988.
New York: St. Martin's, 1988.

The local police are aided by Superintendent Bernal, who is sent to the Costa del Sol where a Basque faction has demanded the withdrawal of all Spanish military from three Basque provinces. It is the height of the tourist season and the police high command decides that plainclothes undercover observation is best in this situation. Bernal goes to Torremolinos where he helps in the investigation of a death on the beach and is soon working on a series of disappearances of teenage tourists.

Steve Shagan*

Vendetta *Lieutenant Jack Raines*
New York: Morrow, 1986.
London: Didgwick, 1986.

A Valentine drawn in spilled cocaine is the calling card of a killer who preys on the stars of pornographic films. In touch with organized crime figures in Bel Air, the trashy film show business, and a Columbian drug dealer, Raines cannot stop a violent war in the streets that erupts with ferocity.

Dell Shannon
(Pseudonym of Elizabeth Linington)

Case Pending *Lieutenant Luis Mendoza and the*
New York: Morrow, 1960. *Robbery/Homicide Squad*
London: Gollancz, 1960.

In a six-month span two young women are killed, strangled, and then mutilated in a special way. Mendoza, though a lieutenant, spends much time doing routine legwork that involves him with the beautiful Miss Alison Weir.

The Ace of Spades *Lieutenant Luis Mendoza and the*
New York: Morrow, 1961. *Robbery/Homicide Squad*
London: Oldbourne, 1963.

The autopsy report on the body of a man who had OD'd from a massive dose of heroin proves the man was no addict but a murder victim. At the same time Alison Weir gets her stolen car back and finds a rare old coin hidden behind the seat. There is a man from Greece who is somehow connected to a missing collection of ancient coins.

Extra Kill *Lieutenant Luis Mendoza and the*
New York: Morrow, 1962. *Robbery/Homicide Squad*
London: Oldbourne, 1962.

A cop dies in what looks to be a random drive-by shooting. Then the body of a suspected embezzler is found in a shallow grave under an apartment where the dead policeman had answered a call the night he was killed.

Both incidents may be tied up with a religious group calling itself the Temple of Mystic Truth.

Knave of Hearts *Lieutenant Luis Mendoza and the*
New York: Morrow, 1962. *Robbery/Homicide Squad*
London: Oldbourne, 1963.

An innocent man is executed for the murder of a college student. The similarities between her death and those of several other young women lead Mendoza to believe a serial killer is on the loose. Add to this his recent break-up with Alison Weir and the plot thickens. Fast paced, professional detection leads the homicide squad to the identity of the murderer only to find that Alison is going to be the next victim.

Death of a Busybody *Lieutenant Luis Mendoza and the*
New York: Morrow, 1963. *Robbery/Homicide Squad*
London: Oldbourne, 1963.

Margaret Chadwick is at the party to celebrate the birth of Sergeant Art Hackett's baby. When she is found strangled the next morning the case looks hopeless with the growing number of suspects. Chadwick was an incorrigible busybody—always minding others' business; it may have done her in.

Double Bluff *Lieutenant Luis Mendoza and the*
New York: Morrow, 1963. *Robbery/Homicide Squad*
London: Oldbourne, 1964.

Laurence S. Winthrop III comes to Mendoza's office to report that his sister is missing and he thinks her husband has murdered her. Central homicide is ordered to investigate. Then Mrs. Ingram is found in her car at the bottom of a steep hill. She died of a blow to the head that occurred before the crash. The people who hope to gain from her death begin to circle as buzzards around a carcass and Mendoza's crew must sort out the truth from all of their stories.

Mark of Murder *Lieutenant Luis Mendoza and the*
New York: Morrow, 1964. *Robbery/Homicide Squad*
London: Gollancz, 1965.

While on vacation Mendoza receives the bad news that Art Hackett has been seriously wounded. When Mendoza arrives in Los Angeles he finds that Hackett had been working on the shooting death of a chiropractor and the slasher cases. Art had gone out to gather more information about the two cases and must have discovered something very incriminating because he was knocked out, tied up, and then pushed over a cliff in his car.

Root of All Evil *Lieutenant Luis Mendoza and the*
New York: Morrow, 1965. *Robbery/Homicide Squad*
London: Gollancz, 1966.

The body of Valerie Ellis was dumped in the parking lot of a parochial school, dead of a codeine overdose. Val had grown up in luxury but when her parents died suddenly she was left with nothing and had to make her own way. When the police search her apartment they find a closet full of expensive clothing and a suitcase loaded with marijuana.

The Death-Bringers *Lieutenant Luis Mendoza and the*
New York: Morrow, 1965. *Robbery/Homicide Squad*
London: Gollancz, 1966.

A series of bank robberies has Mendoza's men frustrated because there are no clues to the robbers' identity. Then a nineteen-year-old woman is murdered. In the middle of a bank robbery police sergeant Bert Dwyer walks in and gets killed. He was a member of Mendoza's robbery/homicide squad.

Death by Inches[*] *Lieutenant Luis Mendoza and the*
New York: Morrow, 1965. *Robbery/Homicide Squad*
London: Gollancz, 1967.

Coffin Corner *Lieutenant Luis Mendoza and the*
New York: Morrow, 1966. *Robbery/Homicide Squad*
London: Gollancz, 1967.

The squad must investigate the death of a patrolman; he was run over by a car and witnesses say it was deliberate. The body of a woman is found in her shop and the autopsy shows she was poisoned. There are the usual robberies to look into and a few other things that keep Mendoza's team busy.

With a Vengence *Lieutenant Luis Mendoza and the*
New York: Morrow, 1966. *Robbery/Homicide Squad*
London: Gollancz, 1968.

The cases the squad is working on range from a child beating that proved fatal to a liquor store holdup, a suicide, and an unidentified corpse. As crime is ever-present in the streets of LA, it comes as no surprise that the odd murder crops up to give Mendoza headaches. The man is found under a tree, strangled with a cord, and in his suit pocket is a card that reads "The Vengeance Is Just." This turns out to be the first of a string of murders, same modus operandi, and the same message left on each corpse.

Chance to Kill   *Lieutenant Luis Mendoza and the*
New York: Morrow, 1967.   *Robbery/Homicide Squad*
London: Gollancz, 1968.

A young man is lying dead in an alley. He has been shot but not before he had been hit over the head. A pair of heist men are on the loose in LA and the Chicago police want them too. Then the body of a young woman is found in a dry riverbed, and when the squad investigates, they discover she is a policewoman on the Los Angeles force. Everyone agrees Bettina's life was exemplary and she had no personal enemies; the murder must have occurred because of something that happened on the job.

Rain with Violence   *Lieutenant Luis Mendoza and the*
New York: Morrow, 1967.   *Robbery/Homicide Squad*
London: Gollancz, 1969.

First a young mother is raped and strangled on her living room floor right next to her baby. Then a prostitute is strangled in a fifth-rate hotel. And two elderly women are beaten to death in their home. Two men are found murdered, both lying in alleys near a bar notorious for drugging and rolling its clients.

Kill with Kindness   *Lieutenant Luis Mendoza and the*
New York: Morrow, 1968.   *Robbery/Homicide Squad*
London: Gollancz, 1969.

When Mendoza gets the measles and must stay at home for a month to recuperate, Mairi, his housekeeper, tells him a funny little tale about an old woman who appears drugged and her nurse, who works for twenty-five dollars a week. The men in homicide are working on the usual assortment of cases: a minister is beaten to death; a man is dead after being tied on a railroad track; and a twelve-year-old girl is raped, with no clues to the identity of her assailant.

Schooled to Kill   *Lieutenant Luis Mendoza and the*
New York: Morrow, 1969.   *Robbery/Homicide Squad*
London: Gollancz, 1970.

The rapist/murderer of two young girls is still free (*Kill with Kindness*) and the squad has no leads on the murder of Mrs. Garcia. The body of eight-year-old Pichens is found in Elysian Park. In the meantime, a young man tells the police a tale of being offered a thousand dollars to kill a woman. And another eight-year-old is murdered.

Crime on Their Hands *Sergeant Luis Mendoza and the*
New York: Morrow, 1969. *Robbery/Homicide Squad*
London: Gollancz, 1970.

A man leaves Dubuque driving a Maserati and crosses into California six weeks later. Actually, this person has been *dead* for six weeks, his body found in the desert in Arizona. The squad must find out who was driving the car. Then a woman is found strangled, a sheep's heart tied up with a ribbon on her chair. A man and a woman are murdered in their house, the rooms ransacked. The dead man had been a janitor at the police academy. And there is another murdered man, shot in the head, who was able to write the word "jewels" as a clue before he died.

Unexpected Death *Lieutenant Luis Mendoza and the*
New York: Morrow, 1970. *Robbery/Homicide Squad*
London: Gollancz, 1971.

In a little alley behind the house where they live, the Hurleys find the body of a woman dressed in a green lace evening gown, her neck broken. Next a Los Angeles woman finds her mother-in-law murdered. Edward Holly is found on the front porch of an elderly widow, who has no idea who he is or why he is on her porch. Mr. Holly was going blind and did not go out at night. The squad must also investigate a particularly vicious murder of a young wife in her own bedroom.

Whim to Kill *Lieutenant Luis Mendoza and the*
New York: Morrow, 1971. *Robbery/Homicide Squad*
London: Gollancz, 1971.

Mendoza and his team are working on several jobs when the body of a beautiful young woman is found in an alley. A trio of men in prison for armed robbery escapes and is believed to be heading toward Los Angeles. Some suicides and a murder/suicide also occur.

The Ringer *Lieutenant Luis Mendoza and the*
New York: Morrow, 1971. *Robbery/Homicide Squad*
London: Gollancz, 1972.

Tom Landers, one of Mendoza's best men, is accused of being the head of a ring of thieves specializing in auto theft.

Murder with Love *Lieutenant Luis Mendoza and the*
New York: Morrow, 1972. *Robbery/Homicide Squad*
London: Gollancz, 1972.

After the earthquake of 1972 the Los Angeles police department is faced with a crime wave. A man opens fire in a travel agency and kills someone. A policeman is brutally beaten. Then a man is found murdered in the room he rented for himself and the young woman accompanying him.

With Intent to Kill *Lieutenant Luis Mendoza and the*
New York: Morrow, 1972. *Robbery/Homicide Squad*
London: Gollancz, 1973.

Two men in different parts of the city are shot. One is left on the sidewalk. He still had his money and his diamond ring when he was found. The second man was killed in his store and his gun was taken. Then a motorcycle cop pulls a car over and is shot by the driver. The body of a woman in the morgue is identified as Alma Slater.

No Holiday for Crime *Lieutenant Luis Mendoza and the*
New York: Morrow, 1973. *Robbery/Homicide Squad*
London: Gollancz, 1974.

The newly created robbery/homicide bureau is headed by Luis Mendoza out of central headquarters. Along with everything else he must keep track of a number of stickups, hijackings, and bank robberies. There is also the murder of a young woman in Exposition Park. It all happened so quickly. She had just arrived in Los Angeles, went to the park, and was strangled. The squad is also working on a Christmas Eve rape, robbery, and murder.

Spring of Violence *Lieutenant Luis Mendoza*
New York: Morrow, 1973.
London: Gollancz, 1974.

Robbery/homicide is working on the usual array of cases; some of them are very strange. A tombstone weighing 500 pounds is missing from a cemetery. There are a few murders, a rape, some robberies. One of the new cases triggers the reopening of an old one.

Crime File *Lieutenant Luis Mendoza and the*
New York: Morrow, 1974. *Robbery/Homicide Squad*
London: Gollancz, 1975.

One of the cases robbery/homicide is working on is the murder of a widow. Nothing was stolen from her apartment, which is old and shabby. Years before she was quite a beautiful woman and had many male friends. A couple has abandoned their child and hospital tests show that the baby was subjected to doses of marijuana. Then there are the robberies at posh restaurants that are going unsolved.

Deuces Wild *Lieutenant Luis Mendoza and the*
New York: Morrow, 1975. *Robbery/Homicide Squad*
London: Gollancz, 1975.

With a heavy caseload of random murders and robberies Mendoza is tired of it all. An old man is beaten and robbed for a few dollars. There are plenty of unidentified bodies in the morgue. A teenager has died of an overdose, a hit-and-run investigation is going nowhere, and there is going to be a gang rumble. Mendoza is used to being the one in charge, able to deal dispassionately with the misfortunes of others, so he is totally unprepared to handle the disappearance of his own twin children and almost incapable of handling the role of victim.

Streets of Death *Lieutenant Luis Mendoza and the*
New York: Morrow, 1976. *Robbery/Homicide Squad*
London: Gollancz, 1977.

A disabled man confined to a wheelchair vanishes, leaving his wheelchair behind. His wife is a beautiful woman, who may have had something to do with her husband's disappearance. A man claims he overheard his neighbor planning a murder and a gang of thugs is robbing elderly men.

Appearances of Death *Lieutenant Luis Mendoza and the*
New York: Morrow, 1977. *Robbery/Homicide Squad*
London: Gollancz, 1978.

Another series of felonies involving rape, murder, and death by overdose.

Cold Trail *Lieutenant Luis Mendoza and the*
New York: Morrow, 1978. *Robbery/Homicide Squad*
London: Gollancz, 1979.

A woman's body is found under a condemned house. All that remains to give the detectives help is her badly rotted handbag. At the site of a domestic squabble there is a spent .32 cartridge but the man has been shot with a .22 caliber gun. The police are also looking into the death of a man in an apartment and a number of unsolved robberies.

Felony at Random *Lieutenant Luis Mendoza and the*
New York: Morrow, 1979. *Robbery/Homicide Squad*
London: Gollancz, 1979.

The squad is working on a number of robberies committed by a man who never speaks, the disappearance of a beautiful little girl, and a messy homicide involving three bodies, one of which is that of a three-year-old boy. The crime rate is steadily rising, keeping the robbery/homicide squad very busy. They are looking at a number of suicides in one location that may be murders and a police sergeant dead in his den.

Felony File *Lieutenant Luis Mendoza and the*
New York: Morrow, 1980. *Robbery/Homicide Squad*
London: Gollancz, 1980.

The robbery/homicide squad is working on the usual cases. A woman is committing perfect heists in area stores, and a man confined to a wheelchair is murdered for the twelve dollars he had on him. A nine-year-old girl is raped and beaten, her body left on the bed in her mother's squalid apartment. Bullock's Department Store is robbed and a woman is murdered in the park.

Murder Most Strange *Lieutenant Luis Mendoza and the*
New York: Morrow, 1981. *Robbery/Homicide Squad*
London: Gollancz, 1981.

It starts out with the vicious beating, stabbing, and rape of a young secretary. The rapist is named Dapper Dan and he is wanted for questioning in at least seven cases. He is getting closer to killing one of his victims as his attacks become more brutal. A man is killed and robbed by someone who had followed him home from the library. Another robber uses a Doberman to hold his victims at bay, and there is a death that is supposed to look like suicide.

Motive on Record *Lieutenant Luis Mendoza and the*
New York: Morrow, 1982. *Robbery/Homicide Squad*
London: Gollancz, 1982.

Between the bank robberies and the many murders, Mendoza and his men are quite busy. A mailman is found dead in an empty lot, a woman and two children are dead in a church, and two girls are raped and murdered.

Exploits of Death *Lieutenant Luis Mendoza and the*
New York: Morrow, 1983. *Robbery/Homicide Squad*
London: Gollancz, 1983.

The usual mix of many cases involving robbery, muggings, and murder. The most complicated is the murder of a young woman found dead in a cheap apartment. Her identification states that she is Ruth Hoffman but Mendoza had met her as Julliette Martin, a woman traveling from Paris to LA to meet her father for the first time.

Destiny of Death *Lieutenant Luis Mendoza and the*
New York: Morrow, 1984. *Robbery/Homicide Squad*
London: Gollancz, 1985.

LA robbery/homicide is faced with the usual number of cases. Jack the Stripper is leaving the cash registers at gas stations empty and the attendants naked, a cop is killed, liquor stores are being robbed, a young man helps old ladies to cross the street and then robs them. Mendoza and crew are also busy working on the brutal murder of a little girl.

Chaos of Crime *Lieutenant Luis Mendoza and the*
New York: Morrow, 1985. *Robbery/Homicide Squad*
London: Gollancz, 1986.

There is a ripper/werewolf-type killer loose in LA. He preys at night on prostitutes, decapitating them, mutilating them. There is also a beautiful redhead and a man robbing stores. There is a man who makes women strip. Then a patrolman is gunned down in a routine pullover of a driver.

Blood Count *Lieutenant Luis Mendoza and the*
New York: Morrow, 1986. *Robbery/Homicide Squad*
London: Gollancz, 1987.

Mrs. Louise Cannady from Indianapolis is murdered. At first it appears she died naturally but the autopsy shows she had a severe skull fracture. No one knows why she is in Los Angeles. The squad is also investigating a series of muggings that leaves the victims without shoes and some hit-and-run cases involving an old model A Ford. Then they get called out because a woman is suspicious of a couple whose baby seems to have disappeared.

Georges Simenon*

Maigret's Mistake *Inspector Maigret*
Included in **Maigret Right and Wrong**
London: Hamilton, 1954.

Included in **Five Times Maigret**
New York: Harcourt Brace, 1964.

A young woman is shot in her apartment. Her clothes are worn and she obviously was poor. Maigret must discover who was paying the rent for her flat as well as the identity of her young lover.

Maigret in Montmartre *Inspector Maigret*
Included in **Maigret Right and Wrong**
London: Hamilton, 1954.

Included in **Five Times Maigret**
New York: Harcourt, 1954.

Maigret and the Strangled Stripper
New York: Doubleday, 1954.

The strangulation death of a beautiful young stripper shocks the Judicial police as she had just been to their station telling of overhearing an odd conversation—a conversation involving jewelry and the possible death of the "countess." When the body of morphine addict Countess von Farnheim turns up, Maigret must solve a very perplexing puzzle.

Maigret Has Scruples *Inspector Maigret*
London: Hamilton, 1959.

Included in **Versus Inspector Maigret**
New York: Doubleday, 1960.

Maigret is paid a visit by a man who tells him that he has found poison in his house and his wife is acting strangely. Next, the wife pays a visit to Maigret and alludes to her husband's unbalanced mental state.

Maigret and the Killer *Superintendent Maigret*
London: Hamilton, 1971.
New York: Harcourt Brace, 1971.

A young man is found lying on the sidewalk outside of the restaurant where Maigret is eating. The man has not been robbed nor was he in any kind of trouble. Then why is he dead?

Maigret and the Flea *Superintendent Maigret*
London: Hamilton, 1972.

Maigret and the Informer
New York: Harcourt Brace, 1973.

The owner of the Sardine, a popular nightclub restaurant, is dumped on the sidewalk. Maurice Marcia has made the Sardine a well-known gathering place, but the police have not forgotten that he used to have ties with crime.

Maigret and the Millionaires *Superintendent Maigret*
London: Hamilton, 1974.
New York: Harcourt Brace, 1974.

The wealthy and famous Colonel Ward is found drowned in his bathtub.

The same evening Ward's mistress, the Countess Paverini, takes an overdose of pills and is rushed to the hospital. These two events lead Maigret halfway across Europe to find out why Ward had to die and what role the Countess played in his demise.

Maigret and the Loner *Superintendent Maigret*
London: Hamilton, 1975.
New York: Harcourt Brace, 1975.

In a rundown old wreck of a building the body of an elderly man is found. The man intrigues Maigret because he is clean and neat even though his clothes are old and ill fitting. There is no identification on the body and his fingerprints are not on file. Someone wanted the man dead, as he had been shot in the chest three times.

Maigret and the Hotel Majestic *Superintendent Maigret*
London: Hamilton, 1977.
New York: Harcourt Brace, 1978.

An American woman, Mrs. Oswald Clark, is found stuffed in a locker in the staff room of the Hotel Majestic. While Maigret checks the schedules of the hotel's staff he discovers that some members were not where they should have been.

V. L. Sims*

Death Is a Family Affair *Sergeant Dixie Struthers*
New York: Charter, 1987.

Detective Pete Willis's niece is missing. She is seventeen, intelligent, beautiful, and has never left home before without saying where she would be. Her mutilated body is found in the Winchester Mystery House in a small closet. She had been tortured, carved-up, and disemboweled.

To Sleep, Perchance to Kill *Sergeant Dixie Struthers*
New York: Charter, 1988. *and Lieutenant Tony DiFranco*

Victor Peters is found dead in his computer room at P/C Enterprises. His partner lies to the police and brings about trouble for everyone concerned. Sergeant Dixie Struthers catches the case, placing her in a bad situation because Peters's partner, David Les Carey, is being represented by her stepfather. Then an executive secretary is murdered in the P/C offices.

Maj Sjöwall and Per Wahlöö

Roseanna *Detective Chief Inspector Martin Beck*
New York: Pantheon, 1967.
London: Gollancz, 1968.

The body of a naked woman is pulled out of Lake Vättern. When Beck and his national homicide team arrive from Stockholm, all they know for sure is that the woman is still unidentified and that she was strangled while being assaulted. The birthmark on the inside of her left thigh is the only clue Beck has. When the break comes it is somewhat of a shock—the dead woman was an American, a librarian from Lincoln, Nebraska.

The Man on the Balcony *Detective Chief Inspector Martin Beck*
New York: Pantheon, 1968.
London: Gollancz, 1969.

Little girls are being murdered in Stockholm and Beck has no clues as to the killer's identity. A vicious mugger who preys on women in the city streets is the only one who has seen the face of the killer. Naturally he is not eager to step forward.

The Man Who Went Up in Smoke *Detective Chief Inspector Martin Beck*
New York: Pantheon, 1969.
London: Gollancz, 1970.

Martin Beck is sent to Budapest to find Alf Matsson, a reporter and television personality who has disappeared. Matsson had been working on a series of articles and the magazine editor is concerned that he has not been heard from in days. Beck finds that Matsson has been involved in some organized criminal activities. It does not help matters that Beck has been sent to Hungary as a temporary member of the Foreign Office staff with no official standing.

The Laughing Policeman *Detective Chief Inspector Martin Beck*
New York: Pantheon, 1970.
London: Gollancz, 1971.

It is November 1967 and Stockholm has just had another riot protesting the Vietnam War when a red doubledecker bus drives through a wire fence into a freight yard. On the bus are eight dead people and one of them is Ake Stenstrom, the youngest member of Martin Beck's homicide squad.

Murder at the Savoy *Detective Chief Inspector Martin Beck*
New York: Pantheon, 1971.
London: Gollancz, 1972.

During a dinner party at the Savoy, Viktor Palmgren is shot by a man who then calmly walks out of a window into the night. Palmgren is wealthy and not without power, so the incident attracts notice from the press. Martin Beck is sent to Malmö to head the investigation after the police in Stockholm lose the killer.

The Fire Engine That Disappeared *Detective Chief Inspector Martin Beck*
New York: Pantheon, 1971.
London: Gollancz, 1972.

A man lay dead on his bed. He had shot himself in the head. The only clue is a pad of paper by the telephone where he had written Martin Beck's name. Beck is chief inspector of the Stockholm homicide bureau but he does not know Ernst Sigurd Karlsson, the dead man, or why he wrote Beck's name. Then a bomb destroys an apartment house and the fire department does not arrive in time to put out the blaze because the fire truck disappears.

The Abominable Man *Detective Chief Inspector Martin Beck*
New York: Pantheon, 1972.
London: Gollancz, 1973.

The man dead in the hospital room is a police captain. Investigating his brutal murder is unpleasant for Beck as the man was sadistic and a very bad police officer. The homicide squad must handle this case gingerly as it has many negative aspects and political overtones as well as potential for generating bad feeling against the police.

The Locked Room *Detective Chief Inspector Martin Beck*
New York: Pantheon, 1973.
London: Gollancz, 1974.

A woman robs a bank and shoots a customer who tries to stop her. Martin Beck has been recovering from a gunshot wound for fifteen months. When he goes back to work it is to investigate a case in which a body was found in an apartment. The death looks like suicide, but certain clues point to murder.

Cop Killer: The Story of a Crime *Detective Chief Inspector Martin Beck*
New York: Pantheon, 1975.
London: Gollancz, 1975.

A woman disappears from the Malmö suburb of Andenslör. Beck is called from Stockholm to conduct the investigation because the chief suspect is

Folke Bengtsson, a convicted murderer arrested by Beck's homicide squad but later released. The woman's ex-husband is a wife abuser and a bully. Then a shootout between three policemen and two young men results in two dead. One of the kids escapes. Now homicide must look for him, too.

The Terrorists *Detective Chief Inspector Martin Beck*
New York: Pantheon, 1976.
London: Gollancz, 1977.

Stockholm is in the grip of unrest as a foreign dignitary plans a visit. In a few weeks the president of a Latin American country will arrive and his country has requested a police representative to help plan the arrangements for his security. In Stockholm a bomb explodes beneath the street killing the president and fifteen others in his motorcade. Then a famous film director is found dead in his bathtub.

Michael Slade*
(Pseudonym of Jay Clarke, John Banks, and Richard Covell)

Headhunter *Superintendent Robert De Clercq*
London: Allen, 1984.
New York: Morrow, 1984.

An insane killer is preying on women in Vancouver. He tortures, mutilates, and decapitates his victims and sticks the heads on totem poles. Along with the main plot runs a stream of consciousness from the killer's mind.

Ghoul *Detective Chief Superintendent Hilary Rand and Inspector Zinc Chandler*
London: Allen, 1987.
New York: Beech Tree, 1987.

Two investigations are going on simultaneously in London and Vancouver. Chief Superintendent Rand is desperately trying to solve the vampire killings in London as her job is on the line. In Vancouver the rock group Ghoul is involved in some very strange activities but what they are into eludes Inspector Chandler. A murderer is stalking Deborah Lane, and when she comes to Chandler's attention, Chandler discovers a link between what is going on in Vancouver and the vampire murders in London.

Ben Sloane

Horn: Hot Zone *Max Horn and Dan Riddle*
Toronto: Worldwide, 1990.

During a robbery Horn and his partner, Dan Riddle, of the crime suppression unit, stop the two criminals and retrieve the satchel full of stolen top-secret documents. Horn takes the satchel home with him; a killer sent to get the papers back kills Horn's wife and young daughter and destroys much of Horn's body. Horn finds a doctor who practices black-market medicine who fits him up with E-mod limbs and a robocop mentality. Soon Horn is on an asteroid in New Pittsburgh, a failing mining station. Here he finds the solution to the case and to some of his troubles.

Horn: Outland Strip *Max Horn*
Toronto: Worldwide, 1991.

In a gambling resort Max Horn, a twenty-first century cross between Robocop and the Six Million Dollar Man, investigates the murder of a cop, which leads him into danger and to truths about himself and his past.

Alison Smith

Rising *Chief of Police Judd Springfield*
New York: St. Martin's, 1987.

Something is not right at the construction site of the new dam in Coolidge Corners, Vermont. The chief engineer drives his car off a bridge and dies. Investigating the scene of the so-called accident, Springfield realizes that this was murder. He must discover what is behind the crime, as well as fight the machinations of the town's politicians.

D(aniel) W(ubert) Smith

Father's Law *Detective Chief Inspector Harry Fathers*
London: Macmillan, 1986.
Secaucus, NJ: Lyle Stuart, 1987.

When a British researcher is found to be missing, Chief Inspector Harry Fathers, head of Scotland Yard's serious crimes squad, is called in. He goes to New York to meet with American officials who believe that stealing sophisticated weaponry is the ultimate goal of the criminals.

Serious Crimes *Detective Chief Inspector Harry Fathers*
London: Macmillan, 1987

Silver Spoon Murders
Secaucus, NJ: Lyle Stuart, 1988.

The party at Granthelm House is interrupted when Granthelm's niece and her boyfriend are found dead in a locked room. The convenient murder/

suicide theory is disproved by the evidence the police gather. The silver collection is missing—help from the serious crimes squad is requested and Harry Fathers arrives to deal with the group surrounding the very important Sir Walter Granthelm. No one is telling the truth and everyone wishes to ignore the fact that evidence of drug use was found.

The Fourth Crow *Detective Chief Inspector Harry Fathers*
London: Macmillan, 1989.
New York: St. Martin's, 1990.

Faced with the reality of a high-level security leak, the British spy organization MI5 and the U.S. Secret Service ask for the help of Chief Inspector Harry Fathers and his serious crime squad. Fathers has enough on his plate with the violent and ugly gang war raging. He soon finds that petty bureauracacy and politics aside, he can trust no one.

Julie Smith

New Orleans Morning *Police Officer Skip Langdon*
New York: St. Martin's, 1990.

Skip Langdon, a policewoman in New Orleans, is assigned to help in the murder investigation of Chauncey St. Amant, who was King of Carnival for Mardi Gras. Langdon knows a number of wealthy and influential people because she went to school with most of them and spent time in their homes. The police use her knowledge and entrée into the world of high society but resent her for having those connections. Skip must prove to all that she is fair-minded as well as a good cop.

The Axeman's Jazz *Detective Skip Langdon*
New York: St. Martin's, 1991.

Two people are killed and the letter A has been written on the wall of their apartments. Detective Skip Langdon, now in homicide, cannot believe that the murderer would write a letter to all the news media in New Orleans announcing that the Axeman, a killer from the nineteenth century, is back. All evidence points to the guilty one being a part of a co-dependency group that Skip joins, but she finds more than she bargained for when she learns her own mother is a member.

Mark Smith*

The Death of the Detective *Detective Magnuson*
New York: Knopf, 1973.
London: Secker and Warburg, 1975.

There is a killer loose in Chicago. The life of the police detective is placed under a microscope by the author in this exhaustive study of the daily existence of a police detective.

Martin Cruz Smith*

Gorky Park *Chief Inspector Arkady Renko*
New York: Random House, 1981.
London: Collins, 1981.

Three people, a woman and two men, are found frozen in Gorky Park. That they have been brutally murdered is evident. Now Chief Inspector Arkady Renko of the Moscow police must try to identify the victims and determine why they were killed. Further complications are rendered by the KGB, the American FBI, and the New York Police Department.

Mitchell Smith

Daydreams *Detectives Ellie Klein*
New York: McGraw-Hill, 1987. *and Tommy Nardone*
London: Century Hutchinson, 1988.

Sally Gaither had been scalded to death in her shower. Sally was a high-priced call girl with a number of wealthy and powerful clients. Gaither kept a list of her customers so a team of specialists arrives from Washington, DC, to aid in the search for the list. Detectives Klein and Nardone of the NYPD are the only ones interested in finding the murderer and the truth behind it. They must battle federal agents (and their own personal problems) all the way.

Stephen Solomita*

Force of Nature
New York: Putnam, 1989.

Detective Sergeant Stanley Moodrow and Detective Jim Tilley

After leading a violent life as a thug and drug dealer, Levander Greenwood, also known as Kubla Kahn, has changed his style to become a one-man killing machine. He is working his way through the roster of pushers on the lower East Side of Manhattan, but has gone underground so the detectives from the 7th precinct are having trouble finding him. That is when Sergeant Moodrow and his new partner (the first in almost twenty years) get drawn into the case. One of five people murdered in what is being called the Delancey Street Massacre was an undercover cop.

Richard Martin Stern*

Murder in the Walls
New York: Scribner's, 1971.
London: Hale, 1973.

Detective Lieutenant Juan Felipe "Johnny" Ortiz

In one day two people are found murdered in peaceful Santo Cristo, New Mexico. The first body is that of a young woman who worked in Sanchez House, a Spanish hacienda built circa 1680, now a whorehouse owned by Flora Hobbs. The second corpse is that of a bail jumper, who is found on an archaeological excavation site run by Cassie Enright of the state museum. The Sanchez House is in the path of a proposed highway and something is definitely going on behind the scenes in the business community and the art world.

You Don't Need an Enemy
New York: Scribner's, 1972.
London: Hale, 1973.

Lieutenant Juan Felipe "Johnny" Ortiz

Miss Lucy Carruthers is dead in her library. One of the last people to see her alone was Cassandra Enright, Johnny Ortiz's girlfriend. Cassandra had had an argument with the dead woman the day before. The murder weapon belongs to Don Hastings, a sculptor and Carruthers's nephew. Cassie lies about Hastings's whereabouts on the murder night, and then she is attacked and beaten so badly she must go to the hospital.

Death in the Snow
New York: Scribner's, 1973.
London: Hale, 1974.

Lieutenant Juan Felipe "Johnny" Ortiz

A man is found dead on a ski slope. His pants are too big for him, and he has no belt, no money, no identification. On the same day three young people are dead of heroin overdoses.

Tangled Murders *Lieutenant Juan Felipe "Johnny" Ortiz*
New York: Pocket, 1989.

Charley Harrington, a brilliant computer hacker with few scruples, is murdered. Ortiz must find a motive for his death, but before he does someone else dies.

Missing Man *Lieutenant Juan Felipe "Johnny" Ortiz*
New York: Pocket, 1990.

Ortiz and Sergeant Lopez are called into the mountains where a man has been killed in a rockslide set off by an explosion. The man was bird-watching and carrying all the necessary paraphernalia. He also brought along several pictures of a nude woman. The dead man had been involved in some shady, expensive real estate deals and he and his partners had been having money problems. When one of their buildings burns down, Ortiz begins to suspect that someone is trying to direct police attention away from himself.

Interloper *Lieutenant Juan Felipe "Johnny" Ortiz*
New York: Pocket, 1990

After Walter Higgins visits Johnny Ortiz to ask him to keep an eye on Leon Bascomb, Bascomb is found shot to death on Elk Ridge. Bascomb, who moved to Santo Cristo from Miami, is wealthy and appears to have a shady past. Now Ortiz must find his murderer.

J. Michael Straczynski

Otherside *Detective Susan Warwick and*
New York: Dutton, 1990. *Detective Jordan Cayle*

People in Los Angeles are dying for no good reason. The majority of the deaths take place in and around Lennox High School. The evil involves things that live in the dark that take possession of humans who sell their souls.

L. A. G. Strong*

Which I Never *Detective Chief Inspector Ellis McKay*
London: Crime Club, 1950.
New York: Macmillan, 1952.

Sent to the country on police business, Chief Inspector McKay gets caught up in a case involving a number of missing girls.

Carsten Stroud

Sniper's Moon *Detective Frank Keogh*
New York: Bantam, 1990.

Frank Keogh is diagnosed as burned out after he and his partner, Pat Butler, take out two members of a Bronx street gang, the Ching-a-Lings, who had killed three police officers and were holding two women hostage. When two murders occur with the same modus operandi, Keogh becomes the prime suspect because one of Keogh's father's most spectacular cases featured the same M.O.

Rob Swigart

Vector *Lieutenant Cobb Takamura*
New York: Bluejay, 1986.

Microbiologist Chazz Koenig moves to Hawaii to try to save his marriage. The new job in a great place seems the perfect solution. But people start dying and Koenig is a suspect in the murder investigation. Soon he meets Lieutenant Takamura, and when the autopsy reveals that one of the victims has a puncture wound containing a poisonous biological substance, Takamura asks Koenig for help.

Toxin *Lieutenant Cobb Takamura and*
New York: St. Martin's, 1989. *Microbiologist Chazz Koenig*

A satellite is falling to Earth and it is very likely to hit the island of Kauai. There is good reason to believe that the satellite is carrying a mutant virus or a new link in the substances used in chemical warfare. There is a panic on the island and in its midst a wealthy businessman is found shot to death.

Venom *Lieutenant Cobb Takamura and*
New York: St. Martin's, 1991. *Microbiologist Chazz Koenig*

Kimiko Takamura finds seven dead bodies aboard a vessel in the harbor where she is swimming. The cause of death is an exotic poison, which Koenig must identify. Then two women are murdered, and the murderer is now after Takamura and Koenig.

Jeffrey Tharp

A Killing in Kansas *Lieutenant John Branch*
New York: Fawcett, 1991.

Murder suspect Eddie Shubitz hangs himself in his cell in the Elk Rapids, Kansas, jail. Lieutenant Johnny Branch, formerly a cop in Kansas City, who believes that Eddie did not commit the murder with which he was charged, now faces some unpleasant facts—he is not on the case, he is involved with Eddie's sister, and something is fishy about the man running for the state legislature.

Donald Thomas
(also Francis Selwyn, q.v.)

The Ripper's Apprentice *Inspector Alfred Swain and*
London: Macmillan, 1986. *Sergeant Oliver Lumley*
New York: St. Martin's, 1986.

Someone is poisoning London prostitutes in a hideous way. Using strychnine to cause the victim maximum pain causes pleasure in the killer. A handwriting analyst (something of a rarity in Victorian England) looks at letters sent to various people accusing them of the murders as well as at notes sent to the police. He concludes that a Spaniard, a woman, and a man have written them. Swain's life is further complicated by his growing attraction to the daughter of his landlady. (Note: This is a fictionalized version of a real case that took place in England in 1891–1892.)

Jekyll, Alias Hyde *Inspector Alfred Swain*
London: Macmillan, 1988.
New York: St.Martin's, 1989.

In Robert Louis Stevenson's book about Edward Hyde and Henry Jekyll there are several unusual questions and a number of puzzles left unsolved. Inspector Swain is assigned the task of showing what really happened and providing answers to the puzzles left in the original novella.

Roderick Thorp

Rainbow Drive *Lieutenant Mike Gallagher*
New York: Summit, 1986.

Five people are butchered in a Laurel Canyon home and the Hollywood homicide squad gets the case. The situation does not ring true for Mike Gallagher as the police were on the scene only minutes after the call for help was placed.

Lawrence Treat*

V as in Victim*   *Detectives Mitch Taylor and Jub Freeman*
New York: Duell, 1945.
London: Rich and Cowan, 1950.

H as in Hunted   *Detective Jub Freeman*
New York: Duell, 1946.
London: Boardman, 1950.

Anthony Weir, radio personality, is murdered. Jub Freeman from the NYPD laboratory goes over Weir's apartment collecting everything that may be of help in the investigation. The story is populated with a great many characters and the plot twists and turns but there is very little procedure here.

Q as in Quicksand*   *Detectives Mitch Taylor and Jub Freeman*
New York: Duell, 1947.

Step into Quicksand
London: Boardman, 1959.

T as in Trapped*   *Detectives Mitch Taylor and Jub Freeman*
New York: Morrow, 1947.

F as in Flight   *Lieutenant Bill Decker and Jub Freeman*
New York: Morrow, 1948.
London: Boardman, 1949.

Alan Vane is shot and killed in the home of Norma Drooscken. Norma does not tell the police that she shot the man nor does she say that he is her husband. The police believe Norma did the killing but they do not know why. They detain Ms. Drooscken and painstakingly piece together what they believe happened. All they have to do is prove it.

Big Shot   *Police Officer Mitch Taylor*
New York: Harper, 1951.

Mitch Taylor has been demoted and sent to a small-town, rural police force as punishment for his problems with the New York Police Department—graft and favoritism have become a way of life for him. He is able to advance from patrol officer to investigator when a local man fails to come home from work. Trying to locate the missing man, Taylor sets in motion the inquiries, but a few things do not add up. The man's wife tells Taylor that their home had been searched a few weeks before. Taylor must get her to tell him whatever she knows so that he can solve the case and thus possibly return to being a detective, while at the same time sidestepping the local crime boss and his illegal operations because he does not want to run afoul of people who can hurt him.

Weep for a Wanton[*]   *Detectives Jub Freeman and Mitch Taylor*
New York: Ace, 1956.
London: Boardman, 1958.

Lady, Drop Dead   *Detectives Jub Freeman and Mitch Taylor*
New York and London: Abelard, 1960.

Vivian Vixen is found stabbed in her cottage. Detective Mitch Taylor thinks that private eye Hank Greenleaf is the killer—his life is a mess and he is mixed up with more women than he can handle.

Joseph Trigoboff

The Bone Orchard   *Detective Alvin Yablonsky*
New York: Walker, 1990.

A beautiful young man who works as a stripper and hustler and possesses a closet full of designer clothes is found brutally murdered. Yablonsky sorts through the sexual perversions of the rich and famous as he seeks the killer.

Peter Turnbull

Deep and Crisp and Even   *P Division*
London: Collins, 1981.
New York: St. Martin's, 1982.

While Glasgow is held captive under a blanket of snow and cold, a killer stalks—someone who is stabbing people to death. His calling card is a small scrap of paper containing the message "This is for Lissu." More women are killed. There are no other clues and no leads for P Division to follow.

Dead Knock   P Division
London: Collins, 1982.
New York: St. Martin's 1983.

A half-million pounds of heroin are coming into Glasgow in packages of prawns earmarked for six restaurants. A Dutch woman is given a massive dose of heroin. The investigation into her death leads the police to another murder in Amsterdam. Eighteen months before, the body of a courier for the drug runners was found in a ditch. The Dutch police know the Triad (Chinese organized crime) is behind the killings; the thugs are holding the murdered man's three-year-old child captive. Then a rapist begins operations in Glasgow.

Fair Friday   P Division
London: Collins, 1983.
New York: St. Martin's, 1983.

The body of a *Clarion* reporter is found in an alley. He had been working on a story concerning the mishandling of funds by an attorney working for people who were trying to buy a home. There is something more here as the trail leads to Glasgow's organized crime world.

Big Money   P Division
London: Collins, 1984.
New York: St. Martin's, 1984.

In a post office robbery the criminals get away with a quarter of a million pounds in used small bills. Inspector Donoghue puts together his investigation team but there are no clues to follow. Then they find a witness who observed the thieves transferring the money from the getaway car to a van; this is followed by a murder that may be connected to the criminals.

Two Way Cut   P Division
London: Collins, 1988.
New York: St. Martin's, 1986.

A constable finds a headless corpse. With no clues, an anonymous corpse, and an apparent random murder, P Division investigates.

Condition Purple   P Division
London: Collins, 1989.
New York: St. Martin's, 1989.

Stephanie Craigellachie, prostitute and drug addict, is stabbed once in the throat, her body left in the alley where she was attacked and died. The meager information gleaned through interviews leads the police to Toni Durchan and a lowlife named Jimmy the Rodent.

And Did Murder Him *P Division*
London: Collins, 1991
New York, St. Martin's, 1991

The body of a young man is found lying in an alley; the murder weapon, a knife, is found farther away. It appears to be a routine killing of one drug addict by another. But upon further investigation and evidence found at the autopsy, it is clear that the man had been murdered elsewhere and his body moved to the alley. P Division must reevaluate the facts and dig into the victim's background to ascertain what lead him to his death.

Long Day Monday *P Division*
London: Macmillan, 1992
New York: St. Martin's, 1993

On the verge of the road just beyond the McWilliams farm is a car that has been parked there for two days. McWilliams calls the police, who then find a mound of freshly dug earth covering the dead body of a woman. When Sergeant Sussoch of P Division sees the scene of the crime, he reacts violently for he remembers investigating a similar case twenty-five years before. He also remembers that that case resulted in the discovery of many dead people buried in shallow graves throughout this rural area. The question for the Division is whether this is the same killer who was operating there years ago or a copycat.

Dorothy Uhnak[*]

The Bait *Detective Christie Opara*
New York: Simon & Schuster, 1968.
London: Hodder, 1968.

A serial killer is preying on woman and Opara is used as bait to capture him.

The Witness *Detective Christie Opara*
New York: Simon & Schuster, 1969.
London: Hodder, 1970.

District Attorney Reardon's daughter, Barbara, plans to join the protest against public housing. Her father forbids her, but then sends Christie Opara to protect her just in case. What starts out as a peaceful demonstration turns into a violent altercation and the leader of the protestors, Billy Everett, is shot with a patrolman's gun. Christie sees who did the shooting.

The Ledger   *Detective Christie Opara*
New York: Simon & Schuster, 1970.
London: Hodder, 1971.

Elena Vargas, a material witness to a murder, is being held in a hotel room while the district attorney's people go through the account books of Enzio Giardino, a big-time drug dealer. Vargas is the only person Giardino trusts, his hold over her is complete. She is invaluable to him. Slowly Opara begins to uncover the real Elena Vargas and the real reason for her worth.

Law and Order
New York: Simon & Schuster, 1973.
London: Hodder, 1973.

This novel is a saga of a New York family, members of which are police officers.

The Investigation   *Sergeant Joe Peters*
New York: Simon & Schuster, 1977.
London: Hodder, 1977.

Kitty Keeler's two children are missing. Kitty is a party girl who loves expensive clothes, jewelry, a fast social life, and who associates with people involved in organized crime. When the bodies of her sons are found in a vacant lot about six blocks from their home, Kitty is the chief suspect. Detective Joe Peters does not believe she did it and sets out to discover the truth. The trail leads him into Kitty's world, where he encounters a politician with the desire to be mayor, a big-time crime boss, ambitious policemen, and the hint of blackmail.

Derek Van Arman

Just Killing Time   *John F. Scott, Director of VICAT*
New York: Dutton, 1992.

The Violent Criminal Apprehension Team (VICAT), a federal law enforcement program, is after a particularly vicious serial killer who destroys every living thing in a family when he invades their domain. At the same time the team is tracking and closing in on two recreational killers who have left a trail of blood all over the South and are now due to arrive in Washington, DC. There is also the case of the boy who finds a body in what was once a bowling alley. The body has been there a very long time, and the use of an exotic killing device reminds Scott, the team director, of the method used in the murder of another young woman who died many years before.

Janwillem van de Wetering

Outsider in Amsterdam *The Commissaris, Adjutant Grijpstra,*
Boston: Houghton Mifflin, 1975 *and Sergeant Rinus de Gier*
London: Heinemann, 1976.

Called to the building housing the Hindist Society, Grijpstra and de Gier find the founder and leader, Piet Verboom, hanged in his room. The only indication that he did not commit suicide is a bruise on his temple and a faint trace of an opiate in his system. All the people living in the building had ample opportunity and reason to kill him.

The Corpse on the Dike *The Commissaris, Adjutant Grijpstra,*
Boston: Houghton Mifflin, 1976 *and Sergeant Rinus de Gier*
London: Heinemann, 1977.

A young man is murdered in his house, shot between the eyes. The motive for his death eludes the police, as the man has led an innocuous life. De Gier and Grijpstra learn that he had a visitor, known as the Cat, who sells things that others cannot. The Cat and a dealer in used clothing must be interviewed. A brothel is also visited for information.

Tumbleweed *The Commissaris, Adjutant Grijpstra,*
Boston: Houghton Mifflin, 1976 *and Sergeant Rinus de Gier*
London: Heinemann, 1976.

The Dutch secret service is interested in a woman who lives alone on a houseboat and entertains three wealthy and important men. Grijpstra and de Gier have been keeping an eye on her, but when she does not appear for several days and her cat is left unattended, a neighbor calls the police.

Death of a Hawker *The Commissaris, Adjutant Grijpstra,*
Boston: Houghton Mifflin, 1977 *and Sergeant Rinus de Gier*
London: Heinemann, 1977.

As a mob is rioting in the streets of Amsterdam, Grijpstra and de Gier are trying to get to the house of Abe Rogge, whose sister has found him lying on the floor of his room—his head bloodied. Rogge is an intelligent man with a nasty penchant for making people see their own weaknesses. He dies, but no weapon is found at the scene.

The Japanese Corpse *The Commissaris, Adjutant Grijpstra,*
Boston: Houghton Mifflin, 1977   *and Sergeant Rinus de Gier*
London: Heinemann, 1977.

A young Japanese male vanishes and his fiancée goes to police headquarters to report him missng. De Gier and Grijpstra call in the Commissaris, who discovers that the man was a member of the Yakuza, the Japanese organized crime syndicate. After a shocking personal loss and breakdown, de Gier goes to Japan with the Commissaris to play bodyguard. The Yakuza are waiting to do business.

The Blond Baboon *The Commissaris, Adjutant Grijpstra,*
Boston: Houghton Mifflin, 1978   *and Sergeant Rinus de Gier*
London: Heinemann, 1978.

During a very bad storm, art dealer Elaine Carnet falls down an outside stairway and dies. But there is something wrong— some small fact, some feeling about the circumstances surrounding her demise that keeps the Commissaris and his men on the case. Their chief suspect is a man who resembles a baboon, drives a 1936 Rolls Royce, and lives in a very expensive seventeenth-century house. He is also the dead woman's former lover. But when new evidence comes to the fore the case changes once again. Then there is the question of who poisoned Carnet's dog shortly before her death.

The Maine Massacre *The Commissaris, Adjutant Grijpstra,*
Boston: Houghton Mifflin, 1979   *and Sergeant Rinus de Gier*
London: Heinemann, 1979.

The Commissaris's brother-in-law dies in an accident in Jameson, Maine, where he lived with his wife, Suzanne. Suzanne calls her brother and asks him to come help her and he does. But the weather is 30 below zero in Jameson and de Gier and Grijpstra fear for their friend's health and well-being. So the chief constable sends de Gier to observe American police techniques in the wilds of Maine. There have been murders there and the Jameson sheriff is very happy to have de Gier in town.

The Mind Murders *The Commissaris, Adjutant Grijpstra,*
Boston: Houghton Mifflin, 1981   *and Sergeant Rinus de Gier*
London: Heinemann, 1981.

Frits Fortune, who is drunk, is thrown into a canal by two policemen.

Sergeant de Gier rescues him, but Fortune, who is lame, attacks de Gier with his crutch. It turns out that Fortune's wife is missing, and all their household possessions gone. De Gier and Grijpstra begin by treating the missing woman as a homicide victim. While searching for some tangible evidence, they discover the body of Fortune's little Poodle. Then, the corpse of a man is found, and the detectives learn that there are many ways to commit murder.

The Streetbird *The Commissaris, Adjutant Grijpstra,*
Boston: Houghton Mifflin, 1983 *and Sergeant Rinus de Gier*
London: Gollancz, 1984.

A vicious and hated pimp is murdered in Amsterdam's red-light district. He was killed with a machine gun, which is hard to believe, but de Gier gets another surprise out in the street when he sees a vulture sitting on top of a building. Complex clues and motivation lead to a surprise ending.

The Rattle-Rat *The Commissaris, Adjutant Grijpstra,*
Boston: Houghton Mifflin, 1985 *and Sergeant Rinus de Gier*
London: Gollancz, 1986.

Douwe Scherjoen is dead. He was shot in the head then burned in an aluminum rowboat in the river. Grijpstra, in a bad mood, gives de Gier minor tasks throughout the investigation while keeping the interesting bits for himself. Soon they know that the murdered man was the kind of businessman who breaks his word and who had made a lot of enemies.

Hard Rain *The Commissaris, Adjutant Grijpstra,*
Boston: Houghton Mifflin, 1986 *and Sergeant Rinus de Gier*
London: Gollancz, 1987.

In the same night, a banker is killed, his death made to look like a suicide, and three drug addicts die of heroin overdoses in their houseboat right outside the banker's mansion. The cases are wrapped up by Inspector Halba, a shady detective from another sector of the metro police. Everyone, from the Commissaris, who is being investigated for fraud, to de Gier, charged with reckless driving, gets suspended from the force.

Peter Van Greenaway*

Doppelganger *Detective Inspector Cherry*
London: Gollancz, 1975.

There have been several strange deaths in the little town of Carby and Inspector Cherry of Scotland Yard is sent from London to cope with them.

A man named Jederman has been seen at the three death sites but he is also known to have been elsewhere when the deaths occurred. His house is either haunted or is a conduit for supernatural happenings. This is the perfect case for Cherry, who deals rather well with the unusual.

The Killing Cup *Detective Inspector Cherry*
London: Gollancz, 1988.

A Christian relic of great value to the Vatican is about to be auctioned at Peachum's for the Marchesa del Deodati. The dealer, Sarinan, is unscrupulous and has in mind his own interest. Scotland Yard is asked to look into the matter of possible wrongdoing and they assign art buff Cherry to see to things. A clairvoyant and a Vatican emissary add to the mystery of what is really going on.

John Holbrook Vance*

The Pleasant Grove Murders *Sheriff Joe Bain*
New York: Bobbs, 1967.
London: Hale, 1968.

The mailman is murdered and the inquiry involves some of the best families in the California town of Pleasant Grove.

Conrad Voss Bark

The Second Red Dragon *Detective Sergeant Lune*
London: Gollancz, 1968.
New York: Walker, 1968.

Zebedee Crunch, leader of a religious sect, and new convert George Hawkes go missing after a murder has been committed. Sergeant Lune and William Holmes are assigned to find them, as there may be ties to terrorism at work.

Per Wahlöö*

Murder on the Thirty-First Floor *Detective Chief Inspector Jensen*
London: Joseph, 1966.
New York: Pantheon, 1967.

The Thirty-First Floor
New York: Knopf, 1967.

When a threatening letter arrives at the offices of a publisher, Jensen is assigned the case. The letter states that an incendiary device has been planted in the building and will detonate at a certain time. The office workers are not to be told of the threat, so work goes on with Jensen unobtrusively poking into things and asking questions.

John Wainwright*

Death in a Sleeping City   *Detective Chief Superintendent*
London: The Crime Club/Collins, 1965.   *Lewis*

A man is shot in the head gangland style. Detective Superintendent Lewis believes that a police force the size of his can handle the investigation so Scotland Yard is not called in. Two more killings occur and the force is thrown into a frenzy of activity trying to find the hired hit men.

Evil Intent   *Chief Superintendent Charles Ripley*
London: Collins, 1966.

Because Detective Superintendent Harris of the Criminal Investigation Division is ill, the head of the uniform branch of Beechwood Brook Division, Charles Ripley, conducts a murder investigation. Three children have found the badly mutilated body of a man lying on a large rock. The man's throat has been cut and he has been emasculated. The scene looks very much like a black fertility rite. Ripley goes looking for witches and finds that Beechwood Brook may be hiding a few.

The Crystallised Carbon Pig   *Superintendent Gilliant*
London: Collins, 1966.
New York: Walker, 1967.

The police know that a huge diamond robbery is being planned and they send Sergeant John Pewter undercover to find out what he can. But the police have been less than candid with Pewter and he finds himself traveling to France and Italy and to a possible nest of Russian spies.

The Worms Must Wait*   *Chief Superintendent Charles Ripley*
London: Collins, 1967.

The Darkening Glass   *Divisional Superintendent Charles Ripley*
London: Collins, 1968.

A seven-year-old girl is missing from the Summerhead section of Beechwood Brook division. Constable William Holt interviews her mother, and learns that her home life is not the best, that she has run away to Leeds twice. But this time, she has not. Her body is found and the scene examined. Charles Ripley, the consummate policeman and head of the division, takes charge of the case, overruling the Criminal Investigation

Department. The police quickly identify the murderer but getting evidence against him is another matter.

Freeze Thy Blood Less Coldly[*] *Chief Superintendent Charles Ripley*
London: Macmillan, 1970.

Requiem for a Loser *Chief Constable Gilliant*
London: Macmillan, 1972.

Since Superintendent Sweetapple took over the North End division crime has doubled. He does not want excuses or reasons—he wants it stopped. The police are looking for a man named Reginald Drover, who eludes them easily. They want him for killing a policeman.

High-Class Kill *Chief Constable Gilliant*
London: Macmillan, 1973.

Wealthy Edmund Shaw falls from the roof of his uncle's mansion during a birthday party for his cousin. The autopsy proves that the young man was murdered—he died before he fell. The pathologist believes that Shaw was frightened to death.

A Touch Of Malice[*] *Chief Superintendent Charles Ripley*
London: Macmillan, 1973.

The Evidence I Shall Give[*] *Superintendent Lennox*
London: Macmillan, 1974.

The Hard Hit[*] *Chief Superintendent Charles Ripley*
London: Macmillan, 1974.
New York: St. Martin's, 1975.

Death of a Big Man *Chief Superintendent Charles Ripley*
London: Macmillan, 1975.
New York: St. Martin's, 1975.

Charles Ripley, retired, alone, confined to a wheelchair, is offered a chance to eliminate Paul Tinther, a clever, ruthless crook.

Square Dance *Detective Superintendent Lennox*
London: Macmillan, 1975. *and Chief Inspector Bardoph Sawyer*
New York: St. Martin's, 1975.

Harry Ogden is released from prison after serving ten years for the murder of his neighbor's wife. Sawyer, the officer in charge of the old case, wants to warn Ogden that the police are watching him. Ogden is involved in a severe auto accident. All the players in the old drama gather at the Swan's Nest, the cottage of Pamela Ogden, Harry Ogden's wife, where they are joined by Lennox.

Landscape with Violence   *Detective Chief Superintendent Robert Harris,*
London: Macmillan, 1975.   *Chief Superintendent Blayde, and*
New York: St. Martin's, 1976.   *Detective Superintendent Lennox*

The village of Robs Cully, an upper-middle-class real estate development on an island created by several rivers, is taken over by a gang of Americans who want the son of their ringleader released from prison. Despite the author's faulty concept of American gangster slang, the tension builds to a spectacular climax involving Harris, Blayde, and Lennox.

Pool of Tears   *Detective Superintendent Lennox*
London: Macmillan, 1977.
New York: St. Martin's, 1977.

A taxi has disappeared and with it its driver. When the police find the cab, it is burning, totally destroyed. Nathaniel Emmerson has won a large sum of money but he cannot enjoy it as his son has been kidnapped.

Brainwash   *Detective Inspector Lyle*
London: Macmillan, 1979.
New York: St. Martin's, 1979.

The book is told in the format of an interrogation of a prisoner. Detective Inspector Lyle questions the suspect about a rape and murder. The man could be a child molester and killer so Lyle must bring all his skills to bear.

Take Murder . . .   *Inspector Chris Tallboy and Inspector*
London: Macmillan, 1979.   *Edmund Caan*
New York: St. Martin's, 1981.

When the first streetwalker is strangled a task force is formed headed by Chief Superintendent Lennox, the legwork to be done by Inspector Chris Tallboy and Inspector Eddie Caan. Suspicion falls on Constable Turnbull when another prostitute is murdered.

Duty Elsewhere *Inspector Lyle*
London: Macmillan, 1979.
New York: St. Martin's, 1979.

Inspector Lyle had attended Adam Cooke's funeral three years before when he sees him walking down the street. Lyle and Blayde, joined by Lennox and two others, form a duty-elsewhere team and go looking for Cooke, a most dangerous and vicious criminal.

Dominoes *Detective Inspector Lyle, Detective Chief Superintendent*
London: Macmillan, 1980. *Lennox, Chief Inspector Chris Tallboy, and*
New York: St. Martin's, 1980. *Chief Superintendent Robert Blayde*

Tony and Hannah are teachers in a mediocre school for girls. While driving home with a friend, Tony hits a woman riding a horse. The stress is too much for Hannah, who commits suicide. During three days of unabashed lust in Page's home while his wife is away, Nick Page and Angela Warton are murdered by a burglar. Beechwood Brook divisional police conduct the investigation. Lennox and Tallboy know almost immediately that Ben Cooley is the perpetrator but what has happened to bring these people to their deaths is another matter.

All on a Summer's Day *Chief Superintendent Robert Blayde,*
London, Macmillan, 1981. *Chief Inspector Tallboy, and*
New York: St. Martin's, 1982. *Assistant Chief Constable Harris*

Twenty-four hours of the activities of the Soworth police station are dramatized. Everything is included, from a double homicide to the maiming of two policemen in a deliberate explosion, the confession of a murderer, and the arrival of a biker gang in town, intent on mass destruction. In staccato fashion Wainwright fires scene upon scene into a narrative told from all the policepersons' points of view.

Blayde R.I.P. *Chief Superintendent Robert Blayde*
London: Macmillan, 1982.
New York: St. Martin's, 1982.

Robert Blayde goes from a poor family environment to the military to being a policeman. He quickly rises in the ranks until he becomes chief superintendent. Blayde is ruthless, honest, hard, and often unfeeling. Not a procedural, this is more the story of the life of a cop step by step.

Their Evil Ways   *Detective Chief Superintendent Ralph Flensing*
London: Macmillan, 1983.   *and Detective Chief Inspector David Hoyle*
New York: St. Martin's, 1983.

Fred Kelly's burial is postponed because the gravediggers find another body in the grave. Chief Superintendent Flensing is new to Lessford as he takes command of the constabulary previously headed by Blayde. The dead man was a neighborhood womanizer, who may have gotten the wrong woman pregnant. The three men last seen with the victim are hunted down, and in the process the investigation becomes more complicated.

The Ride   *Detective Chief Superintendent Ralph Flensing*
London: Macmillan, 1984.   *and Detective Chief Inspector David Hoyle*
New York: St. Martin's, 1984.

There is one suspect in the murder investigation of a homosexual but not enough evidence to convict him. Flensing and Hoyle arrange to have him driven from London to Lessford with a motor patrol sergeant, CID sergeant Bellamy, something of a loose cannon, Constable Clarke, who is sympathetic, and Hoyle, who holds it all together. Bellamy is to badger the confession out of the guilty person.

Cul-de-Sac   *Lessford Divisional Police*
London: Macmillan, 1984.
New York: St. Martin's, 1984.

John Duxbury keeps a diary to be read by his son. In it he writes all his secret thoughts, all the things that were wrong with his marriage, his hopes, and his dreams. While on vacation Maude, his wife, falls off a cliff to her death. Sergeant Harry Harker conducts the investigation. There are witnesses to the fall and the possibility of murder. Did John Duxbury push his wife?

All Through the Night   *Detective Chief Superintendent Harry Barstow*
London: Macmillan, 1985.   *and Inspector James Riddle*
New York: St. Martin's, 1985.

The night shift at Radholme is shaken up when three people break into a pharmacy and begin shooting at the police who have arrived to arrest them. The ensuing flap results in a murder and two wounded policemen doing a juggling act between loyalty and justice. All in an evening's work, the personal as well as professional problems of the police are discussed and meshed into a coherent piece illustrating the realities of daily police life.

Portrait in Shadow *Lessford Divisional Police*
London: Macmillan, 1986.
New York: St. Martin's, 1986.

The narrator is a killer. He murdered the gamekeeper at his school when he was fifteen, then goes on to become a high-priced hit man. The story seesaws between the killer's reminiscences and the policemen who are hunting him.

The Forgotten Murders *Lessford Divisional Police*
London: Macmillan, 1987.
New York: St. Martin's, 1987.

The same morning that a murdered woman's body is found in the middle of the road, a helicopter crashes into the town library causing many deaths and a destructive fire. The investigation into the helicopter crash is stopped by higher-ups from London, but a constable and a sergeant solve the murder.

A Very Parochial Murder *Detective Chief Inspector Lyle, Detective*
London: Macmillan, 1988. *Inspector Faber, and Detective*
New York: St. Martin's 1988. *Sergeant Jackson*

The town ruffian, Jimmy Doyle, is murdered. As the investigation proceeds, suspicion is that the police are not doing a thorough job because Doyle was the primary suspect in the murder of Bob Jackson's mother-in-law the previous year.

The Man Who Wasn't There *Chief Inspector Lyle*
London: Macmillan, 1989.
New York: St. Martin's, 1989.

In a span of nine months three murders—two men and one woman—have been committed in Lessford; all three victims were members of organized crime. The crimes were being investigated by Superintendent Colladine, but a car ran him down and killed him. Now Chief Constable Gilliant has hired Chief Inspector Lyle to find out what is going on in his Lessford territory. Lyle must ferret out the crooked cop on the force—one capable of stopping his colleagues, one who is in league with the crime lord.

Hangman's Lane *Superintendent Lyle*
London: Macmillan, 1992
New York: St. Martin's, 1992.

Constable Alex Wardle's wife is found in a field by him and his sergeant. Tabitha Wardle had been killed with a shotgun blast to her chest. Obviously the small village of Easedale needs help, and Chief Superintendent Hunt of Lessford constabulary is sent. But Hunt is seriously injured in an automobile crash. Superintendent Lyle is then ordered to sort things out. He finds that Wardle had many reasons to want his wife dead. His daughter, in fact, believes him to be responsible.

Peter N. Walker*

Carnaby and the Hijakers*   *Sergeant James Aloysius Carnaby-King*
London: Hale, 1967.

Carnaby and the Assassins   *Sergeant James Aloysius Carnaby-King*
London: Hale, 1968.

No one suspects that police constable Earnshaw has been murdered when he is found on the moors; that is discovered at the postmortem. Earnshaw had been shot in the back, the blood washed off his body and his clothing replaced, and left on the moors. Commander Pigeon sends Carnaby to Yorkshire to look around but when he arrives, he is told that Superintendent Adams of the murder squad will be joining him. Something dangerous and very strange is going on and Earnshaw has stumbled into the middle of it.

Carnaby and the Gaolbreakers   *Sergeant James Aloysius Carnaby-King*
London: Hale, 1968.

The commando squad knows that there are a number of prison escapes each year. What makes the current year outstanding is that while the police are searching for the convict, someone is carrying out very lucrative robberies. Carnaby goes undercover as a prisoner and plots a daring escape, which has some unexpected results.

Carnaby and the Conspirators*   *Sergeant James Aloysius Carnaby-King*
London: Hale, 1969.

Carnaby and the Saboteurs*   *Sergeant James Aloysius Carnaby-King*
London: Hale, 1970.

Carnaby and the Eliminators   *Sergeant James Aloysius Carnaby-King*
London: Hale, 1971.

Mr. Justice Broughton of the criminal assize court of Parchester is shot amid a crowd of civilians, tourists, and officers of the court. Scotland

Yard's murder squad is dispatched to oversee the investigation because Mr. Justice Felstead of the civil court has asked for help from the secret commando squad. That same day a vicar of the church and a doctor are murdered. The killings are claimed by a group of religious fanatics who are to be infiltrated by undercover detective sergeant Carnaby.

Carnaby and the Demonstrators*   *Sergeant James Aloysius Carnaby-King*
London: Hale, 1972.

Carnaby and the Infiltrators*   *Sergeant James Aloysius Carnaby-King*
London: Hale, 1974.

Carnaby and the Kidnappers   *Sergeant James Aloysius Carnaby-King*
London: Hale, 1976.

When three young women, each the daughter of a Member of Parliament, are kidnapped, the Yard authorities decide the situation is serious enough to send the commando squad, and Carnaby goes to York. Carnaby checks on the kidnapped Caroline McDonald. He meets and interviews her former boyfriend, a student who is a member of a militant black group.

Carnaby and the Counterfeiters*   *Sergeant James Aloysius Carnaby-King*
London: Hale, 1980.

Panda One on Duty   *Police Constable Jock Patterson*
London: Hale, 1971.

Fossford is involved in a number of automobile thefts. Then someone begins assaulting little girls. The police have a prime suspect, who is beaten by an enraged policeman. The suspect and a little girl disappear.

Panda One Investigates*   *Police Constable Jock Patterson*
London: Hale, 1973.

Witchcraft for Panda One   *Police Constable Jock Patterson*
London: Hale, 1978.

Jock Patterson of Panda One figures out that the items being stolen in a series of small robberies are all related to witchcraft ceremonies. When Patterson tries to get a look at the ritual he is apprehended by the gamekeeper of the estate where it is taking place. That interference leads to the man's death.

Siege for Panda One   *Police Constable Jock Patterson*
London: Hale, 1981.

Patterson is given the job of investigating a pair of men who go to the homes of old people and buy an item of their furniture for a fair price. The men then haggle over another item that they say is worthless but are willing to remove from the house. The owner sells it for a small sum and the men turn around and make a huge profit on it because it is the genuine antique. While on this job Patterson has seen a beautiful young woman around Fossford. When she goes missing he learns that she is the daughter of the wealthy and influential Sir Randolph Coulton, who has considerable interests in the Middle East. The kidnapping has ugly political overtones.

Randall Wallace

Blood of the Lamb *Detective Investigator Scarlet McCullers*
New York: Bantam, 1990. *and Detective Thomas Ridge*

LAPD detective Scarlet McCullers is out on a cruising expedition with her partner and two senior detectives. When they make a stop the situation gets out of hand and McCullers, in a shootout with four drug dealers, kills them all. Thomas Ridge is a homicide specialist who chooses his own cases. He is working on a drowning death that may or may not be suicide when Cully kills the four men. A student at U.C.L.A. is killed and his girlfriend is kidnapped. All of these incidents may be connected to a drug ring in Los Angeles.

Where Angels Watch *Detectives Scarlet McCullers and Thomas Ridge*
New York: Bantam, 1992.

Jack the Ripper, Los Angeles style, is on the loose in the city. He preys on women of the streets, brutally murdering and mutilating them. The Los Angeles special homicide squad is given the case. Tom Ridge and Scarlet McCullers must race against time to find the perpetrator before he kills more women.

Joseph Wambaugh[*]

The New Centurions *Police Officers Serge Duran, Gus Plebesly,*
Boston: Little, Brown, 1970. *and Roy Fehler*
London: Joseph, 1971.

The story follows three rookie cops through five years of training and routine police work. Their lives, both professional and private, are scrutinized.

The Blue Knight *Officer William A. "Bumper" Morgan*
New York: Little, Brown, 1972. *and Sergeant Cruz Segovia*
London: Joseph, 1973.

Bumper Morgan has been a beat cop in Los Angeles for twenty years. He is planning to retire, marry, move to the San Francisco area, and work for an electronics firm as its security chief. This is a walk-through story of the everyday life of a cop. The reader follows along as Bumper goes about his daily duties, as he reminisces about his youth, and as his future becomes his reality. His relationship with his best and oldest friend and his new sergeant, Cruz Segovia, is the backbone of the novel.

The Choirboys* *Commander Hector Moss*
New York: Delacorte, 1975.
London: Weidenfeld, 1976.

The Black Marble *Detective Sergeant Valnikov*
New York: Delacorte, 1978.
London: Weidenfeld, 1978.

Madeline Witfield's champion stock Schnauzer Vickie is dognapped at the Brown Derby while on the way to her first dog show. The dog show was to prove that Vickie is a champion in all respects. The man who grooms and trains dogs for showing has the little female and wants $85,000 in cash. Sergeant Valnikov must try to get the dog back while fighting his alcoholism, his natural tendency toward Russian moroseness, and a growing attraction to his new partner, Natalie Zimmerman, who has been planted to keep an eye on Valnikov.

The Glitter Dome *Sergeants Al Mackey and Martin Welborn*
New York: Morrow, 1981.
London: Weidenfeld, 1981.

Captain Woofer is unhappy that the police have made little headway in the four weeks since the murder of Nigel St. Claire, one of the heads of a major film studio. Woofer assigns Sergeant Mackey and Martin Welborn to the case because they are already working on the murder of another celebrity.

The Delta Star *Sergeant Mario Villalobos*
New York: Morrow, 1983.
London: Macdonald, 1983.

Missy Moonbean, a Los Angeles hooker, is pushed from the roof of a local hotel, and homicide detective Villalobos and the squad from Rampart station must investigate. Her trick book (the book listing the names and telephone numbers of her clients) contains some interesting phone numbers. Meanwhile the Bad Czech, one of the most hardboiled cops to come out of fiction, is having a hard time explaining why he has a dead man's credit card.

The Secrets of Harry Bright　　*Sergeant Sidney Blackwell, Detective Otto*
New York: Morrow, 1985.　　*Springer, and Chief of Police Paco Pedroza*
London: Joseph, 1986.

Twenty-one-year-old Jack Watson, U.C.L.A. student and son of wealthy Victor Watson, disappears from his father's house in Mineral Springs just outside of Palm Springs. Two days later Jack is found in his car in the desert, the car and body burned beyond recognition. The autopsy shows that a .38 bullet lodged in Jack's brain. Seventeen months later Victor Watson asks Sidney Blackwell to look into the case. Blackwell, still recovering from his own son's death and now a heavy drinker, reluctantly agrees.

Fugitive Nights[*]　　*Detective Lynn Cutter*
New York: Morrow, 1992.

Hillary Waugh[*]

Last Seen Wearing　　*Chief of Police Frank Ford*
New York: Doubleday, 1952.
London: Gollancz, 1953.

Everyone who knows her reacts with disbelief when Lowell Mitchell disappears from Parker College in Bristol, Massachusetts. Yet she is gone without a trace. Considered a classic police story, this, however, is not a true procedural. The police go through the investigatory motions until they piece together the secret her disappearance has hidden.

A Rag and a Bone　　*Captain Mike Danaher and*
New York: Doubleday, 1954.　　*Detective Dan Malone*
London: Foulsham, 1955.

The mutilated body of a woman cannot be identified because her face has been destroyed. Detective Dan Malone knows that someone will be reported missing so he commissions a wax face reconstruction, using bits and pieces of what is left of the woman's head. Pictures of the reconstructed face are circulated, which eventually leads to an identification.

Sleep Long, My Love　　　　　　　　　　*Chief of Police Fred C. Fellows*
New York: Doubleday, 1958.
London: Gollancz, 1960.

Jigsaw
London: Pan, 1962.

The torso of an unidentified woman is found in a house that had been rented by a man who has left little trace of himself. Patient police work and careful adherence to procedure lead to the identity of the woman and the killer.

Road Block　　　　　　　　　　*Chief of Police Fred C. Fellows*
New York: Doubleday, 1960.
London: Gollancz, 1961.

The job is to steal the payroll of the Grafton Tool and Dye Company. The thieves have a man on the inside who for $5,000 will leave the door open for easy access to the safe. About a third of the book is Lloyd Ragan planning the robbery, and the rest is Fred Fellows trying to catch him.

That Night It Rained[*]　　　　　　　　　　*Chief of Police Fred C. Fellows*
New York: Doubleday, 1961.
London: Gollancz, 1961.

The Late Mrs. D.　　　　　　　　　　*Chief of Police Fred C. Fellows*
New York: Doubleday, 1962.
London: Gollancz, 1962.

Celia Donaldson died at age twenty-nine of an abscessed liver. The same day, the First Selectman of Stockford received a letter warning him that something was not right with Celia's death. She just happened to be the third Mrs. Donaldson; the two previous wives of Dr. Henry B. Donaldson also died. The day after Celia's death the good doctor tells Chief Fellows that he has every intention of marrying again—after all, he has been disappointed three times, maybe this next time he will get lucky. A coroner's inquest is ordered but Celia Donaldson's body has disappeared.

Born Victim　　　　　　　　　　*Chief of Police Fred C. Fellows*
New York: Doubleday, 1962.
London: Gollancz, 1963.

Thirteen-year-old Barbara is missing from her home. She had gone to a dance Friday night, then spent the next day at home alone. When her mother got home from work, Barbara was gone.

Death and Circumstances[*]　　　　　　　　　　*Chief of Police Fred C. Fellows*
New York: Doubleday, 1963.
London: Gollancz, 1963.

Prisoner's Plea*
New York: Doubleday, 1963.
London: Gollancz, 1963.

Chief of Police Fred C. Fellows

The Missing Man*
New York: Doubleday, 1964.
London: Gollancz, 1964.

Chief of Police Fred C. Fellows

End of a Party*
New York: Doubleday, 1965.
London: Gollancz, 1965.

Chief of Police Fred C. Fellows

Pure Poison*
New York: Doubleday, 1967.
London: Gollancz, 1967.

Chief of Police Fred C. Fellows

The Con Game
New York: Doubleday, 1968.
London: Gollancz, 1969.

Chief of Police Fred C. Fellows

One of Stockford's businessmen reports buying a $9,000-insurance policy from George Demarest. Now the Demarests are missing. Gradually it comes out that Demarest and his wife offered a few wealthy couples a chance to make big money. Each couple tells a different story of what happened.

"30" Manhattan East
New York: Doubleday, 1968.
London: Gollancz, 1969.

Detective Frank Sessions

When Monica Glazzard, a newspaper columnist, apparently commits suicide, there are one or two funny things that make the police on the scene call in the homicide squad. They also notify the medical examiner, who suspects asphyxiation. The homicide squad looks seriously at Monica's daughter, Linda, because she hated her mother and will inherit everything. Then they discover that several people had visited the Glazzard apartment before Monica's death. One of the visitors was a man friend, but no one knows who.

The Young Prey
New York: Doubleday, 1969.
London: Gollancz, 1970.

Detective Frank Sessions

An early novel about teenage runaways. A young girl leaves home and heads for New York City, where she falls into a predator's hands. The story ends in sadness and tragedy.

Finish Me Off *Detective Second Grade Frank Sessions*
New York: Doubleday, 1970.
London: Gollancz, 1971.

Linda Howard is a heroin addict and a prostitute. She and a man are found dead in a hotel room. Linda kept her addiction secret from her roommate, Gloria, but had told Gloria about the money she owed Max, a wealthy drug pusher. The action becomes a tangled story of Gloria, Frank Sessions, and the murders.

Irving Weinman*

Tailor's Dummy *Detective Inspector Lenny Schwartz*
New York: Atheneum, 1986.

Lenny Schwartz, Harvard graduate and supercop, has fallen on hard times. He made a big mistake in the bribe department and now gets fewer and fewer real cases. His ex-partner, the deputy chief of detectives, assigns Schwartz a murder investigation—a Brooklyn art dealer has been killed. The rough side of the New York gay scene is explored.

Pamela West*
(Pseudonym of Pamela West Katkin and Samuel Leonard Rubenstein)

Yours Truly, Jack the Ripper *Detective Inspector West*
New York: St. Martin's, 1987.

Each of the brutal murders of Jack the Ripper is related in the diary of Inspector West, the investigating officer. Here are the Victorian police at work.

Robert Westbrook

Nostalgia Kills *Lieutenant Nicky Rachmaninoff*
New York: Crown, 1988.

Big-time music video producer Jay Jeffries is murdered in his Beverly Hills mansion. Years before he had been a member of the rock group the

Perceptions, who broke up when the lead singer, Billy Leon, drowned in his bathtub in Rome. Whether that death has anything to do with the current murder is a puzzle to Rachmaninoff. The Perceptions still have a number of enemies.

Lady Left *Lieutenant Nicky Rachmaninoff*
New York: Crown, 1991.

Susan Merril, big-time movie star and Rachmaninoff's ex-wife, decides to become a communist. She persuades Nicky to go to Nicaragua with her and their fourteen-year-old daughter, Tanya. Everything becomes tense as Tanya gets into trouble, and the possibility of a political rebirth of the Sandinistas involves Rachmaninoff in the murder investigation of an American professor.

John Westerman

High Crimes *Detectives "Tree" Nelson and Jimmy Tibaldi*
New York: Soho, 1988.

The Seaport, Long Island, police have their hands full when Rastafarian drug dealer Gladstone Lanier comes to town to take over the growing narcotics operation from the Hispanics and organized crime. Nelson and Tibaldi are in deep trouble as the Jamaicans mark them for death, and the policemen haven't a clue as to why they are in the limelight as they are both rather lazy and unambitious.

Exit Wounds *Police Officer Orin Boyd*
New York: Soho, 1990.

Orin Boyd, for his sins of alcohol abuse, is sent to the 13th precinct of the Nassau County (New York) police department, where all the cops are greedy and corrupt, getting rich and indulging their proclivities for vice. Now Boyd is there to battle for good and retard the 13th's appetite for excess. A drug lord and a vicious cop are pitted against him.

Sweet Deal *Detective Jack Mills and*
New York: Soho, 1992. *Detective Claire Williamson*

Jack Mills, lately of the community affairs department, frequently seen on billboards as the most photogenic cop, handsome, ex-jock, is now assigned to homicide. A retired cop gets killed in a particularly brutal fashion. His body is found in Suffolk County but because he is a former Nassau County cop, both forces take the case. Mills, considered by many to be a real airhead, is assigned the case in the hope that he never solves it because it will expose the corruption, greed, lust, and viciousness that the force wants to keep quiet.

Collin Wilcox*

The Lonely Hunter   *Sergeant Frank Hastings*
New York: Random House, 1969.
London: Hale, 1971.

Frank Hastings, a sergeant on the homicide squad, has problems with his ex-wife and moves from Detroit to San Francisco to make a new life for himself. His former wife calls to tell him that their teenage daughter is in California but no one knows where. Then the body of a young man is found on the grounds of the Presidio. Since he is dressed in the hippie style of the late Sixties, the police believe him to be a civilian and not military personnel. The murder may be connected to the death of a woman who was killed six weeks before. Hastings wonders if the sale of LSD has something to do with the murders, all the while worrying about his own daughter's safety.

The Disappearance   *Lieutenant Frank Hastings*
New York: Random House, 1970.
London: Hale, 1971.

Carol Connoly, the wife of an influential businessman, disappears. As Hastings investigates, he discovers that Carol had a lover, a wealthy male friend who could be another lover, and a husband who is not concerned about any of it.

Dead Aim   *Lieutenant Frank Hastings*
New York: Random House, 1971.
London: Hale, 1973.

Susan Draper, a young wife and mother, is mugged and beaten to death outside her home. Her husband, who had neglected to leave the door open for her, found her body. When a daughter of a wealthy man and her boyfriend are killed, Hastings digs into the backgrounds of the victims. These are not random killings as they had been tortured first.

Hiding Place   *Lieutenant Frank Hastings and*
New York: Random House, 1973.   *Senior Co-Lieutenant Pete Friedman*
London: Hale, 1974.

A teenage girl is dead in Golden Gate Park. There are several suspects right from the start. Several hundred dollars are found hidden in the girl's bedroom—money she should not have had. Suspicion falls on a man who lives in the neighborhood who has a background of mental illness.

Long Way Down *Lieutenant Frank Hastings*
New York: Random House, 1974.
London: Hale, 1975.

In this fast-paced story Hastings is called to the San Francisco main library where the Governor of California has been shot while at a rally. The suspect, a Mexican-looking man, flees with Hastings in pursuit. The assailant takes cover in a house divided into apartments, and the subsequent action follows procedures that deal with a hostage situation. The second case Hastings is working on is that of a knifing victim who produces commercials. All the evidence points to a black man as the perpetrator but Hastings believes that solution to be too pat and looks deeper for the real killer.

Aftershock *Lieutenant Frank Hastings*
New York: Random House, 1975.
London: Hale, 1976.

Ann Haywood, Hastings's long-time girlfriend, is being threatened by James Biggs, a psychopathic genius. Lieutenant Friedman wants Hastings to stay away from Biggs so he assigns him to the murder of Flor Gaines, a seventy-year-old with a penchant for young men. Meanwhile, Biggs is getting closer to Ann all the time.

Doctor, Lawyer *Lieutenant Frank Hastings*
New York: Random House, 1976.
London: Hale, 1978.

The note on the murdered body read "Doctor, Lawyer, Merchant, Chief" and was signed "The Masked Man." The dead man had been a doctor. The killer is demanding $100,000 or he will kill again. He does not get the money so he next kills a lawyer and the ante goes up. Lieutenant Hastings, working against the clock, knows that more people will die if he does not catch this killer.

The Watcher *Lieutenant Frank Hastings*
New York: Random House, 1978.
London: Hale, 1979.

Just as he is leaving on a vacation with his fourteen-year-old son, Frank is accused of taking a bribe. Everyone believes he is being set up. A killer is waiting in the mountains to extract vengeance for what he perceives

Hastings has done to him. More a novel of survival than a procedural, the book details the story of a father and son fighting to stay alive.

Night Games *Lieutenant Frank Hastings*
New York: Random House, 1979.

James Haney is found stabbed to death in the hallway of his home. Hastings is called to the scene and realizes that this is no run-of-the-mill killing. Haney had been stabbed with a ceremonial dagger from Morocco. Haney's young stepdaughter knows something but is too terrified to speak. His wife, Katherine, says she saw a young black male leaving the house shortly after her husband was killed. But there are problems presented by Katherine Haney's lifestyle—she has ex-husbands and a current lover.

Mankiller *Lieutenant Frank Hastings*
New York: Random House, 1980.
London: Hale, 1981.

Rock singer Rebecca Carlton has been murdered at the Cow Palace just before her last performance. When she does not appear the crowd begins to riot. Interviewing witnesses is a nightmare but the investigation soon centers around those close to Rebecca. Her novelist father and her stepmother, also a writer, are scrutinized as are her multimillionaire ex-husband and her brother. Then another woman is killed and the case turns upside down.

Stalking Horse *Lieutenant Frank Hastings*
New York: Random House, 1982.
London: Hale, 1987.

A threat has been made against the life of Donald A. Ryan, majority leader of the U.S. Senate. The senator is recovering from a heart attack so no one wants to tell him what is happening. Hastings is commandeered to stop the threat. He, FBI agents, and the Secret Service are working together. Then the senator's daughter receives a phone call telling her that she can save her father's life.

Victims *Lieutenant Frank Hastings*
New York: Mysterious, 1984.
London: Hale, 1986.

Charlie Quade has been killed in the home of high-powered, wealthy attorney Alex Guest. Quade is a former detective who worked on Hastings's homicide squad. Guest is one of those domineering men who has driven his daughter to drink and to the divorce court twice. Now he is out to get control of his grandson.

The Pariah *Lieutenant Frank Hastings*
New York: Mysterious, 1988.

Amy MacFarland, a San Francisco prostitute, is murdered and the next day special agent Draper from the FBI shows up talking about his study of serial killers. The MacFarland murder matches some that Draper is profiling. He and Hastings share information and soon realize that the murderer is based in Los Angeles and travels around the country in search of victims. The prime suspect is someone linked to the popular television evangelist Austin Holloway.

A Death Before Dying *Lieutenant Frank Hastings*
New York: Holt, 1990.

Meredith Powell, a childhood friend of Hastings, is the proverbial unhappy woman married to money, but hating every moment of her existence. When she becomes a homicide victim, Hastings takes the case even though he knows that a cop should never investigate a crime involving someone he knows.

Dead Center *Lieutenant Frank Hastings*
New York: Holt, 1992.

A street person walks up to millionaire Tony Frazer and shoots him twice. When he realizes Frazer is not dead, he puts another bullet between his eyes. The weapon used is a .22 caliber automatic fitted with a silencer. More deaths occur and Lieutenant Frank Hastings is faced with identifying a killer of wealthy men. He must find out why they are dying.

Charles Willeford*

Miami Blues *Sergeant Hoke Mosley*
New York: St. Martin's, 1984.
London: Futura, 1985.

When Freddy Frenger gets out of San Quentin he heads for Miami and the good life. He hooks up with Susan, a strange young woman who goes along with his violent behavior. A member of a Hare Krishna group is killed at the Miami airport, which brings Hoke Moseley into the psychotic world of Freddy Frenger.

New Hope for the Dead *Sergeant Hoke Mosley*
New York: St. Martin's, 1985.
London: Futura, 1987.

Sergeant Mosley is going through fifty old cases still pending, looking for something new, some way to solve them. He is concerned about his partner, who is pregnant, and homeless since her strict family asked her to leave. Hoke's two teenage daughters have arrived to take up residence, presenting him with a new twist on life.

Sideswipe *Sergeant Hoke Mosley*
New York: St. Martin's, 1987.
London: Gollancz, 1988.

Mosley, in the throes of a life crisis and mental breakdown, leaves home for a less stressful place than Miami. He gets a job as a building manager on the island where he grew up and soon realizes that crime is wherever people are. There is a parallel story concerning an old man and a sociopathic killer. Soon all of their paths cross in a violent manner.

The Way We Die Now *Sergeant Hoke Mosley*
New York: Random House, 1988.
London: Gollancz, 1989.

Commander Henderson tells Sergeant Mosley to grow a beard and head south, where the migrant workers toil and apparently die. Mosley goes underground to check out stories that workers are treated more like slaves than anything else.

Timothy Williams

Converging Parallels *Commissario Pietro Trotti*
London: Gollancz, 1982.

The Red Citroën
New York: St. Martin's, 1983.

Shy little six-year-old Anna Ermogni has disappeared. Anna is Commissario Trotti's goddaughter so he begins an investigation. Italy is in turmoil because of the kidnapping of Aldo Moro. While Trotti is looking for the missing girl and clues to the identity of the Red Brigade members who may be living in his city, a murderer is hacking up his victims and soon becomes another problem for the Commissario.

The Puppeteer *Commissario Pietro Trotti*
London: Gollancz, 1985.

The Metal Green Mercedes
New York: St. Martin's, 1985.

Commissario Trotti, on vacation in the little town of Gardesana, is having his morning coffee when a green Mercedes pulls up and a person riding in the car shoots the man sitting next to Trotti. The dead man is the son of a criminal Trotti sent to jail. Soon everyone is after the Commissario, looking for money stolen from a bank in Milan. And the Carabinieri believe that Trotti knows more about the murder than he has admitted.

Persona Non Grata *Commissario Pietro Trotti*
London: Gollancz, 1987.

The White Audi
New York: St. Martin's, 1987.

When a twelve-year-old girl is attacked in her parents' apartment the police believe that she was mistaken for her older sister. Add to this the mysterious death of Trotti's older brother during World War II, which somehow is related to the killings currently going on in the village where Trotti was born, and the present becomes a search for answers that become very personal for Trotti.

Walter Jon Williams*

Days of Atonement *Police Chief Loren Hawn*
New York: TOR, 1991.

The mining company that practically owns Atocha, New Mexico, lays off all its workers, closing down the copper mine that is the primary basis of employment in the town. The twenty-first-century has bypassed the area and left all its small town ways intact. But things change when Police Chief Loren Hawn realizes that the man who has just died in his arms had already died twenty years before. All of the morality and religious thought prevalent in Atocha cannot combat the realities being created in the technological laboratory outside of town.

David Wiltse*

The Serpent *Lieutenant Sandy Block and*
New York: Delacorte, 1983. *Detective Lou Florio*

Just married, Sandy Block, a lieutenant in the New York Police Department, realizes while viewing the scene of the murder of an actress that the murderer was totally out of control. This is a killer who hates women and kills them sadistically. The murders continue, as it becomes clear that all of the victims are specifically targeted by the fact that they are pregnant.

Prayer for the Dead *Special Agent John Becker*
New York: Putnam, 1991

Serial killer Roger Dyce keeps his victims drugged until he kills them; he then draws the blood from their bodies, grooms them, and dresses them up in his dead father's clothing. Becker's friend Tee Terhune, chief of police in Clamden, New Jersey, where Becker lives, realizes that his nephew is missing and fears that he will be the next victim of the killer because he fits the profile of the killer's victims. Then Dyce is mugged and Tee and Becker think he was supposed to be the next victim.

Close to the Bone *Special Agent John Becker*
New York: Putnam, 1992

Becker, who has killed several people in the line of duty, has a certain reputation for being hard and able to get his man. The terrorism unit wants Becker to help them find an international hit man named Roger Bahoud, who has assassinated several prominent statesmen. Bahoud is on his way to the United States to kill a diplomat who is crucial to the team that is trying to develop peace in the Middle East.

The Edge of Sleep *Special Agent John Becker*
New York: Putnam, 1993

On medical leave, agent Becker is called on by deputy assistant director Karen Crist to help her. She is heading an investigation of a series of murders of young boys. She needs Becker because he can get an impression of the serial killer's mind and method and has a proven track record for hunting them down. Becker and Crist establish that the boys are being taken from shopping malls but until they figure out how and where the boys are kept before they are killed, they cannot solve the crimes. The boys disappear for weeks and are then found in trash bags thrown along the highways in and around New Jersey.

Anne Wingate*
(Byline of [Martha] Anne [Guice] Wingate; also Lee Martin, q.v.)

Death by Deception *Mark Shingata, FBI Agent*
New York: Walker, 1988.

Two women are killed in one evening. They are stepsisters, and one of them is the ex-wife of FBI agent Mark Shingata. When he returns home from work he discovers Bayport's one detective waiting for him. Shingata is the prime suspect and his twelve-year-old daughter is missing.

The Eye of Anna *Chief of Police Mark Shingata and*
New York: Walker, 1989. *Sergeant Al Quinn*

While Hurricane Anna is preparing to touch down in Galveston, Shingata must investigate a multiple murder. Three women have been killed in the apartment of Gwen Hardesty. Next the wife of Dr. Richard Weston is found dead in her bedroom. Shingata and Quinn must decide whether the same killer is at work in both places and what his motive is.

The Buzzards Must Also Feed *Chief of Police Mark Shingata*
New York: Walker, 1991.

Three years ago Steve Hansen came home to find his house full of police officers and his wife, daughter, and dog dead. The police chief, who just happened to be Hansen's wife's ex-husband, looked no further than Steve as the murderer and arrested him. Now free after a car accident that occurs as he is being transported back to prison after a court appeal has failed to stay his execution, Hansen determines to kill the now-former police chief.

Pauline Glen Winslow*

The Brandenburg Hotel *Detective Sergeant Capricorn*
London: Macmillan, 1976.
New York: St. Martin's, 1976.

During WW II, England found itself with pockets of displaced Germans living on British soil. The Brandenburg Hotel housed just such a group. When a young woman is found murdered there, Capricorn is sent to investigate because his background is military intelligence.

The Witch Hill Murder* *Detective Chief Superintendent Merle Capricorn*
London: Collins, 1977.
New York: St. Martin's, 1977.

Coppergold *Detective Chief Superintendent Merle Capricorn*
London: Collins, 1978. *and Detective Inspector Al Copper*
Copper Gold
New York: St. Martin's, 1978.

Crime figure Charlie Bonomi dies of heart failure but his wife believes he was murdered. Bonomi was a heavy investor in the club owned and operated by Jess Parker, live-in friend of Inspector Copper. Then Jess is murdered and Copper arrested.

Ted Wood*

Dead in the Water   *Chief of Police Reid Bennett and Sam*
New York: Scribner's, 1983.
London: Collins, 1984.

Reid Bennett served in Vietnam and was a homicide cop in Toronto until he killed a man who was raping a sixteen-year-old girl. He begins a new life in tiny Murphy's Harbour where he and his dog, Sam, are the entire police force. A young woman reports her lover/traveling companion missing. Bennett finds the man dead. Also, a gang of motorcyclists is on the way to the village to terrorize its people.

Murder on Ice   *Chief of Police Reid Bennett and Sam*
New York: Scribner's, 1984.

The Killing Cold
London: Collins, 1984.

The second annual Murphy's Harbour Water Carnival is in full swing when the Queen of the Carnival disappears. In an attempt to find her Bennett goes to the Muskellunge Motel and finds the body of a young woman hanging from the shower rail in one of the rooms. In town at the same time are members of C.L.A.W., or Canadian League of Angry Women, who are trapped by the fierce storm raging over the area. The bad weather is also keeping a number of other folks in town, including the murderer.

Live Bait   *Chief of Police Reid Bennett and Sam*
New York: Scribner's, 1985.

Dead Centre
London: Collins, 1985.

While Reid Bennett is on vacation a friend from Toronto invites him to help in a particularly ugly case of guarding a construction site in the city. Bonded security has been hired to make sure nothing happens at the site but property is being damaged and the watchmen have been attacked. Bennett finds the guilty thugs with little trouble but he then agrees to stay longer in order to find what is behind the problems.

Fool's Gold *Chief of Police Reid Bennett and Sam*
New York: Scribner's, 1986.
London: Collins, 1986.

Bennett and his dog, Sam, travel to Olympia, Ontario, to investigate the death of a geologist who has made a big gold strike. There are a number of murders and Bennett must figure out why people are dying.

Corkscrew *Chief of Police Reid Bennett and Sam*
New York: Scribner's, 1987.
London: Collins, 1988.

One-man police force, Reid Bennett and his dog, Sam, have their hands full looking for a missing thirteen-year-old boy and keeping a gang of bikers in order. After two murders Bennett begins to see what lies behind the violence and in his unique way averts more tragedy.

On the Inside *Chief of Police Reid Bennett and Sam*
New York: Scribner's, 1990
London: Collins, 1990.

Reid Bennett is asked to go undercover to investigate reports of police corruption on the Elliot, Ontario, force. Joining as a constable, Bennett quickly finds that Chief Harding and Sergeant Ferris appear to be very much involved in murder and accepting bribes. Aided by his wife, Freda, and his dog, Sam, Bennett makes inroads into the corruption of the police force, placing them all in extreme danger.

Flashback *Chief of Police Reid Bennett and Sam*
New York: Scribner's, 1992.

Much is happening in tiny Murphy's Harbour. A gang is swarming through the town stores and one of them kills a dog with a baseball bat. A car is pulled out of the harbor and the body of a woman is found in the trunk. A few hours later the body of a Toronto attorney is found in the bathtub of his hotel room. While Reid is working with the Ontario State Police to try to figure out where and why a crime wave has come to his small town, Freda must go to the hospital to have their baby.

Daniel Woodrell[*]

Under the Bright Lights *Detective Rene Shades*
New York: Holt, 1986.

Councilman Alvin Ranbin is shot to death in his own home. Detective Rene Shades has to find out who killed him in what looks like a burglary.

Shades, whose older brother owns a seedy bar in a bad area of town and whose younger brother is an assistant district attorney, is caught in the middle of an ugly situation.

Stuart Woods*

New York Dead *Detective Stone Barrington*
New York: HarperCollins, 1991.

New York television personality Sasha Nijinsky falls twelve stories to the street below but she survives. As she is being transported to the hospital a fire truck broadsides the ambulance and Nijinsky disappears. The mystery of how she could fall so far and not die is solved when Barrington finds that Nijinsky was a skydiver and knows how to minimize damage in a long plunge. The television star had been receiving letters from a man who hounded her until she got a restraining order against him. Barrington's work is cut out for him.

Eric Wright

The Night the Gods Smiled *Inspector Charlie Salter*
London: Collins, 1983.
New York: Scribner's, 1983.

David Summers is in Montreal for a convention of English professors when he is struck on the head and killed in his hotel room. Because he is from Toronto the Montreal police ask Salter to investigate the local angles. The night before he was killed Summers had been euphoric. It is up to Salter to discover why and perhaps save his own career from the limbo it has been in since he backed the wrong man for deputy chief and, as a result, has been languishing behind a desk.

Smoke Detector *Inspector Charlie Salter*
London: Collins, 1984.
New York: Scribner's, 1985.

A secondhand dealer is found dead when fire fighters come to put out the blaze in the basement of his shop. Superintendent Orliff assigns Salter, as all homicide detectives are busy. Soon the Toronto detective learns that few people liked Drecker and the investigation leads Salter to suspect that there is something strange, perhaps even shady, about the way he did business.

Death in the Old Country *Inspector Charlie Salter*
London: Collins, 1985.
New York: Scribner's, 1985.

Charlie Salter and his wife, Annie, are vacationing in England when they are involved in a head-on collision. They stay at Broomewood where a guest has seen a prowler. Then the murder of the hotel owner adds to the "comfort" of their stay.

A Single Death *Inspector Charlie Salter*
London: Collins, 1986.

The Man Who Changed His Name
New York: Scribner's, 1986.

Salter cannot say no to his ex-wife, who asks him to look into the murder of one of her friends. Salter, who works in General Duties, reluctantly agrees to have a word with homicide about the rape and strangulation of Nancy Crowell. He juggles his ex-wife's inquisitiveness and his current wife's developing jealousy.

A Body Surrounded by Water *Inspector Charlie Salter*
London: Collins, 1987.
New York: Scribner's, 1987.

While he is vacationing on Prince Edward Island the local Mounties invite Salter to help with their investigation into the death of a man who was negotiating the purchase of the Great Seal of the Island, which was once lost for two hundred years. Now it has been taken again. The case involves Salter's father-in-law.

A Question of Murder *Inspector Charlie Salter*
London: Collins, 1988.
New York: Scribner's, 1988.

Assigned to make sure a Royal Princess shops safely in the upscale Yorkville area of Toronto, Charlie Salter does just that. But the threatening letters received by the shopkeepers are for real. The Princess goes about her business but a bomb explodes close to her intended route. Salter must discover if the Princess is in danger or whether the merchants are the intended victims.

A Sensitive Case *Inspector Charlie Salter*
London: Collins, 1990.
New York: Scribner's, 1990.

Salter investigates the murder of Linda Thomas, a masseuse whose clientele included powerful people. Suspects are not forthcoming, and to add to the pressure at work Salter thinks his wife is having an affair.

Final Cut *Staff Inspector Charlie Salter*
London: Collins, 1991.
New York: Scribner's, 1991.

Salter is given the job of police liaison and watchdog on a movie set. But someone is out to sabotage the production by committing little acts to disrupt the filming. The question is, how far will the person go to shut down the movie?

A Fine Italian Hand *Staff Inspector Charlie Salter*
New York: Scribner's, 1992.

First the motel clerk finds the Volkswagen Jetta parked behind the motel—only a woman's scarf left in the vehicle. Then he finds a dead man in room 5 and calls the police. The man was Alec Hunter, an actor. He has been strangled. The deputy chief puts Salter in charge and moves him to a temporary spot in homicide. There has been a fuss in the media and Toronto's Italians are up in arms because as room 5 had been rented to a person who looked Italian, all Italians are suspects—or so the media imply. To make matters worse, Salter's wife is out of town and his old girlfriend comes back into his life.

L. R. Wright[*]

The Suspect *Staff Sergeant Karl Alberg*
New York: Viking, 1985.
London: Hale, 1986.

Eighty-six-year-old Carlyle Burke is dead. His head has been smashed with a bookend. Staff Sergeant Karl Alberg of the Royal Canadian Mounted Police is the investigating officer.

Sleep While I Sing *Staff Sergeant Karl Alberg*
New York: Viking, 1986.
London: Collins, 1987.

A young woman who had been hitchhiking is found murdered at the side of the road. Sergeant Alberg investigates and the case becomes complicated because his friend Cassandra Mitchell is romantically, almost obsessively involved with his prime suspect.

A Chill Rain in January *Staff Sergeant Karl Alberg*
New York: Viking, 1990.
London: Macmillan, 1990

Zoe Strachan is leading a comfortable life in British Columbia until her long-lost brother shows up at her door. He tells her that he has found her old diaries and wants money to keep quiet about what is in them. Another woman, Ramona Orlitzki, is in a nursing home and hates it, so she escapes, returning to the one home she has loved, which happens to be a cabin on Zoe Strachan's property. Then Zoe's brother has a fatal accident and Alberg must conduct an investigation. He becomes involved with both women in different ways because they intrigue him.

5

Period of Story (1700–1992 and Beyond)

1700–1720	Keith Heller	
	Man's Storm	
1720–1729	Keith Heller	
	Man's Illegal Life	
	Man's Loving Family	
1820–1829	Vincent McConnor	
	I Am Vidocq	
1850–1859	Anne Perry	
	The Face of a Stranger	
	A Dangerous Mourning	
	Defend and Betray	
	Francis Selwyn	
	Cracksman on Velvet	
	Sergeant Verity and the Imperial Diamond	
	Sergeant Verity and the Blood Royal	
	Sergeant Verity and the Swell Mob	
1870–1879	Alanna Knight	
	Enter Second Murderer	
	Blood Line	
	Deadly Beloved	
	Killing Cousins	
1890–1910	Richard Grayson	
	The Murders at the Impasse Louvain	
	The Monterant Affair	

1890–1910 (continued)

    Richard Grayson (cont.)
        The Death of the Abbé Dodier
        Crime Without Passion
        Death en Voyage
        Death on the Cards
        Death Off Stage

    Ray Harrison
        French Ordinary Killing
        Death of an Honourable Member
        Death of a Dancing Lady
        Deathwatch
        Harvest of Death
        Tincture of Death
        Sphere of Death
        Patently Murder

    William Marshall
        Faces in the Crowd

    Michael Pearce
        The Mamur Zapt and the Return of the Carpet
        The Mamur Zapt and the Night of the Dog
        The Mamur Zapt and the Donkey–vous

    Donald Thomas
        The Ripper's Apprentice
        Jekyll, Alias Hyde

    Pamela West
        Yours Truly, Jack the Ripper

1930–1939   Max Allan Collins
        The Dark City
        Butcher's Dozen
        Bullet Proof

1940–1949   John Creasey
        Inspector West Takes Charge
        Inspector West Leaves Town
        Inspector West at Home
        Inspector West Regrets
        Holiday for Inspector West
        Triumph for Inspector West
        Battle for Inspector West
        Inspector West Kicks off

Period of Story (1700–1992 and Beyond)

                James Ellroy
                    The Black Dahlia

                David J. Murphy
                    Inspector Malone Sails In

                Georges Simenon
                    Maigret and the Hotel Majestic

                Lawrence Treat
                    V as in Victim
                    H as in Hunted
                    Q as in Quicksand
                    T as in Trapped
                    F as in Fugitive

1950–1959   Gwendoline Butler
                    Dead in a Row
                    The Dull Dead

                John Creasey
                    Inspector West Cries Wolf
                    Inspector West Alone
                    Puzzle for Inspector West
                    A Case for Inspector West
                    Inspector West at Bay
                    Send Inspector West
                    A Gun for Inspector West
                    A Beauty for Inspector West
                    Inspector West Makes Haste
                    Two for Inspector West
                    Parcels for Inspector West
                    A Prince for Inspector West
                    Accident for Inspector West
                    Find Inspector West
                    Strike for Death
                    Murder, London–New York
                    Death of a Race Horse
                    The Case of the Innocent Victims

                James Ellroy
                    Clandestine

                Chester Himes
                    For Love of Imabella
                    The Crazy Kill
                    The Real Cool Killers

1950–1959 *(continued)*

    MacKinley Kantor
        Signal Thirty-Two

    Bill Knox
        Deadline for a Dream
        Death Department

    Ed McBain
        Cop Hater
        The Mugger
        The Pusher
        The Con Man
        Killer's Choice
        Killer's Payoff
        Lady Killer
        Killer's Wedge
        'Til Death
        King's Ransome

    J. J. Marric
        Gideon's Day
        Gideon's Week
        Gideon's Night
        Gideon's Month
        Gideon's Staff

    Maurice Procter
        The Chief Inspector's Statement
        I Will Speak Daggers
        The Pub Crawler
        Hell Is a City
        Midnight Plumber
        Man in Ambush
        Killer at Large

    Georges Simenon
        Maigret's Mistake
        Maigret in Montmartre
        Maigret Has Scruples

    L. A. G. Strong
        Which I Never

    Laurence Treat
        Big Shot
        Weep for a Wanton

Hillary Waugh
  A Rag and a Bone
  Sleep Long, My Love

1960–1969   John Ball
  In the Heat of the Night
  The Cool Cottontail
  Johnny Get Your Gun

Roger Busby
  Robery Blue

Gwendoline Butler
  Death Lives Next Door
  Make Me a Murderer
  Coffin in Oxford
  Coffin for Baby
  Coffin Waiting
  Coffin in Malta
  A Nameless Coffin
  Coffin's Dark Number

Jon Cleary
  The High Commissioner

Thomas H. Cook
  Streets of Fire

John Creasey
  Murder on the Line
  Death in Cold Print
  The Scene of the Crime
  Policeman's Dread
  Hang the Little Man
  Look Three Ways at Murder
  Murder, London–Australia
  Murder, London–South Africa
  The Executioners
  So Young to Burn
  Murder, London–Miami

E. V. Cunningham
  Samantha

Harold R. Daniels
  The House on Greenapple Street

1960–1969 (continued)

Robert L. Fish
The Fugitive
Isle of the Snakes
The Shrunken Head
Brazilian Sleigh Ride
The Diamond Bubble
Always Kill a Stranger
The Bridge That Went Nowhere
The Xavier Affair

Nicolas Freeling
Love in Amsterdam
Because of the Cats
Gun Before Butter
Double-Barrel
Criminal Conversation
The King of the Rainy Country
Strike Out Where Not Applicable
Tsing-Boum

Joseph Harrington
The Last Known Address
Blind Spot
The Last Doorbell

Laurence Henderson
With Intent

Olga Hesky
Time for Treason

Chester Himes
All Shot Up
The Big Gold Dream
Cotton Comes to Harlem
The Heat Is On
Blind Man with a Pistol

E. Richard Johnson
Silver Street
The Inside Man

Hamilton Jobson
Therefore I Killed Him
Smile and Be a Villain

Bill Knox
- *Leave It to the Hangman*
- *Little Drops of Blood*
- *Sanctuary Isle*
- *The Man in the Bottle*
- *The Taste of Proof*
- *The Deep Fall*
- *Justice on the Rocks*
- *The Tallyman*

Roy Lewis
- *A Lover Too Many*

Elizabeth Linington
- *Greenmask*
- *No Evil Angel*
- *Date with Death*
- *Something Wrong*
- *Policeman's Lot*

Ed McBain
- *Give the Boys a Great Big Hand*
- *The Heckler*
- *See Them Die*
- *Lady, Lady, I Did It*
- *Like Love*
- *Ten Plus One*
- *Ax*
- *He Who Hesitates*
- *Doll*
- *Eighty Million Eyes*
- *Fuzz*
- *Shotgun*

J. J. Marric
- *Gideon's Risk*
- *Gideon's Fire*
- *Gideon's March*
- *Gideon's Ride*
- *Gideon's Vote*
- *Gideon's Lot*
- *Gideon's Badge*
- *Gideon's Wrath*
- *Gideon's River*
- *Gideon's Power*

1960–1969 *(continued)*

    Jennie Melville
        Come Home and Be Killed
        Burning Is a Substitute for Loving
        Murderer's House
        There Lies Your Love
        Nell Alone
        A Different Kind of Summer

    Gil North
        Sergeant Cluff Stands Firm
        The Methods of Sergeant Cluff
        Sergeant Cluff Goes Fishing
        More Deaths for Sergeant Cluff
        Sergeant Cluff and the Price of Pity

    Laurence Payne
        The Nose on My Face

    Robert L. Pike
        Mute Witness
        Quarry
        Police Blotter

    Joyce Porter
        Dover One
        Dover Two
        Dover Three
        Dover and the Unkindest Cut of All
        Dover Goes to Pott

    Maurice Procter
        Devil's Due
        The Devil Was Handsome
        A Body to Spare
        Moonlight Flitting
        Two Men in Twenty
        Death Has a Shadow
        Rogue Running
        His Weight in Gold
        Exercise Hookwink
        Hideaway

    Hugh C. Rae
        The House at Balnesmoor

Dell Shannon
- *Case Pending*
- *The Ace of Spades*
- *Extra Kill*
- *Knave of Hearts*
- *Death of a Busybody*
- *Double Bluff*
- *Mark of Murder*
- *The Death-Bringers*
- *Root of All Evil*
- *Death by Inches*
- *Coffin Corner*
- *With a Vengence*
- *Chance to Kill*
- *Rain with Violence*
- *Kill with Kindness*
- *Schooled to Kill*
- *Crime on Their Hands*

Maj Sjöwall and Per Wahlöö
- *Roseanna*
- *The Man on the Balcony*
- *The Man Who Went Up in Smoke*

Lawrence Treat
- *Lady, Drop Dead*

Dorothy Uhnak
- *The Bait*
- *The Witness*

John Holbrook Vance
- *The Pleasant Grove Murders*

Conrad Voss Bark
- *The Second Red Dragon*

John Wainwright
- *Death in a Sleeping City*
- *The Crystallised Carbon Pig*
- *Evil Intent*
- *The Worms Must Wait*
- *The Darkening Glass*

Per Wahlöö
- *Murder on the Thirty-First Floor*

1960–1969 *(continued)*

    Peter Walker
        Carnaby and the Hijakers
        Carnaby and the Assassins
        Carnaby and the Gaolbreakrs
        Carnaby and the Conspirators

    Hillary Waugh
        Road Block
        That Night It Rained
        The Late Mrs. D.
        Born Victim
        Death and Circumstances
        Prisoner's Plea
        The Missing Man
        End of a Party
        Pure Poison
        The Con Game
        "30" Manhattan East
        The Young Prey

1970–1979
    John Ball
        Five Pieces of Jade
        The Eyes of Buddha
        Then Came Violence
        Police Chief

    James Barnett
        Head of the Force

    Dallas Barnes
        Yesterday Is Dead

    K. Arne Blom
        The Moment of Truth

    Rex Burns
        The Alvarez Journal
        The Farnsworth Score
        Speak for the Dead
        Angel of Attack

    Roger Busby
        The Frighteners
        Deadlock

Period of Story (1700–1992 and Beyond) 307

    A Reasonable Man
    Pattern of Violence

Gwendoline Butler
    A Coffin from the Past
    A Coffin for the Canary

William Camp
    The Jacobs Park Killings

Robert Chambers
    The Neon Preacher

Jon Cleary
    Helga's Web
    Ransom

K. C. Constantine
    The Rocksburg Railroad Murders
    The Man Who Liked to Look at Himself
    The Blank Page

John Creasey
    A Part for a Policeman
    Alibi
    A Splinter of Glass
    Theft of Magna Carta
    The Extortioners
    A Sharp Rise in Crime

E. V. Cunningham
    The Case of the One-Penny Orange
    The Case of the Russian Diplomat
    The Case of the Poisoned Eclairs

Robert Daley
    To Kill a Cop

Frank DeFelitta
    Oktoberfest

Nelson De Mille
    Ryker #1: The Sniper
    Ryker #2: The Hammer of God
    Ryker #3: The Terrorists

Robert L. Fish
    The Green Hell Treasure
    Trouble in Paradise

1970–1979 *(continued)*

    Nicolas Freeling
        Over the High Side
        A Dressing of Diamonds
        What Are the Bugles Blowing
        Lake Isle

    Paula Gosling
        A Running Duck

    Alfred Harris
        Baroni

    Mark Hebden
        Death Set to Music
        Pel and the Faceless Corpse

    Laurence Henderson
        With Intent
        Sitting Target
        Cage Until Tame
        Major Enquiry

    Peter Hill
        The Enthusiasts
        The Washermen

    Tony Hillerman
        The Blessing Way
        Dance Hall of the Death
        Listening Woman

    John Hough, Jr.
        The Guardian

    Jon A. Jackson
        The Diehard
        The Blind Pig

    Hamilton Jobson
        Naked to My Enemy
        The Silent Cry
        The House with Blind Eyes
        The Sand Pit
        The Shadow That Caught Fire
        Contract with a Killer
        The Evidence You Will Hear

      Waiting for Thursday
      Judge Me Tomorrow
      To Die a Little
      Exit to Violence

E. Richard Johnson
      Case-Load Maximum
      The God Keepers

Cyril Joyce
      The Information Man
      Seize the Passing Stranger

Herbert Kastle
      Death Squad

Bill Knox
      Children of the Mist
      To Kill a Witch
      Draw Batons!
      Rally to Kill
      Pilot Error
      Live Bait

Michael Z. Lewin
      Night Cover

Roy Lewis
      Error of Judgment
      Secret Singing
      Blood Money
      A Question of Degree
      A Part of Virtue
      Nothing But Foxes

Herbert Lieberman
      City of the Dead

Elizabeth Linington
      Practice to Deceive
      Crime by Chance
      Perchance of Death
      No Villain Need Be

Ed McBain
      Jigsaw
      Hail, Hail, the Gang's All Here!
      Sadie, When She Died

1970–1979 *(continued)*

> Ed McBain *(continued)*
>> *Let's Hear It for the Deaf Man*
>> *Hail to the Chief*
>> *Bread*
>> *Blood Relative*
>> *So Long As You Both Shall Live*
>> *Long Time No See*
>> *Calypso*
>
> James McClure
>> *The Song Dog*
>> *The Steam Pig*
>> *The Caterpillar Cop*
>> *The Gooseberry Fool*
>> *Snake*
>> *The Sunday Hangman*
>
> William McIlvanney
>> *Laidlaw*
>
> J. J. Marric
>> *Gideon's Sport*
>> *Gideon's Art*
>> *Gideon's Men*
>> *Gideon's Press*
>> *Gideon's Fog*
>> *Gideon's Drive*
>
> William Marshall
>> *Gelignite*
>> *The Hatchet Man*
>> *Thin Air*
>> *Skulduggery*
>
> Ian Kennedy Martin
>> *Regan*
>> *Regan and the Manhattan File*
>> *Regan and the Deal of the Century*
>
> James Melville
>> *The Wages of Zen*
>
> Jennie Melville
>> *A New Kind of Killer, An Old Kind of Death*
>
> Gil North
>> *A Corpse for Kofi Katt*

Period of Story (1700–1992 and Beyond) 311

Lillian O'Donnell
   The Phone Calls
   Don't Wear Your Wedding Ring
   Dial 577 R-A-P-E
   The Baby Merchants
   Leisure Dying
   No Business Being a Cop

Freny Olbrich
   Desouza in Stardust
   Desouza Pays the Price

D. J. Olivy
   Never Ask a Policeman

Jack Olsen
   Night Watch

Paul Orum
   The Whipping Boy
   Nothing But the Truth

Robert L. Pike
   Reardon
   The Gremlin's Grandpa
   Bank Job
   Deadline 2 A.M.

Joyce Porter
   Dover Strikes Again
   It's Murder with Dover
   Dover and the Claret Tappers
   Dead Easy for Dover

Hugh C. Rae
   The Shooting Gallery

Julian Rathbone
   The Euro-Killers

Shepard Rifkin
   McQuaid
   The Snow Rattlers

Jack Ripley
   Davis Doesn't Live Here Any More
   The Pig That Got Up and Slowly Walked Away
   My God How the Money Rolls In
   My Word You Should Have Seen Us

1970–1979 (*continued*)

    Lawrence Sanders
        The First Deadly Sin
        The Second Deadly Sin

    Jack S. Scott
        A Better Class of Business
        The Bastard's Name Was Bristow
        The Poor Old Lady's Dead
        The Shallow Grave
        A Clutch of Vipers

    David Serafin
        Saturday of Glory

    Dell Shannon
        Unexpected Death
        The Ringer
        Whim to Kill
        With Intent to Kill
        Murder with Love
        No Holiday for Crime
        Spring of Violence
        Crime File
        Deuces Wild
        Streets of Death
        Appearances of Death
        Cold Trail
        Felony at Random

    Georges Simenon
        Maigret and the Killer
        Maigret and the Informer
        Maigret and the Loner
        Maigret and the Millionaires

    Maj Sjöwall and Per Wahlöö
        The Laughing Policeman
        Murder at the Savoy
        The Fire Engine That Disappeared
        The Abominable Man
        The Locked Room
        Cop Killer: The Story of a Crime
        The Terrorists

Richard Martin Stern
Murder in the Walls
You Don't Need an Enemy

Mark Smith
The Death of the Detective

Lawrence Treat
Lady, Drop Dead

Dorothy Uhnak
The Ledger
Law and Order
The Investigation

Janwillem van de Wetering
Outsider in Amsterdam
The Corpse on the Dike
Tumbleweed
Death of a Hawker
The Japanese Corpse
The Blond Baboon
The Maine Massacre

Peter Van Greenaway
Doppelganger

John Wainwright
Requiem for a Loser
High-Class Kill
Freeze Thy Blood Less Coldly
A Touch of Malice
The Evidence I Shall Give
The Hard Hit
Death of a Big Man
Square Dance
Landscape with Violence
Pool of Tears
Brainwash
Take Murder...
Duty Elsewhere

Peter N. Walker
Carnaby and the Saboteurs
Carnaby and the Eliminators
Carnaby and the Demonstrators
Carnaby and the Infiltrators

1970–1979 (continued)

    Peter N. Walker (continued)
        Carnaby and the Kidnappers
        Carnaby and the Counterfeiters
        Panda One on Duty
        Panda One Investigates
        Witchcraft for Panda One

    Joseph Wambaugh
        The New Centurions
        The Blue Knight
        The Choirboys
        The Black Marble

    Hillary Waugh
        Finish Me off

    Collin Wilcox
        The Disappearance
        Dead Aim
        Hiding Place
        Long Way Down
        Aftershock
        Doctor, Lawyer
        The Watcher
        Night Games

1980–1999   Thomas Adcock
        Dark Maze

    Warren Adler
        American Quartet
        American Sextet
        Senator Love
        Immaculate Deception
        The Witch of Watergate

    Gary Alexander
        Pigeon Blood
        Unfunny Money
        Kiet and the Golden Peacock
        Kiet and the Opium War
        Deadly Drought
        Kiet Goes West

Noreen Ayres
: *A World the Color of Salt*

John Ball
: *Singapore*
: *Trouble for Tallon*
: *Chief Tallon and the S.O.R.*

James Barnett
: *Backfire Is Hostile*
: *Palmprint*
: *The Firing Squad*
: *Marked for Destruction*

William Bayer
: *Switch*
: *Pattern Crimes*
: *Wallflower*

Paul Bishop
: *Citadel Run*
: *Sand Against the Tide*

Eleanor Taylor Bland
: *Dead Time*

Peter Blauner
: *Slow Motion Riot*

John Brady
: *A Stone of the Heart*
: *Unholy Ground*
: *Kaddish in Dublin*

Anthony Bruno
: *Bad Guys*
: *Bad Blood*
: *Bad Luck*
: *Bad Business*
: *Bad Moon*

James Lee Burke
: *The Neon Rain*
: *A Stained White Radiance*

Rex Burns
: *Strip Search*

1980–1999 (*continued*)

    Rex Burns (*continued*)
        Ground Money
        The Killing Zone

    Roger Busby
        The Hunter
        Snowman

    Gwendoline Butler
        Coffin Underground
        Coffin in the Black Museum
        Coffin and the Paper Man

    Robert Cain
        Cybernarc
        Cybernarc: Gold Dragon

    William J. Caunitz
        One Police Plaza
        Black Sand
        Suspects
        Exceptional Clearance

    Nick Christian
        Ronin

    Martin Claridge
        Nobody's Fool

    Ernest Clark
        Fatal Rose

    Jon Cleary
        Dragons at the Party
        Then and Now, Amen
        Babylon South
        Murder Song
        Pride's Harvest

    Andrew Coburn
        Off Duty
        Love Nest

    Michael Connelly
        The Black Echo

K. C. Constantine
    Always a Body to Trade
    Upon Some Midnight's Clear
    Joey's Case
    Sunshine Enemies

Thomas H. Cook
    Tabernacle
    Sacrificial Ground

Susan Rogers Cooper
    The Man in the Green Chevy
    Houston in the Rear View Mirror
    Other People's Houses
    Chasing Away the Devil

Patricia D. Cornwell
    Postmortem
    Body of Evidence
    All That Remains
    Cruel and Unusual

E. W. Count
    The Hundred Percent Squad

Bill Crider
    Too Late to Die
    Shotgun Saturday Night
    Cursed to Death
    Evil at the Root
    Booked for a Hanging
    Blood Marks

E. V. Cunningham
    The Case of the Kidnapped Angel
    The Case of the Murdered Mackenzie
    The Case of the Sliding Pool

Jack Curtis
    Point of Impact

Claire Curzon
    I Give You Five Days
    Masks and Faces
    The Trojan Hearse
    The Quest for K
    Three-Core Head

1980–1999 (*continued*)

    Claire Curzon (*continued*)
        The Blue-Eyed Boy
        First Wife, Twice Removed

    Robert Daley
        The Dangerous Edge
        Hands of a Stranger

    John Danica and Lucy Freeman
        Lerza's Law

    O'Neil de Noux
        The Big Kiss
        Blue Orleans

    Joseph P. De Sario
        Limbo

    Michael Dibdin
        Ratking
        Vendetta

    D. J. Donaldson
        Cajun Nights
        Blood on the Bayou

    Alison Drake
        Black Moon
        Lagoon
        High Strangeness

    John Kevin Dugan
        Badge of Honor

    Robert L. Duncan
        The Serpent's Mark

    Susan Dunlap
        Karma
        As a Favor
        Not Exactly a Brahmin
        Too Close to the Edge
        A Dinner to Die For
        Diamonds in the Buff
        Death and Taxes

John Dunning
   Booked to Die

Lew Dykes
   Choke Hold

Jack Early
   Donato and Daughter

John Eller
   Rage of Heaven

James Ellroy
   Blood on the Moon
   Because the Night
   Suicide Hill

Earl W. Emerson
   Black Hearts and Slow Dancing
   Help Wanted: Orphans Preferred

Richard Fliegel
   The Art of Death
   The Next to Die
   The Organ Grinder's Monkey
   Time to Kill
   A Semiprivate Doom

Peter Fox
   The Trail of the Reaper

Edward J. Frail
   Cult

Kristopher Franklin
   Silvercat

Nicolas Freeling
   Castang's City
   Wolfnight
   Back of the North Wind
   Cold Iron
   Not as Far as Velma

Joe Gash
   Public Murders
   The El Murders

1980–1999 (*continued*)

 Kenneth Goddard
  Balefire
  The Alchemist

 Paula Gosling
  Monkey Puzzle
  Hoodwink
  The Wychford Murder
  Death Penalties
  Backlash

 Laurence Gough
  The Goldfish Bowl
  Death on a No. 8 Hook
  Hot Shots

 James Grady
  Razor Game
  Just a Shot Away

 Bill Granger
  Priestly Murders
  Newspaper Murders

 Michael Grant
  Line of Duty

 W. E. B. Griffin
  Badge of Honor: Special Operations
  Badge of Honor: The Victim
  Badge of Honor: The Witness

 Ken Gross
  Rough Justice

 Batya Gur
  The Saturday Morning Murder

 A. B. Guthrie, Jr.
  Playing Catch-Up

 Jean Hager
  The Grandfather Medicine
  Night Walker

 Nan Hamilton
  The Shape of Fear

Thomas Harris
> *Red Dragon*

Cynthia Harrod-Eagles
> *Orchestrated Death*

Roy Hart
> *Seascape with Dead Figure*
> *A Pretty Place to Die*
> *A Fox in the Night*
> *Remains to be Seen*
> *Breach of Promise*
> *Robbed Blind*
> *Final Appointment*

James Neal Harvey
> *By Reason of Insanity*
> *The Headsman*

John Harvey
> *Lonely Hearts*
> *Rough Treatment*
> *Cutting Edge*
> *Off Minor*

Mark Hebden
> *Pel Under Pressure*
> *Pel Is Puzzled*
> *Pel and the Staghound*
> *Pel and the Bombers*
> *Pel and the Predators*
> *Pel and the Picture of Innocence*
> *Pel Among the Pueblos*
> *Pel and the Pirates*
> *Pel and the Party Spirit*

Sue Henry
> *Murder on the Iditarod Trail*

Nat Hentoff
> *The Man from Internal Affairs*

Joan Hess
> *Malice in Maggody*
> *Mischief in Maggody*
> *Much Ado in Maggody*
> *Madness in Maggody*

1980–1999 (continued)

   Joan Hess (continued)
      Mortal Remains in Maggody
      Maggody in Manhattan

   Tony Hillerman
      People of Darkness
      The Dark Wind
      The Ghostway
      Skinwalkers
      A Thief of Time
      Talking God
      Coyote Waits

   Timothy Holme
      The Neopolitan Streak
      A Funeral of Gondolas
      The Assisi Murders
      The Devil and the Dolce Vita
      At the Lake of Sudden Death

   Ruby Horansky
      Dead Ahead

   Robert Houston
      The Fourth Codex

   Gary Hunter
      Death Warrant

   Jack D. Hunter
      Judgment in Blood

   Joe Hyams
      Murder at the Academy Awards

   Peter Inchbald
      Tando for Short
      The Sweet Short Grass

   Graham Ison
      Confirm or Deny

   Jon A. Jackson
      Grootka
      Hit on the House

Michael Jahn
> *Death Games*
> *City of God*

Bill James
> *You'd Better Believe It*
> *The Lolita Man*
> *Halo Parade*
> *Protection*
> *Come Clean*

J. A. Jance
> *Until Proved Guilty*
> *Injustice for All*
> *Taking the Fifth*
> *Improbable Cause*
> *A More Perfect Union*

Trish Janeshutz
> *Hidden Lake*
> *In Shadow*

Hamilton Jobson
> *Don't Tell the Press*
> *The Sleeping Tiger*

E. Richard Johnson
> *Blind Man's Bluff*
> *The God Keepers*
> *Case Load Maximum*
> *Dead Flowers*

Bruce Jones
> *In Deep*

R.W. Jones
> *Saving Grace*
> *Cop Out*
> *The Green Reapers*

Cyril Joyce
> *Murder Is a Pendulum*

Stuart M. Kaminsky
> *Death of a Dissident*
> *Black Knight in Red Square*
> *The Red Chameleon*
> *A Find Red Rain*

1980–1999 (continued)

Stuart M. Kaminsky (continued)
A Cold Red Sunrise
The Man Who Walked Like a Bear
Rostnikov's Vacation
Death of a Russian Priest

William Katz
Open House

John Katzenbach
The Traveler

Faye Kellerman
The Ritual Bath
Sacred and Profane
Milk and Honey
Day of Atonement
False Prophet

Jonathan Kellerman
The Butcher's Theater

Bill Kelly and Dolph Le Moult
Street Dance
Dream Street
Death Spiral
The Killing Moon

Bill Knox
A Killing in Antiques
The Hanging Tree
The Crossfire Killings
The Interface Man

John Lantigua
Heat Lightning

Lynda La Plante
Prime Suspect
Prime Suspect 2

Philip Lauben
A Nice Sound Alibi
A Surfeit of Alibis

John Leslie
Killer in Paradise

Bob Leuci
    Captain Butterfly

J. R. Levitt
    Carnivores

Michael Z. Lewin
    Hard Line
    Late Payments

Roy Lewis
    A Relative Distance

Herbert Lieberman
    Nightbloom
    Shadow Dancers

David L. Lindsey
    A Cold Mind
    Heat from Another Sun
    Spiral
    In the Lake of the Moon
    Mercy

Elizabeth Linington
    Consequences of Crime
    Skeletons in the Closet

Jayson Livingston
    Point Blank

Tom Logan
    Detroit P.D.: Sword of Samos

Mike Lundy
    Raven

Ed McBain
    Ghosts
    Heat
    Ice
    Lightning
    Poison
    Tricks
    Lullaby
    Vespers
    Widows

1980–1999 (*continued*)

 James McClure
  The Blood of an Englishman
  The Artful Egg

 Vincent McConnor
  The Provence Puzzle
  The Riviera Puzzle
  The Paris Puzzle
  Limbo

 Sharyn McCrumb
  If Ever I Return, Pretty Peggy-O

 Jill McGown
  A Perfect Match
  Redemption
  Death of a Dancer
  The Murders of Mrs. Austin and Mrs. Beale

 William McIlvanney
  The Papers of Tony Veitch
  Strange Loyalties

 Joseph D. McNamara
  The First Directive
  Fatal Command
  The Blue Mirage

 Michael Malone
  Uncivil Seasons
  Time's Witness

 Anthony Mancini
  Talons

 Terry Marlowe
  Target Blue

 Margaret Maron
  One Coffee With
  Death of a Butterfly
  Death in Blue Folders
  Baby Doll Games
  Past Imperfect

 Max Marquis
  The Twelfth Man

William Marshall
- *Sci Fi*
- *Perfect End*
- *War Machine*
- *The Far Away Man*
- *Frogmouth*
- *Out of Nowhere*
- *Manila Bay*
- *Whisper*

Lee Martin
- *Too Sane a Murder*
- *A Conspiracy of Strangers*
- *Murder at the Blue Owl*
- *Hal's Own Murder Case*
- *The Mensa Murders*
- *Deficit Ending*
- *Hacker*

Edward Mathis
- *Only When She Cries*

Archer Mayor
- *Open Season*
- *Borderlines*

Henry Meigs
- *Gate of the Tigers*

James Melville
- *The Chrysanthemum Chain*
- *A Sort of Samurai*
- *The Ninth Netsuke*
- *Sayonara, Sweet Amaryllis*
- *Death of a Daimyo*
- *Death Ceremony*
- *Go Gently, Gaijin*
- *Kimono for a Corpse*
- *The Reluctant Ronin*
- *A Haiku for Hanae*
- *The Bogus Buddha*

Jennie Melville
- *Murder Has a Pretty Face*
- *Making Good Blood*
- *Witching Murder*

1980–1999 (*continued*)

> D. R. Meredith
>> *The Sheriff and the Panhandle Murders*
>> *The Sheriff and the Branding Iron Murders*
>> *The Sheriff and the Folsom Man Murders*
>
> Hugh Miller
>> *An Echo of Justice*
>
> Rex Miller
>> *Stone Shadow*
>> *Iceman*
>
> John Minahan
>> *The Great Hotel Robbery*
>> *The Great Diamond Robbery*
>> *The Face Behind The Mask*
>> *The Great Pyramid Robbery*
>> *The Great Harvard Robbery*
>> *The Great Grave Robbery*
>
> Kirk Mitchell
>> *With Siberia Comes a Chill*
>
> Marcel Montecino
>> *The Crosskiller*
>
> Stephen Murray
>> *A Cool Killing*
>> *Salty Waters*
>> *The Noose of Time*
>> *Fetch Out No Shroud*
>> *Fatal Opinions*
>
> Ed Naha
>> *On the Edge*
>> *Razzle-Dazzle*
>> *Cracking Up*
>
> Janet Neel
>> *Death's Bright Angel*
>> *Death on Site*
>
> David Nemec
>> *Mad Blood*

Christopher Newman
Sixth Precinct
Midtown South
Knock-Off
Midtown North
19th Precinct
Backfire

Fridrikh Neznansky
The Body in Sokoliniki Park

Kyotaro Nishimura
The Mystery Train Disappears

Jack O'Donnell
Box Nine

Lillian O'Donnell
The Children's Zoo
Cop Without a Shield
Ladykiller
Casual Affairs
A Private Crime
Pushover
The Other Side of the Door

Freny Olbrich
Desouza in Stardust

Jerry Oster
Internal Affairs
Sweet Justice
Nowhere Man
Club Dead
Saint Mike

T. Jefferson Parker
Laguna Heat

James Patterson
The Midnight Club

Paul Patti
Silhouettes

Barbara Paul
You Have the Right to Remain Silent

1980–1999 (continued)

 Ridley Pearson
  Undercurrents
  Probable Cause
  Hard Fall

 Dave Pedneau
  A.P.B.
  D.O.A.
  B.O.L.O.
  A.K.A.
  B & E: Breaking and Entering
  N.F.D.

 Gerald Petievich
  One-Shot Deal
  To Die in Beverly Hills
  The Quality of the Informant
  Earth Angels

 Tom Philbin
  A Precinct Siberia Novel: Cop Killer
  A Precinct Siberia Novel: Street Killer
  A Precinct Siberia Novel: Death Sentence

 Joyce Porter
  Dover Beats the Band

 Erica Quest
  Cold Coffin
  Death Walk
  Model Murder

 Derek Raymond
  The Devil's Home on Leave
  He Died with His Eyes Open
  How the Dead Live
  I Was Dora Suarez

 Robert Sims Reid
  Cupid
  Benediction

 John Lawrence Reynolds
  And Leave Her Lay Dying
  Whisper Death

Peter Robinson
> *Gallows View*
> *A Dedicated Man*
> *A Necessary End*

Charles G. Rogers
> *1199*

Robert Rosenberg
> *Crimes of the City*

Dennis St. Pierre
> *The Marshal*

Lawrence Sanders
> *The Third Deadly Sin*
> *The Fourth Deadly Sin*

John Sandford
> *Rules of Prey*
> *Shadow Prey*
> *Eyes of Prey*
> *Silent Prey*

J. G. Sandom
> *Gospel Truth*

Soledad Santiago
> *Undercover*

Eric Sauter
> *Skeletons*

Alan Scholefield
> *Dirty Weekend*
> *Thief Taker*

Monte Schulz
> *Down by the River*

Jack S. Scott
> *The Gospel Lamb*
> *A Distant View of Death*
> *An Uprush of Mayhem*
> *The Local Lads*
> *All the Pretty People*
> *A Death in Irish Town*
> *A Little Darling Dead*
> *A Knife Between the Ribs*

1980–1999 (*continued*)

> David Serafin
>> *Christmas Rising*
>> *Madrid Underground*
>> *The Body in Cadiz Bay*
>> *Port of Light*
>> *The Angels of Torremolinos*
>
> Steven Shagan
>> *Vendetta*
>
> Dell Shannon
>> *Felondy File*
>> *Murder Most Strange*
>> *The Motive on Record*
>> *Destiny with Death*
>> *Exploits of Death*
>> *Chaos of Crime*
>
> V. L. Sims
>> *Death Is a Family Affair*
>> *To Sleep, Perchance to Kill*
>
> Michael Slade
>> *Headhunter*
>> *Ghoul*
>
> Alison Smith
>> *Someone Else's Grave*
>> *Rising*
>
> D. W. Smith
>> *Father's Law*
>> *Serious Crimes*
>> *The Fourth Crow*
>
> Julie Smith
>> *New Orleans Morning*
>> *The Axeman's Jazz*
>
> Martin Cruz Smith
>> *Gorky Park*
>
> Mitchell Smith
>> *Daydreams*
>
> Stephen Solomita
>> *Force of Nature*

Richard Martin Stern
> *Death in the Snow*
> *Tangled Murders*
> *Interloper*

J. Michael Straczynski
> *Otherside*

Carsten Stroud
> *Sniper's Moon*

Rob Swigart
> *Vector*
> *Toxin*
> *Venom*

Jeffrey Tharp
> *A Killing in Kansas*

Roderick Thorp
> *Rainbow Drive*

Joseph Trigoboff
> *The Bone Orchard*

Peter Turnbull
> *Deep and Crisp and Even*
> *Dead Knock*
> *Fair Friday*
> *Big Money*
> *Two Way Cut*
> *Condition Purple*
> *And Did Murder Him*
> *Long Day Monday*

Derek Van Arman
> *Just Killing Time*

Janwillem van de Wetering
> *The Mind-Murders*
> *The Streetbird*
> *The Rattle-Rat*
> *Hard Rain*

Peter Van Greenaway
> *The Killing Cup*

John Wainwright
> *Dominoes*

1980–1999 (*continued*)

    John Wainwright (*continued*)
        All on a Summer's Day
        Blayde R.I.P.
        Their Evil Ways
        The Ride
        Cul-De-Sac
        All Through the Night
        Portrait in Shadow
        The Forgotten Murders
        A Very Parochial Murder
        The Man Who Wasn't There
        Hangman's Lane

    Randall Wallace
        Blood of the Lamb
        Where Angels Watch

    Joseph Wambaugh
        The Glitter Dome
        The Delta Star
        The Secrets of Harry Bright
        Fugitive Nights

    Irving Weinman
        Tailor's Dummy

    Robert Westbrook
        Nostalgia Kills
        Lady Left

    John Westermann
        High Crimes
        Exit Wounds
        Sweet Deal

    Collin Wilcox
        Mankiller
        Stalker Horse
        Victims
        The Pariah
        A Death Before Dying
        Dead Center

    Charles Willeford
        Miami Blues

    New Hope for the Dead
    Sideswipe
    The Way We Die Now

Timothy Williams
    Converging Parallels
    The Puppeteer
    Persona Non Grata

David Wiltse
    The Serpent
    Prayer for the Dead
    Close to the Bone
    The Edge of Sleep

Anne Wingate
    Death by Deception
    The Eye of Anna
    The Buzzards Must Also Feed

Ted Wood
    Dead in the Water
    Murder on Ice
    Live Bait
    Fool's Gold
    Corkscrew
    On the Inside
    Flashback

Daniel Woodrell
    Under the Bright Lights

Eric Wright
    The Night the Gods Smiled
    Smoke Detector
    Death in the Old Country
    A Single Death
    A Body Surrounded by Water
    A Question of Murder
    A Sensitive Case
    Final Cut
    A Fine Italian Hand

L. R. Wright
    The Suspect
    Sleep While I Sing
    A Chill Rain in January

2030–2039   Ben Sloane
             Horn: Hot Zone
             Horn: Outland Strip

2040–2047   Greg Bear
             Queen of Angels

             Walter Jon Williams
             Days of Atonement

6

Locations

Police procedurals take place anywhere there is a police force. Every kind of location is used. Some are fictional, others quite real, a few have had their names changed and now masquerade under an alias. They are big and little, village, urban, and suburban.

Africa
   Gil North
      A Corpse for Kofi Katt

Australia
   Jon Cleary
      The High Commissioner
      Helga's Web
      Ransom
      Dragons at the Party
      Then and Now, Amen
      Babylon South
      Murder Song
      Pride's Harvest

Belgium
   Julian Rathbone
      The Euro-Killers

Brazil
   Rio de Janiero
   Robert L. Fish
      The Fugitive
      Isle of the Snakes
      The Shrunken Head

Brazil/Rio de Janiero (*cont.*)
   Brazilian Sleigh Ride
   The Diamond Bubble
   Always Kill a Stranger
   The Bridge That Went Nowhere
   The Xavier Affair
   The Green Hell Treasure
   Trouble in Paradise

Canada
  British Columbia
  L. R. Wright
   The Suspect
   Sing While I Sleep
   A Chill Rain in January
  Vancouver
  Laurence Gough
   The Goldfish Bowl
   Silent Knives
   Hot Shots
  Michael Slade
   Headhunter
   Ghoul
  Ontario
  Ted Wood
   Dead in the Water
   The Killing Cold
   Live Bait
   Fool's Gold
   Corkscrew
   On the Inside
   Flashback
  Prince Edward Island
  Eric Wright
   A Body Surrounded by Water
  Toronto
  Eric Wright
   The Night the Gods Smiled
   Smoke Detector
   A Single Death
   A Body Surrounded by Water
   A Question of Murder
   A Sensitive Case
   Final Cut
   A Fine Italian Hand

Columbia
Robert Cain
Cybernarc
Cybernarc: Gold Dragon

Denmark
Copenhagen
Paul Orum
The Whipping Boy
Nothing But the Truth

Egypt
John Minahan
The Great Pyramid Robbery
Cairo
Michael Pearce
The Mamur Zapt and the Return of the Carpet
The Mamur Zapt and the Night of the Dog
The Mamur Zapt and the Donkey-Vous

England
Stephen Gallagher
Down River
Bill James
You'd Better Believe It
The Lolita Man
Halo Parade
Protection
Come Clean
Hamilton Jobson
Smile and Be a Villain
Naked to My Enemy
The Silent Cry
The House with Blind Eyes
The Sand Pit
The Shadow That Caught Fire
Contract with a Killer
The Evidence You Will Hear
Waiting for Thursday
To Die a Little
Exit to Violence
Don't Tell the Press
The Sleeping Tiger
R. W. Jones
Saving Grace

England (*continued*)
- *Cop Out*
- *The Green Reapers*

Cyril Joyce
- *The Information Man*
- *Seize the Passing Stranger*
- *Murder Is a Pendulum*

Jill McGown
- *A Perfect Match*
- *Redemption*
- *Death of a Dancer*
- *The Murders of Mrs. Austin and Mrs. Beale*

Jennie Melville
- *Come Home and Be Killed*
- *Burning Is a Substitute for Loving*
- *Murderer's House*
- *Here Lies Your Love*
- *Nell Alone*
- *A Different Kind of Summer*
- *A New Kind of Killer, An Old Kind of Death*
- *Murder Has a Pretty Face*
- *Making Good Blood*
- *Witching Murder*

Hugh Miller
- *An Echo of Justice*

Joyce Porter
- *Dover One*
- *Dover Two*
- *Dover Three*
- *Dover and the Unkindest Cut of All*
- *Dover Goes to Pott*
- *Dover Strikes Again*
- *It's Murder with Dover*
- *Dover and the Claret Tappers*
- *Dover Beats the Band*

Maurice Procter
- *The Chief Inspector's Statement*
- *I Will Speak Daggers*

Jack S. Scott
- *A Better Class of Business*
- *The Bastard's Name Was Bristow*
- *The Poor Old Lady's Dead*
- *The Shallow Grave*
- *A Clutch of Vipers*
- *The Gospel Lamb*

    A Distant View of Death
    An Uprush of Mayhem
    The Local Lads
    All the Pretty People
    A Death in Irish Town
    A Little Darling Dead
    A Knife Between the Ribs
L. A. G. Strong
    Which I Never
Peter Van Greenaway
    Doppelganger
    The Killing Cup
Peter N. Walker
    Carnaby and the Hijackers
    Carnaby and the Assassins
    Carnaby and the Gaolbreakers
    Carnaby and the Conspirators
    Carnaby and the Saboteurs
    Carnaby and the Eliminators
    Carnaby and the Demonstrators
    Carnaby and the Infiltrators
    Carnaby and the Kidnappers
    Carnaby and the Counterfeiters
    Panda One On Duty
    Panda One Investigates
    Witchcraft for Panda One

Cornwall
Roger Busby
    New Face in Hell

Cotswolds
Erica Quest
    Cold Coffin
    Model Murder
    Death Walk

Dorset
Ray Harrison
    French Ordinary Murder
    Death of an Honourable Member
    Death of a Dancing Lady
    Deathwatch
    Harvest of Death
    Tincture of Death
    Sphere of Death
    Patently Murder

England *(continued)*
  Roy Hart
    Seascape with Death Figures
    A Pretty Place for a Murder
    A Fox in the Night
    Remains to be Seen
    Breach of Promise
    Robbed Blind
    Final Appointment
London
  Roger Busby
    The Hunter
    Snow Man
  Gwendoline Butler
    Death in a Row
    The Dull Dead
    Death Lives Next Door
    Make Me a Murderer
    Coffin for Baby
    Coffin Waiting
    A Nameless Coffin
    Coffin's Dark Number
    Coffin from the Past
    A Coffin for the Canary
    Coffin Underground
    Coffin in the Black Museum
    Coffin and the Paper Man
  John Creasey
    Inspector West Takes Charge
    Inspector West Leaves Town
    Inspector West at Home
    Inspector West Regrets
    Holiday for Inspector West
    Triumph for Inspector West
    Battle for Inspector West
    Inspector West Kicks Off
    Inspector West Cries Wolf
    Inspector West Alone
    Puzzle for Inspector West
    A Case for Inspector West
    Inspector West at Bay
    Send Inspector West
    A Gun for Inspector West
    A Beauty for Inspector West

Inspector West Makes Haste
  Two for Inspector West
  Parcels for Inspector West
  A Prince for Inspector West
  Accident for Inspector West
  Find Inspector West
  Strike for Death
  Murder, London–New York
  Death of a Race Horse
  The Case of the Innocent Victims
  Murder on the Line
  Death in Cold Print
  Scene of the Crime
  Policeman's Dread
  Hang the Little Man
  Look Three Ways at Murder
  Murder, London–Australia
  Murder, London–South Africa
  The Executioners
  So Young to Burn
  Murder, London–Miami
  A Part for a Policeman
  Alibi
  A Splinter of Glass
  The Extortioners
  Theft of Magna Carta
  A Sharp Rise in Crime
Jack Curtis
  Point of Impact
Keith Heller
  Man's Illegal Life
  Man's Storm
  Man's Loving Family
Laurence Henderson
  With Intent
  Cage Until Tame
  Major Enquiry
Peter Hill
  The Washermen
Peter Inchbald
  Tondo for Short
  The Sweet Short Grass
  Or the Bambino Dies
Graham Ison
  Confirm or Deny

England/London *(continued)*
- Cyril Joyce
  - *Seize the Passing Stranger*
- Lynda La Plante
  - *Prime Suspect*
  - *Prime Suspect 2*
- Max Marquis
  - *The Twelfth Man*
- J. J. Marric
  - *Gideon's Day*
  - *Gideon's Week*
  - *Gideon's Night*
  - *Gideon's Month*
  - *Gideon's Staff*
  - *Gideon's Risk*
  - *Gideon's Fire*
  - *Gideon's March*
  - *Gideon's Ride*
  - *Gideon's Vote*
  - *Gideon's Lot*
  - *Gideon's Badge*
  - *Gideon's Wrath*
  - *Gideon's River*
  - *Gideon's Power*
  - *Gideon's Sport*
  - *Gideon's Art*
  - *Gideon's Men*
  - *Gideon's Press*
  - *Gideon's Fog*
  - *Gideon's Drive*
- Ian Kennedy Matin
  - *The Deal of the Century*
- David Murphy, Jr.
  - *Inspector Malone Sails In*
- Stephen Murray
  - *The Noose of Time*
  - *Fetch Out No Shroud*
  - *Fatal Opinions*
- Janet Neel
  - *Death's Bright Angel*
  - *Death on Site*
- D. J. Olivy
  - *Never Ask a Policeman*
- Laurence Payne
  - *The Nose on My Face*

Anne Perry
  The Face of a Stranger
  A Dangerous Mourning
  Defend and Betray
Derek Raymond
  The Devil's Home on Leave
  He Died with His Eyes Open
  How the Dead Live
J. G. Sandom
  Gospel Truth
Alan Scholefield
  Dirty Weekend
  Thief Taker
Francis Selwyn
  Cracksman on Velvet
Michael Slade
  Ghoul
D. W. Smith
  Father's Law
  Serious Crimes
  The Fourth Crow
Donald Thomas
  The Ripper's Apprentice
  Jekyll, Alias Hyde
Conrad Voss Bark
  The Second Red Dragon
Pamela West
  Yours Truly, Jack the Ripper
Midlands Region
  Airechester (a fictional city)
  Maurice Procter
  The Pub Crawler
  Granchester (a fictional city)
  Maurice Procter
  Hell Is a City
  The Midnight Plumber
  Man in Ambush
  Killer at Large
  Devil's Due
  The Devil Was Handsome
  A Body to Spare
  Moonlight Flitting
  Two Men in Twenty
  Death Has a Shadow
  Rogue Running

England/Midlands *(continued)*
  His Weight in Gold
  Exercise Hoodwink
  A Large Midland City
  Roger Busby
  Robbery Blue
  The Frighteners
  Deadlock
  A Reasonable Man
  Pattern of Violence
  John Harvey
  Lonely Hearts
  Rough Treatment
  Cutting Edge
  Off Minor
Northumberland
  Roy Lewis
  Nothing But Foxes
Oxford
  Gwendoline Butler
  Coffin in Oxford
Richmond
  Peter Fox
  The Trail of the Reaper
Sussex
  Stephen Murray
  A Cool Killing
  Salty Waters
  Fetch Out No Shroud
Thames Valley
  Claire Curzon
  I Give You Five Days
  Masks and Faces
  The Trojan Hearse
  The Quest for K
  Three-Core Lead
  The Blue-Eyed Boy
  First Wife, Twice Removed
Yorkshire
  Jack Ripley
  Davis Doesn't Live Here Anymore
  The Pig That Got Up and Slowly Walked Away
  My God How the Money Rolls In
  My Word You Should Have Seen Us

Peter Robinson
- *Gallows View*
- *A Dedicated Man*
- *A Necessary End*

John Wainwright
- *Death in a Sleeping City*
- *The Crystallised Carbon Pig*
- *Evil Intent*
- *The Worms Must Wait*
- *The Darkening Glass*
- *Requiem for a Loser*
- *High-Class Kill*
- *Freeze Thy Blood Less Coldly*
- *A Touch of Malice*
- *The Evidence I Shall Give*
- *The Hard Hit*
- *Death of a Big Man*
- *Square Dance*
- *Landscape with Violence*
- *Pool of Tears*
- *Brainwash*
- *Take Murder*
- *Duty Elsewhere*
- *Dominoes*
- *All on a Summer's Day*
- *Blayde R.I.P.*
- *Their Evil Ways*
- *The Ride*
- *Cul-de-sac*
- *All Through the Night*
- *Portrait in Shadow*
- *The Forgotten Murders*
- *A Very Parochial Murder*
- *The Man Who Wasn't There*
- *Hangman's Lane*

Finland
Helsinki
Matti Joensuu
- *The Stone Murders*

France
Nicolas Freeling
- *A Dressing of Diamonds*
- *The Bugles Blowing*
- *Lake Isle*

France *(continued)*
    The Night Lords
    Castang's City
    Wolfnight
    The Back of the North Wind
    Cold Iron
    Not as Far as Velma
  Mark Hebden
    Death Set to Music
    Pel and the Faceless Corpse
    Pel Under Pressure
    Pel Is Puzzled
    Pel and the Stagehound
    Pel and the Bombers
    Pel and the Predators
    Pel and the Picture of Innocence
    Pel Among the Pueblos
    Pel and the Pirates
    Pel and the Party Spirit
  Vincent McConnor
    The Provence Puzzle
    The Riviera Puzzle
    The Paris Puzzle
    I Am Vidocq
Nice
  Robert Daley
    A Dangerous Edge
Paris
  Richard Grayson
    The Murders at the Impasse Louvain
    The Monterant Affair
    The Death of Abbé Dodier
    Crime Without Passion
    Death en Voyage
    Death on the Cards
    Death Off Stage
  Georges Simenon
    Maigret's Mistake
    Maigret in Montmartre
    Maigret Has Scruples
    Maigret and the Killer
    Maigret and the Informer
    Maigret and the Millionaires
    Maigret and the Loner

Locations 349

Germany
  Munich
  Frank DeFelitta
    Oktoberfest

Hong Kong
  William Marshall
    Yellowthread Street
    Gelignite
    The Hatchet Man
    Thin Air
    Skulduggery
    Sci Fi
    Perfect End
    War Machine
    The Far Away Man
    Frogmouth
    Out of Nowhere
  Owen Sela
    The Bengali Inheritance

India
  Bombay
  Freny Olbrich
    Desouza Pays the Price
    Desouza in Stardust
  Calcutta
  Francis Selwyn
    Sergeant Verity and the Imperial Diamond

Ireland
  Dublin
  John Brady
    A Stone in the Heart
    Unholy Ground
    Kaddish In Dublin
  R. W. Jones
    The Green Reapers

Israel
  Jerusalem
  William Bayer
    Pattern Crimes
  Batya Gur
    The Saturday Morning Murder

Israel *(continued)*
  Jonathan Kellerman
    The Butcher's Theater
  Robert Rosenberg
    Crimes of the City
  Tel Aviv
  Olga Hesky
    Time for Treason

Italy
  Michael Dibdin
    Ratking
    Vendetta
  Timothy Williams
    Converging Parallels
    The Puppeteer
    Persona Non Grata
  Verona
  Timothy Holme
    The Neopolitan Streak
    A Funeral of Gondolas
    The Assisi Murders
    The Devil and the Dolce Vita

Japan
  James Melville
    The Wages of Sin
    The Chrysanthemum Chain
    A Sort of Samurai
    The Ninth Netsuke
    Sayonara, Sweet Amaryllis
    Death of a Daimyo
    The Death Ceremony
    Go Gently, Gaijin
    Kimono for a Corpse
    The Reluctant Ronin
    Haiku for Hanae
    The Bogus Buddha
  Janwillem van de Wetering
    The Japanese Corpse
  Tokyo
  Seicho Matsumoto
    Inspector Imanishi Investigates
    Points and Lines
  Henry Meigs
    Gate of the Tigers

Kyotaro Mishimura
: *The Mystery Train Disappears*

Luong (mythical country in Southeast Asia)
Gary Alexander
: *Pigeon Blood*
: *Unfunny Money*
: *Kiet and the Golden Peacock*
: *Kiet and the Opium War*
: *Deadly Drought*
: *Kiet Goes West*

Malta
Gwendolyn Butler
: *Coffin in Malta*

Mexico
Robert Houston
: *The Fourth Codex*

Netherlands
Janwillem van de Wetering
: *Rattle-Rat*
Amsterdam
Nicolas Freeling
: *Love in Amsterdam*
: *Because of the Cats*
: *Double-Barrel*
: *Criminal Conversation*
: *The King of the Rainy Country*
: *Strike Out Where Not Applicable*
: *Tsing-Boum*
: *Over the Side*
Janwillem van de Wetering
: *Outsider in Amsterdam*
: *The Corpse on the Dike*
: *Tumbleweed*
: *Death of a Hawker*
: *The Blond Baboon*
: *The Mind-Murders*
: *The Streetbird*
: *Hard Rain*

Philippines
Manila
William Marshall

Philippines (*continued*)
   Manila Bay
   Whisper

Russia
  Stuart M. Kaminsky
   Rostnikov's Vacation
   Death of a Russian Priest
  Moscow
  Stuart M. Kaminsky
   Death of a Dissident
   Black Knight in Red Square
   Red Chameleon
   A Fine Red Rain
   The Man Who Walked Like a Bear
  Fridrikh Neznansky
   The Body in Sokoliniki Park
  Martin Cruz Smith
   Gorky Park

Scotland
  Hugh C. Rae
   A Few Small Bones
   The Shooting Gallery
  Edinburgh
  Martin Claridge
   Nobody's Fool
  Alanna Knight
   Enter Second Murderer
   Blood Line
   Deadly Beloved
   Killing Cousins
  Glasgow
  Bill Knox
   Deadline for a Dream
   Death Department
   Leave It to the Hangman
   Little Drops of Blood
   Sanctuary Isle
   The Man in the Battle
   The Taste of Proof
   The Deep Fall
   Justice on the Rocks
   The Tallyman
   Children of the Mist

To Kill a Witch
Draw Batons!
Rally to Kill
Pilot Error
Live Bait
A Killing in Antiques
The Hanging Tree
The Crossfire Killings
The Interface Man
William McIlvanney
Laidlaw
The Papers of Tony Veitch
Strange Loyalties
Peter Turnbull
Deep and Crisp and Even
Dead Knock
Fair Friday
Big Money
Two Way Cut
Condition Purple
And Did Murder Him
Long Day Monday

Siberia
Stuart M. Kaminsky
A Cold Red Sunrise

South Africa
James McClure
The Song Dog
The Steam Pig
The Caterpillar Cop
The Gooseberry Fool
Snake
The Sunday Hangman
The Blood of an Englishman
An Artful Egg

Spain
Madrid
David Serafin
Saturday of Glory
Madrid Underground
Christmas Rising
The Body in Cadiz Bay

Spain/Madrid *(continued)*
    Port of Light
    The Angel of Torremolinas

Sweden
  K. Arne Blom
    The Moment of Truth
  Maj Sjöwall and Per Wahlöö
    Murder at the Savoy
    Cop Killer: The Story of a Crime
  Stockholm
  Maj Sjöwall and Per Wahlöö
    Roseanna
    The Man on the Balcony
    The Man Who Went Up in Smoke
    The Fire Engine That Disappeared
    The Abominable Man
    The Locked Room
    The Terrorists
  Per Wahlöö
    Murder on the Thirty-First Floor

Wales
  Peter Hill
    The Enthusiasts

United States
  Alabama
    Birmingham
    Thomas H. Cook
      Streets of Fire
  Alaska
  Sue Henry
    Murder on the Iditarod Trail
  Arkansas
  Joan Hess
    Malice in Maggody
    Mischief in Maggody
    Much Ado in Maggody
    Madness in Maggody
    Mortal Remains in Maggody
  California
  William Camp
    The Jacobs Park Killings

Kenneth Goddard
  Balefire
Joseph D. McNamara
  The First Directive
  Fatal Command
  The Blue Mirage
Ed Naha
  On the Edge
  Razzle-Dazzle
  Cracking Up
Jerry Oster
  Rancho Maria
T. Jefferson Parker
  Laguna Heat
Monte Schulz
  Down by the River
John Holbrook Vance
  The Pleasant Grove Murders
  Berkeley
  Susan Dunlap
  Karma
  As a Favor
  Not Exactly a Brahmin
  Too Close to the Edge
  A Dinner to Die For
  Diamonds in the Buff
  Death and Taxes
  Beverly Hills
  E. V. Cunningham
  Samantha
  The Case of the One-Penny Orange
  The Case of the Russian Diplomat
  The Case of the Poisoned Eclair
  The Case of the Sliding Pool
  The Case of the Kidnapped Angel
  The Case of the Murdered Mackenzie
  Gerald Petievich
  To Die in Beverly Hills
  Robert Westbrook
  Nostalgia Kills
  Carmel
  Ridley Pearson
  Probable Cause

United States/California *(continued)*
    Hollywood
    Joe Hyams
    Murder at the Academy Awards
    Los Angeles
    Dallas Barnes
    Yesterday Is Dead
    Greg Bear
    Queen of Angels
    Paul Bishop
    Sand Against the Tide
    Chapel of the Ravens
    Michael Connelly
    The Black Echo
    Joseph P. De Sario
    Limbo
    James Ellroy
    Clandestine
    Because the Night
    Blood on the Moon
    Suicide Hill
    The Black Dahlia
    Nan Hamilton
    The Shape of Fear
    Alfred Harris
    Baroni
    E. Richard Johnson
    The God Keepers
    Faye Kellerman
    The Ritual Bath
    Sacred and Profane
    Milk and Honey
    False Prophet
    Elizabeth Linington
    Greenmask
    No Evil Angel
    Date with Death
    Something Wrong
    Policeman's Lot
    Practice to Deceive
    Crime by Chance
    Perchance to Die
    No Villain Need Be
    Consequences of Crime
    Skeletons in the Closet

Locations

Vincent McConnor
Limbo
Marcel Montecino
The Crosskiller
Gerald Petievich
One-Shot Deal
To Die in Beverly Hills
The Quality of the Informant
Earth Angels
Steve Shagan
Vendetta
Dell Shannon
Case Pending
The Ace of Spades
Extra Kill
Knave of Hearts
Death of a Busybody
Double Bluff
Mark of Murder
The Death-Bringers
Root of All Evil
Death by Inches
Coffin Corner
With a Vengence
Chance to Kill
Rain with Violence
Kill with Kindness
Schooled to Kill
Crime on Their Hands
Unexpected Death
Whim to Kill
With Intent to Kill
Murder with Love
No Holiday for Crime
Spring of Violence
Crime File
Deuces Wild
Streets of Death
Appearances of Death
Cold Trail
Felony at Random
The Motive on Record
Destiny of Death
Exploit of Death
Chaos of Crime

United States/California (*continued*)
    Roderick Thorp
    Rainbow Drive
    Randall Wallace
    Blood of the Lamb
    Where Angels Watch
    Joseph Wambaugh
    The New Centurions
    The Blue Knight
    The Choirboys
    The Black Marble
    The Glitter Dome
    The Delta Star
    Fugitive Nights
    Robert Westbrook
    Nostalgia Kills
    Lady Left
    Orange County
    Noreen Ayres
    A World the Color of Salt
    Palm Springs
    Joseph Wambaugh
    The Secrets of Harry Bright
    Pasadena
    John Ball
    The Cool Cottontail
    Johnny Get Your Gun
    Five Pieces of Jade
    The Eyes of Buddha
    Then Came Violence
    Singapore
    Sacramento
    Jayson Livingston
    Point Blank
    San Diego
    Kenneth Goddard
    The Alchemist
    Charles G. Rogers
    1199
    San Francisco
    Paula Gosling
    A Running Duck
    John Lantigua
    Heat Lightning
    Kirk Mitchell
    With Siberia Comes a Chill

Robert L. Pike
Reardon
Colin Wilcox
The Lonely Hunter
The Disappearance
Dead Aim
Hiding Place
Long Way Down
Aftershock
Doctor, Lawyer
The Watcher
Man Killer
Stalking Horse
Victims
Night Games
The Pariah
A Death Before Dying
Dead Center
San Jose
L. V. Sims
Death Is a Family Affair
To Sleep, Perchance to Dream
Santa Barbara
Bruce Jones
In Deep
Colorado
Kristopher Franklin
Silvercat
Denver
Rex Burns
The Alvarez Journal
The Farnsworth Score
Speak for the Dead
Angle of Attack
The Avenging Angel
Strip Search
Ground Money
The Killing Zone
John Dunning
Booked to Die
Connecticut
Hillary Waugh
A Rag and a Bone
Sleep Long, My Love
Road Block

United States/Connecticut *(continued)*
    That Night It Rained
    The Late Mrs D.
    Born Victim
    Death and Circumstances
    Prisoner's Plea
    The Missing Man
    End of a Party
    Pure Poison
    The Con Game
Florida
Alison Drake
    Black Moon
    Lagoon
    High Strangeness
Paul Patti
    Silhouettes
Derek Van Arman
    Just Killing Time
  Key West
  John Leslie
    Killer in Paradise
  Miami
  Trish Janeshutz
    Hidden Lake
    In Shadow
  John Katzenbach
    The Traveler
  Charles Willeford
    Miami Blues
    New Hope for the Dead
    Sideswipe
    The Way We Die Now
Georgia
  Atlanta
  Thomas H. Cook
    Sacrificial Ground
Hawaii
Rob Swigart
    Vector
    Toxin
    Venom
Illinois
Eleanor Taylor Bland
    Dead Time

Chicago
Joe Gash/Bill Granger
Public Murders
Priestly Murders
Newspaper Murders
The El Murders
Mark Smith
The Death of the Detective
Indiana
  Indianapolis
  Michael Z. Lewin
  Night Cover
  Hard Line
  Late Payments
Kansas
Jeffrey Tharp
  A Killing in Kansas
Kentucky
Philip Lauben
  A Nice Sound Alibi
  A Surfeit of Alibis
Louisiana
James Lee Burke
  A Stained White Radiance
Daniel Woodrell
  Under the Bright Lights
  New Orleans
  James Lee Burke
  The Neon Rain
  O'Neal de Noux
  The Big Kiss
  Blue Orleans
  D. J. Donaldson
  Cajun Nights
  Blood on the Bayou
  Julie Smith
  New Orleans Morning
  The Axeman's Jazz
Maryland
Jack D. Hunter
  Judgment in Blood
Derek Van Arman
  Just Killing Time
  Baltimore
  Lew Dykes
  Choke Hold

United States/Maryland (*continued*)
    James Grady
      Razor Game
      Just a Shot Away
Massachusetts
Andrew Coburn
    Off Duty
Harold R. Daniels
    House on Greenapple Road
  Boston
  John Minahan
    The Great Harvard Robbery
  John Lawrence Reynolds
    And Leave Her Lay Dying
    Whisper Death
  Cape Cod
  John Hough, Jr.
    The Guardian
Michigan
  Detroit
  Jon A. Jackson
    The Diehard
    The Blind Pig
    Grootka
  Tom Logan
    Detroit P.D.: Sword of Samos
Minnesota
  Minneapolis/St. Paul
  John Sandford
    Rules of Prey
    Shadow Prey
    Eyes of Prey
    Silent Prey
Montana
A. B. Guthrie, Jr.
    Playing Catch-Up
Robert Sims Reid
    Cupid
    Benediction
Nevada
  Las Vegas
  Paul Bishop
    Citadel Run
New England
Andrew Coburn
    Love Nest

Jack O'Donnell
  Box Nine
New Mexico
Lee Martin
  Hal's Own Murder Case
Richard Martin Stern
  Murder in the Walls
  You Don't Need an Enemy
  Death in the Snow
  Tangled Murders
  Missing Man
  Interloper
Walter Jon Williams
  Days of Atonement
Navaho Reservation
Tony Hillerman
  The Blessing Way
  Dance Hall of the Dead
  Listening Woman
  People of Darkness
  The Dark Wind
  The Ghostway
  Skinwalkers
  A Thief of Time
  Coyote Waits
New Jersey
David Wiltse
  Prayer for the Dead
  Close to the Bone
  The Edge of Sleep
New York (state)
Edward J. Frail
  Cult
James Neal Harvey
  The Headsman
  Isola (a fictional city much like New York)
  Ed McBain
  Cop Hater
  The Mugger
  The Pusher
  The Con Man
  Killer's Choice
  Killer's Payoff

United States/New York *(continued)*
 Lady Killer
 Killer's Wedge
 'Til Death
 King's Ransom
 Give the Boys a Great Big Hand
 The Heckler
 See Them Die
 Lady, Lady, I Did It
 Like Love
 Ten Plus One
 Ax
 He Who Hesitates
 Doll
 Eighty Million Eyes
 Fuzz
 Shotgun
 Jigsaw
 Hail, Hail, the Gang's All Here!
 Sadie, When She Died
 Let's Hear It for the Deaf Man
 Hail to the Chief
 Bread
 Blood Relative
 So Long As You Both Shall Live
 Long Time No See
 Calypso
 Ghosts
 Heat
 Ice
 Lightning
 Poison
 Tricks
 Lullaby
 Vespers
 Widows
 Long Island
 John Westermann
  High Crimes
  Exit Wounds
  Sweet Deal
 New York (city)
  Bronx
  Richard Fliegel
   The Organ Grinder's Monkey

The Next to Die
Time to Kill
A Semiprivate Doom
Bill Kelly and Dolph Le Moult
Street Dance
Dream Street
Death Squad
Tom Philbin
A Precinct Siberia Novel: Cop Killer
A Precinct Siberia Novel: Street Killer
A Precinct Siberia Novel: Death Sentence
Carsten Stroud
Sniper's Moon
David Wiltse
The Serpent
Brooklyn
William J. Caunitz
Suspects
Ruby Horansky
Dead Ahead
Bob Leuci
Captain Butterfly
Irving Weinman
Tailor's Dummy
Manhattan
Thomas Adcock
Dark Maze
William Bayer
Switch
Wallflower
Peter Blauner
Slow Motion Riot
Anthony Bruno
Bad Guys
Bad Blood
Bad Luck
Bad Business
Bad Moon
William J. Caunitz
One Police Plaza
Exceptional Clearance
Robert Chambers
The Neon Preacher
Nick Christian
Ronin

United States/New York (*continued*)
   E. W. Count
    The Hundred Percent Squad
   Robert Daley
    To Kill a Cop
    Hands of a Stranger
   Nelson De Mille
    Ryker #1: The Sniper
    Ryker #2: The Hammer of God
    Ryker #3: The Terrorists
   Jack Early
    Donato and Daughter
   John Eller
    Rage of Heaven
   Michael Grant
    Line of Duty
   Ken Gross
    Rough Justice
   Joseph Harrington
    The Last Known Address
    Blind Spot
    The Last Doorbell
   James Neal Harvey
    By Reason of Insanity
   Nat Hentoff
    The Man from Internal Affairs
   Joan Hess
    Maggody in Manhattan
   Chester Himes
    For Love of Imabella
    The Crazy Kill
    The Real Cool Killers
    All Shot Up
    The Big Gold Dream
    Cotton Comes to Harlem
    The Heat Is On
    Blind Man with a Pistol
   Michael Jahn
    Death Games
    City of God
   MacKinley Kantor
    Signal Thirty-Two
   Herbert Kastle
    Death Squad
   William Katz
    Open House

Faye Kellerman
Day of Atonement
Bill Kelly and Dolph Le Moult
Street Dance
Death Spiral
Dream Street
The Killing Moon
Herbert Lieberman
City of the Dead
Nightbloom
Shadow Dancers
Anthony Mancini
Talons
Margaret Maron
One Coffee With
Death of a Butterfly
Death in Blue Folders
Baby Doll Games
Past Imperfect
William Marshall
Faces in the Crowd
John Minahan
The Great Hotel Robberty
The Great Diamond Robbery
The Face Behind the Mask
The Great Grave Robbery
David Nemec
Mad Blood
Christopher Newman
Sixth Precinct
Midtown South
Knock-Off
Midtown North
19th Precinct
Backfire
Lillian O'Donnell
The Phone Calls
Don't Wear Your Wedding Ring
Dial 577 R-A-P-E
The Baby Merchants
Leisure Dying
No Business Being a Cop
The Children's Zoo
Cop Without a Shield

United States/New York (*continued*)
    Ladykiller
    Casual Affairs
    A Private Crime
    Pushover
    Jerry Oster
    Internal Affairs
    Sweet Justice
    Nowhere Man
    Club Dead
    Saint Mike
    James Patterson
    The Midnight Club
    Barbara Paul
    You Have the Right to Remain Silent
    Robert Pike
    Police Blotter
    Shepard Rifkin
    McQuaid
    The Snow Rattlers
    Lawrence Sanders
    The First Deadly Sin
    The Second Deadly Sin
    The Third Deadly Sin
    The Fourth Deadly Sin
    Soledad Santiago
    Undercover
    Ben Sloane
    Horn: Hot Zone
    Horn: Outland Strip
    Stephen Solomita
    Force of Nature
    Lawrence Treat
    V as in Victim
    H as in Hunted
    Q as in Quicksand
    T as in Trapped
    F as in Flight
    Big Shot
    Weep for a Wanton
    Lady, Drop Dead
    Joseph Trigoboff
    The Bone Orchard
    Dorothy Uhnak
    The Bait

The Witness
The Ledger
Law and Order
Derek Van Arman
Just Killing Time
Hillary Waugh
"30" Manhattan East
The Young Prey
Finish Me Off
Queens
Dorothy Uhnak
The Investigation
North and South Carolina
John Ball
In the Heat of the Night
Ernest Clark
Fatal Rose
Michael Malone
Uncivil Seasons
Time's Witness
Ohio
Paula Gosling
Monkey Puzzle
Backlash
Cleveland
Max Allan Collins
The Dark City
Butcher's Dozen
Bullet Proof
Oklahoma
Jean Hager
The Grandfather Medicine
Night Walker
Pennsylvania
K. C. Constantine
The Rocksburg Railroad Murders
The Man Who Liked to Look at Himself
The Blank Page
Always a Body to Trade
Upon Some Midnight's Clear
Joey's Case
Sunshine Enemies
Philadelphia
John Danica and Lucy Freeman
Lezra's Law

United States/Pennsylvania *(continued)*
 W. E. B. Griffin
  Badge of Honor
  Badge of Honor: Special Operations
  Badge of Honor: The Victim
  Badge of Honor: The Witness
 Eric Sauter
  Skeletons
Tennessee
 Sharyn McCrumb
  If Ever I Return Pretty Peggy-O
Texas
 Susan Rogers Cooper
  The Man in the Green Chevy
  Houston in the Rear View Mirror
  Other People's Houses
 Bill Crider
  Too Late to Die
  Shotgun Saturday Night
  Cursed to Death
  Evil at the Root
  Booked for a Hanging
 Edward Mathis
  Only When She Cries
 D. R. Meredith
  The Sheriff and the Panhandle Murders
  The Sheriff and the Branding Iron Murders
  The Sheriff and the Folsom Iron Murders
 Rex Miller
  Iceman
 Anne Wingate
  Death by Deception
  The Eye of Anna
  The Buzzards Must Also Feed
 Dallas
 Terry Marlowe
  Target Blue
 Rex Miller
  Stone Shadow
 Fort Worth
 Lee Martin
  Too Sane a Murder
  Conspiracy of Strangers
  Murder at the Blue Owl
  The Mensa Murders

Deficit Ending
   Hacker
   Houston
   Bill Crider
   Blood Marks
   David L. Lindsey
   A Cold Mind
   Heat from Another Sun
   Spiral
   In the Lake of the Moon
   Body of Truth
   Mercy
Utah
   Salt Lake City
   Thomas H. Cook
   Tabernacle
   J. R. Levitt
   Carnivores
Vermont
Archer Mayor
   Open Season
   Borderlines
Alison Smith
   Rising
Virginia
   Fairfax County
   Patricia Cornwell
   Postmortem
   Body of Evidence
   All That Remains
   Cruel & Unusual
Washington
   Seattle
   Earl W. Emerson
   Black Hearts and Slow Dancing
   Help Wanted: Orphans Preferred
   J. A. Jance
   Until Proven Guilty
   Injustice for All
   Taking the Fifth
   Improbable Cause
   A More Perfect Union
   Ridley Pearson
   Undercurrents
   Whitewater
   John Ball

Police Chief
Trouble for Tallon
Chief Tallon and the S.O.R.
Washington, DC
Warren Adler
American Quartet
American Sextet
Senator Love
Immaculate Deception
The Witch of Watergate
Ridley Pearson
Hard Fall
Gary Hunter
Dark Warrant
Derek Van Arman
Just Killing Time
West Virginia
Robert L. Duncan
The Serpent's Mark
Dave Pedneau
A.P.B.
D.O.A.
B.O.L.A.
A.K.A.
B. & E.: Breaking and Entering
N.F.D.

7

Serial Killers

Many police procedurals feature serial killers. In fiction as in real life, the police force's task is tremendous. The perpetrator is basically a cipher, a phantom whose existence is known only through the bodies of its victims. Since there are few or no clues left at the scene of the crime, serial killings are mysteries, often too difficult to solve until the killer becomes careless. More realistically, the guilty one stops killing or moves on, leaving a trail of death with no solution. Serial killings make wonderful subject matter for fictional stories. The challenge to the author, as for the police, is basically to put together a case beginning with nothing but a dead body.

Thomas Adcock
    Dark Maze

Dallas Barnes
    Yesterday Is Dead

William Bayer
    Pattern Crimes

K. Arne Blom
    The Moment of Truth

Rex Burns
    The Avenging Angel
    Strip Search

William J. Caunitz
    Exceptional Clearance

Max Allan Collins
    Butcher's Dozen

Thomas H. Cook
: *Tabernacle*

Patricia Cornwell
: *Postmortem*
: *Cruel & Unusual*

John Creasey
: *The Beauty Queen Killer*

Bill Crider
: *Blood Marks*

Nelson De Mille
: *Ryker #2: The Hammer of God*

D. J. Donaldson
: *Blood on the Bayou*

Robert L. Duncan
: *The Serpent's Mark*

Jack Early
: *Donato and Daughter*

James Ellroy
: *Blood on the Moon*

Richard Fliegel
: *The Organ Grinder's Monkey*

Kristopher Franklin
: *Silvercat*

Stephen Gallagher
: *Down River*

Paula Gosling
: *The Wychford Murders*

James Grady
: *Razor Game*

Bill Granger
: *Pulic Murders*

Thomas Harris
: *Red Dragon*

James Neal Harvey
: *By Reason of Insanity*
: *The Headsman*

John Harvey
: *Lonely Hearts*

Jack D. Hunter
: *Judgment in Blood*

Hamilton Jobson
: *The Evidence You Will Hear*

Bruce Jones
: *In Deep*

R. W. Jones
: *Cop-Out*

William Katz
: *Open House*

John Katzenbach
: *The Traveler*

Jonathan Kellerman
: *The Butcher's Theater*

John Leslie
: *Killer in Paradise*

J. R. Levitt
: *Carnivores*

Herbert Lieberman
: *Nightbloom*
: *Shadow Dancers*

David L. Lindsey
: *A Cold Mind*
: *Mercy*

Jayson Livingston
: *Point Blank*

Vincent McConnor
: *Limbo*

Edward Mathis
: *Only When She Cries*

Rex Miller
Stone Shadow
Iceman

Marcel Montecino
The Crosskiller

Lillian O'Donnell
The Phone Calls
Ladykiller

Jack Olsen
Night Watch

Ridley Pearson
Undercurrents

Maurice Procter
Homicide Blonde

John Sandford
Rules of Prey

Lawrence Sanders
The First Deadly Sin
The Third Deadly Sin

Eric Sauter
Skeletons

Steve Shagan
Vendetta

Dell Shannon
Knave of Hearts

Michael Slade
Headhunter

Mark Smith
The Death of the Detective

Donald Thomas
The Ripper's Apprentice

Peter Turnbull
Deep and Crisp and Even
Long Day Monday

Dorothy Uhnak
   The Bait

Derek Van Arman
   Just Killing Time

Randall Wallace
   Where Angels Watch

Pamela West
   Yours Truly, Jack the Ripper

David Wiltse
   The Serpent
   Prayer for the Dead
   The Edge of Sleep

8

A Lighter Touch

These books are not hard-boiled. They do not contain the hard-core torture and mutilation scenes that abound in many police procedurals. Here some of the authors use humor as a means to soften the effects of crime. William Marshall has perfected that art of carefully balancing the horrendous aspects of murder with the antics of his Yellowthread Street police. Tony Hillerman writes so softly and lyrically that when murder comes the reader is as shocked by it as the author intended. Joan Hess frosts her entire story with what amounts at times to Southern slapstick but underlining themes are timely and of concern to us all.

Please make no mistake here. The books listed in this category are not without crime. In fact a few of them are shocking in their cruel portrayal of thoughtless killing and the waste of human life. I believe that some authors listed below have tried to soften the devastation of murder and have shown the everlasting effects of it upon the victim's family and friends and the police who must deal with this aftermath.

John Creasey
> *Inspector West Takes Charge*
> *Inspector West Leaves Town*
> *Inspector West at Home*
> *Inspector West Regrets*
> *Holiday for Inspector West*
> *Battle for Inspector West*
> *Triumph for Inspector West*
> *Inspector West Kicks off*
> *Inspector West Alone*
> *Inspector West Cries Wolf*
> *Inspector West Alone*
> *A Case for Inspector West*
> *Puzzle for Inspector West*
> *Inspector West at Bay*

John Creasey (continued)
    A Gun for Inspector West
    Send Inspector West
    A Beauty for Inspector West
    Inspector West Makes Haste
    Two for Inspector West
    Parcels for Inspector West
    A Prince for Inspector West
    Accident for Inspector West
    Find Inspector West
    Murder, London–New York
    Strike for Death
    Death of a Race Horse
    The Case of the Innocent Victims
    Murder on the Line
    Death in Cold Print
    The Scene of the Crime
    Policeman's Dread
    Hang the Little Man
    Look Three Ways at Murder
    Murder, London–Australia
    Murder, London–South Africa
    The Executioners
    So Young to Burn
    Murder, London–Miami
    A Part for a Policeman
    Alibi
    A Splinter of Glass
    The Theft of Magna Carta
    The Extortioners
    A Sharp Rise in Crime

Bill Crider
    Too Late to Die
    Shotgun Saturday Night
    Cursed to Death
    Evil at the Root
    Booked for a Hanging

E. V. Cunningham
    Samantha
    The Case of the One-Penny Orange
    The Case of the Russian Diplomat
    The Case of the Poisoned Eclairs
    The Case of the Sliding Pool

The Case of the Kidnapped Angel
The Case of the Murdered Mackenzie

Susan Dunlap
Karma
As a Favor
Not Exactly a Brahmin
Too Close to the Edge
A Dinner to Die For
Diamonds in the Buff

John Dunning
Booked to Die

Robert L. Fish
The Fugitive
Isle of the Snakes
The Shrunken Head
Brazilian Sleigh Ride
The Diamond Bubble
Always Kill a Stranger
The Bridge That Went Nowhere
The Xavier Affair
The Green Hell Treasure
Trouble in Paradise

Nicolas Freeling
Love in Amsterdam
Because of the Cats
Double-Barrel
Criminal Conversation
The King of the Rainy Country
Dresden Green
Strike Out Where Not Applicable
Tsing-Boum
Over the High Side
A Dressing of Diamonds
What Are the Bugles Blowing
Lake Isle
The Night Lords
Castang's City
Wolfnight
The Back of the North Wind
Cold Iron
Not as Far as Velma

Richard Grayson
>   *The Murders at the Impasse Louvain*
>   *The Monterant Affair*
>   *The Death of Abbe Dodier*
>   *The Montmartre Murders*
>   *Crime Without Passion*
>   *Death En Voyage*
>   *Death on the Cards*
>   *Death Offstage*

W. E. B. Griffin
>   *Badge of Honor*
>   *Badge of Honor: Special Operations*
>   *Badge of Honor: The Victim*
>   *Badge of Honor: The Witness*

Batya Gur
>   *The Saturday Morning Murder*

A. B. Guthrie, Jr.
>   *Playing Catch-Up*

Nan Hamilton
>   *The Shape of Fear*

Ray Harrison
>   *Death of an Honourable Member*
>   *Death of a Dancing Lady*
>   *Deathwatch*
>   *Harvest of Death*
>   *Tincture of Death*
>   *Sphere of Death*
>   *Patently Murder*

Roy Hart
>   *Robbed Blind*
>   *Seascape with Dead Figures*
>   *A Pretty Place to Die*
>   *A Fox in the Night*
>   *Remains to be Seen*
>   *Breach of Promise*

Mark Hebden
>   *Death Set to Music*
>   *Pel and the Faceless Corpse*
>   *Pell Under Pressure*
>   *Pel Is Puzzled*

    Pel and the Staghound
    Pel and the Bombers
    Pel and the Predators
    Pel and the Picture of Innocence
    Pel Among the Pueblos
    Pel and the Pirates
    Pel and the Party Spirit

Keith Heller
    Man's Illegal Life
    Man's Storm

Sue Henry
    Murder On the Iditarod Trail

Olga Hesky
    Time for Treason

Joan Hess
    Malice in Maggody
    Mischief in Maggody
    Much Ado in Maggody
    Madness in Maggody
    Mortal Remains in Maggody

Tony Hillerman
    The Blessing Way
    Dance Hall of the Dead
    Listening Woman
    People of Darkness
    The Dark Wind
    The Ghostway
    Skinwalkers
    A Thief of Time
    Coyote Waits

Chester Himes
    For Love of Imabella
    All Shot Up
    The Big Gold Dream
    Blind Man with a Pistol

Timothy Holme
    The Neopolitan Streak
    A Funeral of Gondolas
    The Assisi Murders
    The Devil and the Dolce Vita

Ruby Horansky
: *Dead Ahead*

Robert Houston
: *The Fourth Codex*

Peter Inchbald
: *The Sweet Short Grass*
: *Tonto for Short*

Stuart M. Kaminksy
: *Black Knight in Red Square*
: *Red Chameleon*
: *A Find Red Rain*
: *The Man Who Walked Like a Bear*

Alanna Knight
: *Enter Second Murderer*
: *Deadly Beloved*

Bill Knox
: *Leave It to the Hangman*
: *The Deep Fall*
: *Childred of the Mist*
: *To Kill a Witch*
: *Draw Batons!*
: *Pilot Error*
: *Live Bait*
: *A Killing in Antiques*
: *The Hanging Tree*
: *The Crossfire Killings*

Philip Lauben
: *A Nice Sound Alibi*
: *A Surfeit of Alibis*

Michael Z. Lewin
: *Night Cover*
: *Hard Line*
: *Late Payments*

Roy Lewis
: *Nothing But Foxes*

Elizabeth Linington
: *Greenmask*
: *Date with Death*
: *Something Wrong*

Policeman's Lot
No Villain Need Be

James McClure
The Song Dog
The Steam Pig
The Caterpillar Cop
The Gooseberry Fool
Snake
The Sunday Hangman
The Blood of an Englishmen
The Artful Egg

Vincent McConnor
The Provence Puzzle
The Riviera Puzzle
The Paris Puzzle
I Am Vidocq

William Marshall
Yellowthread Street
Gelignite
The Hatchet Man
Skulduggery
Out of Nowhere
Whisper
Faces in the Crowd

Lee Martin
A Conspiracy of Strangers
Murder at the Blue Owl
Hal's Own Murder
The Mensa Murders
Deficit Ending

James Melville
The Wages of Zen
The Chrysanthemum Chain
A Sort of Samurai
The Ninth Netsuke
Sayonara, Sweet Amaryllis
Death of a Daimyo
The Death Ceremony
Go Gently, Gaijin
Kimono for a Corpse
The Reluctant Ronin
A Haiku for Hanae
The Bogus Buddha

Jennie Melville
- *Come Home and Be Killed*
- *Burning Is a Substitute for Loving*
- *Murderer's House*
- *There Lies Your Love*
- *Nell Alone*
- *A Different Kind of Summer*
- *A New Kind of Killer, An Old Kind of Love*
- *Murder Has a Pretty Face*
- *Making Good Blood*
- *Witching Murder*

John Minahan
- *The Great Hotel Robbery*
- *The Great Diamond Robbery*
- *The Face Behind the Mast*
- *The Great Grave Robbery*

Stephen Murray
- *Salty Waters*
- *Fetch Out No Shroud*

Janet Neel
- *Death's Bright Angel*

Freny Olbrich
- *Desouza Pays the Price*
- *Desouza in Stardust*

Barbara Paul
- *You Have The Right to Remain Silent*

Michael Pearce
- *The Mamur Zapt and the Return of the Carpet*
- *The Mamur Zapt and the Night of the Dog*
- *The Mamur Zapt and the Donkey-Vous*

Joyce Porter
- *Dover One*
- *Dover Two*
- *Dover Three*
- *Dover and the Unkindest Cut of All*
- *Dover Goes to Pott*
- *Dover Strikes Again*
- *It's Murder with Dover*
- *Dover and the Claret Tappers*
- *Dover Beats the Band*

Mary Monica Pulver
> *Ashes to Ashes*

Peter Robinson
> *Gallows View*
> *A Necessary End*

Owen Sela
> *The Bengali Inheritance*

Francis Selwyn
> *Cracksman in Velvet*
> *Sergeant Verity and the Imperial Diamond*

David Serafin
> *Madrid Underground*
> *The Body in Cadiz Bay*
> *Port of Light*

Dell Shannon
> *Case Pending*
> *The Ace of Spades*
> *Extra Kill*
> *Knave of Hearts*
> *Death of a Busybody*
> *Mark of Murder*
> *The Death-Bringers*
> *Rain with Violence*
> *Kill with Kindness*
> *Schooled to Kill*
> *Whim to Kill*
> *Streets of Death*
> *Appearances of Death*
> *Felony at Random*
> *The Motive on Record*
> *Destiny of Death*
> *Exploit of Death*
> *Chaos of Crime*

Georges Simenon
> *Maigret's Mistake*
> *Maigret and the Hotel Majestic*
> *Maigret in Montmartre*
> *Maigret Has Scruples*
> *Maigret and the Killer*
> *Maigret and the Informer*
> *Maigret and the Millionaires*
> *Maigret and the Loner*

Richard Martin Stern
    Murder in the Walls
    You Don't Need an Enemy
    Death in the Snow
    Tsybanu
    Tangled Murders
    Missing Man

Lawrence Treat
    V as in Victim
    H as in Hunted
    Q as in Quicksand
    T as in Trapped
    F as in Flight
    Over the Edge
    Big Shot
    Weep for a Wanton
    Lady, Drop Dead

Dorothy Uhnak
    The Bait
    The Witness
    The Ledger

Peter Van Greenaway
    Doppelganger
    The Killing Cup

John Holbrook Vance
    The Pleasant Grove Murders

Peter N. Walker
    Carnaby and the Eliminators
    Carnaby and the Kidnappers
    Panda One On Duty
    Witchcraft for Panda One

Timothy Williams
    Converging Parallels
    The Puppeteer
    Persona Non Grata

Anne Wingate
    Death by Deception
    The Eye of Anna
    The Buzzards Must Also Feed

Eric Wright
- *The Man Who Changed His Name*
- *A Body Surrounded by Water*
- *A Question of Murder*
- *A Sensitive Case*

9

Police Personnel or Ex-Police Personnel Writing Police Procedurals

Listed here are the authors who have been identified as ex-police officers, currently serve on a police force, or have a close working relationship with a department. Where it is clear in what capacity the author has served and on which force, I have listed that affiliation; where there is little or no actual information, I have left the section blank. I also list a few authors whose parent was a police officer with the assumption that the writer probably has inside contacts to verify procedure.

Dallas Barnes, Los Angeles Police Department
Paul Bishop, Los Angeles Police Department
William J. Caunitz, Lieutenant, New York Police Department
Patricia Cornwell, Fairfax County Virginia Medical Examiner's Office
Robert Daley, Ex-Deputy Police Commissioner for New York City
John Danica, Federal Bureau of Investigation
D. J. Donaldson, forensic pathologist, New Orleans, Louisiana
John Eller, son of a New York City policeman
Earl W. Emerson, firefighter, Seattle, Washington
Kenneth Goddard, forensic scientist, Riverside and San Bernadino County, California
Graham Ison, Chief Superintendent, Scotland Yard
Hamilton Jobson, police officer, England
Bill Kelly, police officer, New York Police Department
Bob Leuci, police officer, New York Police Department
Joseph D. McNamara, Chief of Police, San Jose, California
Terry Marlowe, Detective Sergeant and former S.W.A.T. Captain for Dallas, Texas, Police Department

Lee Martin, former policewoman
David Nemec, New York State parole officer
Fridrikh Neznansky, Moscow Police—criminal investigator
Gerald Petievich, Treasury officer and Secret Service agent
Maurice Procter, police officer, Yorkshire, England
Robert Sims Reid, police officer, Missoula, Montana, Police Department
Lawrence Sanders, Lieutenant, New York Police Department
Dorothy Uhnak, New York City Transit Authority policewoman
Derek Van Arman, VICAT
Janwillem van de Wetering, Sergeant, Amsterdam Police Department
John Wainwright, police officer, Yorkshire, England
Anne Wingate, former policewoman
Peter N. Walker, police officer, England
Joseph Wambaugh, Sergeant, Los Angeles Police Department
John Westermann, police officer for one of the Long Island police departments
Ted Wood, Toronto Police Department

10

Police Agencies

UNITED STATES

Local

It is usually estimated that there are some 40,000 separate public police agencies in the United States. There are village, borough, and incorporated town police, city and township police, and the county sheriffs' departments. The local police can be a small unit headed by a chief of police in a city or town or a multilevel hierarchy in a big city, also headed by a chief of police. The police department is usually divided into the uniform branch, which takes care of traffic and patrolling the streets and in some locales investigating crime, and the detective branch, which investigates crime. The ranks are somewhat military in designation. There might be three levels in the detective rankings, then sergeant, lieutenant, captain, inspector, chief of police, and on up. Generally, civil service exams must be taken for an officer to be promoted.

Since it is next to impossible to find a reference book with a breakdown of the various ranks in a U.S. police department and because municipalities can differ, I called the Cleveland Police Academy to find out how a large metropolitan area divides its ranks. Cleveland has no separate ranking for detectives. The detective is the equal of the patrol officer and both receive the same pay. The only difference is that the detective carries a gold badge. Civil service tests are taken to move up in the ranks, which include sergeant, lieutenant, and captain. Commander, deputy chief, and chief of police are mayoral appointees in Cleveland.

Forensic branches and medical examiners are attached to the police department. Special squads such as the bomb squad and the S.W.A.T.

team, the K-9 unit, the records department, the juvenile division, the internal affairs unit, which polices the police, and undercover agents all go to make up the modern municipal police force.

The state police control state regulatory concerns, such as fishing, hunting, and the sale of alcoholic beverages. As citizens we usually meet the state highway patrol, which is concerned with highway traffic control and criminal investigation, when a state law has been broken.

There are more than fifty federal police agencies. A few of the large ones are incorporated into the Department of Justice, which includes the Federal Bureau of Investigation and the U.S. Marshals. The Bureau of Internal Revenue maintains a large investigative force as does the U.S. Secret Service, the Drug Enforcement Administration, the Postal Inspection Service, and the U.S. Customs Service.

If you are going to write a police procedural novel and you have no experience in law enforcement, you really must contact the police agency you are describing. Duties change, ranks disappear, structure is rearranged. Read books by former police officers. William Caunitz, Bill Kelly writing with Dolph Le Moult, Tom Philbin, and Joseph Wambaugh are good examples.

UNITED KINGDOM

Local Police and Scotland Yard

The United Kingdom has no national police. Since 1829 the Home Secretary has been able to make recommendations to Parliament to change the organization of the police. In the 1970s the British police underwent an examination and reevaluation of its powers. Local police departments were kept and given more autonomy thus making them answerable to the communities they serve. Local forces can seek help in investigating crimes from New Scotland Yard, the municipal police force for metropolitan London.

The London Metropolitan Police is not a national force and is called in less frequently than authors of fiction would lead the reader to believe. The uniform branch of the police is not separate from the criminal department. Police officers can be and are interchangeable since the reorganization of 1972.

There are two police forces operational in London. The City of London police have operated in the financial district of the city since 1839. The Metropolitan Police, commonly known as Scotland Yard, serve the greater London area. The original headquarters was located at 4 Whitehall Place, which was the site of a palace used by visiting kings and queens of Scotland, thus reference to it as Scotland Yard. The present headquarters stands on Victoria Street next to the Houses of Paliament and was opened in 1967. It is frequently referred to as New Scotland Yard.

Scotland Yard is renowned for its forensic and criminal investigation capabilities. The name has become synonymous with the Criminal Investigation Department or CID. The Yard's fingerprinting system was developed in the late nineteenth century and adopted as official procedure by the American Federal Bureau of Investigation on their formation. The flying squad, the fraud and drug branches, criminal records office, forensic unit, and the training school for detectives are all used throughout the world as prototypes of what police work is all about.

The best way to understand the British police force at work is to read the novels of John Wainwright. Peter Turnbull, Bill Knox, and William McIlvanney illustrate the inner structure of the police in Scotland at large and in Glasgow.

To try to understand how a real police force functions, read *Behind the Uniform: Policing in Britain and America* by Ian K. McKenzie and G. Patrick Gallagher (London: Harvester Wheatsheaf; New York: St. Martin's, 1989). The authors compare the British police in all aspects to their American counterparts using the London Metropolitan Police and the New York Police Department as their control groups. They include a history of policing and general organizational charts for the two large forces. There are chapters on bearing arms, civil rights, how a police department works, and the rules and regulations governing both British and American forces. The bibliography is extensive and invaluable.

If you are looking for a procedures handbook try *The Law Enforcement Handbook* by Desmond Rowland and James Bailey (New York and Oxford: Facts on File, 1985). This is a handbook of police procedure that includes patrolling, keeping notes, responding to emergencies, stop and search, accident investigation, criminal investigation, raids, crime by computer, and job stress. Rowland, a British police superintendent, has written the closest thing to a universal handbook on how to do the job.

The Handbook of Criminal Investigation (New York: Arco, 1974) by Colonel Maurice J. Fitzgerald, MPC, U.S. Army, is a text covering most aspects of procedure. Fitzgerald, a long-term policeman in the U.S. army and the New York Police Department, covers all the basics from interviewing witnesses, what to do at the crime scene, surveillance, interrogation techniques, writing reports, keeping files, and profiling repeat criminals. While some of the information may be out of date, Fitzgerald is dealing with the basics; therefore it stands as a good example of what the police officer does to perform his or her duties.

In 1989 Garland published *The Encyclopedia of Police Science*, edited by William G. Bailey. Alphabetically listing all the top subjects related to police work, the volume includes essays on topics ranging from administration, the K-9 unit, important individuals and their contributions, and the FBI to military police, police suicide, U.S. marshals, and video technology. Laws are cited, court decisions are included, and a brief bibliography on the subject concludes each article.

Any number of books deal with a single aspect of police work. I sit up and listen when a police officer recommends a particular title. A former treasury agent once told me that Kenneth W. Goddard's *Crime Scene Investigation* (Reston, VA: Reston Publishing, 1977) is the best single book on the subject. Everything about searching a crime scene, collecting evidence, taking fingerprints, examining fibers, and so forth is included and explained, and in language that laypeople can understand.

Personal accounts of life as a police officer are a growing aspect of nonfiction literature. British reminiscences are usually by high-ranking officers and are easy to find in libraries. Mike Seabrook, author of *Coppers: An Inside View of the British Police* (London: Harrap, 1987), is an exception—his entire career was spent as a police constable. This short bibliography of five authors writing on actual police life includes among them the American Joseph Wambaugh. Seabrook's rationale for including Wambaugh is his belief that his books are extrememly realistic, reflecting a true picture of police life, so much so that they can be discussed in a nonfiction context. Seabrook also considers the lot of both American and British cops enough alike to warrant Wambaugh's inclusion.

Among the many accounts appearing in the United States my favorites are *What Cops Know: Cop Talk About What They Do, How They Do It, and What It Does to Them* (New York: Villard, 1990) and *Pure Cop* (New York: Villard, 1991). Both books are by Connie Fletcher and show life as a police officer in Chicago.

11

One Hundred Classics of the Genre

Since the police procedural dates from the 1940s there is not a great deal of historical perspective. However, once the genre got started authors made up for lost time. For every book included here there are at least two more that I might add to the list on a different day. In trying to be objective, I have probably left a number of excellent writers off this list. In the end any list of the "best" is going to be in some way subjective.

John Ball
    Police Chief

Dallas Barnes
    Yesterday Is Dead

William Bayer
    Switch

K. Arne Blom
    The Moment of Truth

Anthony Bruno
    Bad Guys

James Lee Burke
    A Stained White Radiance

Rex Burns
    Strip Search

William Camp
    The Jacobs Park Killings

William J. Caunitz
: *Suspects*

Max Allan Collins
: *Butcher's Dozen*

Michael Connelly
: *The Black Echo*

K. C. Constantine
: *The Blank Page*

Thomas H. Cook
: *Streets of Fire*

Patricia D. Cornwell
: *Body of Evidence*

E. W. Count
: *The Hundred Percent Squad*

Robert Daly
: *The Dangerous Edge*

Frank DeFelitta
: *Oktoberfest*

Joseph P. De Sario
: *Limbo*

Susan Dunlap
: *A Dinner to Die For*

Lew Dykes
: *Choke Hold*

Earl W. Emerson
: *Help Wanted: Orphans Preferred*

Kenneth Goddard
: *Balefire*
  Alchemist

Paula Gosling
: *A Running Duck*

Laurence Gough
: *Silent Knives*

James Grady
: *Just a Shot Away*

Bill Granger
: *Public Murders*

Jean Hager
: *Night Walker*

Joseph Harrington
: *Blind Spot*

Ray Harrison
: *Tincture of Death*

John Harvey
: *Cutting Edge*
: *Off Minor*

Tony Hillerman
: *The Blessing Way*
: *Listening Woman*
: *People of Darkness*
: *A Thief of Time*

Jon A. Jackson
: *Grootka*

E. Richard Johnson
: *The God Keepers*

Herbert Kastle
: *Death Squad*

Bill Kelly and Dolph Le Moult
: *Death Spiral*

Bill Knox
: *The Hanging Tree*

John Lantigua
: *Heat Lightning*

Bob Leuci
: *Captain Butterfly*

Michael Z. Lewin
: *Late Payments*

Herbert Lieberman
: *Shadow Dancers*

David L. Lindsey
: *Heat from Another Sun*

Jayson Livingston
: *Point Blank*

Ed McBain
: *The Con Man*
: *The Heckler*
: *Jigsaw*
: *Ghosts*

Jill McGown
: *Redemption* (U.S. title: *Murder at the Old Vicarage*)

William McIlvanney
: *Laidlaw*

Joseph D. McNamara
: *Fatal Command*

Terry Marlowe
: *Target Blue*

J. J. Marric
: *Gideon's Staff*
: *Gideon's Fire*

William Marshall
: *Perfect End*
: *Whisper*

Seicho Matsumoto
: *Inspector Immanishi Investigates*

Hugh Miller
: *An Echo of Justice*

Marcel Montecino
: *The Crosskiller*

Christopher Newman
: *Midtown North*
: *19th Precinct*

Fridrikh Neznansky
: *The Body in Sokoliniki Park*

Lillian O'Donnell
A Private Crime

Paul Orum
Scapegoat

Jerry Oster
Nowhere Man

James Patterson
The Midnight Club

Laurence Payne
The Nose on My Face

Ridley Pearson
Hard Fall

Gerald Petievich
Earth Angels

Anne Perry
The Face of a Stanger

Tom Philbin
Cop Killer

Robert L. Pike
Reardon

Maurice Procter
A Body to Spare

Derek Raymond
The Devil's Home on Leave

John Lawrence Reynolds
And Leave Her Lay Dying

Peter Robinson
A Necessary End

Charles G. Rogers
1199

Robert Rosenberg
Crimes of the City

John Sandford
Shadow Prey

Soledad Santiago
: *Undercover*

Steve Shagan
: *Vendetta*

Maj Sjöwall and Per Wahlöö
: *Murder at the Savoy*

Stephen Solomita
: *Force of Nature*

Roderick Thorp
: *Rainbow Drive*

Peter Turnbull
: *Big Money*
: *Condition Purple*

Janwillem van de Wetering
: *The Blond Baboon*
: *The Rattle-Rat*

John Wainwright
: *Landscape with Violence*
: *All on a Summer's Day*
: *The Forgotten Murders*
: *The Man Who Wasn't There*

Joseph Wambaugh
: *The Blue Knight*

John Westermann
: *Sweet Deal*

Charles Willeford
: *New Hope for the Dead*